Sherwood Anderson's Love Letters to Eleanor Copenhaver Anderson

Night

Morning Thanksgiving

[illegible]

dearest darling—

I havnt any words to tell you dear what happens when you come back to me.

Its such a silly word but there is, at last, lightness of the soul.

My body too dear — the sweet smell of your man—

Your hand touches me — O darling one...

Something dancing inside me dear—

Its not what you see. O dear I write for you I could be Apollo. There is a white swift, soft-running thing — man, boy, fawn—

softly — on the carpet of the night — ——

To him — to the dear sweet lipped, sweet beautiful one

You are sweeter than ever. Can you love me? Is it possible? Your eyes shine with love. O the sweetness in you—

dear darling woman.

Edited by
Charles E. Modlin

Sherwood Anderson's Love Letters to Eleanor Copenhaver Anderson

The University of Georgia Press
Athens and London

Athens, Georgia 30602

Designed by Richard Hendel
Set in Sabon
The paper in this book meets the guidelines for permanence and durability of the Committee on Production Guidelines for Book Longevity of the Council on Library Resources.

Printed in the United States of America

93 92 91 90 89 5 4 3 2 1

Library of Congress Cataloging in Publication Data

Anderson, Sherwood, 1876—1941.
Sherwood Anderson's love letters to Eleanor Copenhaver Anderson / edited by Charles E. Modlin.
p. cm.
Bibliography: p.
Includes index.
ISBN *0-8203-1150-2 (alk. paper)*
1. Anderson, Sherwood, 1876-1941—Correspondence. 2. Anderson, Eleanor Copenhaver, d. 1985—Correspondence. 3. Authors, American—20th century—Correspondence. 4. Love-Letters.
I. Modlin, Charles E. II. Title.
PS3501.N4Z4897 *1989*
813'.52—dc20
[B]

89-4895
CIP

British Library Cataloging in Publication Data available

FRONTISPIECE
Letter of 24 November 1932.
The annotations are by Eleanor Anderson.
(By permission of the Newberry Library)

For Mimi and John

Contents

Preface

The 224 letters in this volume are chosen from a collection of some 1,400 that Sherwood Anderson wrote to Eleanor Copenhaver Anderson, beginning with their early acquaintance in 1929 and continuing through their courtship and marriage up to a month before his death in 1941.

Mrs. Anderson left most of the letters with the Newberry Library in 1947 with the provision that, because of their intimacy, they be sealed until after her death. She briefly relented fifteen years later, telling a reporter that she was willing to consider publishing some of them. The story, headlined "Clear Way for Publication of Writer's Love Letters," was prominently reported in the *Chicago Daily News* on 31 March 1962 and elicited interest from *Life* magazine for several months. At about the same time, an exterminator working in the basement of Mrs. Anderson's home in Marion, Virginia, found a tin box containing 66 additional letters, including some of the most impassioned ones of 1930, and apparently their candor convinced her once more to delay release of any of the letters. In early 1964 she added the 66 letters to the Newberry collection and requested that all of the letters to her be resealed. Thus they remained for an additional twenty years. In 1984, the year before she died, Mrs. Anderson gave me permission to open the letters and to begin preparing a selection of them for publication.

The letters, stored in five boxes, were left in varying degrees of organization. A few were arranged, through the efforts of Mrs. Anderson and Amy Nyholm, the former curator of the Anderson collection at the Newberry Library, in chronological order, while many were roughly sorted by year, and still others were in no apparent order. Notes indicated that Paul Rosenfeld had also gone over the original cache of letters and picked out some as publishable in a volume he projected not long before his death in 1946. Mrs. Anderson made notes on many of the letters, providing dates, places, and readings of occasional obscurities of Anderson's handwriting. Except in a few time periods that were apparently confusing to her, she was highly accurate in her annotations, and I have often been dependent upon them, particularly when no other evidence for determining dates or locations was available.

Because of the great number of letters, I have had the advantage of considerable selectivity. Naturally not all of them are of equal value. Many are repetitive or deal with details that are of no lasting interest; Anderson was, after all, often writing two or three times a day and sometimes in great haste. I have chosen letters that seem most successful in displaying some of his most interesting and eloquent writing; in commenting significantly on his life, ideas, and literary career; and in telling the story of an extraordinary love affair.

The letters here are complete except for three short passages, indicated in brackets, that Mrs. Anderson removed. In editing the texts, I have silently corrected misspellings and slips of the pen, slightly altered punctuation when necessary for readability, and supplied omitted words in brackets. The ellipses are Anderson's own. He did not usually give the dates or locations of his letters, but in most cases I have been able to provide them in brackets, using Mrs. Anderson's information or other evidence.

The letters in this volume are published with the permission of the Sherwood Anderson Literary Estate Trust and the Newberry Library. For their aid in the completion of this book, I am grateful for summer fellowships from the National Endowment for the Humanities and the Newberry Library and for support in many forms from the English Department of Virginia Polytechnic Institute and State University.

These books have been especially useful to me: *The Buck Fever Papers,* ed. Welford D. Taylor; *Letters of Sherwood Anderson,* ed. Howard Mumford Jones and Walter B. Rideout; *The Sherwood Anderson Diaries, 1936–1941,* ed. Hilbert H. Campbell; *Sherwood Anderson's Memoirs: A Critical Edition,* ed. Ray Lewis White; Kim Townsend, *Sherwood Anderson* (1987). Ray Lewis White kindly showed me the manuscript of his edition in progress of Anderson's letters-a-day to Eleanor, a journal he kept in 1932.

I want to thank the many librarians who have provided me with information, including Florence Archer, Jo Chanaud, Joan Emens, Dianne Glymph, Kenneth M. Grossi, Charles Haney, Paul Metz, Elizabeth Norris, Patrick M. Quinn, Peer E. Ravnan, Pattie J. Scott, Susan L. Seay, Cecil O. Sharp II, and Robert Zietz. Other contributors whom I gratefully acknowledge are Don Francis, Jean Greear, Josh Greear, Thaddeus B. Hurd, April Kim Russell, and Kathryn S. Weindel.

For their help at many stages of this project, I am indebted to John S. Anderson, Janis Bolster, Hilbert H. Campbell, Madelaine Cooke,

Virginia C. Fowler, Diana Haskell, Marjorie Modlin, Fritz Oehlschlaeger, Karen Orchard, Walter B. Rideout, Marion Anderson Spear, Welford D. Taylor, Kim Townsend, Ray Lewis White, and Gladys L. Williams.

My greatest debt is to the woman who inspired these letters, Eleanor Copenhaver Anderson.

Introduction

Sherwood Anderson and his third wife, Elizabeth Prall Anderson, first came to southwestern Virginia during the summer of 1925 to escape the heat of New Orleans. They stayed at the boardinghouse of John and Caroline Greear in Troutdale. Anderson liked the area so much that with the royalties from the sale of his novel *Dark Laughter* he bought a nearby farm, which he called Ripshin, and built there a fine house of stone and logs. The Andersons moved in at the end of the summer of 1926 and stayed until after Thanksgiving, when they left to spend the winter in France. His publications during this period included *Sherwood Anderson's Notebook, Tar: A Midwest Childhood, A New Testament,* and a series of articles for *Vanity Fair.* In the fall of 1927 he bought, with the help of a loan from his friend and patron Burton Emmett, the two weekly newspapers, the *Smyth County News* and the *Marion Democrat,* in Marion, twenty-two miles northwest of Ripshin. The Andersons moved to town and Sherwood plunged into his new role as newspaper editor and publisher. Elizabeth helped with the papers but did not adapt well to life in Marion; and during 1928 their marriage gradually broke up. Before Christmas Elizabeth left for California and did not return. At about the same time, Robert, Sherwood's older son, who had been working for the *Philadelphia Bulletin,* arrived in Marion to help his father with the newspapers. Restless and tired of the grind, Sherwood began to turn over the business to Bob and to spend less time in Marion, where he still considered himself an outsider. "In Marion," he wrote, "I am something strange and queer" (letter to EC of 29 November 1929).

Anderson, whose birthdate was 13 September 1876, was twenty years older than Eleanor Copenhaver, who was born on 15 June 1896, the oldest of five children. Her father was Bascom E. Copenhaver, who began his career as an administrator and a teacher of mathematics at Marion College, then served for many years as superintendent of schools in Smyth County (of which Marion is the county seat) and raised cattle on farmland near town. Her mother was Laura Lu Copenhaver, who taught English at Marion College, wrote hymns and pageants for the Lutheran church, worked as a publicity agent for the Farm Bureau, and founded the Laura Copenhaver Industries, which marketed local handicrafts. The Copenhavers lived in a large, stately house called Rosemont, reputedly the oldest in town, next door to Marion College, which was founded by Mrs. Copenhaver's father, the Reverend John J. Scherer. Eleanor went away to college, graduating from Westhampton College of the University of Richmond in 1917. After an unpleasant experience teaching for one year at Marion High School, she went on to graduate school at Bryn Mawr College, receiving in 1920 a certificate in social work. In that same year she was employed by the national board of the YWCA; her assignments for the next four years were primarily in programs for working women in the southern and central regions. In 1925 she became secretary of the industrial division of the YWCA in New York, the position she held at the time she met Sherwood.

The sense of strong womanhood that Anderson responded to and celebrated in *Perhaps Women* was present from the start in the career of Eleanor Copenhaver. In her work to improve women's working conditions, she traveled regularly into the centers of labor conflicts and at times had scrapes with violence that worried her parents. In one incident, which took place about 1921 in the South, she was attacked by members of the Ku Klux Klan. In another she was mugged on a street in Chicago—an incident that was picked up by the Marion papers and spread around the town. After she assured her parents that she was fine, her father wrote an admonishing letter (undated, now in the Newberry Library) to Eleanor, who was then in her mid-twenties: "Everybody is asking naturally about it. They ask if it was in the day time. I am ashamed to tell them it was at 9 o'clock at night and that you were out by yourself." He adds: "If it is done again, I want you to realize that you are outside the bounds of propriety, and that besides endangering your life, you are trifling with the rights of your people at home—who have your name, and whom you should help to keep it inviolate." Eleanor knew how to weather such storms, however, and continued on undaunted.

Just a few years later, this stern father was confronted by an even greater assault upon the family name when his daughter became romantically involved with Sherwood Anderson—a man whose recent failure in marriage only added to his rather bohemian reputation in Marion. Copenhaver's reaction this time, however, was complicated by the fact that his own wife and Anderson had already become good friends. They had first met not long after his move to Marion, when, according to

Eleanor, "He walked by the house, was impressed with it, and came to call." She whimsically added: "I think he fell in love first with the house, then with my mother, and then with me" ("An Interview with Mrs. Sherwood Anderson," *Sherwood Anderson: Centennial Studies*, p. 70). As his relationship with Eleanor developed, he frequently stopped by Rosemont while she was away to talk with or read to the personable, highly literate Laura Lu Copenhaver. Anderson's descriptions in the letters of his visits with her occasionally depict her husband's surly, though never openly hostile, reactions. After Sherwood and Eleanor married, he and his father-in-law learned to accept each other, but there was always distance between these two men who were so different in their temperaments and values.

There is no record of the exact date when Sherwood and Eleanor first met, but she recalled, as did Elizabeth Anderson, that it was at Rosemont in 1928. Sherwood described his early visits in a letter to Eleanor of 4 April 1930:

> I used to go up to the house and feel you warm and loving. I felt the living blood going through your body.
>
> "There is one," I said to myself. This was when Elizabeth was still there.
>
> I was terribly puzzled. We went home.
>
> She [Elizabeth] always began talking about the end of things.
>
> Perhaps something in her said . . . "If these two people go toward each other, a new kind of life will come into both of them."

Early in January 1929, following Elizabeth's departure and his return from a trip to Chicago, Sherwood began to confide in Eleanor. While she was back at Rosemont, he paid her a visit, which, in a letter of 27 March 1930, he later recalled for her:

> Like you I felt the naturalness of you and me together from the first. I remember the night when I came up to the house to tell you about Elizabeth. There had been for so long a kind of queer dryness and lack of warmth in that. I started to tell you and could hardly speak. You seemed so warm, so fluid, so all woman, so lovely.

At about the same time he enlisted her in an effort to sell Ripshin, occasioning his first letter to her, one not included in the Newberry collection that is now in my possession. Dated 22 January 1929, it is seven pages typed by a secretary on a Marion Publishing Company letterhead (with Elizabeth P. Anderson listed as manager), beginning: "I am writing you as my representative, for the sale of my country home in the mountains of Virginia." Anderson goes on to describe at length the countryside around Ripshin, the house, the other buildings on the farm, and the possibilities for horseback riding, hunting, and fishing. The letter is virtually a copy of one that he wrote to his publisher, Horace Liveright. At one point, in fact, the letter to Eleanor inappropriately retains a reference to Liveright; in describing his 1925 visit to southwestern Virginia, Anderson writes: "As you know, a couple of years ago I made a good deal of money, for me, out of my books. I had come down into this country to spend a few months, where I wrote the book of mine you published called 'Tar.'" The letter is not included in this volume because it is long, impersonal, and derivative, but the ending is of interest in its brief allusion to the breakup of his marriage: "I would be glad to give you any additional information of any kind about the house. Alas, I must sell it and you know why."

The relationship with Eleanor developed slowly. Anderson's early letters are restrained, yet there is no mistaking his intentions: "Speaking as one of your family—you say you all love me. I hope you may love me a little specially yourself. One of the wonderful things about not being married would happen if you did" (letter to EC of 4 February 1929). Eleanor, on the other hand, was cautious. She had not previously been involved in serious love affairs, having had just one minor romance a few years earlier with a poet in Minnesota. She was also keenly aware that Sherwood was still a married man; she insisted that he destroy her letters to him prior to his divorce from Elizabeth in 1932.

Their activities at first were limited to Eleanor's returns to Rosemont and consisted of short but gradually extended drives around the Marion area. A key event in this early period was their visit to an evening meeting of striking mill workers in Elizabethton, Tennessee, about fifty miles southwest of Marion. The date was probably about a week before he wrote up his account of the trip for the *Smyth County News* on 18 April 1929. The experience, though brief, had an impact upon Anderson's thinking and foreshadowed Eleanor's future role in introducing him to labor problems in the South. In June he visited her at two camps for young working women in North Carolina where she annually conducted classes. While taking great pleasure in her company, he became at times impatient with her busy schedule and, when they were alone together, her sexual reticence.

During the spring and summer of 1929 Sherwood was torn between his new interest in Eleanor and his ties with another woman, Mary Vernon Greer, who had done secretarial work for him in Marion before moving to Maryland in 1928. He visited Greer in April and July, but by the fall he seems to have fixed his attentions solely and permanently on Eleanor. Arranging to see her when she was on YWCA assignments in Washington and Richmond, he began a pattern of meeting her on her travels when possible and keeping up an increasingly intense correspondence with her when they were apart. When he reported to her on 26 December 1929 that he wanted to study and write about the labor movement, he committed himself not only to a new direction for his literary career, as evidenced in *Perhaps Women* and *Beyond Desire,* but also to a closer bond with her as she helped to arrange and even to subsidize his travels in 1930 to southern mills and factories.

Anderson's most memorable trips, however, were not those to mills or factories but, rather, his side excursions into nature, especially when he could share them with Eleanor. On 5 March 1930, a few days after they became lovers in a Georgia pine forest, he wrote to her: "You will always mean pine trees to me, a yellow river, quiet places in the wood. All these in your eyes. . . ." Following an idyllic trip through rural California, he exulted in her "lovely gracious body, so full always for me of hillsides, earth, flowers, soft, rich smells" (letter to EC of 11 April 1932).

In the succeeding series of emotional peaks and valleys as Sherwood intensified his pursuit of Eleanor and began to propose marriage, she was beset by various pressures. There was on the one hand a continued need to conceal the full extent of their relationship from her family. In addition, her friend Lois MacDonald, with whom she shared an apartment in New York, was unsympathetic to Eleanor's deepening relationship with Sherwood. At times he too felt the pressures. After coming to New York in October 1932 to be with her after an operation, he sensed resentment of his presence by her family; and in addition, when Eleanor became fearful of an unpleasant scene should MacDonald visit the hospital while he was there, he decided he had had enough and left to visit his friend Roger Sergel in Chicago.

The other major obstacle was Eleanor's YWCA career, which involved an onerous routine of conferences, meetings, camps, studies, and reports. In addition, from 1931 to 1933 she was enrolled in a graduate program at Columbia University, earning an M.A. in political economy. Her crowded schedule left little time for romance. More important, because of her job, she needed to avoid the appearance of either moral impropriety or dereliction of duty. During Eleanor's long stays in San Francisco in 1932 and Kansas City in early 1933, for example, Sherwood managed to spend some time with her but only at carefully selected intervals and locations.

Anderson's own schedule of activities kept him on the road much of the time as well. He usually enjoyed his speaking engagements, which were extensive in the early 1930s, and always enjoyed the travel (especially when it brought him nearer to Eleanor) and the stimulation of new sights and people. His tours of factories and various activities in the labor movement gave his thinking and writing a new focus, culminating in his attendance at the Amsterdam Peace Conference in August 1932. Anderson's sympathy for the worker was genuine; and he, like many of his contemporaries, was strongly attracted to the ideals of the communist movement. But he was never much of a joiner, and his commitment to "the revolution" began eventually to wane. After 1932 he assumed a calmer individuality, scoffing at radicals and insisting "that our reactions to life shall not be made for us by a party or by any group" (letter to ECA of 1935?). One reason for his change was the advent of the Roosevelt administration. As Anderson traveled the country in 1933–34, writing a series of articles for *Today,* many of which were included in *Puzzled America,* he became interested in the programs and personalities of the New Deal and found them hopeful signs for the future.

Another settling influence upon Anderson was that Eleanor in late September 1932, after many months of indecision, finally agreed to marry him when the demands of her job permitted. He drove her to Kansas City in January 1933 and stayed a few blocks from her at the Puritan Hotel (a name that amused him) while she worked for two months on a YWCA study of women's working conditions. When he returned to Virginia in the spring, he had abandoned his plan to sell Ripshin and, with the completion of a new road to Troutdale, put new energy into opening the house and preparing it for guests. Two of them, Arthur Barton, a playwright, and Louis Gruenberg, a composer, planned to spend the summer collaborating with Anderson—Barton on a dramatic version of *Winesburg, Ohio,* and Gruenberg on an opera about the Mississippi River. They seemed at first to fulfill for Anderson an old dream of using Ripshin as an artists' commune, but actually he sent Barton home early and soon became disenchanted with Gruenberg. Despite the failure of these experiments in collaboration, they did initiate a series of visits during the pleasant summers at Ripshin that provided the Andersons with some of their most enjoyable occasions.

The letters after their marriage, which finally took place at Rosemont on 5 July 1933, are much more sporadic, reflecting the happy fact that the two were now together for most of the year. The letters thus do not provide a sustained record of the Andersons' life during those seven and one-half years. A few from each year, however, do give, at some of the intervals when they were apart, an intimate view of Sherwood's personal world—marred at times by the strain of his relationship with Mary Emmett, Eleanor's disappointment at not becoming pregnant, his discouragement with his writing and embarrassment at depending upon Eleanor's job for most of their income, and his frequent bouts with illness and depression. But there were good experiences to write about as well, such as his visits with old friends in New York and New Orleans, his return to his boyhood home of Clyde, Ohio, his pleasant times at Olivet College in Michigan, and his enjoyment of the harness races in Lexington, Kentucky. And always he returned to expressions of his contentment with and dependence upon Eleanor as the "solid rock" in his life.

The final group of letters covers the difficult period in early 1941 following the death of Laura Lu Copenhaver, the woman who after Eleanor had become Sherwood's dearest friend. While Eleanor attended meetings in Chicago, Sherwood went to New York to do some writing and to make preparations for a trip to South America, where they planned to travel for several months. He was stricken with the flu, however, and spent much of the time in bed. With Eleanor back in New York but busily winding up YWCA affairs before her leave of absence, he made a hurried trip south in an effort to recover from his illness and an accompanying state of depression. He headed for Tampa, where he wanted to practice his Spanish, and on the way was struck with nostalgia driving by some of the old haunts from the "golden days" when he and Eleanor had first fallen in love. After another week of the flu followed by a few pleasant days working on his Spanish in Tampa, he rejoined Eleanor in Marion on 14 February, and his letters to her were completed. They returned to New York and on 28 February boarded the *Santa Lucia* bound for Valparaiso, Chile. By the second day at sea he was taken ill with peritonitis, the result of the perforation of his intestine by a toothpick he had swallowed at a party a day or two before he embarked. His condition became progressively worse, and when the ship reached Cristobal in the Canal Zone, he was removed and taken to a hospital at Colón, where on 8 March he died. Eleanor returned to Marion with his body, and on 26 March he was buried in Round Hill Cemetery on a hillside overlooking Rosemont.

Eleanor subsequently resumed her work with the YWCA, serving as the head of its industrial division (a position she had assumed in 1938) until 1946. In the fall of 1947 she presented her husband's papers to the Newberry Library prior to leaving for Italy, where she served as a foreign secretary for the YWCA until 1949. She helped to organize the Newberry's Anderson collection in 1950 and, in the years following, returned frequently to work with it. In New York she assumed new duties with the YWCA, the United Community Defense Services, and the American Labor Education Service, and served as executor of the Anderson literary estate. In Virginia she assumed the management of the Laura Copenhaver Industries and faithfully preserved Ripshin as Sherwood had left it. She died in Marion on 12 September 1985 and was buried beside her husband.

Anderson's tombstone, which now stands over Eleanor's grave as well, bears an epitaph that he himself had requested: "Life, not Death, is the Great Adventure," his way of expressing the zest for life that is so pervasive in these letters. Similarly, on 11 May 1933, a few weeks before his marriage to Eleanor, he wrote: "I would like to keep our lives open and adventurous to the end." The letters in this volume preserve the spirit of the man for whom life was always an Adventure, and for whom the romance with Eleanor was the greatest Adventure of all.

Sherwood Anderson's Love Letters to Eleanor Copenhaver Anderson

[Marion, 2 February 1929]

Dearest Eleanor—

I am leaving here tomorrow morning—Sunday—for a two weeks loaf south. Burt Dickinson[1] will go with me. We will loaf along, fish and see the country. We want to go quite far down, into Florida, as I want some days of lying in the sun by the sea.

About Mr. Kahn.[2] As a matter of fact I think he is the man who will buy the house.

As for Horace Liveright[3]—he has been down with flu. As soon as he gets up he will have to run off for a month or six weeks in Europe. I do not expect him to do anything—or to be in the way of my real estate lady until April or May.

To return to Mr. Kahn. My relations with him have been peculiar. I have only seen him a few times. Several times I have made appeals to him—always of course for something outside myself.

Only last week, after you left here, I got into my head a scheme for the young painter[4]—whose still life you saw.

I wrote Mr. Kahn and several other men. I enclose a copy of my letter to him. Will you return it after reading?

He responded with a check for $300.00 in the next mail and wrote me a marvelous letter. His address is 52 Williams Street, New York.

What is bothering me is that I rather hate to take advantage, in any way, of his expressed preference for me and all that concerns me.

I think these rich men suffer too much from this sort of thing. Am I silly? I think not.

As a matter of fact the place could be very wonderful in Mr. Kahn's hands. How wonderful if he could have it as a place to send painters in whom he is interested, or young singers. How marvelous that would be for our country down here too. And come himself of course.

But I would hate to say these things to him myself. You see how I feel. Do you fancy you could see him and get the matter before him in such a way as not to leave any feeling that I am trying to take advantage of him—so that he could laugh the whole thing off—and not have it affect our relations?

You who, I imagine, rather live by subtleties, will understand my feeling.

As I have so far taken you into my confidence regarding things I do not want known in Marion, I will tell you something else. When I sell the house and farm I want to buy the old Haller place in Marion.[5] It will be for sale presently. I would restore it just as it is, painted white with green blinds, rose bushes etc. at the side, make the downstairs the newspaper office and library and build a brick printshop on the back, out of sight from the street.

There would be room enough above for small apartments for Bob[6] and me. Would it not be wonderful to have that sweet old house as the headquarters for the paper? If it were known I wanted it, Bob Goolsby, Henry Staley[7] or some of our other sweet souls would try to get in and pinch me.

To love and then not to love is a tragedy always happening to people and that I cannot understand. The not loving, the separation, is like a major physical operation. I feel now like a convalescent.[8]

At the same time how poisonous the air when love is gone. You can't stay on. I am afraid—for me—there is a kind of lack of personal dignity in living on intimate terms with a woman after love leaves that is unbearable. Both are made ugly. Perhaps having children is the only possible justification for marriage. I feel so little love and respect in houses, in relationships.

I plan now to go to New York about March 10th and stay I hope for a month. The only address I can give you for the next two weeks is Delray Beach, Fla.[9]

Won't you write me there.

Sherwood Anderson

1. Burt L. Dickinson was judge of the Court of Juvenile and Domestic Relations and former mayor of Marion.

2. Otto Kahn, wealthy New York banker. SA was trying to sell his country place, Ripshin, and had recruited EC to help him.

3. Head of Boni and Liveright, who had published SA's books since 1925. SA had also asked him to help in selling Ripshin.

4. Charles Bockler, who was living in New York City. SA had asked Kahn and several other men to buy one of Bockler's paintings for $300. The text of his letter to Kahn appears in *Letters of Sherwood Anderson,* pp. 185–86.

5. The Haller place was an old ramshackle frame house on Main Street near the newspaper office. SA's idea was hardly a secret, since he had announced it in the *Smyth County News* on 24 January. The plan did not materialize, however, and the house was later torn down.

6. Robert Anderson, SA's older son.

7. Goolsby, a Marion lawyer, owned the building in which the printshop was located. Staley was a local mill owner.

8. SA refers to his separation from Elizabeth Prall Anderson.
9. He stayed at the Hotel Casa del Rey.

[Murphy, North Carolina,
4 February 1929]

Dear Eleanor

I am writing you this short note, after my long letter of yesterday, hoping they may both be forwarded to you at Greenville.[1]

I did not know our trip south was to take us through Asheville until Sunday morning, when we started—having left the route to Burt Dickinson, who is with me. Then I wired you—from Bristol. We got to Asheville at noon. Had I found you there I would have insisted on staying the rest of the day.

I planned to tell Burt a grand lie about a mysterious real estate lady and side-track him at some hotel other than your own.

Then I hoped to walk about with you, or perhaps take you off in the car on some mountain road.

Thus dreaming, I got into Asheville and on the phone only to find you had gone to Greenville. I hope this and my other letter may follow you.

Sherwood Anderson

P.S. Speaking as one of your family—you say you all love me. I hope you may love me a little specially yourself. One of the wonderful things about not being married would happen if you did.

I am much more absorbed in the idea of having you as a very very close friend than I am in getting semi-affluent by selling the house.

1. EC had just completed a YWCA assignment in Asheville, North Carolina, and had moved on to another in Greenville, South Carolina.

[Marion, late February? 1929]

Dear Eleanor.

Of course it does not follow, my dear. Where love may be life-giving, marriage may be destructive. It is to me.

I feel unclean trying to live so closely to another. It is hard to say all I mean in this.

Women, in their moments of loveliness, are as necessary to me as breath.

I will not go back to that woman nor will she come to me. It has passed.

But there is always this personal remorse. Why was I not more wise, gentle, determined?

You have to realize that the other is suffering the same remorse.

Artists, as you know, live in others. That is what makes them lovers.

I have felt all of her remorse, suffered with her. It is as though every thought passing through her passed through me.

And I am more stupid, wiser too. I see clearly when she does not.

The separation between those who have loved is like a surgical operation. That is what makes people afraid of love.

I did this thing myself, knowing what I would have to pay, knowing it to be the only thing I could do.

That will not be lived again. I am no longer that woman's lover.

Which won't, in the least, prevent the suffering and the ghosts. I would not be much if they did not come.

I shall talk to you of the artist[1] when I do see you. I got $600 for him, which with something he has saved will give him almost a year.

S.A.

1. Charles Bockler.

[Marion, 10 March 1929]

Sunday

Dear Friend

I got your letter from Birmingham this morning. You forgot to put on a stamp—so the postmaster wrote that I could have it for 2¢.

And glad I was.

Dear woman—it is not going to be so simple to sell the property—although it can be sold.

I think the ultra[?] rich man the solution. We may be a year selling it.

The Freeman thing[1] is an old note. To the political radical you are muddle-headed if you do not see as he does. His own sight is clear. He sees to the Bolshevik state—and paradise.

Dell, Upton Sinclair,[2] this man and many others have written of my confusion etc. The truth is that I have perhaps seen as clearly as any man can see in the muddle. At least I have seen and felt, sometimes, what prose is.

I hope you will not be discouraged about the house. It is, I think, a fair gamble. I am almost sure I could tell you how to sell it to Mr. Kahn. We will talk of that when I see you. The thing has so many shades.

Your mother and Mazie[3] are gone. I miss them. There is no house here where one may have conversation, exchange ideas. I keep wondering if, when you are here, you will dare go around with me. I think there is some notion growing up of the failure of my marriage. I don't mind. It will have to come.

I am going to try to get away from here—to be in New York for a few weeks at the end of this week.

With love,
Sherwood Anderson

1. Joseph Freeman's article "Sherwood Anderson's Confusion" appeared in *New Masses* 4 (February 1929): 6.

2. Floyd Dell, former editor of *Masses* and author of *Moon-Calf* (1920), reviewed SA's *Windy McPherson's Son* in "A New American Novelist," *Masses* 9 (November 1916): 17. Upton Sinclair, active socialist and author of *The Jungle* (1906) and many other novels, plays, and political writings, reviewed SA's *Many Marriages* in "Sick Novels of a Sick World," *Haldeman-Julius Weekly*, 31 March 1923, p. 4.

3. Mazie Copenhaver, a younger sister of EC's, then living at Rosemont. She and her mother were in New York.

[Marion, 7 April 1929]

Dear Eleanor—

I have come home from talking with you—and being with you twice today—and I am very grateful to you for the day.[1] It has been one of the few endurable Sundays I have had in Marion.

I do feel however that I have succeeded in putting you in a very embarrassing position. When I first spoke to you about "E,"[2] I had really been without any affection from a woman for two years.

I think you one of the most charming women I have ever met. I was greedy to get closer to you. You must have felt it in the letters I wrote you.

I thought of your coming here and of my having the chance of being with a really lovely woman in this lovely country.

But today I have felt a lot of other things. Tonight, when I was in your father's sick room, I felt keenly his starved life. I think you are very close to him, that he loves you.

I am terribly afraid that any effort I would make to get what I want from you (companionship with you, closeness to your lovely person in lovely places) would only hurt him.

You do not want to hurt him and I love the tenderness in you for him. I think I had better not press you in the matter any more. In the town's eyes I am a married man. Well.

I know you will not think me presumptuous in taking it for granted you want a closer relationship with me. After all I am a nice person. I know that. There have been a good many things gone between us that have not needed words. I have felt you liking me as I have liked you.

Alas we are man and woman, a fact for which I am half glad, half sorry.

Anyway I am not going to force upon you any additional problems now—by saying anything more about your playing about here with me.

Do you know, my dear, it makes me half sorry that our country is so beautiful and that it is spring. It is spring in me too. On many days I love the country here as I might a woman.

I will of course come to the house once or twice more—but any effort to do anything else would be bound to hurt your father.

Affectionately
Sherwood

1. EC had come to Marion on 6 April and spent several days there before returning to New York.

2. Elizabeth Prall Anderson.

[Marion, 15 April 1929]

I cannot help hoping that you got here, from knowing me more closely, a little of what I got. O dear, I'm afraid I am always the busy miller—a restless force lives in me. I use constantly those I love and those I do not love.

From the moment on Walker Mountain and the other moment on cemetery hill,[1] both with you, I got something that came out on the day after you left. It was a short story I called "Ashamed."[2]

You will see it one of these days. The motive was this—that the loveliness of nature often had the odd effect of separating people. We are all ashamed that we are not nicer, more dignified, more lovely.

Suddenly we look at each other with strangeness in our eyes. There is a kind of terrifying possibility in nature and nature is in us too. For some reason we cannot feel deeply enough alone. I think the artist must be the artist because thus he can make love to many people.

How little I feel sometimes before such women as you—in your lovelier moments, before nature, before some men too.

It must be that we want to make love, go down into each other, because thus we draw, or hope to draw, even for a moment, nearer the mystery.

Oddly, it seems to me we achieved so much more, in relation to each other, in the moment on the mountain, and later on the hill, than we did in that other moment in the car on the road, when we had stopped and were holding each other.

I don't believe my book will go so well here.[3] People who are not written up as important figures will feel hurt. Men and women are made important who do not seem so important to others.

I had to follow my own mood.

Does it strike you as odd that I have made your own father more important to the town life than I have your mother? Well.

Your uncle Jay came into the shop and I have given him the same layouts I am sending you today.[4] Please write to me now and then. It will be very lovely if I can be with you away from here sometime soon. I wish you were here. It is lonesome as hell here.

S.A.

Why don't you come soon.

1. Walker Mountain is a scenic ridge north of Marion; the cemetery hill overlooks the town.

2. This story was not published, and the manuscript has apparently not survived.

3. *Hello Towns!* was published by Liveright on 17 April.

4. John Jacob Scherer, Jr., for many years pastor of the First English Evangelical Lutheran Church in Richmond, Virginia, was a brother of EC's mother and frequently visited in Marion. The "layouts" were a drawing of the floor plan of the house and a map of the grounds at Ripshin.

[Marion, 21 April 1929]

My dear Eleanor.

Bob and I went to the farm yesterday—Saturday. The housekeeper we had last year came back.[1] She is rather good. I am letting the farmer[2] go which will cut my expenses. The woman has a son who can do what needs to be done.

It was a hard trip for me—so many of poor "E"'s things yet to be packed. I packed a large trunk and 6 large cases which can go to her now. Mostly clothes. She was a strange little creature in many ways. Bolts and bolts of goods bought and never made up, dresses bought and never worn. I found, stuffed away, enough packets of flower seeds to stock a small store—never planted.

We drove home in the early afternoon because a storm threatened. It did not come then.

I had brought some jonquils, tulips and narcissus and got some rather nice tulips from the park, making a bouquet which I took to your mother.

They were sitting on the porch when I got up there, a cloudy warm evening. Rev. Copenhaver[3] was there but went soon. I am quite sure it wasn't my conversation, although I did mention Doctor Freud.

Bob had gone up with me but went early to work.

Your father seemed much better and was very sweet, as also was your mother.

There was talk of a letter from you and I was jealous of course. I didn't mention it though.

Then a terrible wind came up. The trees fairly danced. You should have seen the tall maples just before the door—how they flung their arms about.

Many many thoughts of you passing through my head all the time. They come so often at night.

It is hard being here but I am going away for a week, just to loaf in the car and look at the spring. I got a new car—traded my old one in. I shall loaf in it and do not quite know where I will go.

I sent 3 copies of the paper having in it the Elizabethton story to your mother for you. The *Nation* bought it.[4]

Mr. Liveright tells me the critics are being very generous about *Hello Towns*.

O Lord, I wish you were not so far away.

Will there perhaps be a letter from you when I get back?

1. A Mrs. Hilton, who, with her son Mendel, stayed at Ripshin.

2. Claude Reedy, the former caretaker.

3. Eldridge H. Copenhaver, Lutheran pastor and recently appointed president of Marion College.

4. "A Traveler's Notes: Elizabethton" appeared in the *Smyth County News* on 18 April; *Nation* published "Elizabethton, Tennessee," on 1 May (128:526–27).

[Marion, c. 22 April 1929?]

Eleanor . . . I found among the books a small book of tales by Turgenev. I had not read it for years. I think they might say of Ivan as they say of me that his short things are best. How delicately he handles words. He never really, dear, lost the point. The reason, dear, that, when for example we go to the clay, what we want doesn't come forth is that there is something wrong with us. I for example am always superimposing myself on others. How would it be if I could always be really alive to what is before me instead. Let it exist. Let it exist. Let it exist. We should stand before everyone and everything in that mood. We can't. Turgenev did it often. He does not try to make people good or bad. He has delight in little turns of human nature. I imagine him sitting among people. Everyone must have felt the essential goodness in him. It wasn't nonsensical goodness. It was quiet and alive.

He heard people talking, noted little turns of speech. Reality popped out of people suddenly and he nailed that.

He is never excited as he works as I am. Why, yes he was but in some way he held down and down. The prose goes on, dignified, quaint at times, always clear. You get a real sense of houses into which he takes you, of fields.

He is like Cézanne. After all Cézanne is best. He is to Van Gogh what Turgenev was to Dostoevsky. You see the river in flood, carrying down mud, stones, rails etc. There is power there. That's Dostoevsky.

But there is Turgenev, a clear stream. Lights dance in the waters. You see the trees reflected and the sky. You sit down beside it, wade in it. You go back again and again. If I could be like that. I can't. I go on for a day or two all right and then I get all muddy. Then again I have to wait a long time, like a fisherman, for the water to quiet down and get clear again.

[Marion, probably
29 April 1929]

Dearest Eleanor.

I went away from Marion nervous and upset and came back in the same mood. I think you upset me some. You are so nice and I was so lonely. I always want to do too much.

The last six months have really been hell for me. When I got home there was a letter from the princess E. It was really ugly—she said, in substance, that I never had wanted her for anything but a drudge—now that I had got Bob I did not need her as drudge, etc.

I don't know whether it is true or not.

Perhaps to relieve my own mind I plunged into the novel[1]—wrote some 15000 words in a week, then a short story and other things.

Again I got into the terrible state—not sleeping, nerves all over my body on edge.

I got in the car and rode and rode, all over Virginia.[2]

I may have been near you. I went to Washington and took part in a christening, a man in the diplomatic circles.[3] All night I drank champagne and danced. The next day I walked about Washington. People all seemed ugly to me and I seemed ugly to myself.

The point is that I do not at all know that anything I have said to you is sincere.

I do know about the really deep liking because that was there before. My experiences make me rather afraid of doing anything to draw anyone—particularly of your sex—nearer me. "Don't, don't," I keep saying to myself.

Presently I will wear through this time. Human relationships cut so deep. Afterward there are always wounds that keep opening.

The *New York Times* were wonderful Sunday about *Hello Towns*.[4] I shall not think any more about it selling or not selling. It has registered, as a definite thing. That is all I could have asked out of this year.

S.A.

1. Probably "No God," a project SA abandoned by the end of the year.

2. During the week he visited Mary Vernon Greer and, according to another letter, stopped at Civil War battlefields and the University of Virginia in Charlottesville.

3. The party was given by Mr. and Mrs. Chauncey Hackett, Washington friends of SA.

4. Percy Hutchinson, in "The Village Oracle Speaks" (*New York Times Book Review,* 28 April 1929, p. 1), wrote that "again we have it impressed upon us that Mr. Anderson is one of the truly striking figures today in American literature."

[Marion, c. 7 June 1929]

My dear—I must write you another letter before you leave that conference for the next one.[1] As a matter of fact the sentence in your letter that you would be less busy at this conference than the second one came near starting me on the road at once. All my strong mindedness leaked out at my finger ends.

However I had invited some men to the farm for next Sunday. And Mimi will come next Wednesday.[2]

I am planning now to come to the other place arriving on the evening of the 21st—Friday—and coming back here the morning of Monday the 24th. You must not fail to tell me again just the place the second conference is to be held. You did tell me but I was so interested in something else—your dear self—that evening that I do not remember. I do seem to remember that it begins on the 19th.

As for bringing Mimi with me—I don't know. I want in particular one day with you alone—that we may get in the car together and go off to the woods. Do you think that can be managed if she is there? If you do I will bring her. She is a lovely child and it would be fun to take her on the trip to see that country. I dare say the girls would take care of her for our day. What do you think?

It was so silly not to take you down. I have done nothing in particular, being here. How silly our virtues are. And half the time they are not appreciated. I have been reading old Sam Pepys and the Boccaccio.[3] On the whole Sam is more fun. The Boccaccio is often quite dull. Sam never was.

I think it is a good thing I have not tried to write this last year. I have been such a sad excuse of a man. I do not want to write out of that mood. My dear woman, at least let us try to get joy out of our love. But I do not need to tell you that. It is myself that need telling. I have felt such fine strength and health coming from you when I have been with you. You are the beautiful one. The feel of your body under my hand, the sweet strength of it. O my dear, if you could have the lover you deserve, you would never have me.

But I will be none the less grateful if you do have me.

I have known for so long that I wanted a definite and sweet personality, outside myself, to which I could give myself. All my life becomes sweeter because of you. That evening as we sat together, the sweet country there before us, you so much a part of its sweetness and yourself too. It is hard to say all I mean. But you know so well.

I shall write again with gusto and a swing and if I do you will have no small part in it. Already, because of you, I already begin to walk with a new swing, breathe deeper, love life more again. Today I went out and spent four hours just walking over hills, through the deep grass, loving the cattle in the fields, feeling new strength in myself. That you thought me at all beautiful, that there was any male daintiness in me you felt and to which you responded, gives me more pride and joy of life than I have had in me for a long long time. O my dear, you are very good and very sweet to me.

1. EC was working at a YWCA conference for working women at Blue Ridge, North Carolina, and was to go to another at Camp Merrie-Woode, on Lake Toxaway, near Sapphire, North Carolina. SA had visited her at Black Mountain, a few miles from Blue Ridge.

2. SA's daughter Marion ("Mimi") had just graduated from high school in Michigan City, Indiana, and was visiting in Marion.

3. I.e., Samuel Pepys's diary of the years 1660–69 and Giovanni Boccaccio's *Decameron* (1348–53).

[Marion, 12 June 1929]

Dearest Eleanor—

I am writing you thus, with a pencil, in the middle of the night. It is 3 A.M. My pen is down in the shop.[1] I have been sleeping a little but now am broad awake.

I am sure you never had what I have—an outbreak of hives. They itch terribly and I am supposed to be strong-minded and not scratch.

I want to come to that other place,[2] leaving here next Thursday and getting there Thursday evening. We would stay Friday, Saturday and Sunday. I know you will be busy but I shall be seeing you. Perhaps your evenings will not all be busy.

Do get us rooms as near you as you can.

Of course I have been thinking of you day and night. I do rather think I have been run down. The emotional struggle of last winter has left these marks. I dare say this hive business is a part of it. I have so needed your warm embraces and your love.

I think you would be amused if you knew all that has gone on in my mind. I fancy every lover is partly the hunter. He thinks constantly of the deliciousness of the body of his beloved—how to attain to the innermost parts of her. (I must constantly stop writing to scratch these welts on my legs. Why are you not here to touch them with your hands?)

(Did anyone ever tell you how marvelously expressive and lovely your hands are? Or is it a discovery of mine?)

It is lovely to think how delightful our morning was. Certain scenes in life are impressed on the mind to never be lost. It is so with that woodland path. Already I have seen it all a thousand times—the trees, the soft light under the trees, the squirrels in the leaves—you, your body leaning forward, your face against a tree trunk—the troubled look in your eyes.

What is good is that, after the evening, which was in a way a failure on both our parts, the morning brought us close as we never were before.

I think it must have been just the sense of failure in each of us. You had failed to give yourself—your body—to your lover, in spite of all difficulties and risk, as something in you cried out to do, and your lover had failed in gentleness and in patience. It was the mutual sense of failure that brought us so close. Failure and what is called "sin" are such lovely things sometimes, Eleanor my love.

I am alone in the apartment. Mimi came today and Bob took her with his guest[3] to the farm for the night. Mimi is very charming. You will love her.

As a matter of fact, I think my hives are leaving. That may be what makes them itch so insanely.

It is a little insane to think of you so much, to be always touching in fancy your lips, your cheeks, your legs, your sweet breasts. I should be more strong.

I should even not come down there next week to disturb you, which I will do, but I know I will.

Your lover

1. SA and Bob were living in an apartment above the printshop.

2. Camp Merrie-Woode.

3. John Lineaweaver of Lebanon, Pennsylvania, Bob's former classmate at the University of Virginia.

[Marion, c. 15 June 1929]

Dear One—I got both your letters this morning. It happens that we were all up at your house last evening. That queer young school teacher who used to come to see Mazie last winter was there. Of our outfit, Bob, Mimi and myself. The four youngsters played cards and your father, mother and I talked until eleven. Of course we talked about God. It was the first time your father has not gone away when the conversation drifted to religion. I was trying to say what I felt.

The substance of it is that I have always felt that if I could understand God and his purposes he would not be God—or else I would be God. I did say that I thought that any belief on which anyone could lean was all right and should not be disturbed. I also spoke about success and how it had ruined every man I knew to whom success had come. I think it touched your father closely. He is really that fine thing, a truly modern man.

Bob and Mazie had got into a jam and Bob was rude. After he came home he was so upset he could not sleep.

As a matter of fact I told your father and mother of my plan to take Mimi and come to the conference of working girls. I saw no reason why I should not. Of course they know I am interested in you. People are not stupid about such things. They let themselves know what they want to know. It is only decent not to tell them more than they want to know. Do you think anyone seeing us together would not know, if they wanted to, that we loved each other? Well.

I am of course not exactly clear as to what you meant—the reference as to the lack of understanding of your position. I do know that, when I am not with you, it becomes absurd that so much emphasis should be put on one thing.

But when I am with you—of course. Well, you know that you set me physically afire. Of course the one thing becomes all important then. It probably will remain so, when we are together, until we love—if we do.

I have an idea then that things can take their relative positions more truly. A new test of relationships comes then, I fancy.

I'll bet you Tom[1] sensed our interest in each other too. I don't care of course. I would always be proud of you as a beloved one. I am glad he liked me as of course I did him.

Don't worry about any discomforts and of course I want all the time with you I can get but I know you will do the best by me you can.

Mimi and I will start early on the morning of the 20th as I want to take her by Mt. Airy to see Fancy Gap, a lovely drive.[2] It will no doubt take us all day to get there but we should see you that evening in the camp. You can look for us about six. It will be a chance to do something for her before I go away.

I am in much better spirits, gayer in my mood, happier. You are the cause of that.

I do not want you, my dear, to look upon our relation as a problem nor do I want to make anything difficult for you. Well, you know that. I am of course thinking of you constantly, night and day. It's nice. You are nice to think about. Mimi's being here is a help. I love the child. She is so pretty and sensible and fine. I love you too, God bless you, dear.

1. Tom Tippett, leader in the southern labor movement and author of *When Southern Labor Stirs* (1931), who was a participant at EC's camps.

2. SA had returned by that route after his visit with EC earlier in the month, stopping off at the Blue Ridge Hotel in Mt. Airy, North Carolina, to write her a letter.

[Marion, 25 June 1929]

Dearest Eleanor—I am at home at last. This is four o'clock on Tuesday. After we left camp I drove until we reached Asheville and then let Mimi take the wheel. She had not had it more than a half hour than, in going around a sharp corner, she lost her head and went into a heavy lumber truck. This was about twenty-five miles north of Asheville. In the crash the steering rod was jammed and we darted across the road and into a ditch. Of course it was just a bare chance we were not all killed. We darted into the ditch and hit a stump. No one hurt at all.

Well, I can't run the lives of my kids on the safety-first plan. It's all a gamble anyway. I don't mean just that—I do mean that life is an adventure.

You will hardly believe it but as we dashed across the road and into the ditch I was thinking of you so I grabbed the emergency brake, pulled as hard as I could and continued my thoughts.

Here is what I was thinking . . . you said I had you on Sunday, if I had only pressed my advantage etc. Damn, I knew that. There isn't any point to my just penetrating you physically—although there is no doubt of the physical delight—if I do not make a deeper penetration. There are no morals in this. It lets you out a bit too easily. If it all doesn't turn out as lovely as we hope, well . . .

Too easy for you, Eleanor, to say to yourself—"He took me when I was helpless." The whole pagan delight of it could then be shifted to me. I guess I won't have it, never intended to have it so.

If you ever come to me, you have got to come. You know I want you. Well, why not you saying, "Sherwood, I want you, come in." The house that is your body throw open or not. Why should I force myself in? I can love you for something else. I have made up my mind to that.

There has been too much caution, fear, I guess. I don't just mean fear of being caught. I mean trying to discount the future. "Will it succeed or will it not?" etc. etc.

If you ever become my woman I guess you will be my woman but you do not need to, you know that.

After the wreck I sent Mimi on with Margaret[1] on a bus to Elizabethton and got some country mechanics to work on the car. They had to dismantle it and take certain parts to Asheville so the car would run at all. Then I had to sit beside the road from noon until eleven that night, when the car was got going after a fashion, and I limped home, arriving just now.

There was nothing to eat but a can of beans, got from a little general store, and when the car did start there was a heavy fog lying over the mountains so I drove, with a bent steering rod, fifty miles at night. It was all kind of glorious. I wish I had had you and could have taken you on one of those mountain tops in the fog.

I am sending Tom [Tippett] *Hello Towns* and *Poor White*. Ask Tom the name of that book on rayon making. Write me c/o Horace Liveright, 61 West 48th, New York. I am leaving here Thursday. Of course I love you. You are marvelous in everything but love and, isn't it odd, you are a born lover. You will be fine in that too—if not with me, with some lucky man.

1. A friend of EC's at camp who had asked SA for a ride to Elizabethton.

[Marion, c. 26 June 1929]

My dearest Eleanor—

I must write you again after my so ugly letter. How brutal it was of me. I was, I dare say, driven to it by my passion for you—physically. I was so much aroused when I saw you, you were so surrounded, you seemed so to come toward me and then go flying away.

You yourself had told me how this was a part of your nature and had explained how you came by it but I was tired when I wrote. We had smashed the car and I had gone through all that weary waiting and dangerous driving afterward. I should have waited—to get things in perspective again—before writing.

I think what stung me was your saying afterward—"You had me, at such and such a moment."

There seemed to me the implication that I was to show my manhood by forcing you over a certain line.

The implication of this did seem to me afterward that the future happiness and loveliness of our relationship would be up to me.

You will know what I mean. I do admit that to take or be taken is not a casual happening between such people as ourselves.

And even in those moments, when I might have pushed through to possession of you—by that lovely lake at night or in the green close wood in the rain—well, my dear, at least you do know enough of the technique of love-making to know that the tight little white trousers were a kind of insurance policy on your virginity. They left about as much freedom for the exercise of the rites of Eros as manacles about your ankles.

I am going away to the country now[1] and perhaps I shall not even write, although I shall think constantly of you. You have come into me to stay although I have not come into you.

1. SA spent most of July and early August with Charles Bockler and his wife, Katharine, at a rented farm near Dykemans, New York.

[Danbury, Connecticut?,
late July 1929]

I think it is mighty fine of you that you took my remarks as you did. I was baffled and upset. Of course it wasn't just the remark. I was having dreadful doubts of myself too, my sincerity and everything.

The past year and in particular the last winter and spring have been dreadful times.

Mixed up in it was a rather deep-seated fear and distrust of all women.

I rather guess I was too much for the princess E[lizabeth]. There is in me sometimes too much hotness of physical life and fancy. My mind darts about. If I do not work I become vicious.

About as far from Jesus as a man in this world could be—Satan rather. Tom like most radicals is a dear but a bit sentimental, eh. Bless him for a good man.

The idea of meeting the doctors excites me but I do not think I had better do it now.[1] Some day perhaps I shall tell you the story of these weeks. You'll laugh.

Marion depressed me. Thoughts of the princess, gone away to her island on the Pacific, haunted me. God knows I did not want her back. Too much persistent sadness.

She wanted in some way to make me something I am not. After she left there were all her clothes to pack—dead dreams. Like becoming an undertaker.

The little apartment full of death. When I saw you I wanted life—now, now, now.

Not some other time.

A kind of insanity of wanting.

I thought perhaps you knew. "Damn you," I thought.

I did some hot inner cussing at you too—

All conferences, rights of man, YWCAs, people tugging at you, eating up the sweet life within.

"To hell with them too," I thought.

The wreck was a kind of satisfaction. "Smash the God damn thing"—that sort of feeling.

I began writing—a little excitement. It was pitched too low. The words came but not the music of words.

I wanted something in this book, laughing, fancies playing. "There was some prose I wrote once," I told myself. It was in *Many Marriages*. There has been no such prose written by another hand in my time. The damn fools do not know it yet even.

I wanted that back, with added years lived, new defeats, a kind of laughter like stars laughing, buried down in the prose.

So I had got into a place with a poor young painter. Poor cuss. This is not the one I got the money for but another.[2] We went to a little farmhouse.

Well, just before I came, his wife went and got pregnant. They were in hellish trouble, having no money. It would be a bother for me to stay and would hurt their feelings if I didn't.

I stayed.

I began to write. The whole thing was pitched too low. I wrote perhaps ten thousand words.[3]

Then I went to work, utterly miserable.

The pregnant woman was sick, vomiting as women do, trying to cook for two men.

The painter, seeing his summer in the country, my financial contribution was to help realize, shot to pieces.

Do you know, my dear, in the midst of this I began to write, really, something of the prose I want now. It has been flowing. That is why I won't go to the woman and the doctors now.

I probably won't write you any more. If the prose keeps flowing, every hour, every ounce of energy in me, will be wanted.

I won't want to divert my mind with other thoughts, other impulses, until all this has flown out of me. It will be a novel if it comes on as it is coming.

Will you in some way convey all this to your friend and through her to the doctors, keeping the thing open for me later? I shall have to come back to M[arion] about Aug. 10—and will try if it will keep on running there. Bless you for a dear friend.

This fall and winter I will be more in the East. I sent this to Bob—to mail for me—not being very sure of your address.

1. Apparently EC had proposed that SA interview a group of physicians who had treated factory workers.

2. Bockler was the painter SA got money for; see letter of 2 February 1929 and note 4. SA was probably attempting to conceal the fact that, while visiting with Charles and Katharine Bockler, he was also paying court to her sister, Mary Vernon Greer, formerly SA's secretary in Marion.

3. "No God."

[Dykemans, New York, 31 July 1929]

Dear Woman—We poor novelists certainly are provided with a world of material. What a shame we do so little with it.

At any rate your letter makes it seem as though the C[openhaver] household were all alive with terrible suppressed things these days.

Aug. 1st—I awoke to a clear cool morning. There was a wind blowing into my bedroom window. The only reason I have not given you my address here is that I do not want Sherwood Anderson mail here. There is a thin postmistress who may possibly be literary.[1]

It is nice to move unknown, "a man in a brown coat."[2]

The novel came to a stopping place. It is however growing in my mind. It seems to open out, a real challenge to me.

Yesterday I wrote a short story—one of the best I have done. I called it "Other Worlds."[3]

As for the morning—Aug. 1st—my mind was full of poor M and the poor man too.[4] Little seems to have been said about him. He remains in my consciousness a somewhat colorless light man.

And poor M is such an eager passionate one. I have always thought of your whole family as being that way—passionate, eager—not too clear-headed, holding down and down.

You yourself frightened—bold only up in your head. I wonder what would have happened had I got you instead of poor E.

There is nothing more dreadful for a man not too vital than to have got a woman who is vital, eager and not too clear-headed.

These thoughts in my head. Our thoughts about poor M and her man.

Then thoughts of little Suzanne Bloch.[5] Perhaps Bob told you of her. If not you might ask Bob to show you her letter.

My whole day full of thoughts of Mazie and her man—the two perhaps standing up—saying words.

Flesh of my flesh.

Bone of my bone.

It is being done everywhere all the time of course.

You have to face that. You can't live the other fellow's life.

Well, it's a gloomy letter. The day is clear and cool. Some days are terrible. Nature is terrible on some days. It seems to be laughing at people.

I remember a bright morning by that lake down there in N.C. You coming along with piles of papers in your arms, going to a conference.

Tom speaking.

The lake laughing, the trees, the grass. Anyway, if I can write this novel it should have that kind of laughter in it.

As for poor Stark Young—he is made that way.[6] Everything must be indirect. It was so with the Princess E too.

It happens here that just now the whole countryside is full of magnificent mulleins. Do you know them? They have soft thick luscious green leaves.

They are so phallic. The stems with their yellow tiny blossoms stand up so erect.

Nature is all like that to me these days.

But I would like it to be delicate. The mulleins are. Why cannot man be . . . without being forever indirect, evasive?

S.A.

1. Again SA seems less than candid; he probably did not want mail from EC at the Bocklers' because Mary Vernon Greer was with him.

2. SA's "The Man in the Brown Coat" was published in *Little Review* 7 (January-March 1921): 18–21, and reprinted in *The Triumph of the Egg*, pp. 97–101, and *A New Testament*, pp. 71–76.

3. The story was not published, and the manuscript has apparently not survived.

4. Mazie Copenhaver married Channing Wilson in the yard at Rosemont on 2 August.

5. Suzanne Bloch, formerly of Cleveland, Ohio, and later of New York, whose family SA had known for many years, had written him on 24 July about her separation from her husband.

6. Possibly a reference to a disparaging review of *Hello Towns!* by Geoffrey T. Hellman, "Hello, Sherwood!" in *New Republic* 57 (15 May 1929): 365. Young, an editor of *New Republic*, apologized to SA for the review.

[Washington, D.C.,
28 September 1929]

Saturday night

My cold has about passed off and I am feeling more fit than I have for a long time. I have been at work again.

Here I know practically no one. It has its advantages and certainly its disadvantages. The days pass. I work until I am tired and then walk, sit in some little park, read a book etc.

I read Bowers' book about the period after the Civil War—*The Tragic Era.*[1] It was surely a sordid time.

Such a greedy ugly scheming for power. It still I fancy goes on.

Last night I did dine with a newspaper man and his wife, people I used to know ten years ago. The man told me a story of how Hoover got his money. Have you ever heard it? God knows whether or not it is true but it sounds probable.

Well, by this tale, he simply stole it, in China, during the Boxer time out there.[2]

It would be so sweet if you were here tonight. Can't you come next weekend? We could go out to some small town. The country is lovely now.

I am lonely here, as I was in Marion, but it isn't the same thing. Perhaps this kind of loneliness is rather good for me now.

At home I know so many people, after all. I am tempted to go to someone. Well, I go. There is conversation.

It is conversation without being conversation at all. Like always kissing a lady you love and never drawing closer. Words without any thinking and not much feeling back of them.

Newspaper men are a queer lot. I am thinking of the man here. He is disillusioned about everything and goes cheerfully on just the same. Why doesn't he shout or scream or commit suicide—or quit?

He doesn't. "What I am going to do today is rotten," he says and then goes right on and does it.

I don't dare talk about my work. I am working. That's all I dare say.

Please do plan to stop here. If you are going to New Orleans I shall be mightily tempted to go also.

Love to you—dear woman.

Sherwood

1. Claude G. Bowers, *The Tragic Era: The Revolution after Lincoln* (1929).
2. Herbert Hoover was a mining engineer and adviser in Tientsin, China, from 1899 to 1901.

[Washington, 6 October 1929]

Dear Eleanor.

It is a puzzle. I don't blame you. I dare say I was crude.

The truth is that I like you more than anything I have been able to say would indicate. I wish we could be together.

When I think of being with you I always think of it in that way—not in any other way.

Then, when I am with you, the male in me does respond to the woman in you. It is true of you too.

Your instincts may be quite right. Any feeling I have now may not be deep enough for you to take risks. I fancy it was really my loneliness, just now, that was calling to you.

I really won't urge you any more, dear.

I wish you wouldn't think of me as a "woman's man." A phrase in your letter about my experience and your lack of it had that sound. It really isn't true.

I expect I had sounded too sure you wanted to come, too casual. I didn't feel that way.

Let's not let it hurt either of us or our naturally nice feeling for each other. I do not feel very chesty these days.

Dear Eleanor, be a sweet woman and forgive me if I have been crude.

With love,
Sherwood

[Washington, 21 October 1929]

Dearest Eleanor—

I hope you will not be bothered by a stream of letters. I keep wanting to write you, feeling you, in some odd way, a part of what I am trying to do.

Temporarily the tone of the book has slipped. It is because now I must get ahold of something else.

The two people directly concerned are Jim LaForge and Mildred Edgerton.[1] He is forty and she is 22.

I have now to bring her more fully into the picture, make her live in it.

Of course the only thing I can do is to go right on. I will have to see if she is willing to come to life in the pages.

I think Jim has rather.

You have said, with that turn of yours for saying things that sometimes miss but sometimes do strip pretensions bare, that I was a woman expert. Of course you must know, being a woman, that I am a muddler in that field. If a man has got, as that mill woman said, a few women between the sheets, that doesn't mean much.

In that other thing I wrote before I left home and that I repudiated later, I over-emphasized the importance of what goes on between sheets. I knew that afterwards, or at least was pretty sure of it.

Just the same it can be very lovely, bringing out the loveliness of people.

Maybe that's all we want of each other, the niceness inside, when it is inside, given.

I wish you had told me, in your letter, why I inhibit you. It would be so fine of you if you would just write it all out.

Besides being whatever I am, I am also, must be, a bit of a scientist too. Dear one, I presume I have muddled so much and so long in the world of feeling that just now I want to see.

I mean I want people to tell me things.

I have been trying here, when I have seen people, to stand a little aside. I have tried to say to myself—"Now be nice. Don't condemn people or judge them. Stop, look and listen."

Perhaps I am trying not to be hit by any more trains.

If I knew more about what you felt about me, I surely would know more of what Mildred felt about Jim.

He takes women but is afraid of them. He has had a marriage that turned out badly. "There is no use," he thinks, "saying, 'It was her fault or my fault.'"

His wife is dead. He has been living alone for a long time. He sees this woman Mildred.

He is drawn to her but is suspicious of his own feeling. If, being with her outdoors, the landscape becomes suddenly lovelier because she is there, he remembers that it was once so with him because of the presence of another woman.

Look out.

Am I getting into another mess of lies?

I wish you were here so I could talk to you. I know you could tell me a lot. I shall just have to work on and perhaps, when I see you again, seeing you will make me know whether I am going right or wrong.

There is a kind of intelligence down in you and is deeper seated than in anyone else I know.

Is that an illusion?

1. Characters in "No God."

[Washington, 22 October 1929]

Tuesday

Dear Eleanor—It was so thoughtful of you to call me last night. It had got to the place where I felt terribly lonely and cut off from you—not knowing just where you were etc.

I hope you are not too tired or haven't been too upset by the outcome down there.[1]

I am sending you to read a copy of a story written last week and just sent off to *Vanity Fair*.[2] I think it rather rings the bell, being about the tone I am after now.

I mean everything a bit more objective. I have always tried too hard to bore in and in. Doing it got me some results, I'm sure of that.

But often it carried me away off too. It was the sort of thing that led to the misunderstanding between us.

Often too, too often, I myself became nothing, a kind of shaking mass of nerves, half crazy a lot of the time.

I am just trying, that is all, to be a bit more objective.

The trouble with the other, too often, was that, having gone as far as I could, too far, along the road of feeling, I did wrong to everyone about. I'm not going to spend my time now blaming myself but the fact is that these women who have failed, trying to live with me, were not to blame.

I asked too much—that they try to follow me in my moods when, often, I did not know myself where I was going.

I am trying a swing of the pendulum now, to objectify, stand a little aside, use more my outer senses.

To hear more and see more for a time . . .

Like a painter who has gone far into the maze of color and having got lost (color you see might better be taken for feeling rather than sex, as I once said to you. Holding it all to sex is like trying to make all red)—having got lost in color, the painter comes back, takes up drawing again.

I submit this piece, dear, as a straight piece of drawing.

It would be terribly nice if, when you head north, toward Richmond, you would let me meet you somewhere for a day together. When you are in Richmond I will only be able to see you a little, I'm afraid. I need to see you.

I don't think you will ever be upset by the prospect as you were.

[Across margin] Wire me here if you can on Saturday what your address will be next Monday so I can wire you my Richmond address.

1. EC was in meetings at Charlotte, North Carolina.

2. Probably "These Mountaineers," *Vanity Fair* 33 (January 1930): 44–45, 94, reprinted in *Death in the Woods,* pp. 161–71.

[Washington, 22 October 1929]

I think I have come out of my slump. It's odd what you have to do to yourself when you are working, when you are in the midst of something, as I am now.

You have to hold yourself up and up.

Well, you get going. Pretty soon you are just sliding along, making words, your attention not centered.

A grand chance for big holes in your book later. Hardly any of my long books are quite free from these holes, places where I wasn't giving all I had.

I want this book to be pretty tight when it is a book.

I went into a book store yesterday. Wyndham Lewis, the Englishman, has written a long book, mostly centered about [D. H.] Lawrence and myself, proving by us the decay of the whole of western white civilization.[1]

It's a pretty large order. He makes your poor friend cover a lot of territory.

It isn't all nonsense though.

Only I had beat him to it. What he had seen I had seen. It is what I have been talking to you about, what I have been fighting about the last two years.

It would be curious, my dear, if you were the first woman, in all my life, I had really known.

And God knows I don't mean I have fathomed you.

I only mean that I do, I think, take you as you are, for yourself, liking you just so, not wanting in any way to remake you.

I don't want to even take you physically if you don't want me.

But wait. I'm not so sure of that.

And anyway I guess you do, having the same hungers I have sometimes.

But I do mean not wanting to make you hold me up—not wanting to be mothered.

Not expecting you to give me what I can't get, because I am so often slovenly and weak and afraid, out of life itself, nature and people.

I'll get the Lewis book and send it to you, or bring it to Richmond where we can speak of it.

Lordy, I wish I were going to see you tonight—

And tomorrow.

And the next day etc.

1. *Paleface: The Philosophy of the "Melting Pot"* (1929).

[Washington, 26 October 1929]

Dear Eleanor—

Your telegram came early this (Saturday) morning and I shall wire you from Richmond tomorrow although I am pretty certain I shall be at the Westmoreland Club there. I would be quite sure but that my card for the club is supposed to have been sent by John Buchanan[1] and you know John.

Jim and Mildred are going along and Mildred is sure in it now. I think you are bound to like her. I really think I got her, the feel of her, from Mimi.

—stop—

Good—just then a knock on the door. There is a tall Swedish girl who is on the desk at this hotel. Do I want ice water, my clothes pressed, does a letter come, up she comes with what I want. She speaks a little brokenly and grins. "I wouldn't do this for anyone but you," she always says. Every time she brings a letter she says, "Here's a letter from your sweetie."

Of course what happened at that trial just makes you ill.[2] It's like seeing a child run over by an automobile—and the jails—of course. I wish you would get Bob to take you into the one at Marion when you go home sometime.[3]

I used to get Andy Funk[4] and we would go over there in the evening sometimes to sit with the boys. There are bootleggers, chicken thieves etc.—just humans.

I wonder what you will feel about "These Mountaineers." I'm mighty curious. In it is bound up something of the new tone I am after now in writing. You will see how much less I am in it as a personality. It is surely more objective. I think the writing gains strength by it.

As to the people. It doesn't seem to me that you lose sympathy for the girl. I tried to make her stand alone, without relation to anyone, a portrait.

I don't mean by this, dear, that I want to give up feeling. You will know what I mean. If you go too far with feeling it becomes personal. Your own feelings get on top, they ride on top of everything.

I understand Lewis is up to doing a labor novel.[5] You know what it will be. It doesn't matter which side he takes, he will draw a caricature.

When I have got through this book I will be more a free agent than I have been for years. Some time when this thing is cracking somewhere (it will keep cracking in the mill towns for [a] long time) I'll go with you.

You know now I think what I feel about seeing you. If it's too much fuss or makes you feel too much disconcerted, just let me take my chances, seeing what I can of you in Richmond with other people.

The devil—it isn't like being alone with you, having you in my arms, feeling your lips on mine.

But you know that.

I'm crazy about you, woman.

1. Marion attorney and former state senator.

2. Probably a reference to a controversial trial in Charlotte while EC was there, in which seven strikers and union organizers were found guilty of murdering the police chief of Gastonia, North Carolina, on 7 June at the headquarters of the Textile Workers Union in Gastonia.

3. SA had complained in the Marion newspapers about the overcrowded conditions at the jail, which was located across the street from his apartment and the printshop.

4. Charles H. ("Andy") Funk, a Marion lawyer and good friend of SA's.

5. Earlier in the month, Sinclair Lewis had visited Marion, North Carolina, to investigate a strike of mill workers and had published a series of newspaper articles and a pamphlet, *Cheap and Contented Labor* (1929), on his observations. SA resented Lewis's involvement in the labor movement and later wrote an article about it (see second letter of 2 March 1930 and note).

[Marion, 29 November 1929]

Friday . . . I suspected Nick[1] was like that. He is the man who wrote the article about my coming to Marion and made me out a kind of little Santa Claus. After all it must be nice to be like that. Nothing can ever touch such a man.

There has been heavy snow here. I have not tried to work since I came home. Almost every day I have gone hunting or for a long walk. There is nothing very fierce about my hunting. I so seldom hit anything when I do shoot and half the time, when something flies up, I forget to shoot. There is however something very wonderful about being alone outdoors. We have been hunting pheasants. The man I am with goes up one gully and I up another. There is a small stream through the gully. Some of them are from a half to a mile deep. You go up there and sit down on a log. This isn't however a way to get pheasants. There are sounds in the forest, a sense of mystery. A queer kind of spell comes over you. I used to get it out in the open on the desert too. What a place that would be to get acquainted for two people like you and me. Of course I think about you constantly. We meet in this queer casual way.

Almost always there is misunderstanding to clear up. There is your background and mine, so different, giving birth to different thoughts. I think of you perhaps more clearly when I am not with you. I imagine your warm presence. We are always at peace in such imagined scenes. There is perfect understanding. I feel your warmth, your goodness. The strong insistent demand to come to ultimate grips with you physically, that makes you confusing to me and me to you, is not there.

What a mess the man in the magazine article makes of Mann.[2] I can't believe that Mann thinks of himself in that way. He has a fine delicate mind. He was the man to get the award. It is this kind of writing about a man's work that makes men refuse, after a time, to read most of things written about him.

We are in a strange transient time, Eleanor dear. I have just been reading *Middletown*.[3] What a terrible picture it makes. I wonder how true it is. I have to believe that it does not get it all. There would be little left but suicide if that expressed it all. Which is most true, a picture like that or the picture made by *Winesburg*?

I have been more lonesome here than I have ever been. What a queer thing you told me, that you never get lonesome. If that is true how lucky you are. In Marion I am set aside. They think of me here as something strange and queer. I have the sense that this feeling, as regards me, is growing. They are so much more satisfied with Bob. Even the paper he makes for them is better for them.

I am leaving on Tuesday for Chicago. My address there will be c/o Ferdinand Schevill,[4] Hotel Flamingo, 5520 So. Shore Drive. I will send you a better address after I get there. Ferdinand and Clara his wife are very charming people. I will be glad to be near them.

I am afraid sometimes that, when I make such suggestion, as for example about your coming to Chicago while I am there, you will think me being brash and masculine. I do not mean it that way. I am just hungry to see you and be with you. That's all. God knows whether it will ever work out.

A heavy snow today. The world is white. It is still snowing. Bob will return here on Monday.

1. Probably Nick Carter, a writer of advertising who worked at the time for the chamber of commerce in Richmond, Virginia. His first wife was a cousin of EC's.

2. Possibly Joseph Wood Krutch, "The Dualism of Thomas Mann," *Nation* 129 (4 December 1929): 679–80. Krutch writes about Mann, who had received the 1929 Nobel Prize in literature: "Perched upon the pinnacle of his magic mountain he sees a titanic struggle going on below him, but he cannot be sure which side ought to win and in the confusion he cannot even distinguish with certainty the disposition of the troops" (p. 679).

3. *Middletown,* a study of Muncie, Indiana, by sociologists Robert S. and Helen M. Lynd, was published in 1929.

4. A close friend of SA's, a history professor at the University of Chicago.

[Chicago, 5 December 1929]

Thursday—Chicago has changed tremendously since I have been here. I have not been downtown yet but this place where I am now is very familiar. I lived for years in this neighborhood. I should have known you then.

Many odd adventures in my life, almost within sight of where I am now sitting. It is at 55th Street, where it projects out into the lake, all new land. I see the lake, obscured by the morning mist, to my right. Droves of cars, like crazy sheep running swiftly, are going along the outer driveway.

I slept well but awoke early, to sit at the window and look out.

I was gloomy. I had been reading Montaigne.[1] Most of his essays were written when he was an old man. He talks of death too much.

There was one sensible essay though, praising suicide as a sensible thing . . . when you have outlived your usefulness . . . rather than to sit about and mourn. I liked that.

I have not seen Mimi yet but will today.[2]

I think I shall work. The novel will have to be extended, heightened, its points brought out.

I want to get the consciousness of the two things . . . in the one person. Mildred pregnant . . . wanting to use her pregnancy to make the man marry her . . . at the same time not wanting to take advantage . . . doing it just the same . . . aware . . . rather laughing at herself.

Jim not wanting to marry . . . afraid of marriage . . . wanting her though.

As it would have been sweet this morning to have you . . . in the dawn here by the window . . . looking out over the lake with me . . . your body against mine.

We might have made love in the night and would have been quiet.

Myself really living in your body, feeling the movement of your blood, your breasts, as you breathed.

We humans . . . male and female . . . are so strange to each other . . . so precious sometimes . . . so irritating to each other sometimes.

Sometimes there is, for a time anyway, complete acceptance . . . the one of the other . . . that is about the sweetest experience there is in life I guess.

I haven't any plan here except to work. Something is not in the novel that must get in before I can let go of it.

I wish you were coming here for a few days. I presume it is a hopeless dream. It is such a gamble too. O my dear Eleanor, what puzzling things we are.

1. Michel Montaigne (1533–92), whose *Essais* first appeared in 1580.
2. Mimi was a student at the University of Chicago.

[Chicago, 12 December 1929]

Dear E—Poor Barton[1] is an ass. God knows what such men have in their minds. I always think of them as eternally whistling in the dark, to keep up their courage.

If they let go for one moment, let themselves think, "Here I am. My God, what am I?" they would be gone forever.

Of course, if you begin to say, "Here we are. There is the artist class, or the labor crowd," or any crowd for that matter, you do find, in general, pretty much the same shallowness and cruelty.

There do seem to be individuals, a few of them, who have something else shining in their eyes. I have seen it in your eyes. That's why I love you.

There is a heavy cold fog over the lake and the city. Chicago is in one of its dark days. I walked over to the park, thinking of the night we walked round and round the park in Washington, thinking how nice the presence of another sweet to you can be.

They are tearing down the old Field's Museum. Rosenwald, the Sears Roebuck one, is giving a million to rebuild it.[2] No one seems to know whether or not it is to be a replica of the old one. I hope so. You remember how lovely it was on summer nights. I used to go sit on the steps at the rear and see the moon shining on the lagoon. I dare say you have done that.

I am afraid the whole book will have to be pretty much rewritten if it is to get anywhere near what I want. That doesn't make me as sick as I thought it would. I am seeing very few people, rather holing myself up and seeing what I can do with it. It's something to do, at any rate, something in which to absorb myself.

No, I won't be at Marion for Christmas. I shall be sorry not to see you there.

And yet I don't know. When I see you I have this physical yen for you and it would have to go unsatisfied.

I dare say it confuses me because it is unsatisfied.

When I sit thinking of you, as I am doing at this moment, I just think what a nice person you are.

I wonder how anyone gets so nice and stays so nice.

1. Possibly Ralph Barton, who later committed suicide (see letter of 21 May 1931).

2. SA refers to what is now the Museum of Science and Industry. The earlier structure, called the Field Columbian Museum, was being renovated in preparation for the Century of Progress Exposition in 1933. Julius Rosenwald, president of Sears, Roebuck, actually contributed about $5 million.

[St. Petersburg, Florida,
20 December 1929]

Friday
Dearest Eleanor.

Here I am, down here in this southern place, on the Gulf. It is a pretty town and I have a room that looks out over the bay. I arrived here last night after a strange trip down.

I was in Chicago two weeks. All the time I was there it was dark and gloomy. What that had to do with what happened to me I don't know.

At any rate I got into one of my own particular kind of fits of depression. They are rather hard to explain to any sensible normal person. When it comes, the thing grows and grows on me. There is an overwhelming sense of futility. I try to think of other things, I walk about. Sometimes during such times it seems to me as though all the ugliness of life . . . so much of which is in me . . . were a great beast sitting on my back and pressing me down and down.

I dare say, my dear, this is all a question of nerve force. When my nerves are all right, I can usually throw the beast off. I hope, my dear, you will forgive me for telling you all of this. It is a kind of relief to speak of it, as though speaking of it brought you in here to me, into this room. Almost, as I write, I can feel your presence, hear your voice, see your kind eyes. I feel your hands in mine. You are one of the people in life who have come close to me. In spite of the confusion between us, brought about by the fact that we happen to be man and woman, I feel you always warm and close and friendly, willing to give your warmth and courage to me.

I dare say there are many people who would give me something if I could let them. Why I can't I don't know. Everything, when one of these fits comes on me, seems strange. I walk along the streets seeing thousands of people and they all seem a million miles away.

Well, I am in a hotel room. The furniture of the room even seems strange. I walk across the room and touch a chair with my hand. I actually want to assure myself there is a chair there, that the walls of the room exist, the bed over there, this table.

Does it all sound a little crazy, dear? It is.

That sort of sense of nothingness, of myself a part of a world in which nothing is true, nothing real, comes. You must take this all not [as] a fancy but, while it lasts, as very real. All the way on the train coming down here I had terribly this feeling.

Will I get over it here? Well, my dear, I have some sort of faith in sunshine and the sea. It may all be a matter of curing over-tired nerves.

What a letter to write to a woman at the Christmas time.

What could Christmas mean if we could believe in it?

If, for example, my dear, I could feel, at times like this, that life had any purpose, that there was any meaning to anything?

I know it is silly to ask that. I ought to take the sun, the wind coming over the water, as enough for me, I ought to take the fact that there are people like you as enough.

I do normally I think. I am only trying to describe what has happened to me . . . walking this way on the dark ground through another of these dark places.

But I really believe now, dear, that I shall be better. I am going to stay outdoors all I can. Perhaps, if I can once go through such a time in any manly way, I shall get from it, in the end, a new kind of self-reliance, some real manhood in myself.

Forgive me for telling you of this strange time. I should not think too much about it. I hope you will have some fun being at home for Christmas, and of course I hope that being in this warmer place and seeing the sun will make me whole again. Dear Eleanor.

S.A.

[Across margin] Hotel Detroit, St. Petersburg, Fla.

[St. Petersburg, 25 December 1929]

Dearest Eleanor . . .

I have not written you for some days, but do hope you had a nice Christmas. It is a horrid day really, so much fakiness clustered about it in churches and houses. I rather detest it. On the night before Christmas here . . . it was stinging cold . . . three or four middle aged men and women singing in the hotel here about Christ in voices so dead, so ugly, so meaningless, that it made you ill to hear it.

I haven't written because I have been in an ugly mood but am over it now. Am working again.

However my saying that I had got through the book was all bunk. It hadn't really much life or swing or joy in it. There has been a bit more of these qualities to what I have written these last few days.

I think I do not have this feeling about Christmas because of the Christ idea. There is really, at bottom, a good deal of God love in me.

I've an idea too that the Christ story is one of the finest ever written. There are artists back of it and they did fine delicate work.

I could take it, the figure of Christ I mean, as a fine bit of statuary or a lovely painting. I can respect too men like your father who say . . . "If Christ did not actually rise from the dead, I have no hope."

Only I haven't such hope. I can see nothing in my life that should make it valuable enough to save or continue.

The God idea is to me something else. It is the Absolute, the thing beyond human comprehension, like art itself when it is beautiful, the mystery . . . It . . . call it what you will . . . the mystery of the thing that makes two humans, with all complications of life on them, love each other.

A man and woman loving for example. Sometimes they do seem to skirt the edge of infinity.

Christmas never was lovely to me. It wasn't at home when I was a child. I suppose we were too poor. We shivered through it, saying "damn" under our breaths.

Odd how much nicer people are just going along, doing what work they have to do, than they are on Sundays and on what they claim is Christ's birthday. Children do right to hate Sundays and I am sure we do right to hate what the world, by advertising, gift giving etc., does to Christmas.

I sank pretty low these last weeks. Perhaps had there been someone near to talk to, to love a little, I would have got through better. I suppose I just realized that my book was not lovely and I shrank from beginning again—

A kind of cowardice in me, dear.

Today, Christmas day, it had grown warmer and the sun came out warm. I went and sat on the end of a pier, where there were some men fishing, and sat there a long time, looking out to sea. If I could have had someone's hand to hold, it would have been quite perfect.

Love to you, dear.
Detroit Hotel, St. Petersburg.

[St. Petersburg, 26 December 1929]

Dear Eleanor.

The hankies were lovely, I don't care who made them. You sent them.

No, my dear woman, I am not ill, at least not physically. I admit I am—in the head.

The trouble with the novel goes pretty deep I fancy.[1] I have been trying to write another story of men and women in love. For some reason I can't quite explain, that isn't my central interest any more. I think I accept love as a thing in the world. It may be the central, the absolute, thing . . . I don't know. It affects people in different ways and they react to it in a multitude of ways. There are stories there, novels no end . . . I can think of fifty within a week.

But as I have suggested, Eleanor, it is no longer my central interest.

There is however something I want to do. I have been getting nearer and nearer it the last year. I think you know, Eleanor, that I have made a mess of my own life so far. What there is left of it I would like to use.

I would like to get into the labor movement. More and more as I have thought of it, seeing the little I did see at Elizabethton, talking to you and Tom, I would like to give myself to it.

Of course, my dear, I can't be a labor leader. I wouldn't know how and I am not a natural leader of that sort.

I think anyone will admit that I have a certain talent. For example I would like to devote the next year or two [to] going about to factory towns. I would like to go into factories, into strikers' homes, visit with them, talk to them, talk to employers, to strike breakers.

Then I would like to devote the rest of my life to writing books and articles about what I find.

There wouldn't be any money in this but I don't believe I am going to need a lot of money the rest of my life. Bob can run the papers at Marion and I dare say some day I will sell the farm.

However, I would need some backing for two or three years at least, perhaps longer. Do you suppose some rich woman could be interested in this, I mean to back me while I go about and absorb what I need to absorb?

I have very naturally the notion that the central inner story of labor and capital is not being told. I think it can best be told in the simple human tales of people caught in both sides of it.

There are these masses of people, men and women, young boys and girls. The thing was done in one way in *Middletown* but there is a better and deeper way to tell it.

As for myself, Eleanor, and the novel. It was all right and just wasn't right. I haven't really been centrally interested in it. There is no use my going over old ground. I suppose, when I wrote *Dark Laughter* and some of the other later novels, I did still believe that in the love, as between man and woman, there might be found a way out of the tangle of existence.

I don't believe it any more. The figures of Russell and Powys[2] both become a little absurd to me. Like you I like Russell the least. In some queer way he isn't at bottom nice.

I wonder if it would be necessary to have someone help me financially in what I would now like to try to do. Surely it would not need to cost much. I think, for example, of myself in a cheap car perhaps drifting from town to town let us say in the southern mill country. I would like to have a certain feeling of leisure. It would be all right in one way I fancy to be able to do the job, as I at first thought of it, for some newspaper or syndicate of newspapers but, having talked to two or three newspaper men, I am not now so sure of that.

There would be lacking a certain freedom. I do not want quite the newspaper point of view.

I think, to speak a little for myself, not for you but for someone who might be interested, that, in the body of my work already done, there are indications of my capacity for the thing I want. It would be, I think, generally admitted that, in my *Winesburg, Ohio,* I did do something to give people an insight into the lives of people of the small towns.

My *Poor White* was the story of the coming of the modern industrial world to such another town. Neither of these books, when published, were financially successful. At that time, when I was at work on them, I did not depend, as I am rather foolishly I think doing now, on novel writing for a living. I went every day to an advertising office in Chicago and wrote advertisements to make a living. I rather doubt now whether or not I have the reserve physical strength for that, although I have determined to get out of my present position of depending on feeding out novels to the public to live.

If I cannot get someone to back me in what I would now like to try to do, I will go to work at something other than novel writing anyway.

As for the two books mentioned above. Although, at the time of their publication, they brought me little or no money, they have since, through cheap editions, been distributed, as you know, by hundreds of thousands.

I think you will know why I came to you about this matter. You are the only person I know who is in touch with both sides of this matter. I thought it entirely possible that you could, when I got into it, steer and help me toward making the contacts I will need in the world of workers and could perhaps also interest someone in helping me financially to accomplish my purpose.

As you know, Eleanor, I came out of the world of workers. I feel more comfortable there than anywhere else. Already, at the thought of doing some such work, the deep depression that has hung over me so long passes and I feel content within myself. It is as though life had meaning to me again.

Please, my dear, think about this whole matter. Write me just what you feel. Do you not agree with me that there is a job to do that I might do? Surely, in this whole situation, capital on one side and labor on the other, there should be a place for the artist who wants merely to be open-eyed, to receive impressions and make his pictures, wanting to serve only the central inner story and not one side or the other.

What do you think?

I will stay here until I hear from you. In some way I am going to do it but it would tremendously simplify everything if I could have a backer to the extent of say a few thousand a year to give me freedom.

As always
Sherwood

1. SA had abandoned "No God."

2. Bertrand Russell and John Cowper Powys. Russell's *Marriage and Morals* and Powys's *The Meaning of Culture* were published in 1929.

[St. Petersburg, 26 December 1929]

Dear Eleanor.

I had just written you the enclosed letter when news of this came.[1]

It is a deep hurt. It only confirms me in my feelings about the matter set forth in the letter just written you.

Would you mind wiring me, after reading the enclosed, and telling me whether or not you think there is a chance of getting backing for what I propose.

Sherwood

1. The "enclosed letter" was the preceding one. The "news of this" is probably the telegram he had just received about the death of Tennessee Mitchell, his second wife, from an apparent overdose of sleeping pills in her apartment in Chicago. SA had talked to her on the telephone when he was there earlier in the month but had refused to go see her.

[St. Petersburg, c. 30 December 1929]

Dear Eleanor.

Your letter came today and the wire and as you are to be there until the 4th I will address you there.

I think, after going over the matter a little more in my mind, that you had better do nothing about it until I see you and we have a talk. As suggested I have given the novel up and have notified Liveright. On the other hand I have full $500 in hand and shall probably have more. I can live very reasonably as I am living.

My present plan is to stay out of Marion all winter. I will probably go over to Miami about Jan. 15th and may stay about there for a month. If you were going to be in New Orleans in early January, I would be strongly tempted to go over there. Lord, wouldn't I love two or three days with you about that old town. However, I suppose that won't work out.

I will have some money coming in Feb. 1st and in fact there should be at least $500 more by then.

When I think it over, I realize that I would not want to take any money from any fund that, if I did not take it, would go to the workers. I suppose I had in mind a rather special thing. I thought of some rich dame who might be willing to put up a guarantee of a few thousand a year . . . if needed . . . say $3000.

I would be glad to go over things with such a one and explain my present financial status. The chances are I think a little better than 50-50 that I wouldn't need any of it.

Having such a guarantee would I think help me over rough spots and most of all would give me a feeling of security. There is something middle-class in me, Eleanor. When my resources get down below $300 I begin getting in a money panic.

What I want to do, after February—or perhaps in February—is to go into some of the mill towns, visit some mills. If the strike at Marion is still on[1] or there is a strike at another place, I will go there. I want to get acquainted with some of the strikers. I fancy it won't be hard. I would depend on you helping me do all that.

After I gave the novel up I got at once, with an intense feeling of relief, into short stories, did one which I am having typed and am on a long one. I call one of them "A Dead Dog," the other "Horns"—about a man putting horns on his friend.[2]

I also began sketching a labor thing. I want to build a book, this summer if I can, about some little mill girls, such types as we saw at Elizabethton, and already the book begins to form in my mind.

I just have, you see, the feeling that these people going through this thing, young kids and old people, in the south make up the richest and best material in America today.

Suppose for example that you and Tom (the blanket room being in my mind)[3] fell in love, Tom married, the complications of that. It might be quite rich material, I mean any such human problem (after all, Eleanor, we are, however, middle-class)—such problems are middle-class problems. Compare them with the vitality of the problem faced by some of these southern white families.

I want some sort of vital grip with that material if I can get it. I have a feeling it belongs to me rather than to any other writer in America. I don't know that the labor crowd will like my point of view on it. I just have this deep feeling that they are my people. It seems to me now almost as though I had been wandering all these years when I have been fooling with anything else.

If it did not eat up funds so and you were going to be anywhere in the south where I could see you and have a day or two to talk with you before Jan. 15th, I'd come. Tell me where you are going to be in the first two weeks of January and could you put in two days somewhere talking over my plans with me.

At any rate do nothing until we do talk—I mean about money.

I promised to go off on a two-weeks jaunt after Jan. 15th with my Miami laundryman friend[4] and would rather like to do it. My nerves did a little go to pieces . . . fool-like trying to force myself into the handling of materials that had gone a little dead to me . . . the kids in that union room we saw that night at Elizabethton haunting me all the time.

I think I thought I would write a novel that would be popular, get the money that way, like a woman going on the streets to get money so she will look nice to her lover in a new dress, something like that.

Write me before you leave Marion if you can and give me if you can your itinerary and tell me if you think it would be sensible to meet somewhere now & talk—and if so where and when.

You will see I am rather treating you as an agent. Well, it's a good cause. You are a darling.

The Tennessee thing[5] had some cutting sad things in it for me that I'll tell you about when I see you.

1. The strike of cotton mill workers at Marion, North Carolina.

2. "A Dead Dog" appeared in the *Yale Review* 20 (1931): 554-67. "Horns" was not published.

3. EC had written SA earlier about a conversation with Tom Tippett in a hotel blanket closet. SA teased her about the incident in several letters.

4. Maurice Long, who also had a home in Washington, D.C., where SA often visited.

5. Tennessee Mitchell's death.

[St. Petersburg, 6 January 1930]

Dear Eleanor.

It is Monday noon—the 6th, and I just got your fine letter. I think it would be rather foolish of me to go on to Miami and that I had better come and see you, say at Greensboro next Sunday. That should be within striking distance of where I want to be. However, I will put it all into your hands. If you are too busy there, [I] could come to Salisbury or anywhere you say.

I want of course to get the dope from you, where I ought to go, what I ought to see, people I ought to meet, etc. I'll go look at the big labor people here but had already concluded, from things heard and from the pictures in the newspapers here about what they were.

About Washington etc., Eleanor, I shall let you alone about that. There is no use my lying to you. You know I adore you. Well, it is in your nature that you cannot do the Isadora Duncan sort of thing. Your body arouses me. It is adorable to me. I love to touch it.

To do so upsets you. I know that. We'll forget it. Anyway, my dear, if I had you in that way I dare say I wouldn't be faithful to you. The feeling might pass after a time. It has happened to me with other women. Perhaps it always passes.

That doesn't need to prevent me loving you, as a person. I can do that and let you alone physically.

Besides, my dear, I saw as well as you did how, at Washington, Richmond and down there at camp, my going after you in that way upset you, knocked you out of your work, raised the devil with you in general.

However, I have to love women. It is in me. I'll love you anyway. You have a thousand things in you to be loved besides your dear body.

So that's that. I mean it. We'll be friends.

Any[way], Eleanor dear, I'm not one to be taken too seriously. I'll never, I dare say, be faithful to any one woman. There are too many facets to my nature I suppose.

You'll see how well I'll behave really. If you should really give yourself to me, wholly, as women sometimes do to men and as it is in you to do, it would be an unlucky day for you. I'm really not a monogamist. And I'm so damn grateful to you for all you are doing to help me out.

I guess also, dear, that it is all foolishness for me to stay down here trying to cure my nerves. There may be nothing in the world wrong with me but boredom.

I am writing some days and on other days just lying stale and flat here.

I have to get out of myself, have an absorbing interest outside myself. That will cure my nerves. I think these people will do it. Here everyone is aged, middle class, self-satisfied.

I realize, as you must, dear, that I cannot get into what is wanted all at once but am sure you can help me make the connections I want and start me off. Suppose, when you get this, you just wire me, telling me when and where to meet you. I'm sure you will get this by Thursday at the latest. I'd like, if I could, to go over all my plans with you and have you advise me.

Incidentally, Bob says . . . in a note I had from him . . . that you are more lovely than he ever knew you to be. He says he had hard work not to fall in love with you himself.

You know Bob. He's nice though.

Poor Tom's letter sounds pretty blue, doesn't it. Is there any place where the labor movement in these towns is at all hopeful?

However, you will tell me all these things when I see you.

Really, dear, don't worry about the other. I'll be a good boy. I don't want to upset you. That, I assure you, hasn't been in my mind in wanting to see you. Of course you won't mind my loving to be near you.

I'm too grateful to you to want to upset you that way again, dear woman.

I shall wait, full of hope, to hear from you, telling me where and when to come. It's really the best shot I've got to bring me out of my lethargy and make me again alive and a worker.

With love,

S.A.

Savannah would be fine if you could manage a day or two there.

Then afterward I could perhaps be at Charlotte, N. C. when you are there for the 4 days 22 to 26th.

Savannah, Georgia,
[14 January 1930]

Tuesday
Dear Eleanor—

What a lonesome day this has been. It rained quite hard after you left,[1] until about two. When you got on the bus I began to curse myself for my caution. I wanted so much to go with you (and here was the bus quite empty) but decided to be wise and cautious. I do dread the thought of anything happening to you, as you work, through me.

Then I had another disappointment. I worked until about three and then went to the river front. There was a small steamer going up river to Augusta and leaving at 4. It was 10 minutes to four when I found it. It takes nearly three days and nights, stopping all the way up at little towns and plantations on the way. It would have been such a rare chance to see the interior, off the railroads and highways, talk to people. I dare say the boat would have been a bit dirty, with perhaps bedbugs, but had I but known of it in time would not have hesitated to take it. It would have just suited me, in my pensive mood.

What is the use my trying to tell you what the visit here has meant to me? To be sure I am sad and lonely tonight, as I can't help half hoping you are too. You were so alive, so lovely . . . I have never seen you so beautiful, Eleanor dear. I dare say it will always be like this . . . seeing you rarely, coming a little close to you and then either you or I gone. It may be that life is like that . . . that is all of it.

I am trying not to promise myself much of anything from these next three months. I want, as far as I can, to loaf and look, be, if I can, quite relaxed, in rather a horizontal position I fancy as regards everything. My fancy has this way of racing ahead. Already I am in cotton mills, seeing the machinery, the thread and yarn flying. I want, if I can, to stop this trick of racing ahead, let what will happen to me.

Don't, my dear, think any more about me and don't expect too much . . . or rather anything. If the little gods are good and will just creep into my fancy and my pen.

I went and copied all that off James Oglethorpe's monument.[2] A class of school children had been sent to copy it. There we all were, the little boys and myself, scribbling away. "Gee, it's long," the kids said.

What had happened was that, instead of "Horns,"[3] I had begun playing with the thought of a man come back here. He was a rather whimsical cuss, as I thought of him, brought up as a boy in one of these old houses here. As he stands by the monument, amused by George II's pompous English, giving these people all that territory "west to the South Seas," he begins to think that, after all, the thing happened [as] George II and his ministers intended. They intended to wipe out the Indians and spread the benefits of Anglo-Saxon civilization "west to the South Seas," and behold, with the coming of the airplane, radio, talkie etc., they have done just that.

I imagined my man the great great great grandson perhaps of one of those who came here with Oglethorpe . . . George Carpenter gentleman[4] perhaps.

I spent two hours playing with all that on paper, the man's fancy playing, the solemn sentences on the monument staring at him, his ironic amusement at the town, America, the Anglo-Saxons, himself and all.

Then, as I say, I went to the river (I put in a piece of blotter as being just about its color . . . it had a golden glow, though, in the late afternoon light). The gulls were flying, dipping and diving, and I thought I would like to be a gull for awhile and have you be one . . . to fly off with you and make love in the air, high above the river. I've no idea whether or not gulls do make love in the air but wouldn't it be wonderful—

To go far far up and then, in the delicious ecstasy of love, to fall and fall—at last catching yourself and falling gently on the river's breast.

Surely that is poetry. You made me feel like that.

A workman joined me and we talked. He is an electrician. He began telling me about a great place owned by an automobile man named Coffin.[5]

Also Henry Ford has bought great stretches of country near here.

"What for?"

"He's got so much money he doesn't know what to do with it. He just fools around a lot," the working man said. He was a tall raw-boned man. He said Ford was monkeying with the idea that he could raise some kind of plant out of which he could get cotton.[6]

"They'll make Bolsheviks of us yet, these fools," he said.

He didn't think unions were much good though. "They just get us into strikes and sell us out," he said. He thought unions were much less powerful than they used to be and rich men more respected.

I am taking the sleeper to Macon and, having looked at the hotel register, decided on a hotel called "The Southland." Macon is also in the tourists' belt I think. First-class hotels are a bit too expensive. I'll stay at the Southland unless I write you about a change.[7]

You have been a dear. It has been a lovely time for me.

1. They met briefly in Savannah while EC was attending a meeting there.

2. A statue of James Oglethorpe in Chippewa Square in Savannah. Inscribed on the pedestal is the text of King George II's proclamation establishing the colony of Georgia.

3. See letter of c. 30 December 1929 and note 2.

4. One of the men, including Oglethorpe, who were named by the king to be trustees of the colony.

5. Probably a reference to Howard E. Coffin, automobile and aviation magnate and developer of Sea Island, a beach resort about fifty miles south of Savannah.

6. Ford had a winter home, Richmond Hill, on a large tract of land west of Savannah where he conducted various agricultural experiments.

7. He did change to the Lanier.

[Macon, Georgia], 17 January [1930]

Dear Eleanor.

I must write to tell you of my first impressions at Macon and the prospects for getting at least something of what I want.

I saw Miss Cliff[1] yesterday and we lunched together. She has no car. At once I decided I would inevitably have to have one. Without one it would be quite impossible to visit outlying mill villages and go places I would want to go.

So I phoned Bob at Marion, telling him to buy me a Ford there, about like Randolph's,[2] to be delivered by the dealer here, thinking I could make Col. Tate[3] carry me for a part of its cost. This Bob found couldn't be done so I will just try to fix up a deal somewhere down here.

A young man, friend of Miss Cliff's, who reads my books, loaned us a car for the afternoon and we visited several villages here, clustered about mills . . . some pretty terrible, others not so bad. Miss Cliff had in the meantime phoned the manager of the Bibb plant[4] asking permission for me to go through. They put her off until three and then turned her down. I was represented as just a friend.

I decided to try a mill on my own and drove up to one and went to the gate. I tried to pass myself off as a tourist interested in manufacture, who had never been in a mill etc. There was a man with a broken leg at the gate and he hobbled off on his crutches and presently came back saying the superintendent had refused—"on account of insurance," he said.

The broken-legged man and I discussed what that meant. "I didn't want to set the place afire, just see it," I said. He laughed. We had got on good terms. He thought it was silly.

The truth is that Miss Cliff, like your honorable self, is I'm afraid under suspicion. This I got from a young newspaper man later. He seemed to think I had better . . . as regards seeing the inside of plants etc. . . . let such questionable characters as you and Miss Cliff alone.

I'll get in the plants O.K.

As regards the plant of the broken-legged gate man . . . there have been AF of L men in here making speeches etc. and the probabilities are that the sup. looked out a window and, seeing me, took me for one of them. I have been often taken for actor, thief, gambler, race track tout, but this is the first time I've been taken for an AF of L. From what I saw of them at St. Pete, I'm not flattered.

Talking with the hon[orable] Bob on the phone, I found he was really seriously thinking of marriage. He has too many vitamins in him, that boy. I wrote him pages of austere advice. It comes so well from me.

Miss Cliff and I had stopped at the public library to get *Life of Wm Gregg*.[5] I signed S Anderson—Marion, Va. The Marion, Va. gave me away. The poor child who got me the book was afterward scolded for not making a fuss over me. She should have kissed me, I gather, and afterwards, if that happened to be my mood, taken me into some nearby blanket room.[6] Fame is fame, my dear. I am in the newspaper this morning and tomorrow must go to a literary breakfast. I must go because it is for Julian Harris[7] and, knowing Julian, I know that, if I don't go, being here, he'll have his feelings hurt. He is that way. I've a hunch it will be a mess of Annabelles.[8]

A young newspaper man came to see me, University of Ga. man. He is a native of a little mill town up north in the Georgia hills and has a Ford. He and I are going there in his Ford. He promises me the inside of two or three mills on the way up. Also having been raised in a mill village, I shall have the opportunity of two or three days conversation with him going and coming.

I retouched "A Dead Dog" and got it off.

In the evening a Mr. Robinson,[9] English Dept. the college here . . . a somewhat silly man . . . came to call.

Later I went to a square dance, mill girls, and stayed until midnight. A good day I call it.

I'll get what I want all right.

The article, or rather story, "These Mountaineers," is in current *Vanity Fair,* also there is a story "In a Strange Town" in current *Scribner's.*[10]

I can see I'm going to have a good time. Don't know though about people like you and Miss Cliff. You are a bit disreputable. Perhaps I had better not get too thick with your sort.

1. Cliff Taylor was industrial secretary at the Macon YWCA.

2. Randolph Copenhaver, EC's younger brother.

3. James Tate of Chilhowie (near Marion), Virginia, a Ford dealer.

4. The Bibb Company produced cotton yarn.

5. A biography by Broadus Mitchell, published in 1928. Gregg was a pioneer in the establishment of the southern cotton industry.

6. See letter of c. 30 December 1929, note 3.

7. The son of Joel Chandler Harris. He had recently resigned as editor of the *Enquirer-Sun* in Columbus, Georgia, and was living at the time in Atlanta.

8. A reference to Annabelle Buchanan, a prominent Marion musician and wife of John Buchanan. SA complained of her social airs.

9. Joseph Robinson of Wesleyan College.

10. "In a Strange Town" appeared in *Scribner's Magazine* 87 (January 1930): 20–25.

[Macon, 23 January 1930]

Notes for Eleanor.

Your letter has not come yet. This is early morning. I have not slept well.

I feel ashamed that I do not seem to be able to avoid thinking of you as a woman. I am constantly afraid I will do something to upset you . . . I mean to affect the effectiveness of your work . . . which God knows I do not want to do.

Perhaps I had better take me a little mill girl . . . as I dare say most men down here do. There are plenty of them that have the flair . . . that give men the wicked eye.

I have become acquainted with two girls here, waiters in a cheap restaurant, genuine troupers. They are the nicest and the toughest pair you ever saw. I go over there and sit on a stool. They haven't figured me out. "What are you, guy, anyway?" they say. They have got to telling me stories about men who come in, how they stall them off, get money out of them etc. They are both the strangest combination of toughness with gentleness you ever saw.

Went with Miss Cliff to the overall factory. It is infinitely better than the mill I was in. I will talk to you about the mill. You are all right to fire at the mill as the central evil now. Little Cliff is fine with the girls. She is O.K.

I suppose a man like myself does need a woman. In the first place I need the warm fact of love. I suppose also, dear, that I have this direct physical need that upsets me when not gratified. It results in sleepless nights and flatness and inability to think and work clearly the next day. I dare say you have avoided it by the simple expediency of never having had that kind of fulfillment.

There are plenty of women to function with, God knows, but that sort of thing is too debasing. I'm rather a wreck today because I did not sleep last night. I hate not being on my toes when life is as absorbing and interesting as it is now.

I understand what you mean by social sense. I can love whole rooms full of these working girls, the feeling being almost physical in me, without it in the least centering on one of them.

I've an idea that you, in getting me into this, have done the nicest thing anyone ever did to me.

Later

Have made a failure of an attempt to write this morning. All morning I have been full of you. Last night I went to my room early and sat there or walked around. You were so long calling. Of course I knew you were up to your ears in things and I want you to be. I want you to be just what you are.

Just the same, dear, I have the faults that go with my virtues. I imagine too much always. I thought of the flood of letters you would get at Charlotte.[1]

Then I thought that after S[avannah] you might feel as you did after W[ashington].

I wish I could explain W to you. It rather looked as though I had jockeyed to get you into a room. The hell of it is that I did too, and didn't at the same time.

Why, after S I was happy as I think you were.

I suppose even if we grow to love each other more and more (I know there is a kind of gigantic assumption in my supposing you will love me more and more but I do, for some queer reason, assume it), even if we grow to love each other more and more, so that we feel free and happy in a room together, so that clothes do not play such an important role, so that the technical difference between 1/2, 1/3, 1/4, 1/16, 1/32 and the whole means little or nothing, I suppose, in any event, we probably won't want to have children, set up an establishment ever, etc.

I can fancy we might sometimes run off together for a week, seeing mountains and roads together.

But I think, dearest of women, that I am sincere, as far as sincerity in me lies, in saying that I am going to spend the rest of my days in this working people's field and I've an idea you will.

Dearest, it won't hurt you to go the whole singing tower.[2] I'm enough of a pagan to know that. When you have done it, when you have dropped the bars in that respect, you will be all the happier and nicer for it.

There is a whole world of feeling and joy in life, two people, being male and female, loving each other, can explore together.

I myself want what is Beyond Desire a damn sight more than climbing a singing tower, or being buried under one either.

I am a poet after all and you are a woman, and, my senses all tell me, a strangely generous, sensitive, fine woman.

Perhaps you won't be able to help saying to yourself—"But he has done this to other women, bringing them unhappiness, maybe telling them the same thing."

Maybe it's true. I don't know. I have to spend my life seeking, as you do. I don't think that has anything to do with it.

Darling, I won't rape you, or unnecessarily frighten you, or anything. I won't let Henry Staley see you. Tom's O.K. but the industrial revolution isn't going to come off on Sunday Jan. 25, '30,[3] so let's let Tom stew this once.

I'll be generous . . . I mean about future blanket rooms.

As for Rome, Athens, Alexandria, Carthage, Moscow, Marion and Kalamazoo,[4] suppose you just come to Atlanta on that train Sunday . . . wire me if you will.

Back of all my desire to see you and be with you is something surely beyond W or S. You know that.

Sometimes I think . . . you said once that you were straight as anything about people in the mass but terribly muddled about people as individuals . . . why not let me help you in what I do understand as you help me constantly in what I am trying to understand.

I guess it's just a plain case of a man who loves a woman saying to her—"Come here."

One thing your lover knows, if you admit me as lover, is that it's all an adventure.

What, tell me, my dear, more is life?

Wire me, Eleanor dear, that you are coming to Atlanta and I'll be at the train there when you get off.

1. EC had meetings in Charlotte on 22–26 January.

2. I.e., sexual intercourse, a meaning SA derived from the phallic suggestiveness of the Singing Tower at Mountain Lake, Florida.

3. SA wanted her to meet him in Atlanta on that day.

4. A playful reference to EC's travel schedule. She was to be in Rome, Georgia, on 29 January.

[Macon, 23 January 1930]

Notes for Eleanor

I presume it is what happens to you as you get older. You are inclined to be too easy on yourself. I wasn't any good today but after I wrote to you, or rather after I got your letter, I felt better.

I went over to see my two troupers. I go there for hot soup at noon. There is a long counter, at which you sit on stools—two in fact with a high fence-like wall like a spite-fence between.

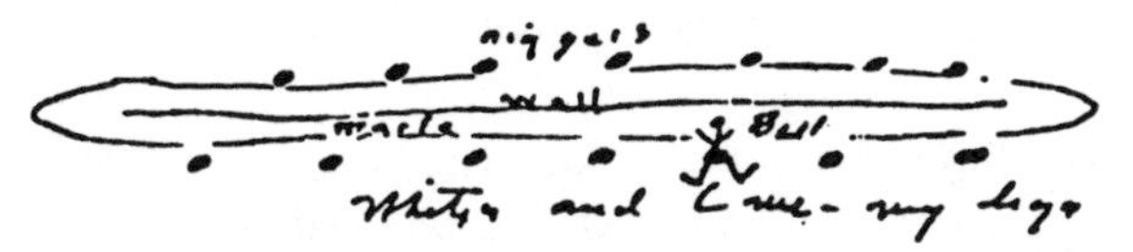

The two troupers are Belle and Marie. I told Belle my troubles. "Belle," said I, "I love a lady and don't know whether she loves me or not."

Belle—"Well, where is she? Go and ask her."

Me—"I can't. She isn't here. I feel bum. I didn't sleep last night. Were you ever like that?"

Belle—"I sure was. I found out he was two-timing me though. I'll bet this lady is two-timing you too."

Belle is 32 and has 3 children—all girls. One of them is already in a factory. She says her old man got to two-timing her and she got a divorce.

"Did you get any alimony?"

"Well, the judge said I could have some but I just took his word for it and let it go. He didn't have any dust on him. He was clean as a plate.

"Besides he had got his new woman already in the barn. I knew she was going to get hers without me making it any worse for her."

Marie has two children also but she hasn't been married. You should see her walk. She is a big raw-boned woman, with amazing grace.

"Marie, you're good-looking, do you know it?" I said to her.

"You ought to see me stripped," she said.

Belle has a lot of rings on her two fingers. She says she gets them off railroad guys who come in. I gather that railroad men are unusually generous with women. Marie doesn't know why railroad guys always fall for Belle and not for her.

"I'm best on brown-eyed ones, like you," Marie said.

They can't decide whether I am connected with Mrs. Harry Payne Whitney's racing stable—it winters here—or Sparks Circus that also winters here.[1]

"I'm Harry Payne Whitney himself," I said, but they said if I was they would guarantee I'd never get out of that restaurant alive.

As I couldn't write, thinking of you, thinking of the letter I wrote you, wondering if you would understand that it didn't really make so much difference whether it was W or S or X or Y or Z so long as I could have you all to myself, where I could be with you for hours, and as the troupers had spoken of the racing stable and the circus, I went to these two places.

This would have been a joy to you. The horses were lovely creatures. An old Irishman took me around. He was elaborately polite, led the horses out for me to see etc.

I couldn't understand at first, then I got onto something. It seems Mrs. Whitney now and then must tell some friend, going to Palm Beach I presume, to stop and see her colts.

It must be the way I dress or something of the sort, dear. Working people never take me for a business or professional man. They put me down as something anyway out of the beaten track. The old Irishman, after he had shown me all the colts and I had given him a half dollar, winked. "You tell the lady everything is O.K.," he said.

"I don't know her."

"Yes you do. I've seen you, mister. You're just the kind she's always got around."

There wasn't anything open at the circus place but a big dog barn where they train dogs during the winter for circus acts during the summer.

They train pigs too. They train pigs to run up a ladder like this

and slide down a shute like this.

I've got a horrid mind. I couldn't help asking what happened to a trained pig after he has been trained and has put in his season as a circus performer. My dear, they bring him, or her, back here, fatten him or her and butcher him or her. Fact. The same trainers eat him or her while they are training some more the next winter.

There were lovely greyhounds, whippets, leapers, runners, barrel rollers, leapers through hoops, climbers of ladders.

They train performing leopards and lions but I don't want to see that. I always hate to see wild animals made into performers. It hurts me.

You see I'm just prattling on so that I won't think. If I stop to think, I'll be asking myself whether I did right in putting the case so strongly for your coming . . .

And it's such fun to prattle to you.

I'm going to another working girls' dance tonight.

1. Gertrude Vanderbilt Whitney, a sculptor, and her husband, a New York banker, invested some of their great wealth in horse breeding. The Sparks circus was known for its variety of animal acts.

[Columbus, Georgia,
29 January 1930]

Wednesday
Notes for Eleanor

I hardly know where to write to you—O flea.[1] You must give me addresses. I presume it will be New York after this.

And meetings—and resolutions passed—and God knows what.

I've been all afternoon in a cotton mill here. A mill owner with a queerly sensitive face. We had cigarettes together and talked. "What do you want?" said he.

Well, I wanted the rhythm of cotton mills, the machinery, girls and all.

They laughed. Men came in from other offices. What do you think of this guy? He wants the rhythm of cotton mills.

We talked economics, a lot of stuff.

These men even seem willing to let me go and sit in mills if I want that.

They seemed to know—what perhaps you and I don't always know—that economic laws work, regardless of you and me and Tom and Sinclair Lewis and everyone. We are only fleas hopping on the surface of a river.

Have you ever been in a place where they dye whole bales of cotton, blue, red, green and all?

There it lies in great heaps . . . the air filled with steam . . . a place to drive a painter crazy.

A great room with what seemed to me ten thousand looms. Clatter, clatter, clatter.

Where is truth? O Truth where art thou?

I was talking to a little weaver woman, with the strongest little body, the brightest eyes. That is the weaver's knot, she said, making the knot.

Her fingers were so fast, so accurate.

I spoke of them. "You have marvelous fingers, marvelous hands," I said. I had to lean down close to her face to make her hear. She had hands surprisingly like the hands of one Eleanor.

"I've been in the mill thirty years," she said.

"You look too young."

"Then we used to go in young. I went in at twelve."

She refutes every argument of Tom and you in some queer way. After 30 years of it she was so alive, so young.

I'm just telling you. I'm taking impressions, as honestly as I can, as they come.

There are so damned many cross-currents to life, my dear.

The afternoon in the house of the great rich man of all this section . . . his name is Jordan[2] . . . a man 80 . . . such life in him . . . we drank corn whiskey together . . . he started a cotton mill here in 1867.

The woman in you would have loved him. He's hard-boiled & cruel though.

In some queer way tonight I'm sorry for Tom and all the radicals. They are so often such a loose thinking lot.

There is so much to learn. You have sure put me in the way of one of the most interesting winters of my life.

I find this story,[3] stuck between sheets of this cheap paper . . . so I send it to you.

1. SA called her a flea, he explained in another letter, because she hopped about so in her YWCA work.

2. G. Gunby Jordan, leading citizen of Columbus, whose many business interests included textile mills, banks, railroads, and real estate. He died on 9 May 1930 at the age of eighty-four.

3. The story, no longer with the letter, is not identifiable.

[Greenville, South Carolina,
9 February 1930]

Sunday evening
Dear Woman

As I write, you are on the train bound for New York. It was sweet to hear your voice. When you called I was in the office of the hotel here, talking to Mr. [William G.] Sirrine, a lawyer, lawyer for the cotton mill owners association. I think he was feeling me out. He was laying the town at my feet etc. He has sworn to take me through a mill at night, take me into any mill I want to go into, etc.

I stopped talking to him to run into the booth to you. My dear, you should be in the movies. You have so much IT.[1] At least you have for me. At the sound of your voice a thrill goes all through my body.

I become alive in a new way. You dear, you dear.

How foolish that I haven't a car. If I had one we would just get in it, when you come down here, and drift through the country, go into the hills and into the woods.

Have you any notion where we might go together? Look at the map. It will be marvelous to be with you again. Bear in mind I can go anywhere, meet you anywhere you say anytime.

The man, the lawyer, said—"We will take you anywhere you say. We will introduce you to workmen. I know an old fellow."

"But I do not want to meet workmen through you. Through you I want to go in the mills. I'll find my own way to the workmen. I don't want them from your point of view."

"Are you against us?"

"I am neither for you or against you. I'm an artist."

"Are you a communist?"

"No. Are you?"

He is balanced between being afraid of me, sore etc. and interested.

He asked me about Elizabethton. "Did you write about that?"

"Yes. I am sorry I haven't it here. Look it up."[2]

I told him frankly that I might be what he and his associates would call a dangerous man.

My frankness seems rather to disarm him. I don't know.

Doctor Fewell[3] told me a marvelous story about a minute man brought down here. He followed a woman weaver to the toilet, stood outside the door with a watch in his hand.

Her husband was a weaver in the same room.

He rushed upon the minute man and beat him up. There was a near riot in the room. I have worked it up into a kind of grotesque dance, the looms in the room dancing, the weavers dancing with wrath.

Stomping on the minute man's watch, on his glasses, on him.

All to the tune of the looms.

I'll send it when I have had it typed and reworked.

My long thing blew up—the Marion thing.[4] I'm getting too many impressions now for long things. I'd better stick to short quick flashes. You are a darling.

I've thought what I will do if we can have a few days. Through Dr. Fewell here I'll meet an auto dealer. I'll rent a car and drive to Atlanta, or wherever you say to meet you. We'll go off together and have a jaunt out of doors. That will be the best thing.

1. An allusion to the 1927 movie *It,* starring Clara Bow, in which *it* is defined as "that quality possessed by some which draws all others with its magnetic force."

2. See letter of 21 April 1929, note 4.

3. William S. Fewell, M.D. SA used his story in "Loom Dance," *New Republic* 62 (April 1930): 292–94, which reappeared in *Perhaps Women,* pp. 30–40.

4. An abortive work dealing with the strike at Marion, North Carolina.

[Greenville, 11 February 1930]

Tuesday

Had a rather jolly dinner party last night at the home of a Mr. A. S. Bedell. I met his sister Mrs. Haynesworth on the west coast ten years ago. He is in a big firm of engineers and mill builders. They are the people who acted as arbitrators in the strike here.

A. S. Bedell is to take me through a mill at midnight.

A Mrs. McKissick[1]—3 generations of mill owners in her family—is to take me up in the country to a mill on Thursday.

Practically every mill owner in town has called me up, invited me to lunch, to go through his mill etc.

This is a pretty good chance to get their angle. Here I have not made you or Miss Callahan responsible. I have just come in here, gone to Dr. Fewell on my own etc.

I have been honest with these men too. I have tried to let them see where I stand.

I spent all afternoon yesterday in the Dunean Mill—2 hours in the big loom room, with 1800 looms going. The superintendent, a very capable man . . . he reminded me of old Pop Geers, a famous race horse driver I used to know . . . kept saying sarcastically—"You see how hard these mill slaves have to work, eh."

After he said it five or six times, I took hold of his arm. "You may be a fine mill superintendent but you are a bum psychologist."

"Why, what do you mean?"

"When you mention this matter of these girls five or six times, you tell me you have got it on you mind, your conscience, just as I have."

He shut up on that.

What gets these men is that they feel in me the response to the beauty and wonder of the machinery. That gets them. It makes us in some way brothers. This man kept giving me little presents, a handkerchief, a piece of silk cloth etc.

I am still shattered, that is, my nerves are still shattered from the two hours in that room. Of course the mill girls don't get it like that. They would all be dead in a week.

I will just have to have the little vacation with you. Last night, all night, the looms clattered in my head.

I think that mill sup. thought I was a bit crazy. We stood at the end of the great loom room and I began to dance on the floor. "Come on," I said, "let's do a loom dance."

He had to laugh though. "They do dance, don't they," he said. "I had never noticed that."

I am going to dine with Doctor Fewell and his wife tonight. There is a terrible story. Dr. Fewell is gradually going blind. He has an incurable disease of the nerves of the eyes. A friend told me. You would never know it from him. He's a real man.

My dear, there is so much to get. This afternoon I am to spend in a mill village with a school teacher who is teaching grown people how to read and write. She goes every day to mill villages and will take me whenever I want to go.

Dear One—you have pushed me off into an ocean. I swim as well as I can. I love you for having done it.

1. Mrs. Margaret Smyth McKissick, prominent civic leader in Greenville.

[Greenville, 12 February 1930]

After your letter came—Wednesday. The first letter after you got back to N.Y.

First of all don't let me get you distraught and upset about the visit we may have together.

I dreamed of getting a car, meeting you at some small town out of Atlanta—we going off then for 3 or 4 days out of doors. It would be near March 1st. Spring would be showing its face. We would stop at little towns. No need occupying the same room if you think it is better not.

Or we could just meet at some town. Spartanburg would be all right. I thought of the older town of Augusta—for no reason other than that it is older. Greenville is terribly middlewestern. It would be nice to be with you in a place that had more charm—if you think it best not to spend the time in a car wandering through the country.

I am anxious not to awaken in you the feelings . . . that do not come from your head or your immediate reactions but from old deep ones I fancy. They reflect in me too.

You must bear in mind always, dear, that I do not have these feelings. It is partly because I am a man and I presume a peculiarly direct, unconventional man. But I get everything you feel, through you, later because I am terribly sensitive to you. The thought of you at night arouses me. I do not dare let myself think of your physical loveliness to me.

I want to have it nice for you. You make the plan. I will stay here. I will be ready to go anywhere, do as you suggest. This because your plans will necessarily be more subject to other things than mine.

I think maybe I will have John[1] & Bob drive down here for a day with me before you come. I want to see them both.

After you come, I may possibly go down to New Orleans for the month of March and then home in April.

In as much as I have not sold the property and there is no immediate prospect, I suppose everything will depend on money coming in.

It seems to me, dear, that what I am trying to do is terribly important. It would be nice if I could do it with sufficient money to be easy. I ought even to be able to have a secretary.

I have been reading Mitchell[2] and others. These professors, touching industry, are too dry. They get no feeling into what they do.

On the other hand, men like Tom feel enough but wobble terribly when it comes to facts. It is for that reason they are so easy to put aside. More brains. More brains. I do believe that, in the end, if I can do the thing right, it will catch the fancy of people. It is so far and away the biggest thing in America.

But it might take time. I think of how I wrote *Winesburg*, so well known now. I got altogether some $50 or $60 out of all the stories published in little radical magazines, and the book, later, had its big sale in cheap editions, out of which I get almost nothing.

I did this out of my experience as a boy and a young man in a small town. While I did it I made my living writing advertisements. I can't do that now. There are too many places to go to.

Later I want to see the automobile industry, rubber, steel etc. I want to sing the song of the machine. If I could show really the strange and terrible contrast, the glories of the machine contrasted with the workman.

It needs so much nerve force. On several days here I have been nearly wrecked. The machine itself seemed to stretch out its hands to me, pick me up and shake me. I fairly stumbled out of one factory.

Eleanor dear, at least I have got a new feeling of manhood out of all this. I am tackling a man's-sized job. I can lose myself in it. Although I am very tired some nights, from all the things I have felt and seen during the day, I feel basic health in me . . . a thing I had not felt for two or three years before I got into this.

It does seem absurd, doesn't it, that, with all the excess money thrown here and there, there should be any question of money, but money is made a strange force too. It is the symbol by which those in control stay in control.

God knows I am willing to leave them in control if they will let me look and feel and I can get strength and power to put down what I feel.

Lots of love, dear.

1. His younger son, John, had moved to Marion and was working with Bob in the print shop.

2. Broadus Mitchell and George S. Mitchell published *The Industrial Revolution in the South* in 1930.

[Greenville, 12 February 1930]

Wednesday

After I wrote you today I was called to the office of old Sirrine.[1] He is a big mill engineer. More than that he is the man who organized the textile industry of the South.

He is a remarkable old man—a kind of old lion. We got down to hard pan. After the softness of some of these men, always talking of what they are doing for the mill people etc., this man was a relief.

We had a good cross fire.

He set forth the industrialists' point of view. It was like talking, say with a Henry Cabot Lodge.[2]

Do you believe this?

Yes.

And this?

Yes.

And this?

No.

Do you set yourself up as knowing more of these people than I can know, having lived with them all my life?

Yes. You know your thing and I know mine. I would know more of any clerk in your office in ten minutes than you could know in your whole life.

At least, dear, I think I have got these people feeling that they have got someone on their hands.

He said something about entering mills. "We're touchy I know," he said. "I think you are safe."

"Don't be too sure of that," I said.

At least, dear, I have made them no concessions. I don't know how it will all come out.

Anyway I saw a look of admiration, of respect and a kind of friendliness in this man's eyes. At the end he said to me—"After all, I'm glad I'm an engineer, not just a mill owner."

"I have built some good mills," he said.

"And I have written some good books," I replied.
I don't believe he is afraid of me.

1. Joseph E. Sirrine, older brother of William.
2. Lodge, a conservative U.S. senator from Massachusetts, died in 1924.

[Augusta, Georgia,
26 February 1930]

Dear

I could write to you for hours on the subject of seeing you, as against a river trip or a European trip or even a cotton mill. I won't. You surely felt it in me how happy I was being with you.[1]

The afternoon passed, a strange, vivid time. We went right down through the heart of the cotton cropper country. Not a painted house most of the way, roofs falling in, such towns. I could see from the car window the marvellous little pine grove we were in and the stretch of sand that got like a lake in the evening light.

Perhaps all we can do is to build up in ourselves memories of such moments. I remember writing that at the end of *Poor White*.

I made the man standing with some little colored stones in his hand, glad for them.

I like Augusta and you will.

I laid awake a long time thinking of our hours together, our talk.

There is much I want to say to you yet.

Please, please come.

1. SA apparently met EC in Spartanburg, South Carolina, while she was en route to Atlanta, where she was assigned from 23 February to 1 March. SA proceeded to Augusta and checked in as "Will Grove" at the Hotel Richmond.

[Augusta, 2 March 1930]

(Conversation on way back to hotel from train on which I saw you off at A[ugusta])[1]

It was still raining. In the wet street near the station the taxi just missed a collision with a Ford. A young man and woman were in the Ford.

Taxi driver. "Did you see that? He was looking at that girl, not at where he was going."

Myself. "Well, she was nice looking. Don't be sore at him."

T.d. turning to grin. "That's right. You can't blame anyone if they feel that."

Myself. "Don't you feel it anymore?"

T.d. "I do more than I ever did. It may be the outdoors, driving a taxi like I do. I was a clerk for 30 years."

Myself. "You feel it more, the need of it more?"

T.d. "Yes only I'm not like I used to be. I'm more particular, more choosy. If it means anything at all to me, it means ten times more than it ever did."

(We had got back to the hotel.)

I can't write and tell you much but would like to have a little note for you there when you get home.

I can't write much because you know everything I do. You seem to me, dear, to have been so perfect about it all—from the beginning. There has been a queer and very real penetration of me by you. I wonder if you know how little of what I have thought of as male and female there has been to it all.

Almost as though I could say—"Which is woman and which man?"

A sense of my body belonging to you, as I fancy a woman might feel toward a man lover.

But in all this no feeling of assertion in you.

It was a little (and very sweetly to me) as though you, having guarded something better, were saying, "I know you offer but I'll take when it is offered purely."

Does this sound overly subtile? I don't believe you'll think so.

There should be men and women in the world like that, the purer one making the other pure, impregnating the other with fineness like seed. I do feel impregnated by these hours with you. I'll try not to lose what you gave me to keep warm.

I wanted to say it. I've always believed it. It's time for men and women to do to each other what you did to me. I need that. I should be a fine man. I guess I've found out I'm not strong enough to be alone.

I wish you would pick up *Winesburg* and read a little thing called "Tandy." It was a cry out of me long ago for the feeling you left with me here.

1. On 1 March EC met SA in Augusta. They rented a car and spent the afternoon in a nearby pine woods where their first lovemaking occurred. She left the next day on a train to Marion, and on 3 March SA left for New Orleans.

[Augusta, 2 March 1930]

Sunday

It rained steadily after you left and harder and harder, as though all the little gods were saying . . . "See how kind we were."

I stayed in my room, worked a little, read a little and stared out the window a lot. I didn't even go down to dinner.

That feeling that comes so rarely in life was on me . . . as though I held in my hand some beautiful and fragile vessel and that I might break it if I moved.

It is so absurd . . . if you say things like that to most people, they think you mean they are too delicate and fragile. What I suppose I think is that the delicate and fragile thing must be in everyone.

Perhaps I have failed because I wanted too much to have it out where I could see it. It has slipped out of my hands so often. Crash it went.

There are fragments enough around.

How, dear, can we ask anything else? They have taken God away from us. We have to find the equivalent in each other some way.

How delicate and beautiful it was in you. You were like the river that changed constantly in the light. Every moment with you was a new adventure.

E[lizabeth] and others used to say to me . . . "You want only that feeling."

They meant that I wanted only to be sensitized so I would feel changes in the light over a river like voices calling. I mean with new distinction.

If sex aroused that in me, then they said I was only using them for that end.

As though sex . . . to the highly civilized . . . could be a thing in itself.

Suppose the simple want of nature to be that seed be deposited in warm soil.

Nearly everything man does is beyond nature . . . the machine for example.

Suppose I do ask that of you . . . that you give me refuge in your arms, warm me, love me.

Suppose the thing thus brought again to life in me comes out of you through me into song or poetry.

I have never been able to see why two people, a man and woman, should not have other children except flesh and blood children.

The Labor Lewis thing, the machine song,[1] the Loom Dance etc. are as much children of yours as mine. It was what I meant yesterday when I said you impregnated me.

It was as though the other women had said . . . "I want to do it alone, to prove my own individual strength."

No, it wasn't just that they said. They said . . . "You ask too much."

Suppose the real joining of men and women be always to have children. There are all kinds of beautiful children to be had.

Here is all my mysticism, dearest one. In stumbling toward it, I have again and again emphasized sex too much but those who have said it was sex obsession are really stupid.

It is child obsession.

Some days I want the whole world washed with new color . . . all these horrid dirty sordid streets made gay. People dancing. People walking with stately dignity through streets.

I have a little power in me sometimes to make things dance a little.

It never comes alone. That I am sure is why I have so earnestly sought love, in another, that would give love birth again in me.

I have thought . . . I wonder if I am right . . . that the poet . . . when he is the poet . . . is the ultimate, the final, masculine and that the woman, when she loves, is the ultimate, the final, woman.

The dance that may come, the song, the painting, is the child.

I had children thus from Tennessee and E too. After [a]while they did not want to anymore. I don't know just why.

Was it because I asked too much? Children and yet more children until we die.

The children surely, surely yours as well as mine.

Perhaps if I could have said this to them. Perhaps I didn't know it clearly, as you have made me know it.

You were very lovely at the last when I had come to real love of you . . . I had to struggle through my own vulgarity to a kind of beginning of understanding there was no more hesitancy in you than in a warm field . . . no more resistance than in a river into which another stream feeds.

Well, I feel very rich, dearest.

1. "The Labor Lewis thing" is an article which SA originally intended to be an attack upon Sinclair Lewis's participation in the labor movement. He later

removed the references to Lewis, and the article was published as "Cotton Mill" in *Scribner's Magazine* 88 (July 1930): 1–11. "Machine Song: Automobile" appeared in *Household Magazine* 30 (October 1930): 3.

[New Orleans, 6 March 1930]

Dearest

Each day I say to myself—"Today I will not write to Eleanor."

It is because I have the feeling that it is better not to tell the woman you love all your thoughts, feeling etc.

But then I don't. You have made me so alive. My days are full.

A little note to you is like a kiss.

I mean I like to write to you so that I feel it is an indulgence.

My room at this hotel,[1] at the edge of the French Quarter, is on the 6th floor, 679. It is on a corner so that I have 4 windows. Even as I sit writing you, I can look down on the roofs of the Quarter and on the river.

At night the steamers going past, up river to Baton Rouge, keep calling like cattle lost in the dark.

I am trying to combine into one long thing the impression of the factory at night and the story about Jim, the workman who threw the pencil.[2] There is enough to keep me writing for two or three weeks. On Saturday I am going up river to spend a night in a big sugar refinery.

As you will know, I got the Air Mail letter and also the little note about Katharine.[3] She may be vivid, dear, but have you any notion how vivid and real you are?

I have of course moments at night feeling over again that moment under the pine tree when the gates came open. I try not to center on that. I won't, dear. Like you, I know we have something to be treated with delicacy and kept.

Do you know that chapter in the Old Testament when Darius let Ezra rebuild Jerusalem?[4]

And they rebuilt the water gate, and the sheep gate, and the fish gate, and the tower of the furnaces.

There must be, dear, a kind of city wall behind which a man and woman who love can go, even in America now.

The thing in us like a fortified city against ugliness.

We aren't asking too much, are we, dear one?

Write me when you can, whenever you can—for your letters are like a kiss to me too.

1. Hotel Monteleone.

2. Probably "Entering the Mill at Night," *Perhaps Women*, pp. 98–117, although it does not include the story of Jim.

3. Katharine Van Meier, of Stillwater, Minnesota, EC's sister.

4. SA merges two passages of the Old Testament, Ezra 4 and Nehemiah 3.

[New Orleans, 11 March 1930]

Dearest One—

I thought I had better write to Miss Bogue[1] in as much as I had asked you to speak to her and so have sent her the enclosed. I hope you will think it is all right. I guess it is better not to try for money. I wish I didn't get silly frights about it occasionally.

I didn't mean not to tell you my thoughts, dear lover. Sometimes there is an inclination to draw everything out into words. It doesn't happen when I can see you. Then my body can a little express what I feel.

But when I do not see you and know I cannot, a sort of terrible wordiness sometimes takes hold of me. I only meant to say—"Stop talking, Sherwood. Leave something for your lover's imagination."

Of course the Bible has influenced me, dear. I read it all the time. Where else am I to find such fine dignified prose? Prose means little to me without the quality of poetry buried in it. To tell the truth, dear, I have always been sly about this whole matter. I really want only to write poetry but do not want to be called a poet. To be known as a poet is rather too much like being known as a lover.

I try always I think to shift and change and weave the rhythm of words, trying to have the poetry always alive in it but buried down in what seems like prose forms. The old Hebrew poets did that wonderfully. They have taught me a lot.

I think it is always because the rhythm is so important that I must love to work. Unlove is too terrible. I have to have the whole body in it so that I feel the prose down through my body. Not many of the critics have discovered this yet but I don't care.

I suppose that is why it does something so rotten to me to write for money. I tried last week to write something I thought that *Household* magazine out west would like. There was $300 in it. That may be what gave me hives. Don't laugh. I tore it up.

Darling, I don't believe you can quite give me the kiss I like best without coming down here.

P.S. I am afraid I shall have to stay here 2 or 3 weeks yet. I had my poor jaws x-rayed and find there are teeth that must be drilled down into and fussed with. Ain't it hell? More money put into my carcass. I begrudge it so.

Is there any sort of row I could kick up that might bring you here? There are so many lovely things to be seen.

I want to make love to you in the presence of the Mississippi—a gigantic notion but I have it.

1. Anna Bogue was secretary of a committee set up by Mrs. Leonard K. Elmhirst, noted philanthropist and *New Republic* angel, to fund worthwhile social projects. After an initial inquiry by EC, SA wrote to Bogue to explain his work on labor in the South and to thank her for her interest.

[New Orleans, 13 March 1930]

You'll be damned if you do and worse damned if you don't, I guess, dear. It's odd how little after-thoughts come. When I had sent the ring and had said something of it being a symbol of comradeship in my letter, I went along the street, from the post office, smiling at myself because what I felt was pure desire and want of you.

The night before I had made love to you in my dreams.

I went last night to dine at a house here. The woman who had me was once a society girl here.[1] Her people had money. Then they lost it and died.

She went into newspaper work and was nice for a time. I knew her first then.

But they insisted on her doing society and she couldn't or didn't get out of it.

I think she had some idea of saving something nice in herself but perhaps saved it too long. Then suddenly no one wanted her. She became what a friend of mine once spoke of as "the woman whose flesh is no longer sweet." Perhaps we have to pay for it if we try to keep ourselves pure too long. My own notion rather is that, as long as we live, we must drag the past about with us. Every act in life, every thought, I guess, exacts something from us.

I often think of myself as an old house, liking the figure. All my life I have been hanging up pictures on the walls. You'll admit I've been pretty busy.

There is a sweet thing happens in life. Lovely moments in life remain when the ugly ones fade, so that, with Elizabeth and Tennessee now, I keep the finer moments.

There is at least some sense to the notion that the life well lived must be lived dangerously.

I cling to the notion that there is art in relationships too, that love is a fine and delicate art. We blunder at it as we must blunder at any art, but even blundering is better than just standing aside.

That woman with whom I dined is surrounded now with a strange, half-dead flock of homosexual men. The air in her house fairly reeks.

Yet she is, I am sure, what is called Pure.

God save the Mesopotamians.

I don't quite know what I would do, loving you as I do, wanting you sometimes with pure physical want, if it were not for nature.

The river always does something to quiet me and ships going up and down. I can whisper to the river about you. I couldn't to any living person.

I suppose I do say to myself—"Ask as little as you can. Give all you can."

I want as much dignity in life as I can get. There is so little in most people.

I have some notion, hard to express—not to promise myself I will find in one other person what will feed all the hungers in me . . . not to believe in absolute love as a cure for life, to reach for every possible clear sweet moment in love and work.

To ask for the absolute . . . a thing I have done so much . . . is to be asking for what I myself cannot give.

There is one question I do keep asking over and over.

When may I see her again?

When may I see her again?

1. Probably Mrs. Joel Harris Lawrence.

[New Orleans, 20 March 1930]

Sweetheart

Your Monday note came. It is dear of you to send me these little letters out of your busy days. I was foolish last night but it was fun.

I went to dinner and then afterwards with the people, all rich men, to a rich people's play place . . . a big gambling place where there was also a cabaret and dancing. The women were rather lovely creatures, beautifully gowned. I stood for a time watching them about the big tables, enough money lost by one of the men to have got me a Ford.

At table I had begun talking of the satisfaction to be got from modern hotel life, as opposed to the home, just to annoy the women.

I do love the dancing. I danced hard.

Today I went to the big Ford assembly plant here. There is a lot to be written about Ford. I stayed there all morning and later lunched in a big working man's lunch room with some hundred of the men. Very sharp impressions. I will need to go to Detroit and see the thing at its head. There is something poison in it all right.

There was a factory doctor with whom I talked a long time. He has gone red. I am going to his house to dine with him some day next week.

It is interesting to try a little sometimes to use what must be the trained historian's way of thinking when listening to people's talk. They are always saying—so and so can never happen in America . . . thinking obviously of the little span of time in which we live as embracing all time—

Because it does for them.

Dear, I'm glad you did not marry the Nashville man. It would be tough having to love you with a husband about.

The rather lovely creatures I danced with last night had an odd effect on me. They made me sadistic. I wanted to hurt them. I deliberately burned one woman with my cigarette and she flew at me. We fought. Of course I had the best of it. Her husband stared at us. It was a queer sort of perverted love making . . . I suppose I'm wanting you so much. Such women do not make men gentle. They are themselves untamed.

The Ford place is something entirely different from cotton or sugar. I haven't been able to do the sugar thing satisfactorily yet.

I am seeing a good many men here. Since I have got into this thing, men seem to understand me better. The machine touches everyone. Nearly every man has some story to tell.

I won't go to Bogalusa.[1] I intend, when you begin going to camps,[2] if it does not throw you out, to be somewhere near. I'll have a Ford by then. I can come sometimes and take you out at night.

I'm happier inside than I have been for years. It is the combination of you and the thing you have got me into. I can think of cotton, steel, paper, sugar etc. as big musical themes . . . each with its own note to be found.

I wasn't so good in the Ford place. The people last night had spoiled me in some queer way. Still the dancing was fun. Do you dance? I'll take you some night to a tough cabaret and we'll dance and drink. Of course you dance.

It is some satisfaction to me to know that I live about on the scale of a skilled factory worker. I don't run much over.

The Nashville man, if he is sensitive, must feel something glorious in you. If you are at all as you were at Augusta, he'll fall in love with you again.

It's half why I keep asking to see you. You are a fountain at which I drink and I am always thirsty.

1. SA had considered touring a paper mill there, probably on EC's recommendation. She had attended meetings there in February.

2. The YWCA summer camps for working women.

[New Orleans, 20 March 1930]

I can't be quite clear about your letter of today . . . your alarm about the Cincinnati meeting.[1] I agree with you, dear, that, if we are going to be lovers, and I take that to mean we are going to frankly accept the fact that we want to be in each other's arms, if we are going to be lovers, we can't stand on a technicality.

As to the nature of the kiss we both want I mean.

Going to hotels together is another matter. I won't ask that of you anymore. I realize the unfairness of it.

And these hotels are far from being exactly lovely places for the meeting of lovers. I felt that at W[ashington] and A[ugusta]. Surely I did not feel it in the pine woods and do not believe you did.

There was the sky and the trees and the good ground underneath, the colors playing in that charming dress you wore against the darker, steadier colors of the ground . . . so that your whole body became a vibrating thing.

If sex itself with me seems wrong or hurtful to you, then we ought to drop it all. We can't be just friends now. That is past. When I am with you, I can't begin to talk quietly of things outside of ourselves until I have had you . . . as woman.

When I talk of comradeship with you, I put that in it.

You have always moved me that way. You know that.

I thought you accepted the sort of meeting we had at Augusta as an acceptable way out. Don't you, dear?

I grant you we have to take others into consideration, so many others.

There isn't any use saying it will be different next summer or the next or the next. When I wrote of Cincinnati, I thought only of a drive out along some river road, you in my arms for a few hours, some place under the spring trees.

If you can't come because of your work, or lack of time, or because you do not want to be in my arms or any such reason at all—

I'll leave out the last one. I know you also are full of physical love for me. Why question that?

I can't make it. It costs too much. It will throw me out at Detroit etc.

Any such reasons I can accept.

I'm puzzled. You seem in your letter to be going back into the moral question. Am I mistaken? Were you only confused, thinking I was again asking you to take the risk of hotels?

I wasn't.

I need a woman, dear. After Augusta I could feed on what happened there for a long time. I need love, direct and real, to release for a time the pent-up things in me, to make the world of dreams and thoughts live in reality for a time anyway.

I think you ought to accept that in me. You have the right to say, "It isn't enough. I don't want it enough."

I accept in myself the fact that, as a married man, I'm not a success. Marriage is outside me. Even with you, whom I want all the time, I would not want close intimate living.

If you want marriage, children etc., I'm no good.

I have been thinking of you as a woman . . . very much woman . . . who had in some way accepted a kind of relationship with life in work . . . the maternal side of you going into that.

I wanted being your lover to bring another side of life to you.

I don't want the power to throw you into strange fluctuations of uncertainty.

I think now sex is more out of hand in you than in me. You say—"If we met now it would be as at W and A or I would let myself go and spoil the chances of comradeship."

I don't know what you mean when you say that. If you love and want me, why not let go? It isn't accepting me much as comrade not to think that I would be as keen as you could be against your doing anything that would spoil the other side of your life.

If we go to a town, stop at separate hotels, or even at the same hotel in separate rooms, we go into the country, make love somewhere under the trees, unseen.

I thought the great risk was to try going to hotels together. I accepted that fully. Haven't you understood my acceptance?

Make it clear to me if you can, dear.

I know that in offering as lover I can bring almost nothing . . . no safety, not even promise of permanency.

I actually can draw away now, say nothing more about it at all if you want me to.

I think I would shake you or beat you a little if I had you here now. It isn't Cincinnati or not Cincinnati. It's saying things will be different next summer or next year. They won't.

It's leaving me uncertain as to whether, within the limitations of what we can have, you accept me or do not.

You can't leave me this way. If I have got to put you out of my mind as my woman, warm and close to me even when you are far away, someone to think of warmly, to fill up my loneliness, then I've got a fight to make with myself and you should set me at that fight.

I don't want to upset you either. What has Lou and his girl to do with you and me? There were a half dozen women picked up and brought into this hotel last night. What have I to do with that?

You know I wouldn't want you at all if you were going to feel guilty because you loved me. If you had said about Cincinnati—"I'll make it if I can, dear," that would have been all I ask, but if it is always to bring, when you see me, a procession of other figures, Lou & his girl, puritanic women, and a whole procession of others who might, if they knew, accuse us, then I'll always be confused.

Did you feel guilty after Augusta? If you did, it's hopeless, dear.

1. EC had an opening in her schedule on 22–23 April, and SA had suggested that she meet him in Cincinnati on her way to an assignment in Detroit that began on 24 April.

[New Orleans, 21 March 1930]

Friday

Such a queer feeling of having been rather ridiculous and hysterical in my notes to you.

It was partly nerves . . . too much dentist, distorted dreams . . . trying to work.

I knew you did not mean any of the things I feared.

There was a kind of lack of faith in you too.

I wanted you here, near me. There is a kind of peace in your presence.

I suppose that is what we mean by love . . . that you being there make the skies different and the earth.

After I wrote you the rather absurd letters, I went out and got drunk. My jaws were throbbing, the Novacaine dying. The drink deadened the throbbing and I slept heavily.

I awoke early and felt so silly. I wanted my silly letters back from you.

I couldn't get them back. I went and walked, had a haircut and here I am.

How hard it is to be dignified and fine. I don't know how.

I ought never to question you. When have you ever lacked fineness with me?

Even if you told me you felt guilty after Augusta, I should know you didn't really.

I won't think about Cincinnati. I suppose I will be hoping. I'm so damned lonesome for you sometimes that I lose control.

[New Orleans, 28 March 1930]

To My Girl—

A grey day. I was in the little alleyway back of the hotel. I go there a good deal. It is a colorful place.

There are all sorts of little cheap places where workingmen out of work, policemen off duty and small gamblers congregate. I suppose they are all bootlegging places. I drink near beer when I go in.

Everyone here gambles on the races. You can lay a bet of 25 cents back there.

I was in there this afternoon and a young workingman, in workingmen's clothes, was drunk and was picked up by the police.

He had in his hand a little brass check, like a baggage check. He has a job in some factory and the check is to show he works there, so he can go in at the gate.

He was very drunk and scared being in the policeman's hands. He kept appealing to the crowd standing about, holding up the check.

He was so drunk I could not understand what he said.

A man stepped out of the crowd and took the check out of his hand and put it in the drunken man's pocket.

"Hell, buddy, you'll lose that. Don't be a fool."

The drunken man began to cry. "Why does he cry?" I asked. "He's afraid his being drunk and found out will get to the ears of the factory people and he'll lose his job," someone said.

The policeman was nice. "Ah, we won't even book him," he said. "I got to get him off the streets. We'll just throw him in for a couple of hours, let him sleep it off and let him go."

I've a feeling, dear, I may get a real novel this summer. I can feel it growing in me but I'll not tackle it yet.

Perhaps I can be somewhere near you for some weeks, and work.

It's about the factory girl but I'm understanding more, why she doesn't want one of the factory men.

Why is it *New Republic, Graphic, Nation,* all of them are so sterile? Please excuse my words. I grow to like them. They all seem dry ass to me.

Scribner's is a better chance.

I went two or three times to *New Republic* lunches—Robert Lovett, Francis Hackett, Stark Young, Edmund Wilson, Herbert Croly.[1]

The whole *Nation* crowd.

James Joyce.

Most of the critics.

They all seem to live up in the head. No physical life.

No physical feel for words.

No pine woods.

No rain. No sunshine.

Dry ass.

I suppose I mean nothing goes down below the shoulders.

I remember during the war. They all ran about being indignant about one thing today, another tomorrow.

Any one of the indignations really felt enough to shake a man to pieces.

They could be indignant, say about starving babies in Belgium, and then go out to a dinner party that night in the most cheerful mood imaginable.

Dry asses.

No juice. No love.

I know I'm only a wreck of a man but anyway a cotton mill or a sugar factory, or a boy like that one arrested in the alleyway this afternoon, shakes me down to my toes.

I can be hurt, thank God.

So can you. I've seen you hurt. I know how tender you are inside.

I know how sweet you are.

I keep being sorry I didn't know you ten years ago but what's the use.

I'm glad I'm going to be your lover, that you are my girl.

I won't hurt you or fake you, dear.

I think I'll get the sugar mill and plantation thing and the cotton mill at night.

I may cut out Birmingham now.[2] It only hurts and dulls me to try to take on too many impressions at once.

I'd better work out what I've got.

If there is any chance our meeting, at Greensboro or some other place, for a weekend, I'll come to you.

That Greear family, poor people with whom I lived when I first went to Grayson,[3] live in a lumber camp up in North Georgia. There are nice country children in the family and John Greear is gentle.

If I can meet you, I'll do it and then go up there until I can meet you again May 1st.

There'll be a racket of children in the house but it will be healthy and clean enough and I'll be out of doors a lot in the woods.

I begin to dream ahead to the time when we can go such places together.

We'll have to marry someday I suppose. I suppose it's the only sensible thing we can do in the end.

If we make good to each other and we will.

1. Lovett, Young, and Wilson were on the editorial staff of the *New Republic;* Hackett was its literary editor from 1914 to 1922; Croly was the founding editor, serving from 1914 until his death on 17 May 1930.

2. SA had planned to stop in Birmingham on his way to Georgia.

3. The John Greear family, formerly of Troutdale, Virginia, with whom SA and Elizabeth boarded during the summer of 1925. The Greears had moved to Helen, Georgia, where they ran a boardinghouse called the Greear Lodge.

[New Orleans, 30 March 1930]

Sunday

A whole afternoon in the big sugar factory up river. There is also a huge farm where the cane is raised. I'm pretty sure I'll get something out of it.

I came home half hoping, of course, for a wire that you could meet me for a weekend, not really thinking you could . . . I know you must be terribly occupied . . . still hoping.

I knew you would if you could.

I got home and went to bed. I've been sleepless again and felt a cold coming on. It has a grip on me this morning, although I slept.

It has been damp and cold but the sun shines this morning.

I went up to the mill with a Jewish woman[1] and talked to her of you. She is an old friend. Of course I didn't tell her who you were. I even gave you another name . . . called you Esther . . . still I spoke of you. It was a kind of relief.

Another note from *Scribner's*. They did not want all the later part of the article cut away, as I had proposed, but only that Lewis personally be buried.[2] I'll try to do it that way.

I'm somewhat afraid that, if I fool with it much more, I'll lose all taste for it.

If I can't see you until May, I'll go to the woods, to Helen, Georgia, at the end of the week, c/o John F. Greear, Helen, Ga.

It seems to me that I need terribly the healing warmth of you. It does not seem to me that just the act of love making is all. In your presence I feel a warm tenderness enfolding me. I seem to sink into you. All seems pure, warm and fair there. I am healed.

I am such a child. At times I am so proud and sure. Then suddenly I am defeated, afraid and ashamed of all the living fact of my life.

The Jewish woman, who is happily married and whom I have known for years, and who in an odd way I think loves me, talked to me of it.

She has seen me often with groups of people during this visit here and formerly when I have been here.

She said—"You constantly let yourself be hurt too much. I have watched you with people. I can see you sensing everyone in the room. The expression of your face changes constantly. In one evening you are hurt, you are glad, old, young.

"Thoughts pass through the crowd. People are ugly or nice. Everything registers on you as on a photographer's plate.

"I wonder sometimes that you can stand living at all."

She advised me of course to be more phlegmatic. I do try. A large part of what she said was true.

I suppose I want the warmth of love as a child wants food. I try to grow up but it doesn't last.

I say to myself—"You're a man. Stand up, man."

Now I find I have rather cast myself into your arms.

I'm ashamed of it sometimes, terribly ashamed. I know so well many people are doing that to you. You are so warm and alive.

I saw it in the camp where you were at work. I see it in Bill and Tom.[3]

Queer little male children coming to your warmth.

I'm as puzzled as you are.

If I were not entangled, I suppose, I know in fact, that I would come to you with an offer of marriage at once. However, I think of the world smiling. Sherwood has done it again.

Implying an injustice done the one I might marry. It would be true too.

In my sane moments I try to think—"What have I to take to her?"

Practically nothing. An almost worn-out man.

Surely she deserves so much more.

It is odd how everyone wants you to feel old and defeated. For ten years the critics have been trying to do that to me. They seem always to be saying . . . "Stand aside. Let the younger man rule now."

There is a kind of conspiracy in America to clap down the impotence of age upon a man. European men are allowed to go on and ripen until the last but here to try doing so seems a kind of offense.

It will not cost me much to be up there in the woods. I shall live for a few dollars a week. If I cannot see you until May, I shall go home from there late in April and then drive to some place where I can meet you when you have finished with Detroit.

If you really want me to.

I'm not as I was last week. I feel queerly small today. I don't want to upset you.

My own happiness seems rather hopeless to me today. Why should I force myself on you?

I feel that way.

I think I do love you . . . if I am capable of love.

Do you think I am, dear?

The tragedy of the dress hurt me. I love the clothes you wear. They always seem so warmly and richly a part of you.

I know I should let you decide just where and when you can see me. I shouldn't always be making plans, proposing meetings, putting you in the position of refusing to come to me.

I really know how difficult it is for you.

But this proud, impatient side of me comes up.

I can't put it down sometimes.

Today I am very humble, frightened and upset about myself. You seem all the warmth and richness of life to me and I seem nothing.

I appreciate your trying to help Mimi[4] but I feel again that it is rather throwing things on you.

I hope you can find a place to be very quiet this summer. I'm going to try very hard not to bother you anymore.

1. Probably Adaline Katz.

2. See second letter of 2 March 1930 and note.

3. William Ross, like Tom Tippett, was a labor leader who frequently participated in the YWCA workers' conferences.

4. I.e., with her college expenses.

[New Orleans, 1 April 1930]

Dearest—I have come into this hotel[1] near my dentist where I am spending I hope the last afternoon. I had some time off. I had to take dope to sleep last night but it was due to my own foolishness. I had slept well 3 nights without. I had this cold and should have gone to bed last night but was lonesome so went to sit with friends. I drank a little and the people rather put me on edge.

Your letter—the special delivery—made me happy. You had better not try the April 22–23rd I suppose.[2] About Detroit—we'll see how you feel.

I think perhaps the woods will be good for me.

It does discourage me when I think that the difficulties will probably be as great next summer and next year but I try not to think of it.

Perhaps the first few months of pregnancy are the worst. I've a feeling you raped me that night going to Elizabethton and probably got me pregnant at Savannah.

I'm trying very hard, dear, to realize, as I should, that the physical difficulties of getting away and meeting me are ten times greater for you than me. I do want to be decent, not demanding. You go at such a pace, I've no right to add any strain at all.

It's a queer little round I'm in. I try to work and begin feeling grand. Then of course it is true that, now that I love, the physical fact of you gets into my imagination at night. Perhaps when I do not get so many new impressions and can be out of doors a good deal in the woods, I'll build up reserve. I'm going to try that now but I'll go on home before May 1st and will go anywhere always to be near you.

I must run back to the dentist now. Will write more later.

Later—Sometimes, dear, I am rather afraid of the child you seem to have me big with. The possibilities of the whole thing stretch out so indefinitely.

There are all sorts of contradictory things in it.

For example I wrote an article here about the local Ford plant.[3] It is run by a hard-boiled guy who was formerly a major in the army. I know a young man there. He hopes to write and has saved up a little money.

Today he went in to see his hard-boiled boss and told him of his hopes.

Whereupon Mr. Hard-boiled breaks down, tears come to his eyes, and he tells my young man that the dream of his life was to be a country doctor, serving people without much pay.

This from a man who has been infinitely cruel to his employees.

How are you to explain it?

Why are we all so afraid of love?

Paul[4] didn't get my feeling about Lawrence quite. He was a lover. He felt as I do that a kind of thing that is maleness was going out of life.

He thought that money and the desire of success made men rotten lovers. He thought the world was going to pieces on that score. The man was a sex mystic as I am afraid I am.

Our love making at Augusta was marvelous for me but I felt a little that [about four lines cut out]

It is one reason why I have so wanted to be more with you, to a little control my excitement.

If I can completely lose myself in you, something will happen to us both.

There is something there to build upon.

Lawrence thought you might start out from that to rebuild all life. He thought it was the only way to go deeply into nature and that going into nature would cure.

He was one of the greatest of all women lovers, which is I suppose what I mean by maleness.

So I loved the man. Once a friend asked him about me. "He's fine but a little too crazy," he said. He may have been right.

It's odd about the bunched arrival of my letters. I write you every day, often twice. When you are to be away, let me know.

If you can write me a little note every day, I'm sure it will help. I know letters are ineffectual but what else have we now?

It apparently isn't in me to be one of the reserved ones.

Do you think that would be a better way to win a woman?

1. The St. Charles Hotel.

2. Subsequent letters show that SA continued to urge EC to meet him then, as she eventually agreed to do. See second letter of 20 March 1930 and note.

3. "Lift Up Thine Eyes," *Nation* 130 (28 May 1930): 620–22, reprinted in *Perhaps Women*, pp. 18–29.

4. Paul Rosenfeld, literary and music critic, a close friend of SA, whose article "D. H. Lawrence" had just appeared in the *New Republic* 62 (26 March 1930): 155–56. SA's review of D. H. Lawrence's *Assorted Articles* was published in *New Republic* 63 (21 May 1930): 22–23.

[New Orleans, 4 April 1930]

Darling—

It's really nonsense for me to say—"I can work here and not there." If I can work, I can work anywhere.

Particularly where you are (this referring to being in Marion when you are).

I shall arrive at Helen, Ga. on Monday afternoon. Helen is on a small branch road, running north from Gainesville, Ga. If anything comes up that would release you for a day even, weekend or any other time, it would be so easy to meet you.

There is a Southern train leaving N.Y. at 1:00 P.M. I have arbitrarily picked out a town, Orange, Va. You would arrive there at 9 that night.

The next night you could get a sleeper to N.Y. arriving there in the early morning.

How absurd. Really, you dear, I am not urging such a wild scheme on you. I am just pointing out possibilities. I will be much nearer you anyway.

You see, if things did happen to break so you could, and wanted to, during April anytime.

I know I swore not to do this to you. Don't be upset by thinking of me depending on it.

It is just a faint hope. I can't avoid that.

Friday.

Alas I'm afraid there will be no letters from you until I get to Helen now.

I am much better. I bought a new light suit, six new blue shirts and six pair of sox all with blue in them.

The man who owns the store is a Jew. He is another of my friends. I seem to know all the Jews here. I got wholesale prices.

He's rich. He has promised to present me with 2 special blue ties he brought himself from Paris. He writes poetry.

The *Scribner* thing is sent off again.[1] I think it nice.

I am through with the dentist. It cost me $150.00—ouch!

The long poem about the automobile racing through the country is taken by the western woman's magazine.[2] They paid $100.00 for it.

I have a long thing for them I wish I could talk to you about. Perhaps I'll keep it until I see you again.

When I get to the woods, I'll work on it and on the thing about the factory at night.[3]

No word from "Loom Dance." If *New Republic* don't take it, I'll try *Mercury*.[4]

It has suddenly turned summer here. My cold is much better but I shall not try to work now until I get to the woods. I want to get completely over it.

My friends here have arranged a big farewell party for Sat. night. There will be much drinking. They are really amazingly sweet people. I wish they could know you.

It is nice anyway. They say, "When you come, we are all dead. Then we begin to write poetry. It is bad poetry but we feel better."

It is what sustains me against the Wyndham Lewis, *New Republic* etc. dry asses. Just people do feel life in me.

The Jewish woman was nice when I talked of Esther.[5] She had tears in her eyes. "I hope she is warm," she said.

She said, "Let life warm you. Don't be afraid to love the woman. I feel her warmth when you talk of her."

I went to lunch yesterday with some men. They all read a lot. They are just men. One of them manufactures corsets.[6] They spoke of *New Republic, Nation,* etc. and it was interesting to hear them.

The corset man said . . . "Everything is up in their heads. They are afraid of feeling. All feeling seems a little vulgar to them—

"They get everything reasoned out and perfectly dry, then they are all right."

I have been reading further into the Rasputin.[7] I'll mail it tomorrow. He was terrible really and yet . . .

At the base of it all, down in him somewhere, he had an odd purifying touch of truth in him.

You will be revolted by him often as I am.

I just in some way admire him against the figures of those about him.

Your letter came, the last one I may get here. Your letters are more and more full of love.

We won't say, "It's done." We'll take our time. Learn to love, test it in ourselves.

There is something in me dancing with joy today. I couldn't work. I'll go walk by the river.

This afternoon I am to go to a rich man's house to see some paintings.

Those who wanted to kill me off had me almost under. They almost convinced me. Everyone kept saying it.

You did not want that. I used to go up to the house and feel you warm and loving. I felt the living blood going through your body.

"There is one," I said to myself. This was when Elizabeth was still there.

I was terribly puzzled. We went home.

She always began talking about the end of things.

Perhaps something in her said . . . "If these two people go toward each other, a new kind of life will come into both of them."

She was puzzled and afraid. She began scolding about nothing.

"There is no life for me," she kept saying.

It was a kind of madness of denial.

Should I have broken through it? I tried time and again but in the end always failed.

Rest all you can, dear. You will have so much to do now. Do not take everything on your shoulders.

Your saying "Go and hurt yourself, be hurt, then come to me" makes me happy.

I say the same to you.

1. "Cotton Mill" (see second letter of 2 March 1930, note 1).
2. "Machine Song: Automobile."
3. "Entering the Mill at Night."
4. *New Republic* did take it; see letter of 9 February 1930 and note 3.
5. I.e., EC; see letter of 30 March 1930 and note 1.
6. Julius Friend, a good friend of SA's and formerly an editor of the *Double Dealer*.
7. Probably M. V. Rodzianko, *The Reign of Rasputin* (1927).

[New Orleans, 5 April 1930]

Saturday
Dearest One

Suddenly I made up my mind I must have at least one evening on the river.

I had found that the steamer *Tennessee Belle* was leaving for Greenville [Mississippi] at 4. An old acquaintance, Captain Barker, was a pilot on her.

He has false teeth. They won't stay in. He found some preparation in a drug store that would make them stick in and they stuck so tight his mouth got sore.

Finally the preparation dissolved.

I am trying to describe his character. He swears beautifully.

When the big flood was on the river, he was pilot on the boat Hoover was on. He does not admire Hoover much. To Capt. Charlie he is just a little fat man.

He disparages all engineers. "They think they are bigger than the Mississippi River," he says.

He seems to think they haven't reverence enough.

You know the lower deck of these river packets lies close down to the water's edge.

When Hoover was on his boat, he stood at the front, on the lower deck, surrounded by secretaries etc. They were outside the river proper in the flooded area. Suddenly the pilot drove the boat into a mass of willow trees. He almost brushed Hoover and all his secretaries off the deck into the water.

They ran ingloriously, all the nigger deck hands howling with laughter.

The pilot said he had struck a cross current and the boat had got out of hand. He lied. He wanted to show the Great Engineer some of the little river tricks.

As soon as the boat had left the dock here, I went up into the pilot house with him. I haven't a picture of the steamer but send one of another much like it.[1] The pilot house *X* is a magnificent place from which to look over the levee at the distant country.

When I was here before and used to ride with him, I gave Capt. Charlie a copy of my *Poor White*. He and other pilots, captains of tugs etc., it seems, have all read it.

He asked me a question.

"Why did Hugh, on the night of his wedding, when the bride was waiting for him in another room, instead of going to her, why did he crawl out a window onto a roof and, leaping to the ground, run away?"

I said I thought it was like this . . . "She had not accepted him. She was marrying him, yes. But marriage does not mean acceptance. He felt that in some queer way his manhood had not been accepted."

"Ah," said Captain Charlie, "I said so. We discussed that and discussed it. I said that was the reason."

Once, after I had left this country down here, I sent the captain a copy of *Moby Dick*.

They all read that.

"It scared me," the captain said. "It was a long book with fine print but I stuck to her. She got better and better."

I spent the whole evening in the pilot house with him. His watch was from 6 to 12. It was a magnificent evening. The river is very full. A little new moon came out through broken clouds.

There isn't anything quite like such an evening on the river. I hungered for you. As it grows darker, the land seems to fade away.

All kinds of queer lights play over the rushing water. The boat was going up stream. It was seeking the easy water. It creeps up on shore, cuts across the river, goes a few miles and then cuts back across again.

Sometimes the easiest place is right in the middle of the river.

I spent the whole evening with the old man in talk. The pilot house up there was all open. We talked of everything. "Don't call me Capt. Charlie," he said, "call me just Charlie," so I did and he called me Sherwood.

We talked and looked at the river until he was relieved at midnight and then walked the decks for another hour talking.

There is fine honesty and simplicity in the man.

At one we both went to bed and at 8 this morning the other pilot landed me on the bank a half mile from a railroad station and I came back here.

I am loving you today. I leave tomorrow.

1. SA attached to the page a photograph of the river boat with the pilot house marked with an "X."

[Helen, Georgia, 9 April 1930]

Dearest Woman

It is ten o'clock, a cold clear morning. The old woman in the house is not dead. She is past 80 and has been at the point of death for a week. She eats practically nothing.[1]

Day by day they have been expecting her death but now, suddenly, she is better.

Yesterday I went to the sawmill here. Back of the sawmill there is a pool. Logs are brought down from the hills by a narrow gauge railroad and dumped into the pool.

By an endless chain arrangement they are picked up out of the pool and travel up a grooved incline to the top of the big mill.

One by one the big logs are released and roll down an incline to the rack that holds them, facing the saw.

The rack is a kind of platform that slides up and down rapidly and jerkily. Three men ride it.

The sawyer sits in a little pit and controls levers.

He flips the log about as though it were a toothpick.

The saw flies through it and boards fall off onto a traveling belt.

There is a whole story here too, in this lumber camp, the inevitable destruction of the forests, the uncertainty of life, the temporary shacks and houses, these people living all their lives in such temporary places.

I reworked and sent off to be copied again the thing I wrote about the Ford assembly plant. I called it "Lift Up Thine Eyes." It is an attempt to be somewhat ironic. I haven't named Ford. I called the car the Bogel car, made at Jointville.

The idea is the effort made to build up the sense in people of a mysterious all-seeing power at the center of these great industrial institutions.

There is at the very heart of it all at Jointville this semi-mysterious figure.

He represents power, therefore the new god.

I think I shall wait before sending it off until you see it. I do hope to have things to show you.

I wonder what we will do when we meet again.

It is difficult when I see you. Then I want just to hold you in my arms.

Do you suppose we will dare go to a hotel room? It seems not so lovely a place for love making as the woods.

On the other hand we would have the hours together within four walls. We would have so many more hours to talk.

I cannot yet shake off a feeling of depression here. It is partly due to uncertainty about seeing you, partly to the depression of the place here. The lumber camp is on its last legs. The cutting is almost at an end. People are beginning to move out.

That means empty houses everywhere, rows of them in the woods. I haven't yet gone back into the camp proper where cutting is still going on. I will in a day or two.

What I feel now is the depression of the town. And alas of the house into which I have come. It is, however, only for about 2 weeks. How long I shall be here will depend partly upon word from you.

If I cannot see you until May, I will go on back to Marion toward the end of the month.

My lover. There may be a letter from you today.

Later

How can I think of you as superfluous in your knowledge. All my own is so much like that.

I do not know why I feel so mean and low some days. Perhaps I need the revivifying power of your love and faith. I do not feel particularly inferior to others about me.

Is it a mistake for me to seek, as I seem to be doing now, purpose and form in life?

Must I be protected always?

Depressing places depress me too much.

Gainesville is a depressing town.[2] There is a prize mill town there. It has been very nicely arranged—trees and shrubs everywhere, fine school and recreation buildings, the workmen's houses superior to any I have seen. I did not go into the mill.

In an odd way it seemed a bit insulting to the town that this isolated industrialized section should be so apart from the town, so superior.

And such tales coming down from the hills, tales of disease, dirt, poverty and ignorance on the backwoods farms here. I talked a long time to the doctor here, a middleaged shy man. He reminds me of the doctor in Turgenev's vivid tale—[3]

I must try to get more like Turgenev, more apart, more sane. It is, I am afraid, the only way.

Something in me hurts so today.

It may be largely loneliness for you.

O, my dear, let's try courageously to do it—to keep love. It can be made such a healing thing. I need it so. Do you? I'm sure you do. I keep asking myself, "Can you give it and keep giving it?"

I'm so afraid of my power to do that sometimes.

But this is one of my bad days.

I must quit writing of my uncertainty and try to work.

If only a letter comes from you today.

Still Later

Your letter came saying there is a chance. Orange Court House, April 22–23. I feel a dog urging you but you won't do it if it upsets you too much. I try to remember how much more your life is filled with details than my own.

I don't know why I called you "darling." I felt funny when I wrote it. It may have been the new blue shirts and socks.

In an odd way it was false. I don't just know why.

Orange Court House is marked on the maps—a flag stop from N.Y. You would have to inquire.

What about Alexandria or Washington?

I can't be very clear headed today. It is one of my bad days when my judgment is no good. I want you too much. I'll have to trust to your judgment about both this meeting and the one at Detroit, or after Detroit.

If you will only feel that I want to go anywhere, anytime to see you and be with you and that what I am trying to do will be helped, not hindered.

It is odd, on these helpless days I haven't much to give you but I do terribly feel the need of you.

Do you mind that?

1. Betsy Williams, a boarder at the Greear Lodge, was dying of cancer.

2. Gainesville, Georgia, about twenty miles south of Helen, where SA had to switch trains.

3. The doctor in Helen was H. K. Phillips. The "vivid tale" was probably "The District Doctor" in *A Sportsman's Sketches.*

[Helen, 10 April 1930]

Dearest Woman

I went off yesterday afternoon to the woods. It was very quiet and charming there. I followed, up an old railroad track, the remains of a lumber road that ran along the river bank. The river is very clear and cold.

There was a little stream that came down into the river and I followed it. It took me up into the hills.

The young leaves are just coming on the trees. The little stream had become a series of waterfalls. The wind, that has been blowing hard here, had died.

I stayed up there in the hills lying on the ground for two or three hours.

I have not succeeded in getting to work here. I suppose I am too impatient. It was lovely in the hills but I was dreadfully lonely for you.

I could not help remembering the hours with you in the woods. Do you remember the place near Spartanburg?[1] Someone had been cutting trees up there. The limbs cut from the trunks of the trees like that are called "slashings." Do you remember how the car down below on the stretch of sand seemed standing in a lake?

I tried to recapture something of the feeling we had together. It was fragrant in the woods. A soft little breeze blew. I tried to imagine the breeze your lips touching me.

The thought made me too amorous. It is dreadful to be so when you are not near. That may be what is wrong with me here. I couldn't stay in the woods. I had to get up and walk. I walked as hard as I could all afternoon.

In the evening an officer of the lumber company[2] came with his wife.

He talked about what a great man Theodore Roosevelt was.

Then he asked the question . . . is it better to be a poor white, back in the hills, unable to read and write, never knowing anything of the world, never having traveled.

Or to travel, see the world and then have to settle down in a lumber town.

"I would rather have seen something anyway," he said.

He went once and stayed four weeks at Mammoth Cave, exploring it.

It is nice at night but very lonely. I sleep beside an open door. I can hear the river. The bed is very hard. I dare say after two or three more nights I will get used to it.

By my calendar April 22–23 are not a weekend.[3] Not that it makes any difference.

This afternoon I am going back up into the woods to where they are cutting trees. The cutting here will end this spring. The man with whom I am staying, John Greear, is taking me. We will spend the night up there, in the lumber camp.

I'm dreadfully lonely for you of course.

1. See letter of 26 February 1930 and note.
2. Charles Miller, the general manager.
3. The days were Tuesday and Wednesday.

[Helen, 12 April 1930]

Saturday

Little David and I got back from the lumber camp in the mountains at ten last night, having driven down in the moonlight over terrible roads in a car without brakes.

Little David is Mr. Greear's son. At the last moment, when we were about to start on Thursday, Mr. Greear had an attack of indigestion and couldn't go.

David is white haired, wears spectacles and is about fourteen. He is amazingly good company. Like most American boys, he knows everything about a car. We broke down twice and in a half hour he had the old machine running again.

I apologized for my own ignorance about cars. "Well, you see," he said, "the kind of cars we can afford to own, you have to know how to do everything to them or you would get nowhere."

The lumber camp was an amazing experience. I slept Thursday night in a bunkhouse up there. Fortunately it had just been de-bedbugged. Bedbugs do raise such hell with me.

We left camp yesterday morning and went on a log train up into the cutting. It was far up a gorge, five miles in from the camp where I slept. There was another camp there where the lumber jacks, tong grabbers, grab drivers[1] etc. stay—bedbugs there of course.

They are such men as you would not think still existed, men who want to avoid civilization, who want a life out of doors without women.

They work furiously and play furiously. All of them give the impression of grown boys who remain boys, capable of infinite cruelty and all kinds of fine generosity.

You should see them in their dining room, storing food away.

Some of the little houses in which they live are on wheels, switched here and there on the narrow gauge railroad. Others are set on the ground beside the tracks.

When they want to move, a crane reaches down, picks up such a house and sets it on a car. I slept in such a house.

But I must write a long thing on lumber camps. It hasn't been done really and has been so real a part of American life. I spent the morning among the men at work. Little David—they call him King David, the white-haired boy of the Israelites, and love him . . .

He was water jack up there two summers.

He went everywhere with me, telling me about everything.

In the afternoon he and I with our fishing rods started down the gorge afoot. The narrow gauge railroad followed the windings of a clear, lovely river and we fished along down, not a house or a farm in sight, the lovely hills all torn and gashed.

This seemingly wanton destruction of young timber seems an inevitable part of lumbering. Even the lumber jacks regret it. I talked to one. By the way, they are called—not lumber jacks—but lumber hicks.

It is a question of economy. Someone up above constantly demands more logs at less cost. To get the logs out, whole forests of young trees are what they call "swamped."

It means ripped out of the ground, torn and mangled by the great log, at the end perhaps of a steel cable, being ripped through.

I must write of all this. It is so characteristically American.

Do you remember the path in the woods at Black Mountain,[2] when we went up a little ways along a winding path? I kept holding you and we were both rather dumb with wonder.

Love coming to us, surging in on us.

I can't tell all you felt. I know that loving you has a lot to do with the queer fear and humbleness that is in me now. O, my dear, I have muddled everything in life so.

Little David and I walked down the gorge the five miles, fishing as we went, although the place was too grand and terrible for much fishing.

Little David, the amazing mountain child, said . . . "I don't care much whether or not I catch fish. I just like to sit and watch the way water tumbles over a rock."

That any people should feel superior to these mountain people. Well.

We got back to camp, ate hurriedly and started for Helen in the rattling old car, over such roads, dodging big rocks, the road often at this angle, [drawing] often like this, [drawing] some 65 miles to go. We made it by ten. I slept 12 hours.

New Republic has taken "Loom Dance."

Scribner's are paying $500.[3]

So that is 600 earned.

God, it will be good to see you.

Don't you think it will be better for me just to come to N York and then let's go somewhere for the two days.

I love you.

1. The grab driver attached chains to logs that were pulled by horses to the loading site. There the tong grabber threw tongs, which were connected to the cables of a crane, on the logs; the crane then lifted the logs onto a railroad car.

2. See letter of c. 7 June 1929, note 1.

3. For "Cotton Mill."

[Gainesville, Georgia, 23 April 1930]

Dearest Woman

You see my good resolution is not so good. I have to wait here three hours for the car north to Helen.[1] I am full of you. What else should I do but write to you?

It is another glorious day but there will be no such days as yesterday—at least not until I can be with you out of doors.

It still seems to me to make everything right that such a day could come out of the muddle of days.

This will reach you in a swirl of things there. Perhaps you will save it and read it in bed. I hope you can have a room of your own. Otherwise I should be brief and I do not feel brief.

My train got off late. It was one A.M. when we left. I was still excited. I began thinking of difficulties . . . all sorts of possibilities that might spoil things. I was beginning to get into one of my sleepless states.

Was that moment in the wood, when the two men and the woman were all there together, before he emptied the bottle, a warning?

Shivers running down through me.

I could laugh when I was with you, now I couldn't.

So much of our fate in the hands of an outsider, a man who might have dragged us off to jail because of the moonshine in my envelope of mss.

I have seen moonshine that same grey misty color.

Then other scenes came crowding in. In all perfect things nature comes crowding in. Is it all imagined? After that day the second.

You did not see closely as I did the miller's wife, the one who told me about the setting of eggs.

She was good, had nice eyes. I said to her, "My lady and I are going into the woods to picnic. Is it all right?"

Perhaps even that other man, that officer, felt something . . . although it wasn't so nice or so perfect that day. "I'm not going to take you for this little liquor," he said. There was something nice in him when he said that. It said, "I am not going to take advantage of you because fate has given me the chance."

Just people, who cannot succeed, aren't "big people," are nice, dear. Lincoln was right.

There is a kind of fundamental niceness and humbleness even in their submission to the silly capitalists and big people.

Intellectuals etc.

I go for Lincoln and Van Gogh.

Napoleon and Gauguin be damned.

The miller's wife's eyes were smiling. She laughed. She also helped to put the niceness in me up in that woods.

As though she had been loved sometime.

The sky and all the fields and woods being so nice in the failing light coming back to town too.

When the plowed red fields went down, touching the lips of the woods, in that swinging line.

It doesn't swing here on the paper although I plow ahead on the paper in a little hotel with a bad pen and worse ink.

Something joyous and playful in me . . . you put there.

The dark pine woods being not of man and the plowed fields being of man.

I ought to get the poetry of all this, I mean man and not man, in everything I write.

Turgenev did it so beautifully.

Woods and plowed fields and little towns and men there.

And factories and people coming into factories from fields.

So much to get, dear.

But you do make me want to try.

I thought I shouldn't sleep at all on the train and didn't care much. That place just above my buttock, where the root of a tree or a limb pressed so hard when you were pressing, made me roll about . . . it's about gone this morning.

I didn't care whether I slept or not. To sleep seemed losing something of you, the precious present.

Once I wrote in a poem, "The Now is a country to discover which I would give all hope, all promise."[2]

It seemed to me I had gone into that country with you.

The time in the woods when the root pressed into my flesh was so absolutely the Now.

You know how sometimes you half turn from me, put your two hands over your face.

You look out of the car window, or off across the wood.

While you are doing that, I look at your alive hands, at your hair, at just the way the strong, clean little neck creeps out of the hair.

At the shape of your head, your almost Slavic face, your beautiful back, your thin, hard legs that can press so beautifully . . . that are not beautiful by standards of beauty set up but that, to me, have the same strong, slender beauty as have your shapely legs.

I remember once, when you were home, seeing you across the street at M[arion]. You had been to some sort of silly dinner. You were like a little cow girl with your legs that should be straddling a racing horse, not under a banquet table—

Love surged through me that day too. The whole of you was so perfect and lovely to me. It must have been just before we went to Elizabethton and I was as cloudy inside as that moonshine that got poured out in the wood.

You see I am writing on and on. Perhaps I'll not write again for a few days. Tell me just when you will be back in N.Y.

I think I'll wire you at Detroit when I leave here.

Sometimes, when you put your hand over your face like that, you put your face at the same time down against me. You curl up so.

It seemed to me that you did that in the berth last night. I felt you there. I went off to sleep and slept beautifully, feeling you there like that.

You will tell me, won't you, just how you feel about the woman thing[3] . . . how it makes you feel.

You know Mrs. Walker, Mrs. Boots Walker, the hotel man's wife at Marion,[4] so huge, so pink cheeked. The man who runs the Dixie Hunt at Gainesville has a wife just like that.

She is walking up and down the hotel lobby as I write.

Now I'll quit writing. I'll go walk around. I'm happy.

I am full of you.

1. SA was returning from his meeting with EC. They stayed at the O. Henry Hotel in Greensboro, North Carolina, and made trips into the countryside near there.

2. "The now is a country to discover which, to be the pioneer in which I would give all thought, all memories, all hopes" (*A New Testament,* p. 68).

3. SA had given her a copy of an essay he was working on, "It's a Woman's Age," which was to appear in *Scribner's Magazine* 88 (December 1930): 613–18, reprinted in *Perhaps Women,* pp. 41–58.

4. Gilbert C. ("Boots") Walker, manager of the Hotel Lincoln in Marion.

[Helen], 24 April [1930]

Thursday

Dearest Woman

I got back here at 3 P.M. yesterday. Full of you all night. A beautiful night of sleep, the whole room pervaded by you.

It had turned very cold. I slept with all the doors and windows open.

A little cheap travelling show had come to this mining town, such a show as George Borrow[1] might have described, a rusty little Ferris wheel and several cheap gambling games.

The lumbermen and country people had gathered in. I went down and stood about for an hour, watching the tricks to get dimes and quarters.

There was a long open meadow with a river running through it. I went to walk in that. It was night, a night of stars. The ground felt good under foot. I could see the lights of the poor little show in the darkness. At a distance the thing was nice, the voices came to me soft and low, mingled with the sound of the water of the river.

We must keep our love out of doors. Not many houses now are fit for love.

Everything is sweet to remember. There is a kind of truth beyond all the moralists, beyond any words I have found.

John writes he will come for me, arriving on Tuesday the 29th.

We will probably start home on the 30th and arrive in Marion May 1st. Why don't you go back to NY that way?[2]

1. English author of *Lavengro* (1851) and *The Romany Rye* (1857), whom SA greatly admired.

2. I.e., from Detroit.

[Helen, 28 April 1930]

Monday

Dearest Woman—

John is on his way up here, will arrive on Tuesday. We will start home Wednesday and arrive there Thursday.

I am vague in my mind as to when you go to New York. Have a faint hope you may stop at Marion. We will have to stand the test of being together in the presence of others.

The tree with the pale lavender blossoms is called the cottonwood tree. Everyone says the blossoms have a repellent smell.

On Sunday with the doctor here to see a little boy who had an eye put out in an accident. He was busy with him for two hours and I walked along a ridge of hills. He thinks he'll save the other eye.

The hill looked over into a wide rolling plain, no one at work, all the fields new plowed—shades of red and yellow. I stood a long time leaning against a tree.

There was no movement. There have been forest fires and the smoke, from far off, made a thin haze.

I have been trying to hold myself. The out of doors and you together have done something to me. I can't help being proud that you find physical delight in me.

You are all mixed up with the out of doors in me, the strange central thing . . . nature . . . God . . . it . . . become alive . . . flesh and feeling in you.

What a vivid real lover sleeps in you.

Not many women can be real lovers.

It's odd about you. Something I felt from the beginning is true.

There was the puritanic background you used to talk of sometimes. It never did go deeply.

I wasn't nice.

You brought out something nicer in me.

The puritanic thing never had got any real hold on you.

It is such a vital experience, physical love. I try to live in you, be you, understand how you must feel.

You awaken that kind of tenderness in me, taking me out of self into you. It must be a part of the secret of the miracle of love.

I had a sudden impulse to go to the little church here—last night after I returned from the trip with the doctor.

I went. They were holding the sacrament—the bread and wine.

Some old pagan mystery, held over, carried down into Christianity. "This is my body—eat of it.

This is my blood. Drink of it."

The preacher, a young man, just out of college, tried to explain the meaning.

He talked such nonsense.

There were small merchants and their wives, farmers, mountain men with their wives . . . a few lumber hicks.

The preacher checked it back to St. Paul . . . that coarse man . . . an intellectual . . . an organizer.

Some of the early Christians had taken over the feast . . . the blood drinking.

They had got together. It became a debauch, flesh of my flesh, blood of my blood.

We have all got it in us.

A night of wild general fucking under trees, women with their clothes torn off, being fucked and fucked.

Men drunk and shouting.

Paul, who was busy putting Christianity on a paying basis, making it go, was shocked.

He hated women, wanted to subjugate them. The Christian notion of the inferiority of women was read into Christianity by him.

It means nothing . . . this Christianity . . . if it does not mean poetry. Christ himself a poem. It must be taken so.

Paul feeling the coarseness of coarse flesh in himself. He would have been a man with a thick red neck, big feet, stiff coarse hair on his head.

I dare say he masturbated in secret.

The sweetness of trees and fields and women's flesh might have frightened him.

I can imagine him having desired some delicate woman who would not have him, not wanting that coarse ugly man bouncing up and down on her.

I wanted to get up in the little church. They sang a song, "Now I raise my Ebenezer."[1]

It was the first time I had been to a preaching for 15 or 20 years.

Now I raise my Ebenezer.

Abner[2] come up.

Let's take it for very flesh, very blood.

Suppose you merchants, lumber hicks etc. made a temple of your bodies, each raising his Ebenezer, if you will.

There is your woman. Take her home. Put your hand on her ass, softly.

Feel flesh sweet.

Women, make yourself sweet.

Wash the doorsteps of your houses.

Wash.

Fuck gentle, strongly, steadily.

Get the orgasm together, the ultimate blending of male and female.

Feel one with animals, flowers, corn growing in fields.

The little buds on the trees in the wood are red and hard. There is pain in them too, trying to burst into leaves.

The little buds on trees must be like the soft unfolding flesh in you, darling, when it hurts, wanting.

Why shouldn't it be taken so? Eat of my flesh, meaning something.

Drink of my blood, meaning something.

If people let themselves become dry ass, that's your sin, your evil.

It comes from fear of life.

Life itself should be the sacred thing.

Our love meaning nothing if it does not make you nicer to all people, me nicer.

How can people live without love?

People feeling it in you and in me.

The man in the wood who poured the liquor out, the miller and his wife.

We ought to forgive all in each other, not ask too much.

Love making, a sacrament. What else is it? The lovely, strong, tender sacrament to life.

They have so often, dear, made me feel ugly. You sweetened me, atop me under the trees, looking down. Such an exquisite loveliness in you.

The tender hurt, the sense of all earth and sky and trees in you, gathered into your woman's body.

Me being male to you . . . hard for you.

I've been trying to avoid that all I could.

If we had each other all the time, we might spoil it . . . fucking just for fucking.

That comes too easily.

It's my central fear of marriage now.

Perhaps we had better go on, at any risk. There isn't any reason why you, in what you are doing, giving love out of yourself to girls in mill towns, being something outside to them, why you shouldn't live outside me, in yourself, in others.

Your coming to me to be made sweet. My coming to you to be made sweet.

The thing in the church had got pretty dry ass.

There was a pile of bread left, "body of Christ."

The wine wasn't really wine.

I kept thinking, "There is bread left. The preacher don't get much."

I wondered if he would take the scraps left home to his chickens.

I got away from the others and went across lots home, across a field.

Out there I walked about in the dark night.

Of course I wanted you. We wouldn't have made love. We would have walked up and down in the field, hand in hand.

I thought of a strange, loose, sweeping sort of novel I might write, all this in it, you and the people in church.

Throwing overboard what they call form.

Finding new form.

Your legs in it, the thin, hard, firm legs I love so, your body.

The drops of blood from you that got on me like your lips or the round little belly of you.

All sacred.

All like rivers, trees, you, night too.

Death that creeps up and takes people.

A woman and a poet, not afraid to be a woman and a poet.

You see what a jumble, darling.

But a nice, a living jumble.

I may work yet . . . in you . . . you atop me if it goes better so . . . making me pregnant.

I'll risk sending this to Detroit.

It will reach you sometime.

I don't need to see you just yet. Perhaps I'll work. When I do need to see you . . . as a sacrament . . . I'll come to you wherever you are.

You do the same. Don't ever be afraid to do that.

If you feel it that way, you will make me feel it so and cleanse me. If I feel it so, I'll make you feel it and it will be good to you, sweet to you.

You darling . . . my woman.

1. "Here I raise mine Ebenezer" is from the second stanza of "Come Thou Fount of Every Blessing," a hymn by Robert Robinson (1735–90).

2. SA and EC, probably influenced by D. H. Lawrence's *Lady Chatterley's Lover* (1928), had named their genitals "Abner" and "Clarisse."

[Ripshin, 7 May 1930]

Wednesday
Dearest Woman

As you will know when you get back to New York, I had rather planned to run off to N.Y. for a few days this week.

I was in town yesterday and went to see your mother for a moment. She told me of a doctor, from Flint, Mich., who was driving down here to see the farm.

This led to talk. Your mother thinks it foolish for me to sell. I did not tell you but of course you must know that all my own feeling, as regards selling or not selling, depends a good deal on you.

Everything has changed so much and so rapidly since I knew you. Things have changed so much as between us.

For a hundred new reasons I am doubtful now about selling at all.

Let me ask you frankly, dear woman, what have you in mind as regards me?

Are you really wanting a man and am I the man?

I want to run off to New York and ask you questions but think I had better not now.

In the meantime a chance to sell may come up.

We are both old enough to talk with frankness.

You know the risk of marriage with any man and especially with a changing, emotional man like me.

This is always presuming you want to take such chances.

I have been walking about here constantly thinking of all this.

Where are we? Where are we going?

There is your mother and father. Do you feel that eventually you will want to be nearer them?

Already I have your mother's promise to come over here for a visit to John and myself. I did not think she looked well yesterday. She was housecleaning and looked excited and tired. I wasn't altogether being crafty—I mean laying the groundwork of a scheme to get you here. I really wanted her.

Eleanor, the farm is so lovely this year. The old bad situation that made me restless and unhappy here is gone. I sit at my desk downstairs writing. On the couch there, within arm's reach, I held you in my arms.

I walk out. There is the place to which we went, down along the creek bank, and laid down, trying to do it.

Not succeeding.

Since, in another woods, in another place, we did succeed, to me with such rich wonder.

It was to you too.

What I mean is that love of you has got woven into this place.

Let me talk of myself a little to you, dear. I have started a novel, a strange, frank kind of book. I may not be able to publish it. I may not care.

I only want to work on it as the mood comes.

I want to go on and do these industrial things.

Then I think of something else. I would like to do, along as I do the industrial things, some other things about poor people in the country.

Little sketches of what happens to people in this life—the rural mountain boot-legger shot in the road by a deputy sheriff—what the sheriff feels. What the man felt as he died.

Things happening to boys planting corn.

The farm girl who gets with child in a car with a country boy.

This is, I admit, laying out an extensive program but I feel that if I could have you, could renew myself in you, I could do a lot the next ten years.

If I felt all your happiness, all your own life, dependent on me, I couldn't let you risk it.

That's why I ask, what of your own life, your own program, your own plans?

Am I in them?

My mind works this way . . . I say to myself, perhaps excusing myself, that if Elizabeth had made a life of her own, aside from me, we could have made it.

She couldn't. The life here, in these simple people for example, seemed just vulgar to her. She stood off from them . . . perhaps having in mind being some kind of refined delicate lady. Lavender and old lace perhaps.

A man came drunken into the yard here. I remember such a thing happening . . . a drunken young farmer, his boots covered with mud. He wanted to tell me something.

As a matter of fact he had cheated me. He wanted to square it.

He was covered with mud and driveled as he talked.

Well, really, darling, there was a kind of man's love he had for me that wanted to get expressed. E said . . . "I can't have such people."

They really did hurt her.

Let's be frank, dearest. She was a bit twisted sexually. She didn't want me or any man in her really.

Fucking for pure joy of skies, river, trees, flesh, man's flesh, woman's flesh, wasn't in her.

She was tainted with something with which the modern race is too full . . . liking death rather than life, limberness before life. Her brother is a homo and one sister a lesbian.

They all go in for gentleness and refinement.

Why then did I marry her? God knows, Eleanor. You perhaps know better than I do. Perhaps she married me wanting escape from herself.

I admit I am restless, always seeking, apt to make such mistakes.

You have changed me profoundly. My dear, you have no notion of the health you have brought into me.

I had got this feeling of impotence toward life. Did she want that—to carry me thus into some dim world of refinement?

Your little hard dark body astride me in the woods beyond the mill—did you know the joy flowing into me through you?

It was so right you should be atop then—I kept laughing afterward, thinking of this delicious, topsy-turvy world—

Thinking, later I'll fuck life and joy into her as she has into me—

Thinking trees skies people.

Thinking how you love people as I do.

Thinking joy being with you.

Even the man taking the bottle from us in the woods fun—because the man did feel us and got nice.

We are so damn nice together, don't you think?

You see what I dare propose—that we make up our minds where we are going.

That we make up our minds whether we are going to marry or not.

We couldn't, wouldn't dare do it, I'm pretty sure, if we were going to settle down here, away from all other life, bottle ourselves up.

For example could you remain industrial secretary of the Y.W.C.A. if you married me?

I'll not take you from others. I want others to have you. You are too valuable to too many people as you are.

Could you go on working as you do work, having me as mate, having this place here with me, near your mother and father, to which to come?

Would you like to be a partner with me in such a place?

It would take say two years to work it out. Altogether I'll owe, after I make the papers over to Bob this fall, something like $3500.

I'll have only this place, for what it is worth, and my books.

John, Bob and Mimi will each have, out of the papers, a $5000 start.[1]

We checked up—Bob and I and the papers will have paid off this fall some 15000 or 16000. It will be easy for Bob, even though he may get married, to pay all out in 2 or 3 years, I mean to John and Mimi.

We should be able to pay out the 3500 in a year or two.

When I have done enough of the industrial things, I'll make a book called "American Money."[2]

Then I'll do a rural life book.

If you could keep on working, go out from here to work, keep on giving the sweetness out of yourself to others—

Go away and leave me.

Let me go away and leave you.

Let us say the union does have its basis in sex, that physical wonder we can give each other.

Why shouldn't you, as a woman, say to yourself, "I'll give it to him so deliciously he'll never want any other woman"?

Why shouldn't I feel I might take that attitude toward you?

Do you believe in it?

I do.

You have made me believe.

As for the farm—to be our home if we do try it—we have a grand woman here.[3] She would run it like a top for us. We could go and come. We would raise pigs, turkeys, guinea hens, chickens, cattle. Already the place fairly teems with new life.

The farm woman just came in to say 16 little turkeys just born.

There were chickens born yesterday, 14 of them.

There are two lovely young female calves in pasture.

There are hams in the cellar, wine in the bins.

We might even have a brat of our own, who knows?

You see, dear, it is all concerned with the question of selling or not selling. Without some such plan to look forward to, I'd better sell.

You don't have to commit yourself. We'll have at least a couple of years to try things out.

But if you believe in the possibility, we won't sell. We'll hang onto it as a place for us near your own people.

As a kind of central place for my own kids too.

I want you to answer at least that far—

Wire me—Sell—or Don't sell. Sign the wire "*Abner.*" Address it to Troutdale.

Address mail there too, instead of Grant. The R.F.D. comes from there now.

You dear.

P.S. It may be a momentous decision but, do you know, old sweet, I don't feel one bit momentous. I'm going in fact right now to put a cock feather in my hat. Shall I send you a hen feather?

O thou sweet dusky little hen—come lay thyself an egg in our hen yard.

P.S. John and I were talking last night. He has an objection. The house is too much grander than the houses of the people about.

He meant what you felt when Tom [Tippett] came to your father's house—you a bit ashamed before Tom that it was so nice.

I said—it depends on how you feel toward people. You can make them feel all people are just people.

The grand house only affects you in the end if it makes you feel grand.

John conceded the point.

Do you?

It's a turkey hen feather [feather attached].

I don't believe you would ever get the grand lady feeling.

You're too small and dark and bowlegged and strong and human. God, I'm nuts about you.

1. On 12 December 1931 SA turned over virtually all control of the newspapers to Bob, who was to pay $5,000 each to John and Mimi. See first letter of 30 December 1931 and note.

2. He did not publish this book but later planned a novel by that name based on the life of his friend John Emerson. He also used the title for a fourteen-page manuscript about his own experience in business.

3. Mrs. Hilton.

[Ripshin, 10 May 1930]

Saturday

We have four old hen turkeys and one young cock—the cock in his first year, got of Felix Sullivan.[1]

It seems best to have a new cock for the hens every year, they do better. This would seem, my dear, to rather justify my own life.

Now, of the three hens, one has a lot of young turkeys and two others are setting. There is one old hen left unoccupied. If she is laying any eggs, they are being laid somewhere in the woods.

The entire attention of the cock has ruined her. You never saw a character deteriorate as hers has. It frightens me about you. As you know, turkeys roost in trees and normally fly down and go seeking grasshoppers and other bugs at dawn.

And here it is half past eight and she is still abed. The cock has been up and down out of the tree three times. He flies heavily up, gobbles, looks puzzled and flies down again.

Poor fellow, he has a hard on, I dare say. You can't do it on the limb of an apple tree, even if you are a turkey. It is done by people in automobiles, a phenomenal thing, but you simply can have no success on the limb of a tree.

At dawn Suzie the cat came to the kitchen door and mewed pitifully. Mrs. Hilton got up and let her in. She had one poor little kitten, its eyes not open yet, in her mouth. Mrs. H made her a nest in a box. We have all handled it. This was at 5. Now it is 8:30. The question is—has she others, in a shed or in a barn, that will be brought in presently?

If she has but one it shall live.

I have not told you of Collie, the dog. She is a beautiful yellow and gold creature, a shepherd dog, I got her for $10 from Miles Newman, the Smyth County game warden.

Miles put one over on me. Collie sucks eggs. He went over to Ander Sullivan's[2] place and gobbled up 19 turkey eggs.

We tried everything. We have given him eggs coated with red pepper, eggs with quinine on them etc. We can't kill him. He is such an affectionate creature.

We have simply to make him stay at home and keep the door to the hen yard closed.

He stays at home the better because recently something happened to him. Like all dogs he likes to run out into the road and bark at passers-by at night. One night recently a drunken man, going muttering along our road, took out a revolver and shot at him. He probably disturbed the drunken man's thoughts. No man likes that.

And here you are, disturbing my thoughts day and night.

Collie came home that evening with a terribly shocked hurt look on ~~her~~ his face.

I don't know why I insist on writing she instead of he for Collie. It may be because of the egg sucking.

But what is an egg when one's affections are involved?

O dear, it seems a long time before June 2nd. Your mother said you would come then. Will you?

I have a sudden difficulty. I get blotches of ink over everything. Perhaps the cat does it.

Another hen has hatched eleven chicks. She had thirteen eggs. That seems good. Think, my dear, of all the eggs men waste.

They say a man has millions.

But pshaw, how ridiculous. Men do not have eggs at all, do they?

Come as soon as you can, dearest, and do not take too seriously what I say about the deterioration of the character of the turkey hen.

Or do not think your own character will be improved by cultivating a lot of turkey cocks either.

If one could ruin you, what could three or four do?

1. A nearby farmer friend who frequently helped out at Ripshin.
2. John Ander Sullivan, Felix's brother, later the caretaker at Ripshin.

[Ripshin, 12 May 1930]

Monday

Still cold and rainy. Little David [Greear] is still here. John is giving him drawing lessons. He goes today to a place called Nathan's Creek.[1] He is a sweet, wise little mountain boy.

It rained, a slow drizzle, all Sunday afternoon. We played dominoes and then went for a walk. I found some trilliums, yellow, red and white azaleas and some big wahoos. You know what these are—the kind of magnolias that grow here. We call them also "cucumber" trees.

Anyway it filled the house with flowers. They were needed. The house-keeper, Mrs. Hilton, has been in a surly mood for three days.[2]

I sense what is going on although she has said nothing. There is a struggle between her and her son Mendel. Mrs. H is a capable, hard-working woman and a good manager. She has something of the same sort of energy as Bob.

Like Bob she wants to run everything. Her husband couldn't stand being with her and lit out, leaving two sons. One of the sons could not stand it and also lit out.

She had one left. The mother and son sleep in the same bedroom here. The boy has grown a lot. He is very strong. On Friday, against my protest, he picked up and carried a 200[-pound] bag of fertilizer.

The mother still insists on treating him as a little boy and of course he resents it. He wants to be thought of as a man now.

He will finally go away and leave her and then she will be desolated. I am waiting until one or the other speaks to me about it, then perhaps I can help them through it a little.

In the meantime this sense of a silent struggle in the house.

It creeps into rooms, pervades everything.

It is like having Elizabeth back in the house.

She used to go about like that, feeling she was losing me I suppose. Instead of trying to make herself quiet inside, she nursed her dislike of people. It grew of course.

I used to go to her—shake her. "Quit it," I'd say.

She would quit. She'd cry. Of course she wanted love. God knows we all do, poor Mrs. Hilton too.

Why, my dear, if you could come into this room where I am to try to work this morning, just be in here reading or writing letters, how it would change the atmosphere.

I have got the door closed to keep the discord out.

E used to cry when I shook her like that and then within an hour perhaps she would be back at it again.

It must have been there was something too strange and far away in me for her. She couldn't warm herself.

I think perhaps it was flesh. She never did accept flesh as you do.

Man's flesh and woman's flesh, a woman's monthly sickness (something nasty about that in her. I suppose the nastiness notion of that has been built up for ages. It must be the reason many women go a little crazy at such times. E would close herself in a room and talk aloud to herself, filling the house with her discordant voice.

Even the Bible speaks of it as uncleanliness.)

What nonsense.

How is it any more unclean than my finger bleeding?

Man's flesh and woman's flesh. How far people are from acceptance.

How far people are from any attempt at understanding. Damn laziness not to try and try anyway.

Last night I was looking at a book of Rubens—reproductions. A riot of flesh there. How he got the sweet fat fold of it. He wasn't afraid.

When he was past 60 he married a girl of sixteen. He gave her what she wanted too—love—acceptance of life. He painted her portrait several times afterward. It was all over her, the sense of drinking at a clear spring, being fed and loved.

Bob in a house does something to it. He is nervous and restless but there is nothing rotten in him. The air tingles when he comes in. He asserts and asserts.

There is no peace in him but there is sweetness.

None of my children yet surly. Thank God. That is the worst of all.

This silent, persistent putting out of poison.

Why will not people learn that they constantly do that—they either give off poison or food for others. We live off each other or we kill each other.

Some instinct, dearest Eleanor, I think guided me, in Marion, to your father and mother's house. It may be true, as you have sometimes said, that they did give you, when you were young, some fear of flesh, but in some way it didn't become poisonous in you.

How sweetly you respond to love. How sweet your flesh, your body, smells and tastes.

Your father's body is nice too, and your mother's, and Randolph's, and Mazie's. Katharine I do not know so well.

Your mother says . . . with that strange restless persistence of hers—"Let's get at the truth of this."

Meaning education, or industry or sex or whatever subject is up.

I don't mind it.

Of course truth isn't to be caught and caged like that.

I look at her and at your father. Love has managed to live in them. It goes on. There is health.

I go into your father and mother's house and I can breathe there. I can think.

I suppose it is a battle and they have in some way managed to survive.

If we in turn can have courage to fight our way through the dark times—not to grow silent and surly.

Settling down to the giving off of poison, being satisfied with that.

Where my great failure lies—it is like a dark shadow—is that I have not stuck anyway.

I know that. I've failed.

I can't bring you anything but failure.

Your love has to heal the failure in some way. You have to think of me as a man full of failure.

You have to know, I suppose, that all the evil things that may be thought or said of me are true.

You have to believe there is a better truth in me.

I haven't a right to ask it.

I do ask it.

The only possible reason for your making a mating with me that I can see is that, in spite of all failure, all impatience, all cruelty and thoughtlessness in me, there is something.

Paul Rosenfeld once wrote of me saying that I had, by my work, a little reestablished in America, where people have been peculiarly and terribly separated, the sense of man in man. I'm not trying to use his words.[3]

If I have failed with certain individuals, I haven't failed altogether in the broader sense.

I know that.

Knowing all this, I thought—"I'll go it alone."

But I can't. I grow too cold.

If I do not mate with you, I'll mate with some woman. I have to have flesh grown sweet and fragrant to me, as yours has.

I suppose I can't promise anything. What good are promises?

At least I can be fairer to you, franker, than I have ever been to another.

I can come just as I am. You are clear headed. You are the best chance I've ever had.

What's the use talking more of it—you know all this.

It is a grey cold morning and there has been this discord in the house between the woman and her son. It makes me grey and cold.

God, Eleanor, sweet dear woman, will people ever learn the simple lesson of what they can do to a house, a room.

Taking the responsibility.

"I am going into this room. What am I going to do to the air of the room?"

Failing and trying again.

Many marriages. Marriages every minute of every day. A marriage between me and this tree, that field, that man.

To take hold and let go.

It has such possibilities.

My dearest one.

P.S. You should see my room, upstairs, in which I now work. It wants only you, to come into it. I can hardly wait until you do come and see it, bring yourself into it too. It wants that.

1. A village in North Carolina, about twenty-five miles south of Ripshin, where the Greears had relatives.

2. On 4 August SA wrote that Mrs. Hilton "finally exploded" and left.

3. Rosenfeld in "Sherwood Anderson" (*Dial* 72 [January 1922]: 29–42) wrote that SA's stories are "flesh of our flesh and bone of our bone; and through them, we know ourselves in the roots of us, in the darkest chambers of the being" (p. 38).

[Ripshin, 15 May 1930]

Thursday

(She chatters—as I do.)[1]

A cold rainy night—almost cold enough to frost. John & I went fishing but had no luck. As usual I fell in. Just when the fishing should have been best, at the end of the day, a heavy rain storm came. We were fishing over near Quebec[2] and so drove home, wet inside and out, and got to bed at once.

There have been almost continuous rains and the roads are pretty bad.

However, I am well and happy these days. I have a feeling that we can work out some sort of partnership and have each other.

I suppose the reason I did not go to see you at Detroit was that I wanted to think things out. The intimacy between us obviously couldn't go on as it was. Something would have happened. It would, in the end, have been disastrous to your work.

As you said once—you are a woiking goil.[3] Thank God for that.

And then I felt that we could hardly get through the summer. Your father and mother, seeing us together, would know—unless they are blind, dumb and deaf.

Dear, I don't believe Bob was sneering at you about the letter that time. Or did you say "leer"?

I think, from little things he says, that he is terribly fond of you really.

About the farm—its expenses etc. I pay Mrs. H $30 a month and the boy, her son, $15.

Now we have a good cow that keeps us supplied with milk, butter etc. and a young heifer, who will know the rapture of the bull for the first time this fall.

Do you know, my sweet woman, that we are far ahead of the animals in this? Did you ever see a cow getting what she wanted? One jump—one mighty thrust—and that is all.

The bull climbs down at once. He wags his tail. A sleepy dreamy look comes into his eyes.

The cow looks a bit disappointed. Perhaps she had hoped for more. She goes to eating grass.

Of course, my dear, you never had to lead a cow to such an affair. She behaves unspeakably, will dash off in any direction, go through fences, almost climb trees.

I hope you never become like that, dear. Still one can't tell.

Mrs. H has cheered up.

To return. I'm so scatterbrained.

Mrs. H raises almost everything we eat and cans all sorts of things. She puts away meat, hams, bacon, sausage, side meat etc. for the year. She cans fruits and vegetables, makes the wine.

We buy nothing but flour, sugar, coffee, salt and such staples.

This year we will have 3 pigs in the pen—have them now in fact.

There is another cow calf that will not lose her virginity until the fall of '31.

Also Mrs. H & her son clear up new land, rescuing it from brush. The farm will never make a cent of money. What we have to consider is what it would cost us to be somewhere else.

Well, you wait and see. It will have to be a partnership affair. There is a kind of joy in growing things. Just now the place fairly reeks of new life.

The turkeys, the dog, the cat with her one kitten—the little tricks they play—their personalities coming out.

The mother feeling in Red—the cow. Her tricks to get at her calf, now being weaned, to be sucked rather than milked.

Hands pulling at her teats, rather than the warm mouth of her child.

It will make you fairly ache to have a calf yourself, dear.

Old Byrd—the farm horse, grown old and rheumatic. She will follow you all over the place, wanting you to rub her sore shoulder.

It is a question of happiness, dear one. If I am happy I can work. I live.

If I can work it is so easy to make a living.

When I speak of your keeping on with some kind of work, it isn't so much earnings in question. It is because of your value to others, I do not want destroyed.

And I think we should not try to be together all the time.

I am too hard on anyone I love. I need the discipline of loneliness too much. If you, as a woman, were looking for the chance to retire, get out of the complex, busy life you are in, I would be the worst man for you.

If it is a question of two workers, wanting the sweets of intimacy sometimes without the damn constraint that besets lovers in America now, then I fancy I am the man for you.

I don't think the farm need be an expense. I could write someday a book about the animals here and pay for it.

They are marvelous creatures.

The three new pigs are Bessie and Alice and Carrie . . . all female you see, a woman's age.[4]

I gave one of them to Mendel, the farm boy, to fatten for a suit of clothes in the fall.[5]

1. SA attached a card with a picture of a magpie, one of a series of "Useful Birds of America" issued by Arm and Hammer bicarbonate of soda.

2. A community on the railroad from Troutdale to Marion, about twelve miles from Ripshin.

3. The allusion is to their lovemaking on 1 March 1930 when, according to SA, EC facetiously said, "You can't do this to me. I'm a working woman."

4. A reference to his article by that name; see letter of 23 April 1930, note 3.

5. This note is written on the back of the sheet: "Dry ass—the worst sort, dear. Alas I know them. They have made a kind of safety-first humanism. When I think of them going on so, I think *fart*. Dry stinking wind. There would be no balm in Gilead if this were the white hope."

[Ripshin, 22 May 1930]

Thursday

I hardly know whether it is Wed., Thur. or Friday. I know the days go. We have had now two such days. There isn't a cloud. No wind blows. The ground has been wet a long time. Now these days have been almost hot.

Everything seems to have been waiting. You can feel growth.

Yesterday there were two Ross boys plowing corn on a hillside—seen from the window of my room. If people could but get a sense of the drama of themselves against nature.

If the boy planting corn could say to himself—"I am beautiful here, walking across this long slanting hill behind this house.

"I am like a man making a lovely painting. The soil was pale yellow across half the field, growing almost purple over there toward the wood, but as my corn plow goes through it, I change the tone of the field."

I went to where John Ander Sullivan is putting out about 15 acres of corn on our other farm—the so-called Swan Farm. The whole countryside calls it that now. Lucile Swan, who is a sculptress, lived there one summer. She was once the wife of Jerry Blum, the painter.[1]

They parted and she was terribly unhappy.

So I gave her the place for the summer. She was a big, handsome woman.

It's odd how women, having known sex, want it more when it is gone.

Lucile told me that was the hardest thing for her. "I'm suddenly vulgar about it," she said. "I'd take any man."

She knew she would get over it and did not try to get me. She seemed to reserve me to talk to. She used to come to the house and get me and we'd walk. E thought her too vulgar. When a man came to see us, Lucile went after him furiously. She laughed to me about it. "I want any man I can get in me," she said.

Perhaps, in mating, a woman makes a new connection with all men, a man with all women—both with nature.

Lucile thought that if she could get a man in her she would get back something she had lost that wasn't just Jerry Blum. She did not want him back. "I wouldn't care now about the man himself," she said.

Country men going past felt the appeal in her. A mountain man here, the father of 19 children, said to me, "If my old woman would die now, I'd never let that woman get out of this country."

At the Swan farm John Ander with his two sons, one 17 one 12, was hoeing corn. He had taken two little baby girls up there to sit under an apple tree. His wife had gone to see old man Cane, who is 90 and is dying.

A good time to die—in the spring—if you are 90. If I were 90, I would like to die in the spring.

Both of John Ander's children—the boys—chew and smoke. He buys tobacco for them. He is a gentle soul and rules his children by kindness. They adore him.

I hoed corn with them awhile, talking with John about various kinds of weeds, about how much the land needed lime etc.

Thinking all the time how nice they all were up there against the hill. I wanted to be with them and at the same time away off, on another hill looking at them—their figures moving slowly across the hill.

The movements of their arms and backs—going in procession across the field—each in his corn row.

You get what I mean. Some people may be painters, others paintings.

Suppose, dear, I could get, through the factories, a sense across to men of their loss—a desire to get it back.

There is no love of country in America. There is no such thing as love of country until you love one piece of ground. It must begin there.

You can't love women unless you love a woman.

You see why I must love.

Do I make you feel prayers in you when I say that?

It not being me, it being men—you a woman—me a man.

Suppose you undertake it all. I've got to be constructive. I can't just criticize modern life.

Everything worth a damn is subtile and difficult.

Perhaps I scatter a good deal now because I am trying to pick up so many threads.

I'm all right as regards people. I can feel that. Suppose E were, at bottom, lesbian. The lesbian and the homo are parasites. They want death rather than life. E wanted to withdraw from all life. She always seemed to be saying—"Come on. Die with me."

People want to die as well as live. There are these two tendencies.

Good and evil.

Heaven and Hell.

God and the Devil.

Mankind has always sensed in himself the two roads.

It is good to be in relation to a hill, a wood, a river, a woman. By that you get into a new relation to all.

In the wood by the mill I got into a new relation with all life. People here feel it. There is a new laughing quality on the farm.

There was pain and hurt and love and joy in a woman's face. I kept laughing afterwards, have been laughing ever since.

Looking up at her—she being herself and me too. I was right in the beginning—the intense connection is good. It has given me something ever since relating me anew to all women, all men, children, animals, the earth.

Do you get the connection of it all, including the factories?

Such a day. Everything here seems waiting for you to come.

I have got a gallon of the finest peach brandy you ever put to your lips.

I have got 20 gallons—more or less—of grape and apple wine. We just opened the kegs—last year's vintage. It is the best we have made. It is a sour wine—not sweet and mawkish—something you can drink at meals. You'll love it, I'm sure, darling.

I am almost afraid to say—I think I have got the tone for the second—the follow-up article to "A Woman's Age." The one to be called "Perhaps Women."[2]

If I have got it, it will make a complete little thing—the two articles. I'll make a little book of it called "Perhaps Women." I'll not send this last one off—if it comes through . . . it is noon now and I have written all I can today . . . I'm quite exhausted . . . I'll not send it off until you see it.

As speaking from the outside, I am going to say some pretty bold things—contrasting, for example, the attitude of YWCA with YMCA, etc.

I'll want you to pass judgment on it.

1. Jerome Blum, a good friend during SA's years in Chicago. Lucile Swan was at Ripshin during the summer of 1927.

2. "Perhaps Women" is the title of three chapters of *Perhaps Women;* SA probably refers to the one following "It Is a Woman's Age," pp. 59–74.

[Ripshin 23 May 1930]

Friday

Dearest.

I shall have to give up writing for today. Fortunately there is a man here, a neighbor, laying up again a bit of wall that fell down. I can go watch him. That will occupy me.

I got up with aching bones.

It is really nerves.

I wrote furiously yesterday and the day before. When I was tired I drank some of the strong peach brandy and kept going.

I had to quit at one o'clock. At such times, when the words, the ideas, the feeling within yourself, when all flow together, you feel very strong.

It seems almost you can conquer the world, conquer all ugliness in yourself and others, find the very central truth and loveliness of all life.

You can't of course.

You can't even go on as long as you wish. It isn't intended. Well, you are like a man walking from one mountain top to another on a tight wire.

It is all balance.

God never intends you to reach the other mountain.

I wrote you a long letter one day recently, trying to explain somewhat the nature of the artist at such times. It is the one I spoke of that I didn't send. The way I expressed it made me out really too bad.

I tried to explain the great difficulty of breaking down, walking again on earth after being up there on the wire.

How a man is sometimes a little crazy and ugly at such times. He appears angry and dissatisfied with people sometimes when he isn't at all.

He is only saying to God—"Why didn't you let me go on, why didn't you let me do it quite, just once?"

A kind of inner feeling of being thwarted, beaten.

Suppose you beat some other man or a woman, just to get even.

You've got to try to remember their difficulties too. I know.

You wanted the stars to sing, the moon, rivers, winds, people, trees.

One great song.

It fell into broken fragments.

God is so baffling in his intentions.

I speak of God thus. I have to surrender to something outside self.

Force.

Love.

Nature.

It.

God.

What difference what we call it, dear?

I grasp more than I ever have what is wanted. My fancy leaps out beyond my hand.

Yesterday, when I was beaten, couldn't go on any more, my nerves trembling, I couldn't stay in the house.

I got in the car and drove to Marion. I wrote some little foolish things for Bob's papers, visited your mother.

We talked of homosexuality and lesbianism. Your mother is a marvel the way she is willing to let her mind open. We talked as two parents. I tried to make her see how you could hate perversion, not hating the pervert. She did see.

I drove home weary.

Your letter had come saying—"Don't count on it."

I didn't answer very well. I said it was simpler than it is.

I don't know how much it matters, about marriage for example. Love is something else.

If you were here today I would go with you into the woods. I dreamed of you. I was lying close to you. Abner stirred a bit, not much.

"Not your time," I said to him. I would have said the same thing had you been there.

It was a growing together time in another way, as would have been had you been there.

Of course, dear, you will have to think and ask questions but your thinking and asking questions won't do any good. Something inside you will or won't as a wind blows or doesn't blow.

Some days I'm very old, very wise, very strong, very weak.

Strong in my male weakness.

God seems to take from me achievement but he gives me knowledge.

I know more often when I can't write than when I can.

I even think it isn't up to you—or me. If some force stronger than us says yes, it will be yes.

I've not so much faith in our wisdom. There is where my wisdom lies.

I'll quit writing now and go sit in the sun, watch the man lay wall. I'll touch no more ink today.

[Ripshin, 11 July 1930]

Friday evening
Notes for Eleanor—

Such a queer mixture of joy and sadness in me coming home. The memory of the tired-spirited look in your father's face. Has he been that way a long time?

The life in your mother's eyes.

Something in you I had not felt—just like that . . . you a little away . . . warm and dusky . . . full of warm shadows.

I didn't just want to touch you. All the way home the smell of dry burned grass. I wanted to stay near you. Tonight I would have liked sitting by you in silence—just letting something go and come between us. There are no words for it.

I found myself saying over words I had said to you—about my morality—the artist's morality. I don't think many care.

Then about the woman's morality—to be and remain beautiful.

It is in the eyes, in the tone of the voice, in little subtile movements of the body.

Inner graciousness—I guess that is it.

I began remembering something I wrote a long time ago. It is in *Winesburg*—the story "Sophistication"—George Willard walking on a summer night with Helen White. I'll bring the book. When he cries out to the girl, "It's none of my business I tell you. I want you to be a beautiful woman."[1]

You have never failed in that with me.

Then, now, all my life, I have sought the woman willing to be beautiful.

Why should it not be to a woman what an artist's work is to him?

They each helping the other.

What if they don't achieve the last ultimate thing?

Maybe I've found out something after a long lifetime of failure. Have I at last learned to love?

I would, it seems to me tonight, pay any price I could for your happiness.

Today I didn't just want to touch you, to have anything touch you. If we had been married, if we could have gone into a room together, I would not have wanted to touch you.

I would have wanted only to be near you, look and look at you.

I have out of all this a new feeling. I don't want to run away from the world, love of a woman, life, as I did last year.

I do want a quiet sanctuary where we two can come—to be together in many moods—facing together your problem and my problem.

Good night—dearest love.

1. *Winesburg, Ohio,* p. 290.

[Ripshin, 20 July 1930]

Thinking in bed—after leaving you.

First of jealousy. I am always imagining you can find somewhere a man younger, more lovely of person, who can also love you with an imagination as strong as my own. Fearing you will.

Thinking all you say is true—that if you marry me I shall always be wanting for you lovely gowns, soft furs about you, soft things under your feet.

Sometimes I furnish in fancy a room for you as I would like it. I see it glowing with soft colors to match the colors in your skin—shapes to match the loveliness of your body. I guess—if it couldn't be that—I'd rather have it very poor and plain.

Thinking—of death—how I shall hate it when it comes to me—wanting more life, more life, more life. I'll try not to be petulant when it comes but to go like a soldier of some mysterious red army.

Good night, lover. It [is] lonesome here. You did make me feel reasons why you should not marry me.

You did touch a deep sadness in me. You were beautifully gentle with me. I felt your love.

[Marion, 13 August 1930]

What I hate about the Virginia Birchfield incident, the remark of Dr. Baughman etc.,[1] is just that it brings you into the picture some people have of me.

It is inevitable if I am to have any hours with you, any life with you.

I am trying to build that life. I begin in my room in the morning. Two things come—you and the book on which I work.

My mind reaches out into the book, trying to unify it, and at the same time I try to create our life in myself.

The two things should go hand in hand in the healthy man. Do not doubt it, dearest woman. My thoughts of you are pure. I want not to lie to myself or you, [but] to face everything, discouragements, failure, the dullness that must come too.

To believe also in the warm glowing fact.

I remember my fight against the conception of life I once had. Out there in Chicago, when I had begun life as a young business man, a go-getter, and when, at last, I knew there was no peace to be had, I struggled a long time.

I used to get drunk, stay drunk, for days, trying to blind myself.

There were little things. I knew that I must not hurry and rush. I had got into that habit.

My speech was sharp and quick and hurried. I began speaking more slowly. My present slow drawl is a built thing.

I had to learn to walk slowly. As Bob now often runs, playing golf, so I did. I began walking slowly through one street at a time. I said to myself—"I will not run. I'll stroll through this street."

My object was to get some inner quiet in which something could grow.

At last I produced a few things that grew slowly in me, as a babe might grow in you. They came out. I felt pure and clean.

The hurried world outside the little inner quiet place took one hurried, casual look at what I had done.

"Unclean, horrid," the cry went up.

I remember the shock to me in all this. It seemed to me the pure real thing should be taken as pure and real. I thought it would be.

I had to learn something new.

Others, for example, will have to judge us by themselves. A Bill Birchfield, for example, cannot think outside the circle of his own experience, his own feelings.

You get our little circle broken into then.

I took a room in Chicago and for a long time didn't let anyone come in. The advertising department where I worked was filled with what seemed filthy men. They weren't so filthy. They were just dull little defeated men.

I was sick of the talk in there. There was never any free play of ideas. I hated the men in there.

I used to do queer physical things. I went home to my room, took off all my clothes, locked the door.

I had got a pail, water and soap. Does all this seem childish?

I scrubbed the floor, I scrubbed the wood work. I opened all the windows.

I wanted cleanliness.

It has been terribly hard to do any beautiful work.

You can't separate yourself from the life of others. You know, dear, how I tried that. I was trying it when you first knew me.

I was pretty bad. I thought, I guess—"Well, I seem to need a woman. I'll have sex with some woman, make it as beautiful as I can."

I didn't intend to let her into the room where I went to pray.

You jerked me out of that. We began. We made love. Even at first I sensed something in you so fine I wanted to preserve it.

I began to love you outside myself.

But life has not been good to me in one way. Almost always, dear, when I have been most faithful to my inner faith and have produced something out of it, there has been, at first, revulsion in others.

There was a cry of "dirt, dirt."

Just as the cry is going up now about poor Lawrence's book.[2]

This often over my cleanest things.

I couldn't function in the little quiet inner place, into which I sometimes got with the women I tried to bring in.

Tennessee was the only one who came near doing it.

All I asked was belief. What else have we, dear, but love?

Everything else is gone.

It's easy enough to believe in love in glowing moments, when you are making love.

You have to believe when people try to muddy you with their thoughts.

You have to hang on through dull times, blindly sometimes.

There is a kind of inner central fact.

Love making, for example.

It is perfect, wonderful sometimes, complete, like a fine work of art.

Then it isn't. You don't know why.

It revolts you even.

It is so easy then to lose all faith.

You know what people do. Why, my dear one, it is the same in love as in art. You can't separate the two.

One of my best stories I tried for over a period of 12 years. One day it came, beautiful, clear and lovely. All the others lost faith. They wouldn't hold on.

I think, dear, we ought to pray to love as to God. We have to build our life new every day.

Sometimes I have thought a man couldn't be true to the two things, work and love. Now I know they are all one.

Without love, a woman, I am a crippled, one-sided man.

I have seen people do it. I know it can be done.

There isn't much belief in love but, now, there isn't much belief in anything. As regards work I have to say over and over:

I believe. Help Thou my unbelief.[3]

Addressed to what?

Life, I guess.

Some dim, faraway feeling of the full life you and I will never reach, except at moments, but for which we must try, fail, and try again.

I don't curse the ones who want as much as Lawrence did. Other artists say I'm softer. I don't know.

I've been so dirty myself.

I would have you, dear, understand my feeling for men like young Charles [Bockler]. It isn't personal. It is just that, in a smarty world, where most young painters get smart, try for cheap effects, he has some of this faith.

What happens between you and me and will happen over and over, doubt and fear coming in, happens to all such men.

Lankes[4] came down here and walked with me all afternoon one day, utterly discouraged, in doubt as to the value of trying to go on any more.

Charles has done that. We walked one night. He said—"I used to have voices that came to me. Now they are all silent. I'm in a dead world. I can't work any more."

The painting I sent up there proves it wasn't true. He hadn't really given up.

I wish you would take that painting up into your room. Keep it, dear. Take it to New York with you.

Such paintings are just proof that love is worthwhile.

All this because, in poor Virginia B—with that man coming for her, I felt the world looking into our inner place.

Their thoughts won't make it so nice. I guess we have to scrub and scrub. Charles had to scrub and scrub himself to get the clean, warm color of that painting.

I love him for it. I'd give my clothes to keep him warm while he keeps the faith.

We have to keep our own faith, believe when there isn't any belief—or it's no good.

So many words. So many words.

It's just a kind of praying—reasserting, reasserting.

Is it madness, dear?

1. Virginia Birchfield was the wife of William Birchfield, an attorney in Marion. Dr. Jess E. Baughman was a Marion dentist. The "incident" is obscure.

2. *Lady Chatterley's Lover.*

3. "Lord, I believe; help thou mine unbelief" (Mark 9:24).

4. J. J. Lankes, woodcut artist of Hilton Village, Virginia, a friend of SA's. He provided the illustration on the dust jacket and frontispiece of SA's *Perhaps Women.*

[Marion, probably 16 August 1930]

Saturday

It has become a necessary part of my day to begin by a note to you—my love—as I would if I could come to you every day.

I slept after 1 o'clock. Before that a long, restless time of half sleep. Thoughts.

You surrounded by people—some of them asking—

What about you and S.A. etc.

Lois[1] half angry and upset.

Brownie[2] curious.

You have to remember it doesn't go as deep with them as it seems. People are concerned with self.

Lois's life is disarranged. All people hate such disarrangements. She has no personal feeling about me, really doesn't know me. She has made an imaginary me.

Against which, I dare say, she contrasts herself, with some satisfaction to herself.

Well.

It is all a part of a general discord in life that exists as definitely as harmony. Perhaps we would live forever if it weren't true.

At any rate, dear, I have never searched my own self as I have since I have loved you. Now I'm going to stop that. I accept my love of you as a part of me like my hand here, my head, my legs, my brain.

I'm going to try to quit mulling over the past too. I've explained and explained.

Really you have no past for me and I haven't for you. When you tell little stories of the past, before I knew you, you seem talking of another person.

I believe it is so with you when I talk of the past.

Love, if it is anything, is a renewal, a rebirth. With you, in your presence, dear, I breathe, naturally and deeply, a new life.

I am half a thing made by circumstances as you are. When my hand touches your body, there, for me, is an experience new in my life.

I want to give myself to this new health honestly and frankly.

[about two lines torn off] it. You give me health but I have not yet had enough of it. I need marriage, years of you. An hour alone with you makes a day possible.

Let's admit all blundering, all evil, all everything they say.

Can you love me? Can you accept me as mate?

I can and do you, dear.

I have written to E[lizabeth]. I'll find out at once if there is to be a struggle. If not, I'll go and get it done.

That will give you time to think too. I'll be away. If you finally and deeply in you decide for me, then we can do it. And begin.

Life not death is the adventure.[3] These my thoughts last night.

1. Lois MacDonald was an economics professor at New York University, who shared an apartment with EC in New York.

2. Brownie Lee Jones was a YWCA associate and good friend of EC's.

3. This is perhaps SA's earliest version of the words that would be his epitaph: "Life Not Death Is the Great Adventure."

[Marion, 3 September 1930]

Notes for Eleanor

I intended to show you the little portfolio of letters—queer half poets, so many of them.

We want to build a world and there is such material. I could not bear most of these people if I were not myself such a half man.

At the fair—elephants performing before the people. They stand on their heads, roll over, fire a toy cannon etc.

It makes me so ashamed. These great animals, with their slow swinging great bodies, standing on their heads, putting their legs up, running up a flag. I stood with Doctor Wright, Lee Cole[1] and others. They saw something on my face.

"Don't you like it?"

"No."

"Why?"

"Those great fine beasts made silly for the entertainment of second-rate people like us."

Anyway it made them all a little silent.

When I am shattered in the morning now, I have you. You are never shattered as you exist in me. You are clear. I feel nothing mean, nothing small.

When I am with you, I make love to you, love to touch you. It is to try to express something of all these hours of feeling when I am away from you.

You are always at my shoulder, at my back. I want my inner life to be something in which you can exist beautifully.

You are near me so much in this way that I feel every thought I have is spoken aloud. I do not want to do anything to betray our love in this world any more than when I am actually physically near you.

There are things so hard to say. This was what I meant last night. I said I didn't want ever to kiss another, be intimate with another.

I meant that I wanted the sweetness of all sweet people through you.

This, my love of you, is at last the love I have wanted. I know it more and more. The others were not really a test of me. My inner life wasn't touched.

I am afraid I used them trying to go toward love.

In you my love has a center. I use you trying to go toward all people.

If I cannot be true to this love now that it has come, then all that has been said of me is true and I am not a sweet man but rotten. I shall not want to live any more if I waver in my love of you. You will understand that.

There is a new inner dignity to my life that I have wanted. It has come most fully since we went together into Jaffe's house.[2] I am afraid I tried to be untrue to something there but couldn't.

It is very mixed.
It is very clear.

1. Dr. George Wright was superintendent of Southwestern State Hospital in Marion. Lee Cole was an auto dealer.
2. Louis Jaffe, a friend of SA's, was editor of the *Virginian-Pilot,* in Norfolk, Virginia. SA and EC had visited him in the fall of 1929.

[Marion, 6 September 1930]

Saturday

In the hotel[1] they have put me over the Lincoln factory, a ragged sea of roofs. The steady roar of the factory fills the room.

Everything in the room is cheap and shoddy. How many fat traveling men with their thoughts have stayed in here.

It is the kind of small town hotel I wrote about in *Winesburg*.

When I awake in the morning like this, I can't know about the day.

I began this morning dreaming about a place—a quiet room somewhere. The large room upstairs at the farm was lovely but I couldn't maintain the farm.

It was too far away, too isolated, too far away from you. I used to get restless and drive to Marion. When I came into town there was your house, where I had seen you. It brought you closer.

Last night you were more lovely than you had ever been, in the car, walking in the moonlight near the car, in the road when we stopped the 2nd time, afterward in the moonlight in the yard at home.

I think, if we could live together now, when we can live together, I will still want to sit in my room in the morning writing these vagrant notes to you.

For the book I need tone now. I may have to wait a little, work on something else for the time.

I sit listening to the steady roar of the Lincoln factory. Is the tone I want buried away down in there?

You challenged something in me in this factory thing. It's odd that I have never been in a factory with you.

I shut my eyes, see the big bright orderly rooms. I always see you there . . .

As though you had become to me the symbol of all women.

Not a rich woman, not an aristocrat, not a working girl—just all of them.

Afterwards in the car you said—we mustn't for a long time. I know what you meant.

You don't want it spoiled or do I.

Being too close too long, too often, would do that.

I think, dear, that being married must be like the practice of an art. We have to work at it, give thought to it.

The lovely thing is to be able to think of someone outside self.

The moments we have, places where we have been lovely together, are like paintings made to hang up in our house.

Building a life together must be like building a house.

Both people must have to want to have it lovely, be willing to take the times when it isn't, without blaming the other.

I'll try now to help you draw away a little.

1. The Hotel Lincoln. The nearby Lincoln factory made furniture.

[Michigan City, Indiana,
27 September 1930]

Saturday
Eleanor dear.

It turned very cold. There has been snow in Wisconsin. Vessels were wrecked on the lake.

I slept outdoors on the porch of Ferdinand's house.[1]

No word has come from you. I am trying to prepare myself for what seems inevitable—that you will have realized my essential selfishness.

Perhaps you will have definitely turned from me.

I shall not blame you.

If it is true I hardly know yet what I will do.

In the night, the wind howling through the woods in which the house sits here, I kept awakening.

I murmured your name.

Eleanor.

Eleanor.

In spite of my selfishness, my continual self assertion, I do in my own way love at last as I never did love.

I can claim nothing for that. I have, dear, inevitably gone back to the terrible self analysis that saps everything out of me.

I seem unable to stop it.

I am trying very hard not to show my friends here the condition I am in.

I can't avoid clinging to you. You are beautiful to me.

I will have to win some kind of inner victory, get back on my feet. If I cannot do it I have no right to clutter up your life.

If I could get clear and work.

Last year I came to these people when I was in much the same condition I am in now. I am ashamed that it has happened again.

Almost, dear one, I am ashamed to be alive.

I have gone since writing the above for a long walk with Ferdinand. We walked for hours in a bitter wind. He let me talk.

I let go, did talk, told him all my doubts. He listened full of sympathy.

What he urges upon me I myself know. I am to let you alone, give you a chance to think for yourself.

Sun.

To the mail box many times yesterday although it was foolish. There are but two deliveries.

I sleep outdoors on the porch. In the night I awoke. A horrid thought. Suppose you are ill.

The thought terrorizes me. It is Sunday. I do not know your apartment address.

There may be a note Monday. Even a note saying you had decided against any further touch with me but that you were well would be a relief.

I got up and walked about at night outdoors in my pajamas.

If you are not ill, if you have turned from me, it will be what I deserve from life. I have not served life well. I have bungled, been irrational.

I remember laughing times, times when I was happy.

I am sorry you found me as you did. There was another man. He lived, worked, played.

He had not become what you found.

I was defeated when you found me. I am afraid I tried to crawl back into life on your dear person.

Have you decided you will not let me? You are right.

It is a question perhaps of survival. Why should I survive?

I am writing these notes now as a kind of record of these days.

On the whole, dear, I am succeeding, better than I did a year ago when I was so desperate—so near suicide, in concealing my depression from my friends here.

I have undertaken that. It is something to do—a task to undertake—

To take my mind a little off the thought of the desolation of life without you, without hope.

I go about and touch things out of doors, trees and bushes. They are cold now in the fall. It seems to me that if I am to lose you I will lose the sense I was slowly getting back of nature, warmth in nature and in life.

I will deserve to lose it if I do lose it.

1. SA was visiting the Schevills at their summer home on Lake Michigan.

Marion, [15 October 1930]

Wednesday eve

Your gorgeous letter of Tuesday came. The Chappells[1] are coming this weekend. I suppose you know this by now. No wire came from you.

Darling, I do not believe it will be hectic when I see you. Something has changed. Perhaps up there at Michigan City, when I went down so low, something changed in me.

I have always felt, since I failed with Elizabeth, that, if I succeeded in coming through this time, I would be different. Perhaps I am a man who develops slowly. You must remember that I was thirty-five before I began to publish.

I begin, dear, really to feel that I may learn to love. More and more I do not want to upset you. I want peace for you, all the loveliness in life I can give you.

Bob and I took a ride in the country. It was lovely.

Surely your mother will return soon.

Dear, when you know about the next weekend—as soon as you know, will you wire me. As you suggest, use any name. This so I can make my plans for the trip next week. If I can see you I will drive straight from Greenville to you.

Thursday morning

I am glad, dear, that you have come to that determination about frankness—in regard to what I write. I would like to have, in the end, a real union with you. Why should there not be marriage of mind and the imagination as well as the body?

Why, my dear, if it were all just the body, it would be infinitely better for us just to get that out of us as fast as we could.

Why, I do not mean just that. The body is lovely too. What in all the world more lovely than your body.

But, dear, I am not young. There is much I may do. I have had, I presume, more than almost any man of my time, a rather wide, varied experience of American life.

All these years of planting. I should harvest now.

As you well know by this time, I have things within myself that constantly destroy my effectiveness. I spend too much time in self-analysis. I destroy myself.

I feel in you a certain health, a certain strength. Would it not be possible for us, a man and woman, to have all the work that may yet pour out from under this pen here, a kind of mutual thing?

I do not think, dear, you need be afraid of me in this. There is after all a certain flexibility to my mind, to my imagination. I would not mind fighting with you for something I felt right.

All this in regard to the *Mercury* thing.[2] It doesn't matter. It is not so important, as a mistake made.

I have made too many mistakes for one to matter.

I have been reading a life of Frederick the Great.[3] Did you know, dear, that he was a boy lover?

What a queer, thwarted, hurt life.

His father was a brute. No doubt when Frederick was a lad he saw too much of sheer brutality.

The whole court was indulging in rather brutal fucking, like animals. It disgusted the boy.

I dare say much of lesbianism among modern women comes from something like that. Why there is this terribly delicate thing, the opening of one person to another.

This strange outside person coming so close. Women of sensibility must know, seeing men about, that there are but few men having the real strength that produces tenderness. Phallic daintiness must be rare.

The escape into the half world, avoiding the challenge, is inevitable almost.

On the other hand, dear, it does destroy. I am sure of that. We must take, I presume, the ultimate challenge, dare all, or we remain half people.

Well, I do not believe that love is impossible, as between man and man, woman and woman. I believe I love Charles [Bockler] and John and Bob and Paul [Rosenfeld]—

And old Alfred Stieglitz—

And Julius Friend—in New Orleans, and Maurice [Long]—

I could name more—men and women.

That queer Jewish woman,[4] from New Orleans, with the impossible husband.

Since I first met her, perhaps ten years ago, she has been sensitive to me.

When they were here we had adjoining rooms in the hotel. One night, when things were so tangled up at the house, you seeing me only half secretly—myself upset as you were—she got out of bed and came into my room.

There was her husband lying in there.

She came and put her arms around me and kissed me. "I've always loved you," she said, "and always will. You may depend on my love."

Why, there was nothing physical about that. I felt nothing of the sort nor did she.

I am only trying to say that there are all these loves [that] can exist and then a final ultimate love.

If there is not that, perhaps the others do have a tendency to become this queer semi-physical thing—lesbianism— homosexuality.

Frederick grew to hate all women.

It led to a kind of cold cruelty with all people.

Just the same there was a really honest mind.

I got a sense, as I read the book, of a kind of danger. Life has always meant so much to me. One of the reasons I have made so many mistakes has been that I have been too eager.

The mistakes have multiplied. There have been so many that I have become afraid.

It has resulted in a kind of drawing away from life. That is one reason I have not worked.

I have drawn away from my materials.

It is love only that can bring things back. I keep praying, dear, that I may gain this maturity—to know that to really love I must learn like a small boy.

Be patient with me, dear. You are more dear to me than I can tell you.

What a muddled letter. It is a day when I have too many thoughts in my head, too much I would like to say to you.

1. Blanche and Bentley Chappell of Columbus, Georgia, whom SA had met while visiting there earlier in the year. Only Mrs. Chappell made the trip; she was interested in buying Ripshin.

2. "They Come Bearing Gifts," *American Mercury* 21 (October 1930): 129–37. Apparently EC did not like the article; see letter of 2 March 1931.

3. Frederic II (1740–86), king of Prussia.

4. Probably Adaline Katz.

[Marion, 19 October 1930]

Dear One . . . Sunday morning is usually a great trial for me and I am in luck if I do not lose my temper. I did this morning. Last Sunday morning the boy who makes our fire did not get here until ten. The house was icy cold and I had been up since seven. It stayed cold until noon—also the shop was cold and the boy had the key to the coal bin. He did the same thing this morning. I was furious because I was in a working mood and could not sit at my desk. He had promised me faithfully he would come this morning and then, at last, when he did wander in at nine forty-five, I used language to him that would have curled your hair, dear, if you had heard it. There was nothing gentle in me, nothing nice, I assure you. There is only one thing apparently that will make me get like this and it always is connected with work. Something crosses me at such a time and off I go. It may be just someone wandering in . . . not someone I care about but some casual person. There have been so many experiences of this sort. There is the casual man or woman. In they come. I try to make excuses but they stay. I get a bit rough. I roar at them. "God damn it, get out of here."

I used to have to try to work in the advertising place where I was employed. At ordinary times, when I was not working at my own work (I wrote a good many of my stories at odd times there in the advertising place), at ordinary times I was all right. I would bear any kind of interruption.

Then suddenly the fever for my own work came over me. A man came and sat down beside my desk. He had done it a hundred times and I didn't mind.

Why, it was all different that morning. I tried to get it across to him. How could I? Suddenly then I turned upon him. Jesus, I could have killed him. He shuddered looking at me, into my eyes. I suppose there was murder there. Why, there are people who never do it to me. There is Bob. When I am at work here he strolls in and out. He is a great fellow for walking naked up and down the room smoking cigarettes. He sings absurd songs, very badly. I do not mind him at all. It may be because at bottom he has a kind of sympathy in him. He cares something for the things I care for.

I become a terrible autocrat at times, dear, and afterwards I am ashamed. I am ashamed now for what I said to that stupid boy this morning. What is it to him whether I work or not?

Bob is going off with the woman [Mrs. Chappell] this morning. It is bright and cold outside. She is, I understand, leaving tomorrow. I suppose soon we will know whether or not she is going to buy it. If, in the meantime, another chance comes up I'll sell.

I am counting terrifically on seeing you next weekend. I have been going at rather a high pitch. It has been a strain having the woman here. She probably doesn't intend it but she does stay in the mind as a person in a strange place who should be entertained.

Why, how different it is going to see your mother. What, dear, are we to do with these rather shallow, good enough people? You must have to deal with dozens of them all the time. Don't you ever get angry, intolerant, harsh? I'll bet you don't.

It is so difficult to be nice sometimes. There is this difficult, always fragile, creative world into which a man does sometimes get. Poor Cézanne got so that when he was painting he got furiously angry sometimes because a man walked along a nearby road. He was trying to catch some very elusive difficult thing. Why, I am not that bad anyway.

Dear, I need you terribly. I've tried not to speak of it too much. What is the use? You would do anything you could for me. It isn't your fault but mine that we can't be together this year. I need to see you now, be with you. Please do work it for the next weekend if there is any chance at all.

If you don't I'll know you can't and I'll take myself in hand again of course.

The need of love that is present physically is terrible sometimes. Just to look into your eyes would be like seeing the sun again after [a] month of darkness. I am stupid, dear, violent sometimes, not nice very very very often.

I love you.

I was with your mother again yesterday and she said that she felt better than she had felt at any time since she came home. Always, in some way, when I am there, I so manage it that your name is brought up. I hear again someone speak of you who also loves you.

[Marion, 28 October 1930]

Tuesday

Confused a bit—when I saw you in the bus—I am always confused when, after an absence, I see you again.

For me a lovely afternoon and evening. Still, this morning, when I saw confusion in your eyes again, I felt like saying—that, I guess, my love of you would be strong enough to give up having you if by doing so I could get peace for you.

I don't know whether this is true or not.

The whole afternoon was like music to me. I shall remember always the trees—the great trunks of them, the birds calling, leaves stirring, the light coming down yellow and golden on brown leaves.

You give me always this sweet new awareness. I become more pagan. The gods always seem to walk in places where you are.

It's what I mean when I keep saying you give me health.

I came home. Bob was asleep. I got into bed and closed my eyes.

A procession of faces came. This has always been happening to me but it happens more often now that I have you.

It always happens when we have been happy together.

The faces come in a stream. They stop before me. I wrote about it once in *A New Testament.*[1]

A face stops before me. Then it moves on and another comes.

I suppose it could be scientifically explained. Mazie might try it.

My theory is this—that there is something down in me more aware than the outer me.

I wrote of that once too. Read again Grotesque—at the beginning of *Winesburg*—an old man with a young knight inside him.[2]

"These," I have said to myself, "are faces of Americans I have seen who want their stories told."

They appeal thus to me.

They are caught up in the flow of life, swept past me.

A thousand stories in me untold, Eleanor dear.

There is some inner sweet truth in almost every man. It can't get release.

How am I to say even this without sentimentality?

I am always speaking of health, crying for it.

I want to do my task—I do so little.

I feel, if I confuse things for you, spoil things for you, I'll spoil my own outlet into life.

Why is this so of you and never with another? I don't know. Perhaps I never loved before. I don't know.

I seem to myself this morning to know nothing. I only have hunger for some sweet peace for you.

I guess I'm the last one could bring that.

Another thing about the faces. Sometimes it seems they are all at the windows of some vast prison. I am swept past them.

"Release me. Help me find the truth in myself."

Voices clamoring.

I have crazy nights sometimes.

I want peace for you. How am I to bring it when there is no peace in me?

I may just be selfish. I may just want the strength you give me. I may be lying to you. I may just want strength and understanding to tell a few more tales—release a few more of these strange unknown people whose faces pop in and out in these queer dream times of mine.

1. Pp. 69–70.

2. In "The Book of the Grotesque" the old man is described as having inside him "a woman, young, and wearing a coat of mail like a knight" (*Winesburg, Ohio*, p. 2).

[Marion, 30 October 1930]

Eleanor dearest . . . I have been trying to formulate things in my mind. It is a kind of necessity. I have asked you to marry me. I have to face the fact that perhaps I am not making you much of an offer. It has happened so often, these last few years, that my attempts of sustained work break down.

Is it because there has begun in me the inevitable breaking down of the man who has passed through his best days? Frankly, dearest, I do not know yet. There are great projects in me. Can I carry any of them off? I haven't given up but I want you to face things with me.

I will not have you marry a man who cannot bring you life and force. Because of a few days' discouragement I am not going to give up. What I want to do is to gird myself up to the doing of all I can.

There is, however, some chance I may have shot my bolt, as a workman, as a man. If that turns out to be true, I will not have you tied to me. There is too much to you, too much strength and loveliness. You are to me the most lovely person I have ever known. Your body is the most lovely of all human things to me.

I just want to know, if I can find out, what I am, what possibilities there are in me. The queer reaction of the last few days has been a physical thing. I have been close to actual illness. These nerve breaks come and go with me. If they grow more prolonged, more frequent, I may have to confine myself to doing little things. In that case, dearest, I would rather have you free. Let me love you but as for yourself do not let yourself be bound to me. That will be what I want. When I am in such reactions I feel very guilty that I have in any way come into your life to disturb it. I want to be able to bring you things, not just take from you.

I am sure I am saying all this without any self-pity. I just do not want you to feel tied to a man who may not come off.

Your Lover

[Marion, late December 1930]

A new fragrance to life. It seems to come out of you to me. I got into bed when Bob came in. He was just going to the dance. He dressed and left. The room became still. I could hear cars outside in the street.

I must have fallen into a half sleep. There was something happened I can only describe as an unfolding. I saw scenes of my boyhood and my manhood. They unfolded one after the other—as faces sometimes come. You know how I wish sometimes that I had my first young manhood to give to you. What happened to it?

It went into nothingness. That happens to most men I think.

There was a little girl by a fence at night.

The seeds from a maple tree are scattered everywhere. They fall on brick pavements.

We destroy so much in ourselves that way. What is finest, most tender, gets kicked about. There have been so many half passions.

It makes me sick for Bob and for other young men. Perhaps John may hang onto the thing in himself. I don't know.

It is a part of something we have talked of—to participate or stand aside. I have participated a lot.

As scenes come back so faces come back. I am an old theater in which many and many a play has been enacted. The players have come in and gone out.

That play is ended. Now they are rehearsing for a new play. Some day a fire will destroy the building or it will blow down.

I tried to talk of that—not very successfully. Perhaps I should have kept still. But with me, dear, the mind, the fancy, is so much a part of every day, every minute.

I tried to say we can't have young love. It has to be a seasoned man who comes to you. If I do not begin to be seasoned and mature now I never will.

I have faith there is something untouched that can be given.

Do you remember when in the poem I wrote—"Individuality gone. Let it go," and you liked it?[1]

You have to do that a little too.

You have to let Tennessee come into you and Cornelia[2] and Elizabeth and others.

There was one named Margaret and a Helen and a Frankie. Others perhaps, more faintly.

I am not a man from whom anything goes. There has been a love of abstract womanhood in me—my mother as real to me as when she died[3]—Mimi, my daughter.

What I am trying to say is that you cannot get in me an untouched man. These others will come back, melt into you sometimes.

Whether or not you remain above and clear from them all depends I suppose on the giving power in you as it depends upon that power alive in me whether I shall live, love and work beside you. The challenge is as great for you as for me.

A man can't cleanse himself from life except perhaps by death. Before you came I really wanted that cleansing. I thought of that a lot. A year ago now I was in St. Petersburg. A wind blew my hat away as I walked on a pier that went out into the sea. Tennessee had just died. Just then I did not think of a kind of cowardice in her, an insistence on self that destroyed what we tried for. I thought only that she was dead and quiet and still.

I'll never be able to tell how I fought the impulse to slip over the side of the pier and swim out and out until I sank. The land at my back was life. Had I enough of life?

I hadn't, because of you. That was all of it. It came down to that. If I hadn't begun to love you I wouldn't be here now.

I say begun. I don't think it's all come yet. I think I have come a ways recently. You have to judge whether it's worthwhile to you.

I mean by that, that the love for you I'm going toward doesn't depend on your taking me. That ought to be I suppose dependent on what helps you to come nearer the thing.

It doesn't depend quite I guess on what people call faithfulness. It gets just a little outside words what it depends on, dear.

What I want you to accept is that I am that old theater. I'll never be a new building into which you can go feeling it all your own. I belong too much to memories, to things done, said, felt, you know.

Perhaps, in the end, you will have to ask her—"Has Eleanor felt enough, been hurt enough, to accept giving up what any young woman would want—new life in a man, comparatively untouched?" I think young women have a right to ask that.

You get what I am at—trying to say. It wouldn't change anything in my feeling for you. I love you.

I love your feet, legs, voice, eyes, ears, hair, breasts, back, neck, belly, mind. I love Clarisse.

I'll be your lover anyway.

1. Apparently never published.
2. Cornelia Lane Anderson, SA's first wife.
3. Emma Smith Anderson, who died in 1895.

[Washington, D.C., 8 January 1931]

Thursday
Darling—

It is only eight in the morning but I am in a room at the DuPont—the little hotel where you once came to dine with me. I went up from your car to mine[1] and lay for a time with the shade up looking out. Now, dear, that loving you has given me back zest for life, I hate missing anything. Ten, fifteen years at most and I shall be dead and very quiet or, worse, old and of no use. I'm not sad about it. What's the use being? Still I want it all—the distillation of it all. I got into bed and lay there. You were so near. I made a little nest, you next the window so you could look out and I could look over your dear black head. I imagined us curled up so, whispering thoughts to each other. It is pretty hard keeping that up when the reality of you is so much sweeter.

You were never so sweet as last night. Dear, you are so much more like myself than any woman I have ever known. Do you think that loving you as I do is a form of self-love? If so it can't be helped.

You absorb things from those about you as an artist does. At home in your mother's house you are one thing, out in the woods and fields another.

When you are where there is a strike, there is something else comes.

You take people into yourself. They are sweetened by you.

You change as a field changes in the light.

My very dear. My love.

You will be hurt a lot, being as you are.

You are so alive, in a dead world.

I slept and dreamed an absurd dream. By some heroic effort I had organized all the motorists in America. There were millions of them. I had issued an edict. No motors were to be run on the streets of Danville.[2] The town had gone back thirty years but there were no horses. The streets were dead and quiet, the merchants beside themselves.

I thought—I had phoned from Roanoke for the two berths. Perhaps the station man said to the pullman conductor—"Here's a man and woman, not married, traveling together." That may have made the pullman conductor bold. He thought—"Maybe I can get a piece."

I wonder about getting notes of things those women said. Could you make me copies of your notes, just as you put them down? I won't use them directly—in connection with Danville.

It was sweetest of all when you said—"I loved you when I was at work."

I stopped here. It is eleven o'clock. I have written another chapter. I have written the face chapter, about the faces that appear to Joe Beard when he lies in bed at night.[3]

It is mostly about him when he had his woman—his lying beside her at night, seeing things and trying to tell her what he sees.

Regarding the speech, I believe I'd just let the more intelligent man there in New York handle the whole thing as best he can. It will be bungled down there. The whole point is not a speech delivered but one thought out, written down.

Not only by me but by many men.

Not only for Danville but for all workers.

Is it too subtile for them to get? Nothing is much good unless it is subtile.

1. On the previous evening SA met EC at Lynchburg, Virginia, where she had attended a meeting, and took the train with her to Washington.

2. He had been preparing a speech to be delivered to striking mill workers at Danville, Virginia, on 13 January.

3. SA was working on "Crazy Book," an experimental novel that he later abandoned. The section he refers to is on pp. 211–16 of the manuscript at the Newberry Library.

[On train,[1] 12 January 1931]

Monday—On train from Wash. It is raining. There is something to be said about the visit to Maurice [Long]. There has been a queer feeling. You must feel it, dear, when you go to Geo. Anderson[2] and such men.

There is something about wealth. Mind, I think Maurice is game. There is in him a streak of the adventurer. If things went all to smash he wouldn't bellyache. He is big and two-fisted. He knows he would get on all O.K. Sometimes—often perhaps—he half wishes it would happen.

I went to his plant.[3] It was nice. There were three girls taking sheets from a great ironing machine. No one seemed tired. The movement of the girls about the big machine was a kind of dance. Something happened that I have so often seen in factories—a kind of dancing thing.

The head man is an old political henchman of Maurice's. He is intelligent, reads books etc. He had read some of my books.

Maurice told a story on himself.

He said—"I got the welfare idea. I spent $18 for plants to set out before the plant."

He drove up to the plant at the noon hour. There were some of his girls sitting in Fords with men. There was petting going on. He thought it undignified.

He had an older woman in his office who had been there for years. He went to her and complained.

She grew a little white, he said. Something flared up in her.

"Do you know what you pay these girls?"

"No."

"$13 a week. It isn't up to you to say how or where they get anything they can get."

I look at Maurice and think. The road he is on is absolutely the road I once tried to follow.[4]

He says, "It's all an adventure, a game."

It is, darling. When you are young, coming up, it's fun, a fight. There are men in a stronger place than yourself. You have to throw out someone above you, root him out by quicker thinking, etc.

You get up a little. Here's where the rub comes. What have you been fighting for?

Just for the privilege of having people work for you at $13 a week so that you may make $25.

You fought to be a robber chief.

Why there you are. What are you to say? You can be honest-minded. "Sure I'm robbing them. I intend to." There's your honest man—Maurice.

Or you can be a canting ass, poison your own mind—a Fitzgerald.[5]

There is something curious about Maurice's house. I can like him, even love him, man to man. I couldn't love you while I was there. All the time I was with him I couldn't love you.

I am on the train now, in the day coach, going to Lynchburg. I love you. Something tender begins to be born again.

Innumerable women trying to love Maurice. He fucks them, holds them. "My darling, my love," he says.

Is everything all one thing, dear?

Once I was in Maurice's position. I could have been a rich man. I got up out of a chair and walked seven heavy dragging steps to a door.[6] Did I make it possible to love you then? I think so.

You learn so slowly, painfully.

Woman after woman has tried to love Maurice. I have seen two or three try. There is something he won't give up.

He'll give money, time, everything but one thing. He knows it.

Give what you have and follow me.

He won't do it.

"I've always associated with rich men," he says. "I know why I do it. It's policy. They know I'm not really radical."

We talked of women in the night. There were two beds close together. I could feel many women lying still in them, having been fucked.

Can I get him? Can I break it down?

"I'm going to save myself," he says.

There was nothing about the $500. He could throw it to me with a laugh. We were two men. We talked of all his rich men friends. They all, as he does, hold onto something.

He sees something else. He says—"You have it, Darrow[7] has it."

He says—"They are fools who think it's money."

"I'm not going to love, to surrender," is what he is really saying. He knows it. No woman now will ever make him do it.

Because he won't, I, your lover, cannot love you, my woman, while I am in his house. I am outside now, going to Danville. Now I can.

It is all strangely pathetic and sad. Am I to be proud? Is this a sign I am noble or that I can keep loving you?

No, dear. We have to leave that to the gods, to tomorrows and tomorrows and tomorrows.

A curious experience. I feel O.K. about the $500. It doesn't count. I can love Maurice in our man to man way. I'm as good a man as he is, I guess. Maybe not.

He says—promise me you'll shoot the works.

"I won't," he says.

"O.K., Maurice."

That's about where it is. I wish I could sit near you for an hour, just touch your arm, or your shoe. I love you again.

1. SA was on his way from Washington to Lynchburg, where he spent the night before going on to Danville.

2. A businessman of New Milford, Connecticut. EC knew him and his wife through YWCA connections.

3. His dry cleaning plant in Washington.

4. SA refers to his own career as president of a mail-order business in Elyria, Ohio, which he abandoned in 1913 to pursue a writing career.

5. H. R. Fitzgerald, president of the Riverside and Dan River Cotton Mills Company in Danville, whose workers were striking.

6. See SA's account of leaving his business in *A Story Teller's Story,* pp. 309–13.

7. Clarence Darrow, the famous attorney, whom SA had known in Chicago.

[Christiansburg, Virginia,[1]
14 January 1931]

Wednesday
Dearest W.W.[2]

I am here at 1:30—having just got in from Danville. I left in a snow storm that has followed me through to here but should be home by five.

Everything at D worked out. I got over there at 2 and went to the commissary. Neither Miss Loving or Lindsay[3] were there but I was told Miss Lindsay was at court. I went there. Miss Lindsay wasn't there.

Hugh Williams[4] was conducting a strike case and I liked him. Presently he came into the hall and I went up to him. He knew me at once.

We walked up and down talking. I asked him about the cases. He said—"They have got the notion over to the juries here that no striker is to be believed."

I said—"You'll hurt yourself in the town."

He laughed. "I don't give a damn," he said. I think he means it.

Court recessed and Williams, the judge, the prosecuting attorney etc. all went with me into the judge chamber. Others came in. We had an hour's free talk—on union labor, communism, socialism etc. The judge thinks it will probably be communism in the end. They wanted me to stay for a party tonight.

Williams went with me to Miss Lindsay at the [Hotel] Burton and we sat in for a half hour on a meeting of the leaders.

I went back to the commissary and talked for a half hour with Miss Loving.

Back to the hotel—5:30—to shave & change my shirt. I called up a Mr. Davidson of the [Danville] *Register*[5] who had been nice to me when I was there before. Tom Tippett was with him.

Tom had stopped at D on his way up from Chapel Hill. He came to my hotel. A young boy from the high school newspaper came in and wanted an interview. Tom said—"Tell him to tell them to read *Marching Men*" so I did.

Williams came back with his car and took Tom and me to the country where we had a drink. We came back and dined. It was 7:30. We went to the hall.

It was packed to the door, men and women standing in aisles, against the walls etc. A man from the textile union spoke and then came my turn.

I spoke as slowly and clearly as I could. They seemed to drink in every word. Tom and Hugh Williams were on the platform with me. Everything was so packed that I just had arm room.

We came away, Tom and Williams saying fine things. I was exhausted and blue, darling. It seemed so hopeless.

Williams left us and Tom and I went to the Danville to see Davidson of the *Register*.[6] Drinks for which I was very grateful.

He obviously wanted to see me alone so Tom went back to the Burton. More drinks. It came out. The man had that day been fired from his editorial job for trying to be a little fair to the strikers. "I only wanted to be a good newspaper man," he said. He was fired abruptly, has a wife and two kids and not much money.

Tom, Miss Lindsay and I went then to a restaurant, talk.

We went to Tom's room. More talk. I was dead tired but got up at 5:45 to go with Tom to the mill gate before dawn to see the workers go in. Our guess is the Fitzgerald is getting all the workers he wants.

The strike is probably beaten.[7] Everyone thinks it will grow ugly now.

So that is that, dear. I can't tell yet what it has done to me. There is a kind of dead inner soul weariness now. I keep asking myself—"Must this be done over and over?" I will dream of those thousands, such good stuff probably, turned adrift now.

Or a month or six weeks from now. God help them.

Dear, I would be better right now if I only had a look at you, could feel your fingers touch me.

I got your sweet little note. God bless you.

Y.M.[8]

1. Driving back to Marion from Danville, SA had stopped briefly at the Virginia Inn in Christiansburg.

2. "W.W." or "Wop Wife" was an affectionate name that SA gave to EC because of what he considered to be her Italian features.

3. Ida Loving, a worker in Danville, and Matilda Lindsay, vice-president of the National Women's Trade Union League.

4. The union lawyer.

5. Arthur D. Davidson, who was later on the staff of the *Richmond Times-Dispatch* and for many years editor of the *Northern Virginia Daily* in Strasburg, Virginia.

6. Davidson lived at the Danville Hotel.

7. The strike was over by the end of the month.

8. Probably "Your Man."

[Marion, 2 February 1931]

Monday morning . . . I am sending the outline of what I thought I would say at Richmond.[1] I don't know whether or not it is worth sending to Edelman.[2] Do send me his full name and address.

The books came. A thousand thanks, dear. They are just right.

I don't know when anything has made me so happy as the note to you from Lucy Mason.[3] I have all the time, dear, been frightened about something . . . it was that I might be the means of destroying or at least badly hurting all of your old friendships. You have to remember that the only reaction I have got before has been from Lois [MacDonald], certainly not very nice, and Brownie [Jones], who made that unlovely crack. Anyway this note from Lucy Mason makes me feel it may not be all lost. If I take you too much away from others, perhaps I will not have anything to give you that can half compensate. That is about what I have thought. You have been so nice about always wanting my own relationships to remain sound. Why, dear, you can see why I want to hug this Lucy Mason.

An odd experience last night. Rhyne[4] comes into the shop a good deal. We have all been riding him a bit. He is quite a cocksure young man. Besides he is young. I don't think a bit of hard riding hurts him. He announced last Sunday night to his congregation that on this Sunday evening he was going to preach and show why God put evil in the world. Your father told me. "I'd like to hear that," I said. So your father told him. At first, your father said, he backed up. However, yesterday he went up to the house and told your father to bring me. Your father called me up and I went.

It was amusing in a way I don't think your father thought of—my going off to church with him. The congregation rather stared. I'll bet they thought—well, you know.

So Rhyne preached. Of course he never touched it. I didn't think he would. How could he? This morning he was in the shop. Funk came in. "Well, how was it?" he asked. We had just stepped out of the shop. I pointed up to the post office. "Suppose there was a bear up there."

"Yes," said Funk. I pointed down the alleyway. "Rhyne went down there after him," I said. Even Rhyne had to laugh.

Bob is well again apparently. Yesterday he took that little Miss Chryst[5] out in the country in my car. I went to walk with Funk. We walked a long time out along the railroad and climbed some hills. Out back of the hospital in the hills we passed an army of the crazy people from the asylum marching along, getting an outing I presume. It was lovely up on the hills. I said to Funk, "Look, they are like the little wrinkles in a woman's belly." "I don't like fat women," he said. He was in a gentle mood and very nice. Bob is in better spirits.

The pain in my head has gone away but last night I lay by an open window and kicked the covers off. It turned very cold in the night and I awoke with a stiff back. It will pass off during the day. I went up and got my stitches taken out. Now I'll get a haircut and will be quite lovely I'm sure. Suddenly this morning I feel as though I had got over a hill again. I mean that the long time away from you is in some way broken. Instead of looking back to when I saw you last, on the train that night, I'll look ahead now. As the financial wizards say, "The bottom of the depression has been reached." Gee, I love you. I'll take the sleeper to Richmond and be there Monday and Tuesday.[6]

Mimi seems to be swimming along O.K. So does John.

Westmoreland.[7]

1. On 3 February SA gave a talk on the topic "Women in Southern Industry" at a luncheon session of a "One-Day Institute" in Richmond sponsored by the industrial committee of the YWCA, the National Women's Trade Union League, and the Richmond chapters of the National Council of Jewish Women and the American Association of University Women.

2. John Edelman, research director of the American Federation of Full Fashioned Hosiery Workers in Philadelphia and editor of *Labor News,* which published SA's Danville speech.

3. The director of the Richmond YWCA and a friend of EC's. She had expressed her approval of SA.

4. Hugh J. Rhyne, pastor of the Ebenezer Lutheran Church in Marion, later the president of Marion College.

5. Mary Chryst, who married Bob on 18 December 1931.

6. Apparently a slip for "Tuesday and Wednesday."

7. I.e., he would be staying at the Westmoreland Club in Richmond.

[On train, 21 February 1931]

Saturday

Darling

I am on the Clinchfield train riding up from Spartanburg—having stored my car there. I got up at Athens at 5. Of course I'm pretty dead as there were two big nights and every minute of the day occupied yesterday.[1]

I think they are doing a good thing down there and I am going to suggest the same thing to our University of Virginia, as a thing to be put over perhaps by the [*Virginia*] *Quarterly Review.*

All states apparently have these associations of publishers but this is a sort of institute inside the association like the Ins. of Public Affairs in Virginia. It attracts the livelier country editors. The big dailies in the state each try to bring in a national figure, the daily paying his expenses etc. Mark Ethridge[2] really runs it. I like him.

The idea is, he says, to subject the country editors to these outside influences. The head of the Northwest school was there.[3] He liked my speech and said he wished I would give the same one up there. Ethridge was good enough to say I had made a success of it for him this year. We were in a little hall where all the speeches had been held. A woman from Savannah[4] was talking. The hall gradually filled up. There was a queer noise outside. Ethridge came and said, "Three times the number of people we can get in here are waiting to hear you." We had to adjourn to a big hall—Ethridge and I leading the big procession bare-headed across the campus. Lots of fun—people laughing and shouting. They filled the big hall and were wonderfully silent. The man ahead of me had urged that Georgia millionaires give to the University so I began by calling attention to the fact that there were 400,000 farmers in Georgia with an annual income of less than $85 a year. "Take the millionaires' money," I said, "but understand where it comes from. Understand that this big institution—this University—rests on the shoulders of the cotton croppers and the cotton mill hands of Georgia.

"When a millionaire gives you his millions, give a cheer for the people out of whose pockets it actually came."

It's nice, dear, how a little plain speaking loosens everyone up. We had a big men's lunch last night—some rich men there. You know Bowers[5] is a big figure in the Democratic party. I kept challenging him on Russia. "If it wins what will happen to our whole system?"

He was a bit drunk, so was I, a little blackish man.

At last, after I had challenged him several times, he shouted, "It will go to hell."

"Do you think it has a chance to win?"

"By God, more than a chance."

That broke bedlam loose. It was royal fun.

Everyone began to call me the communist.

"All right I'll accept that title," I said. Julian Harris, who hadn't been there during the day, came in. He lined up with me as did Ethridge—3 musketeers, for the evening anyway.

Everyone got excited. There was the usual stuff about dirty lousy Russian.

I threw Turgenev at them, Chekhov, Tolstoy. Mark & Harris swung in with Russian thinkers, scientists etc. Julian, who could do it, being native, kept taunting them, giving them a peep at their own underworld of poverty etc.

It lasted until midnight, a whirl of talk, well handled too, no one got sore. The editor of the Atlanta *Journal,*[6] one of the most reactionary of them all, stood up before them all and gave me a toast when we broke up. "I don't care whether he's a Bolshevik or what he is," he cried—"by God, when he comes to Atlanta I want him as my guest."

One of the owners of the *Constitution* was there. "I want half of that," he cried. So we all broke up happy and in fine friendliness. I felt it was something. At noon, at a big luncheon just after my talk, the university dean[7] in a speech said, "I want to see the day when the University of Georgia doesn't have to take any rich man's money," he said.

And the pres. of the Georgia railroad[8] & two bankers sitting there. Mark was good enough to say I hopped him up to it. I don't know. I love you. I think this newspaper thing is going to turn out. Gee I hope there [will] be you or a letter from you at home.

1. SA was returning from a meeting of the Georgia Press Institute at the University of Georgia in Athens.

2. Mark Ethridge, managing editor of the *Macon Telegraph* and chairman of the Georgia Press Institute Committee.

3. H. F. Harrington, director of the Medill School of Journalism, Northwestern University.

4. Jane Judge, literary editor of the *Savannah Morning News.*

5. Claude G. Bowers, who had delivered the keynote speech at the national Democratic party convention in 1928.

6. Major John S. Cohen.

7. S. V. Sanford, dean of the Grady School of Journalism.

8. Probably Charles A. Wickersham, general manager.

[Marion, 22 February 1931]

Darling—

First, I expect to leave here on Wednesday and go back to Spartanburg where I left the car. I'll go to the Cleveland Hotel there and will wait to hear from you. Will get there at 5 Wed. eve.

I can meet you anywhere you think best and drive you anywhere. I can drive you to Rock Hill if you think best too[1]—that is if we could have any time on the afternoon or evening of the 26th.

I am very happy about the 1st & 2nd. I will drive you somewhere where you will make better connections for Tulsa than you did at Augusta.[2]

Darling—now that I am home and have had a real night's sleep and feel rested a little, I realize that such affairs as that at Athens and the coming one at Chicago are going to put me in a different position than I have been in.

I am trying to face it. You know that a part of my impulse in coming here—to S.W. Virginia—was an escape from life. I realized, dear, that I had made one of the bitter mistakes of my life with Elizabeth. It came about through hunger for something. I think you, dearest woman, more than anyone realize what that hunger is.

As I tried to say to you, there on the bank of that yellow river—there has always been that boy in me. He is sensitive, determined, terrible sometimes. I am both old and terribly young, dear brown-eyed woman. I can't settle anything about you, what is best for you.

Both the boy and the man in me want you. I know that.

I go to such a place as at Athens. No newspaper report is going to tell what happened there. The boy rushed out to those people and was received by them. Something nice happened.

Then the boy wanted to run away to your arms, saying, "Eleanor, don't let them or me coarsen it." I did run to the hotel and did kneel down there for a few minutes, surrounded by whiskey glasses, and pray to you.

Saying, "Hold me a moment, dear. Believe. Believe."

I succeeded pretty well there in not coarsening anything.

1. EC was to attend a conference at Winthrop College, Rock Hill, South Carolina, on 27–28 February. SA did drive her there.

2. On 1 March they went on to Atlanta, where she took a train to meetings in Tulsa, Oklahoma, and Houston, Texas. She had left from Augusta the previous year (see first letter of 2 March 1930).

[Macon, Georgia, 2 March 1931]

Dearest

I wanted to ask you something yesterday. The central point I want to emphasize—in the first of the Chicago talks[1]—is the willingness, even the desire to be little instead of big. This does not, it seems to me, preclude the desire to do good work. I think it should be emphasized in people to counteract all the strong pull the other way.

There is something else. Do I, in this thing, have a tendency to laud myself? There is something difficult to do—in just the right tone. I am telling personal experiences . . . as I am trying to do here. There is always, unconsciously, the desire to represent the figure of yourself, in all these scenes, as rather charming.

It can be just a very subtile way of selling yourself. Do I do that? I know the tendency is in me. It is in all of us some. I did it I'm sure in "They Come Bearing Gifts." We were both somewhat ashamed of that.

What I want to do, without being too obvious, is to sell human life.

How beautifully Turgenev could thrust himself in and yet not be obtrusively in. He was like a little shadow in there, like a wind blowing across the scene he describes.

I would like you, dear, to be my sharpest critic in such things. I will, I'm quite sure, always understand now your love of me. We both will want the best that can be given out of me.

Try to remember the impression left from reading you the speech. Was I subtly trying to sell myself? Did it have any of that feeling?

I am trying to get at a broad basis for anything I may do—in articles, speeches, stories. I can't be an economist, a politician, a thinker. I would like—always in a subtile way—to insist and insist on the human thing.

It seems to me that every good thing I do has that predominant in it.

Do you think so?

1. SA was to lecture on journalism at Northwestern University and the University of Chicago on 20–24 April.

[Macon, 3 March 1931]

Tuesday

Darling—

Your letter came—the one you wrote right after breakfast on the train—from Atlanta.

Dear, I do not think you have ever, by any word or anything, led me to think you really accept the idea of marriage with me. I have never got it that way. You have been lovely with me. I think you love me. I feel it. It makes me live to feel it.

On the other hand I love you . . . if there is any love in me. I think I am clear about all this you speak of. Do not have it on your mind.

I think, dear, that with me it is rather like this . . . I have found my woman. There you are. I love you. You are something for me to take hold of. I came along to you, after all these adventures, trials at life you know of. I can't give you my youth . . . all the years of struggle . . . hurt done others, hurts done me . . . will always I fancy have to be to you a little like a book read.

I could really say to you, Eleanor darling, as I can say of life, that you owe me nothing. I want you to feel that way. If you should find another man you feel could give you more of what you want, I want you to feel free to go to him.

On the other hand, darling, if, when the times comes, you feel that I am the man you want with you and by you—while I live—then you marry me.

I don't think there need be any bargain or even understanding.

You are finally and definitely my woman and will be until I die anyway. That is my point of view. I don't want to force it on you. I mean that.

I worked—and wrote you—at Atlanta and then drove here. Picked up a rather charming Irishman—a furniture salesman, whose car had broken down. He talked of communism and he told me that, as a young man, he was a socialist. The priests talked him out of it. Now he says he is going back to it.

The peach orchards are just getting ready to bloom. The plum orchards are in full bloom.

Dined with [William T.] Anderson—who owns the *Telegraph*. We went on to Ethridge's house. He was having a party—very nice people—with several lovely women. I came home at half past 12. I have a big light room, newly painted.

I've got a habit, dear. I do it every night. Of course I do want to live with you. You know that. I come into the room and close the door. I try to conjure you.

"Eleanor."

"Eleanor," I whisper, I hold little conversations with you, try to tell you of my thoughts. When I get into bed and the lights are out I open my arms. I try to imagine you creeping close. It's child's play, I know. I am a child about that. I want you every minute, every day.

But, darling, that doesn't commit you. You will never have to come because I want you. That is my story.

If you ever come to want me near like that, every night, every time you are alone in a room, then I suppose you'll want to marry me no matter what anyone thinks.

[Macon, 3 March 1931]

Late Tuesday night
Dear W.W.

In spite of what Randolph, Mazie, Katharine and others may think and say (there is something delicious to me in the idea of any of them daring to set up to judge for you), in spite of all you say about your own respectable background, job etc.—I know this—that in the secret, intimate moments between us—all this counts as nothing.

Our own struggle is to keep something fine and clean that belongs to us and no others.

[five lines torn off bottom of page]

The intimate loveliness of us—in ultimate intimate moments . . .

That goes out beyond anyone but us. That's where our battle will be fought out, where we'll win or lose.

Our marriage is a thing beyond anyone but us. The formal marriage is merely a matter of whether in that secret, sweet struggle for all the real sweetness of life you want to be in the struggle with me or another.

Whether you think with me the chances are better than with any other, you are likely to have the chance to make that struggle for the real. I think that's it. Don't you?

This anyway is true of me . . . that with you, in me . . . it is all involved with all life, all feeling for life. I only know sometimes a little how much more rich and varied it all is in me compared with other men when I have been with other men in fields and outdoors, as I have been today. Then sometimes I am not ashamed that it is me and only me I have to offer to you.

Sweet flesh. Goodness in you. My woman. Don't be afraid.

Morning.

I worked until 3. Aaron Bernd, a keen, intelligent young Jew here, and Ben Johnson came in.[1] We talked for an hour. Ben and I went to ride in the Chevy. It was a gorgeous road—a grey day—all the colors very vivid . . . peach trees coming into bloom . . . cypress swamps, red fields, men plowing. One of our days.

What struck and rather hurt me was Ben's insensibility. He seemed to have no touch with his own country.

I went to dine with Anderson of the *Telegraph*—after taking Ben home and meeting Mrs. Ben again. After dinner I went with Ben, Aaron and a young man I had seen here before . . . the most alive man I've seen here. There was pretty good talk. Ben and Aaron in the field of intellect, books etc. are keen and alive.

Outdoors they are just nothing.

A beautiful intimate letter from Paul [Rosenfeld] at last . . . that made me happy because I love the man. As I really knew all the time, he has all the time had the same feeling I have had. He is like you. I complain sometimes that you do not sit down as I do and pour yourself out in words, forgetting it is not natural for you to do so. When I am with you, your eyes tell me things. There is a language of your body. I feel the flesh change under my fingers, love and feeling flood through it.

I have never believed you lost anyone really loved . . . like Charles [Bockler], Paul, Ferdinand [Schevill] etc. I understand your confusion—that you do not always quite know whether you want that final marriage with me. There are, dearest, Many Marriages. Only one with the woman.

I won't quite forgive you if you haven't sent me a new schedule.[2] Yes I will.

1. Bernd and Johnson were on the staff of the *Macon Telegraph*.
2. I.e., a schedule of her engagements.

[Macon, 9 March 1931]

Darling—

Events—I have been having what I think must be flu—eye balls aching—back aching etc. It is not severe. I fancy it is what you had at Rock Hill.

I went into the first of the Vaughn Moody lectures[1] but it exploded in my hands. It may have been due to flu. I got your letter about the speeches but decided to hold them till I saw you in New Orleans. I thought you could take them all on with you and read them after Montgomery—if it is not too much of an imposition. The only way I can write them, or deliver them, is that they shall, in some way, be works of art too. If I were just to become a preacher, dearest, I would be nothing.

I suppose you have to aim at the exceptional one. You can't say, "Life is so and so." You can only say, "Here is a slant on things. Take it for what it's worth."

I have no notion, dear, that my own humility is anything like that of Van Gogh, although, as between the two, I am on his side rather than on Gauguin's side. Cézanne perhaps struck nearer the true course. And as for Gauguin—how are we to know how much he suffered beneath his strut?

I was a little wild yesterday—hungry for you—more than I have ever been. I was ill but couldn't sit in my room so I filled up with whiskey and spent the whole day with people. A woman gave a big reception for me in Sidney Lanier's old home. I behaved.[2] It was queer. It was a day when, fortunately, people didn't get in. I felt all day like a piece of stone on a seashore on which waves were beating. All the time there was a cry in me for you.

There is a cry of this kind in me sometimes that, in the end, will smash me maybe unless there is sometimes the same cry, the same bitter need in you.

I sent a good many letters to the Rice Hotel—Houston.

Today you are with your friend.

In the end I couldn't have Maurice [Long] come. I am in no mood for him. There would be some rich friend. There would be too much talk of women. I wired him I had the flu and not to come. I shall leave here tomorrow morning.

In the afternoon, before going to the rich woman's house, where all those people were gathered, I went with Aaron the Jew to a little Primitive Baptist negro church. There was a foot washing.

There was swaying and singing and beautiful prayers. It got me pretty hard. I hope you do not mind that the swaying black women were you too. Everything was you. I kept drinking and taking soda. A New York newspaper man—the *Herald-Tribune*—was here and he, Mark and I drank away the evening. I slept. I am better today. I love you.

1. SA was to deliver the William Vaughn Moody lectures at the University of Chicago on 21–24 April.

2. An allusion to an incident at a similar occasion in Greenville, South Carolina, the previous month when he gained notoriety for shoving an annoying woman in the face.

[Knoxville, Tennessee,[1]
23 March 1931]

Monday morning
Darling W. W.

It is 9:40 and I have had my breakfast, the room is made and I am going to work. I'll work this morning and drive home this evening. It was a lovely night, full of you. You know how I felt when you left. So few people, dear, have ever been patient with me. I think of all the things I must have put you through—the record back of me—my failures . . . the state of mind I was in when you first knew me . . . that queer hour in the Jaffe house . . .[2]

The whole story of my life in that—pressing forward too eager toward the absolute—failure—fear—myself so often not understanding.

I've tried to tell people. There is a boy—a kind of eternal youth in me. In such a world as we live in it is perhaps insanity to let him live on. It was his death I guess I wanted when you first knew me. Elizabeth did an ugly thing to him. He goes toward you. He tells me over and over—"Trust her. Go toward her." It's all so silly to reasonable people. How can they understand? Why expect it? It may be a form of insanity—this wanting the clean—the real—in the face of all this unreality.

An upside-down world. Money isn't real, fame, success and all that. Reality only peeps out now and then. This world in which we have lived for three days, six days really—the last three have been the most real—it's all as real as the other.

I drove up a dark street. Three policemen were standing. I called to them and two of them came to the car.

I began asking for the hotel. Then I thought, for once, I'd tell someone.

So I told them I'd taken my sweetheart to the train and was confused. I told them I didn't care much whether I found the hotel or not. They laughed. They didn't think I was drunk. One got in and drove around to the hotel with me. We sat and talked. He said he was married and had three kids and told me about a daughter in high school, how smart she was.

So I got here a little crazy but alive.

In bed [the] feel of your head again, as it was in the light last night, the hair, your breasts, your strong back, to lift me up and thrust—

Toward marriage. The time of many marriages.

Your legs—the feel of them against me when we stood under a tree by the river—the sailor—ride her cowboy—the night in the rain—you puzzled—me puzzled—

The black sticks of lumber in that little street—houses there . . . people living in houses . . . a girl going down the dark street.

Life loved in others because it can be so sweet sometimes—in anyone.

You know how I feel—what I feel—love—you feel it too.

1. SA had met EC in New Orleans and had driven her to Knoxville, where she took a train to New York.

2. See letter of 3 September 1930 and note 2.

Bristol, Virginia, [23 March 1931]

Darling—

I think I will have dinner here and drive home in the evening as I have not eaten since breakfast. I had a good morning of work after I wrote you and left K[noxville] about 12:30. I drove along moderately and got here at 4:30 but lose an hour here so it is 5:30 now.

I rather regret getting back. The world outside our little world will flood in—letters etc. I've lived in our world all day, thinking in it, feeling in it.

It's as real as this hotel lobby,[1] that radio grinding away etc.

There were alternate stretches of sunshine and shadows all along the road, the shadows fleeing ahead, my catching them and coming out into sunshine as we did the other day.

I thought a lot of what had happened to me and you. Now I sense that it has really happened to you. I never did before. It makes it all oddly different. I don't take it at all, dear, as some compliment to something in me. I don't think merit or lack of it has much to do with it. It makes me feel closer to you—in an odd way more friendly and understanding of you.

Knowing you will have the sharp, lonely times, will hunger at night for me there, for my touch, as I do for you. It takes me more fully out of myself and into you.

I shall work more consistently. It is hard to tell you what all you have given me to work and rest and live in.

I thought about the others too, a lot, who love you. If it is what I feel now, the real man and woman coming together, it puts them all a bit outside. That is an odd thing I didn't realize before.

I don't know just what I'll say to your mother when I see her, what I feel, I think . . . that is to say that we are not engaged but that we will marry. We will I think if I live. Odd that I do not ever think of you as anything but living. I can't.

I killed a little dog belonging to some country children, coming here. I couldn't help it. He dashed out from among the children and right under the wheels. It made me sick. He was dead at once. Poor dog. Poor kids.

I came to this hotel because we have dined here. Dear, it will be wonderful if, someday, there is a house, or just some room, where everything has been touched by you.

1. The Hotel Bristol.

[Marion, 25 March 1931]

Wed. morning—a lovely morning with a sharp wind blowing. I talked to your father. He seemed about as usual. I guess your feeling that there is any special new feeling is all wrong. There is a kind of general resentment against being disturbed I guess. That's all. Such things are such a queer mixture. It will be all right when we come to it but he will always be a bit resentful of it all. Life hasn't exactly worked out for him either. I'm sorry. I never have had any impulse to change anything on that account.

My whole attitude is different. You are my woman. There is a way the flesh tells when the mind can't. I think of the lives of all people—how difficult they are. Ours are not really different, only a different set of circumstances.

I am not even any more ashamed of the past—even against this man's past. There has been, I'm pretty sure, a kind of generosity toward life, lack of caution if you please. It has produced what people resent and are afraid of along with some beauty.

I even think, dear, there is value in that kind of lives. They began—I'm sure—with a feeling the flesh was evil. They went through troubles together, mistakes etc.—the matter of your poor sister[1] and all.

Two strong people. What life might have been. Your father must have been fine in his young physical strength. Your mother lovely too. They must have hurt each other a lot.

I get traces of it all in you. Randolph & Mazie—Randolph may well turn out to be the cautious one. The adventure spirit may lie on the feminine side of your house.

You have been simply marvelous with me, daring everything. Coming home in the car from K[noxville], the whole thing went through my mind, the feeling I had when I first found you, the way you had handled it and all.

I came to a kind of something in my own manhood. It is a kind of gift you have given back to me. Along with it goes a kind of inability to be ashamed anymore. I take the past, with its mistakes, as a part of the pattern. I think that, if I had ever touched the flesh of another woman with the feeling in my fingers, in all my body, I have when I touch you, you would know it. I think, if you had not become my woman, I'd know it in your touch. Our purity is just as real as any purity.

I even feel an altogether clean man, coming to you. I'm not going to let anyone make me unclean by thoughts without a fight.

So you see, dear, you have aroused the man in me. It is the most precious gift a woman can give her man.

Bob has got Grace[2] making beer. It is very very good. Later I shall try to induce your father to try it. He would love it. There is enough German in him for that.

The N[ew] O[rleans] coffee is fine. I'll make some for you and your father.

I'll take the little cream pitcher to your mother when she gets home.

The town is in a turmoil this morning. The woman who left her baby came back and wanted it.[3] She turned out to be a working woman who said she deserted her baby because she was broke and out of a job. She says her husband deserted her. She had taken up with a workman who came back with her. They are not married. The town clapped them both into jail.

He may be tried under the Mann Act—transporting her. She says quite frankly that she and the workman slept together at Knoxville. They were going to Pulaski. The man got a job there, so did she, as a servant. Then she got him to come back here, bring her back to get her baby.

Now they are both in jail. Mrs. Dent Staley[4] has the baby. Everyone is busy being judge.

My mail is nice.

1. A younger sister, Laura Eugenia ("Jean"), suffered from schizophrenia and was institutionalized in Williamsburg, Virginia. She died there in 1970 and was buried in Richmond.

2. The maid.

3. A woman had abandoned her baby at a local tourist home.

4. Nannie Frazier Staley. Her husband, Denton, owned a hardware store in Marion.

[Marion, 27 March 1931]

Friday morning—rain—a steady drizzle. It is an ironic situation. You, who are so busy that I am sure you do not get time to read all I write you, can only find time to send me cablegrams while I, after I have worked until I can work no more, must wander about the street hungry for details of your own doings, your words, thoughts etc., which I cannot have.

You seem worried about your family, dear. The word I get is that your mother will be at home Sunday or Monday. I can't go there when just your father is there. After all, dear, you can't sit with a man who only, in your presence and in the midst of a conversation, turns on the radio and listens not to you but to Andy and whoever it is in the taxi business with Andy.[1] You just can't.

I think probably what has happened is that they do suspect we have met more often than we have told them, as we have. I think they hope you will give me up. Your mother is driven back and forth by two worlds. She doesn't quite comprehend your life—doesn't really know what you believe, feel etc. They probably think you are just temporarily fascinated by me. They half hope it is temporary.

They are like all people not wanting to be disturbed. Your father has become a chronic no-sayer to life. You see that always. He always says no.

Your mother feels guilty. Her natural inclination is to like and trust me but there are a good many forces against her. She thinks perhaps, when I am not with her, that the others may be right, that I am really some sort of a wild man.

You see I may all along have been too frank with them. People do not understand frankness. After I knew I loved and wanted you, I felt a cheat, coming into their house merely as your friend.

So I told them and stirred all this up.

It's my way. I can't help it.

On the other hand you have never put your foot down firmly—saying—"This is my man. If you reject him you reject me. He is part of me—of my flesh and spirit."

You haven't been ready to do that.

I think naturally that, if you were ready and did do it, all would change. I can't urge you to do it until you are ready.

There is this uncertainty. Your father doesn't actually dislike me. I disturb him. He doesn't like being disturbed, is too tired of spirit. Love of you is all mixed up with self-love—hurt pride etc.

I think parents do have a way of looking on their children always as children. That is confusing too. To me you are a mature woman. I can't conceive of either your father or mother as more mature. There is something left out of me perhaps. I do not look upon my own children so. If tomorrow Mimi were to write me she had fallen in love with Frank Lloyd Wright I don't believe I would presume to advise her. I would hope it was really love.

I think your father and mother would respect that. The real statement of it, to be effective, would have to come from you. I thought, when I was with you, that I would say something of the sort to your mother when I saw her but I'd better not. I oughtn't to speak for you.

Why, I am talking seriously to you, my woman. I hope to God you are my woman. Life will be quite ugly and meaningless to me if you are not.

Something has happened. It happened seeing you this time. Life has been pretty cruel to me too, dear. The poet also has his kind of manhood.

I have been unable to accept half love. I think I can be as true to real love as I have been to the thing I have always been after in my work. I don't believe at all that I am a fickle man.

On the other hand, when I first found you my manhood was pretty much gone. I had lost all faith in self—in the simple right of a man to live and work and love. So many people had analyzed me, telling me that I couldn't love, that it had affected me even physically.

I have got it back. You gave it back to me.

You can see, dear, that I cannot be toward your father and mother like Henry or Channing.[2] I am not a young boy, coming to ask for one of their daughters. The woman I want is a woman of thirty-four and I am—well, at least, dear, not a young man.

As regards your father and myself—there is something wanted as from man to man. It can't be denied. I am ready. It's rather up to him now. You see my difficulty. I heard him discuss poets once.

You see, dearest woman, I think back of all this is something. You have more or less remained one thing in their minds, particularly in your father's mind, while, in reality, you have been developing into something else. Your real friends have been people like that taxi driver,[3] Tom and others while you have remained, in a vague way anyway—in their minds—a southern lady. I don't blame you for this confusion. You didn't want to hurt or jar them. There was no occasion.

But you see, my dear, it is a bit absurd that I should be putting myself in the position of a young suitor. Randolph passing judgment in my world, Mazie doing it, Lois [MacDonald] doing it.

My world is my own world. It is, dear, an old and an honorable one. It has nothing to do with respectability, the old South, ladies and gentlemen, etc. I belong with Turgenev, Balzac, Cézanne, Rembrandt.

There's a long list. As an artist I always have been in the tradition. Men like me have gone on for hundreds of years, adding some of us a lot, some of us a very little. If we add anything sound, we belong. I have added sound things. There is work of mine as solid as a rock.

And the inner secret of my manhood lies here, dear. Do you remember, in *Poor White,* when Hugh crawled out an upstairs window and went away from the woman he loved?

He wanted his own kind of manhood recognized and it hadn't been.

I'm not asking you to do all this suddenly, dearest. It's a decision to be made. I guess you have to decide that you would take me, with all the faults and the past on me, rather than any other living man, that you would take me if it meant even the end of your relations with your own family.

It's a lot to ask. I don't ask it. The point is that, in giving me my manhood back, you have changed things as between your people and me. I think I am ready to give them a lot if they want me. I can't beg of them.

Why what a preachment. Your asking again about the attitude of your family etc. brought it on you, dear. I don't know, you see. I haven't thought much about it. My thoughts have been of you.

Notes

Don't forget to have me tell you the outcome of the baby story.

I'll tell you what I think of the little YWCA dinner booklet when I see you. It's all mixed up in my mind with thoughts of communism, Robert E. Lee, the middleclass notion of the good, the true and the beautiful. O Lord. Patience is a rock in a weary land, isn't it lover?

1. "Amos 'n' Andy," the popular radio series.
2. Henry Van Meier and Channing Wilson, EC's sisters' husbands.
3. Identified in other letters only as "Abe," he seems to have worked with EC in New York labor organizations.

[Marion, 30 March 1931]

Monday

Sunday was a bitter cold day. I guess you had the same kind of weather there. There was a chill dampness in the air and the wind cut. I had hoped your mother would come as I wanted to see her. I presume she will come this morning. No letter from you. I wrote Tom.

I went with Funk to walk and we walked out the Rye Valley tracks. He wasn't nice at first but later got nice. We went to the brick yard, out toward the old Killinger place.[1] They had taken the fire from a kiln on Saturday and it was still warm. We huddled against it to keep out of the wind. A man came out of the brick yard.

Funk began to tell about the man. Some years ago he took as wife a young girl of sixteen. He went about town selling her to anyone who wanted her, negroes or whites. The man made his living selling the sixteen year old white girl that way. She was brought before the court. "Are there any men here your husband sold you to?" the judge asked. She began pointing out men, rather wildly, Funk thought. Perhaps she couldn't remember. Funk said he got nervous, as did all the men who had gone in there out of curiosity. He was afraid she might suddenly point her finger at him. "I was new here," he said. "You can't tell what people will think."

I went to bed early. Bob had gone out and I was alone. I tried to make you come near by talking to you. I was very lonely for you. I read a book about Anatole France by a secretary. I didn't like France. He had a queer smart aleck attitude toward life. However he wrote deliciously sometimes. I got up early, still hungry for you. The days seem so long when I am away from you. When I can work I am lost and all right but I can't work all day. My desk is heavy with unopened mail. I kept saying to myself . . . "Next Sunday she will be here." France says it is absurd to write letters to a woman you love but what am I to do? He says women care nothing for such letters. Maybe. You tell me honestly sometime.

It is one of my little days. I feel very small. Everything seems big except me. The sky is big and the houses and the streets. I went to the PO and still no letter from you. I think you are cruel and then I think . . . how can she be? She doesn't know yet what it means to you, I say.

People in the street frighten me. I hope no one will speak to me. I do not dislike people. I am afraid of them.

I used to get this way often when I was a child. I couldn't go to school. I ran away to the woods, even in winter, and walked about all day. Afterwards in Chicago, when I was a business man. Sometimes in the morning I went down to the office building where I worked. I couldn't go in. I went and sat at the back of some saloon.

If you should quit loving me I might get this way. I have seen men who spent their lives hiding from others. Why? I don't know. It is because they feel so small, as I do today.

I wouldn't get this way if you were around or I could see you. You would cure me. I would let myself be a child. "What is it, dear?" You would be big. "I'm afraid." "Don't be silly." "I can't help it. I don't want to be so. Hold me in your arms."

You do. If you have a child by me it will get this way sometimes. Treat me as though I were a child. It will teach you how to treat your child when it comes. A woman should learn thus from her lover how men are. She may have a man child.

It's all nonsense about men being brave. They are only bold sometimes. Bravery and boldness are not the same things. Sometimes you are bold only because you are afraid.

I feel very far away from you. You are warm as always, kind as always, but you have not got me in your arms. I am trying to make you see how I am today.

Your mother is here. I talked to her on the phone. I will see her this afternoon. She says she is well.

1. They were walking west of the town.

[Marion, Easter, 5 April 1931]

What your father & mother ought to do is as far beyond them as the stars—or as God.

It isn't their fault. It's the terrible gap between.

They ought to realize we are already married and say: "To hell with everything. You, Sherwood, if she, our daughter, wants you, come here and sleep with her in the room upstairs.

"Hold her tight."

I don't expect any such thing, Eleanor darling. I can't expect much of anything, except from you.

But suppose people took what Christ meant—let's say on Easter day, when he arose from the dead.

You can't approach God until you give up everything.

Until you are willing to be in the dregs.

Suppose they, or us, or anyone, could chuck everything.

Respectability.

Morality.

Honor.

Everything.

I don't ask anyone to do it. I think sometimes we, in our little secret life, where we don't give a goddam, may.

You love.

You sweet flesh. That's a new name I got for you. Ain't it nice.

Winston-Salem, North Carolina,
[11 April 1931]

Saturday
Darling
Sweet flesh.

Tired. It would be better perhaps if I did not try to write today. I do so want to though. I'm full of it.

I wrote a travel note—largely about the colored chamber maid.

I listened for your voice this morning and it did not come. Then I had bad luck. I went down to breakfast and you called while I was gone.

I am to see you tonight.[1] Bless God for that.

I think it is the bulk of work done since Knoxville that has tired me. There has been a flow, a constant little stream of thoughts, like a river, running through your man. Cannot you see, darling, why women turn from such men as myself?

We so exhaust ourselves sometimes in that strange, unreal, real world.

Thinking, as I write this, what I owe to you. I have tried to say a little of it.

In some queer way you have brought my manhood back to me, set me on my two legs again.

A man has to respect himself, and his own work. He has to believe dimly that it is of some little consequence.

In reality that other E [Elizabeth] did not believe in it. There was something about my work too direct—embracing life too closely.

She wanted another, dimmer world.

I always felt that what I was trying to get at never could mean anything to her.

This while I was trying to build up something deep and real between us. It never got built.

It left me with shattered hands. Everything fallen down.

I have so needed a mate.

I feel one in you. The test is that when I am tired, no man much outward—knowing that, if you were here, I would be dull—I love you constantly.

Your voice comes into the tired air of the room over the phone and makes streaks of gladness in here.

I'll love you while I live, dearest.

1. EC had a meeting in Winston-Salem on the next day.

[Chicago,[1] 21 April 1931]

Tuesday morning
Darling Woman—

Such a morning. I am just up and have breakfasted. It is cold and rainy outside but I am warm inside.

Your lovely letter came from Marion—the one of Sunday morning—the nice picture of you in bed, the trees just coming into leaf, the sun shining.

I suspect your father and mother will be glad to have you once without me. I don't blame them. I know how nice it is to be with you.

Also the letter written on Monday, just after our marvelous day—about Tom and the lady he renounced.

Alas, dear, I never do quite swallow that. I'm afraid they renounce when they want to renounce anyway.

But I must tell you of the speech, which went off gorgeously. I had dined at the University Club with Baker Brownell, an ex-*Chicago Tri-*

bune editorial writer who has become a professor, Koch the university librarian and a professor Frederick, from University of Iowa.[2]

They told me that, in spite of the rain, they had been compelled to change the meeting to a larger hall. It was filled, largely with students.

I was in a state of dread before speaking and the hall was ugly but it was a grand crowd, mostly kids. They seemed to fairly jump out at me. There was a lot of laughter, closeness, that peculiar nice thing that happens when you get close.

I believe I am not going to mind this sort of talking. It doesn't invade the inner life in which I write and in which I love you. There is no dragging of a lot of people into that close place. They ask questions but about newspapers.

One charming girl with flushed cheeks came running up. "I'm going to live that way," she said excitedly. "I don't care what father and mother say, I'm not going to get into the money making game." It touches you. They are nice—if naive.

Brownell took me, after the lecture and after we escaped the crowd, in his car to Koch's house where we had a drink. His wife feels as your mother does about whiskey, but Koch, a great lover of fine printing, had a bottle of old whiskey hidden. Out it came. He declared himself. "With Anderson in my house I strike for liberty," he said laughing.

His daughter, a charming girl, was having *Winesburg* in her high school course.

Brownell insisted on bringing me clear south to 57th St. in his car. Downtown Chicago was marvelous in the rain and mist. Lordy God, I must bring you out here with me.

I dreamed of you in the night. Abner misbehaved. I had to get up and read. He wouldn't go to sleep.

I have decided that I shall have to come east for a weekend with you in May. It is going to be too long away from you.

Brownell, who has been a city newspaper man, told me a good deal about the men with whom he has worked and the McCormicks and Pattersons.[3] "It is amazing how you have got at them," he said. He is a liberal and a bit shaky now. Communism both attracts and repels him.

Now that the ice is broken, I shall not, I'm sure, mind the lectures. At any rate I will succeed in attracting attention to the country papers. It will get down to them and perhaps arouse and give more courage to the men & women already in the game.

If I could only have you here with me. My quarters here are so large and elegant. I love you.

Darling—I've no notion the novel[4] will stop. I feel it in me all the time, like a child growing. It's a bit odd, a bit upsetting to the ordinary processes. You happen to be the father and I the mother in this case. You impregnated me. You are always doing it. God how I love you.

1. SA was giving lectures at Northwestern University and the University of Chicago.

2. Theodore Wesley Koch, noted bibliophile and longtime librarian at Northwestern. John T. Frederick, formerly a professor of English at the University of Iowa, had moved to Chicago in 1930 to concentrate on the magazine he was editing, *Midland*.

3. Two prominent families who controlled the leading newspapers in Chicago. At the time Robert R. McCormick owned the *Tribune* and Joseph Medill Patterson the *Daily News*.

4. *Beyond Desire*.

[Chicago, 22 April 1931]

Wednesday
Notes for Eleanor

I sent you some Yardley's—from Marshall Field's.

Lemon soda. Dish ice cream.

I got a new cloth hat. You'll like it, I'm pretty sure. You wait & see.

Tonight, after the lecture, I am to dine with Frederick—editor of the *Midland*, a magazine out here—Mimi & the Sergels.[1]

The second lecture is the hard one to put over . . . I'm pretty sure. It contains the most dynamite.

I was very tired last night. It got cold. Even a bit of snow fell. If you are a celebrity, alas, groups quarrel over you like dogs over a bone.

Some man wants to give a party and have you as star. It is pathetic really. You feel sorry for such starved lives.

I thought I had got again the thing I had at the beach, when the queer headaches came on. There was the same tightening across the forehead and the eyeballs ached. I had taken with me the bottle of sleeping pills you left with me. I took one right after the lecture.

At least it relaxed me. I sat for 3 hours later among a lot of people, took part in conversation etc. & yet was no part of it all. I was relaxing.

Afterwards I slept.

My host is a man who has grown rich. I knew him out here when we were both boys and broke. He has a big house. His wife looks tired.

We drove down this morning in a Lincoln. He stopped on the way down to pick up his mistress.

I said to him—"Are you not afraid your wife will find out?"

"She doesn't want to find out," he said. He said she didn't dare find out.

He thought I was a fool. He said as much quite seriously. "You have taken women too seriously," he said.

He went on like that. "You might have been in the game, a successful man. We all respected you. You're sharp. You have [a] keen enough business mind."

"So?"

"Yes. You know it."

I thought of hours we have had together and will have. I didn't answer him. What was the use?

Dear, there is very little hope in these business men.

1. Roger and Ruth Sergel, good friends of SA's.

[Clyde, Ohio,[1] 27 April 1931]

Darling—

Here I am—as you see in my native land. No note from you last night but I am hoping for the morning.

We spent the evening walking about, seeing people I used to know. A man took us to dine at his house—the local manufacturer.[2] We went later to the home of my own special boy friend, who is now a fat man, a grocer.[3] He has two grown sons.[4]

There I found some early photographs of your lover that may amuse you. I borrowed them and will have copies made for you.

The town is very pretty and it's now spring green and has changed little. Fortunately it is one of the towns that has not succeeded industrially. My own fancy, dear, has played over and about it so much that it seems all unreal to me.

Your man

1. SA spent the night in Clyde at the New Nichols Inn.
2. Robert B. Jones, president of the Clyde Cutlery Company.
3. Herman Hurd.
4. Thaddeus, an architect, and Hiram, a painter.

[Elizabeth, New Jersey,[1]
12 May 1931]

Notes for Eleanor—

I like it & shall work here. There is a feeling of you near. I had a queer night.

Too many dreams—of horses racing, of a queer new kind of sales machine. I'll tell you about that . . . a kind of last hour of the machine dream.

It was in a restaurant. A man came in and set the machine down. He began talking into it, a queer monotone. He set the machine down and it began running from guest to guest. Inside its bowels it had printed all the man had said into it. It ran to each guest, coughed and spat forth printed circulars in the faces and laps of the guests.

There was a revolt—someone smashed the machine with a chair.

That started something. In my dream I was in some place, like this room, standing & I could hear a roar and rumble in the distance—as of a thousand factories being destroyed.

It may all have come from what that chemist said, of 2 elements being mixed to destroy the world.

The dreams of horses were lovely. There were a lot of beautiful horses on a track and suddenly you knew that all the drivers were cheats and liars and that the horses weren't.

I wish it were possible to get a kind of purity. There is such need for you in this room. It would make everything better in here if you had actually been in here. If I were a scientist I would try to find out what it is that makes that need as real as the need for food and water.

If I could get you in here without the confusion of thoughts, fears etc. . . . it all being quite clear that I would probably make love to you but that that would not be the real point.

Just the same you are not to get confused about my letter of yesterday—[2]

Meaning that you are not to come if something inside you tells you strongly not to come.

I awoke with a queer kind of nervous exhaustion. I stay half tense so long when I am away from you for a few weeks . . . then when I see you . . . and love really comes back—as a living thing . . . as it did suddenly in the car yesterday morning.

Imagine a stream dammed. It is pushing & pushing against a wall. Then the wall breaks and the water rushes on its way. I am sure a kind of exhaustion comes then.

It was interesting to have that man, that scientist, say that thing about the music or rhythm of inanimate things. It is getting at something so baffling to artists. Why is this room I am in here all right while another would not be? What is in that bed there, the table on which I write to you? Who has been in here?

I was with you in the presence of your mother, your brother, your sister.

You can't quarrel with people because the curve they make is not your curve—quite—.

Don't laugh. It is a fact as much as that building over there.

Why are people hurt and so exhausted by life? Will anyone ever know why?

It isn't because people are bad or good.

You take Lois [MacDonald] for example. She is neither bad or good as compared with me. We disliked each other the moment we saw each other the first time. She might not agree. She would rationalize her dislike now.

Anyway I could not let go and just love you until I was away from the others and alone with you.

What I am trying so hard to find out is whether, for you, my tune, or curve, or whatever it is, is curative and good for you, as yours is for me.

So that your life may all be better because of me.

That goes out beyond all morality, all right and wrong.

It is so much so with me that even the physical fact of your being 30 miles from me, instead of 400, makes the difference almost as between light and darkness.

Your letter did not come in the morning mail and there is no other before 2 P.M. I got up late. I will work a little today.

1. SA had come to Elizabeth to be near EC; he was staying at the Elizabeth Carteret Hotel.

2. In his letter of 11 May, he had written, "I need to see you—to renew myself in you."

[Elizabeth, 14 May 1931]

Evening

Darling—I am tired tonight as I worked much longer than I thought I would.[1] Then it was a difficult chapter I wrote. It was rather the reverse of what I said to you in my letter. It was a queer dark chapter. A woman who has tried several men and hasn't found what she wanted.

Another woman who has given up the idea that there is anything real to be got by a woman from a man.

The one woman practically assaults the other—a kind of attempt at a lesbian rape—but the younger of the two women escapes it.

It has come into my head that what I am attempting really is something like this—a series of what are practically short novels, all built upon people whose lives touch one person—that red-haired young communist who is killed later in a strike.

You know how *Winesburg* was built up so, out of short stories—all about the figure of George Willard. Red Oliver should occupy something of the same position in this book—or it may be series of books.

The village—the sense of which I tried to give in *Winesburg*—was comparatively simple.

I want to give the impression of something infinitely more complex—modern life—

Its queer mixtures and futilities now.

Dear, it is a terribly ambitious plan. It frightens me a bit when I sense its possibilities. It is a group of large forms all making a larger form. Will I have courage and life for it?

You must help me to keep up my courage for the job, dearest one. If you were with me tonight—I having gone through this hard emotional task today—I would ask you to let me lie quietly in your arms.

I hope for the sun tomorrow. Perhaps I'll not try to work. There is only one more chapter to do—in this section of the book.

I'll be in town,[2] perhaps by 12.

I love you.

1. SA was working on *Beyond Desire.*
2. I.e., Manhattan.

[Elizabeth, 16 May 1931]

Saturday
Darling—

We were funny yesterday. We each had so much to say and didn't say it. It is so exciting being with you.

After I went to Leigh[1] I rode on a bus down to Washington Park and, tearing two fly leaves out of Dreiser's *Dawn*,[2] wrote you a letter. I went and tore it up.

It didn't say really what I felt.

I went to Paul [Rosenfeld] at 6:30 & had an hour with him before anyone came. After nearly 3 years it was strange to see him. He has a new small apartment & I could not forget the old room—filled with paintings, where I had gone to see him for 15 years.

There was something to break down. Did you ever have the odd experience of being suddenly not yourself? I felt heavy and fat. There was something, a man much lighter, quicker, more alive, who had stayed with you. My thoughts were still all of you. What had come to Paul was not the nicer me. We had an hour.

We talked. It began to be better. He quickly sensed you. He doesn't miss much. I got nicer—in some way took him in too.

"You love," he said. "Yes," I said.

"I sensed it in things you wrote."

Paul has had a woman for many years. For a long time he had two. That perhaps prevented a marriage. Perhaps they brought him two different things. He used to send for me and we would walk when he was troubled and broken up.

He has been working on a novel. We spoke of that a little. I was still with you. Perhaps he felt that.

We went to a speakeasy to dine—[with] a New England writer—queerly grey of skin, rather nice—several generations of New Englanders back of him. There was no warmth in him I could feel.

His wife was again one of those women who have married and you feel all is as it would have been had she never married. We had cocktails and then wine with dinner.

I realized I had to leave you and took myself in hand. We went back to the apartment.

I began challenging everyone—in a queer way. There was a storm of discussion, myself against the whole room.

It got exciting, rather fun. I took an absurd strong position and then, for fun, defended it.

There was a clash of wits. It got more and more furious and was rather fun.

It was broken by [Edmund] Wilson's coming with his wife.[3] Queer—they were grey too. My mind kept flying back to you—the warm rich glow of your skin, your eyes, your lips. Wilson is short & rather pudgy—a still sensitive man.

He and his wife are like two friends. I liked them together. They drink a lot of gin. Get drunk together. She is short, solidly built and broad. I liked them.

Here's Wilson's story. He came out of Princeton with a good mind and a rather short pudgy body. He fell terribly in love with Edna Milay (that isn't the way to spell her. I mean the poet).[4]

He worshipped her and she evidently played him. She always was promiscuous, dear. Get me to tell you of my own breakfast with her once. Wilson couldn't stand it. She would leave him suddenly—go to bed with some man and then come & tell him . . . a kind of sadistic thing.

He went quickly and married a woman he didn't love but whom he admired.[5] There were some terrible years, his trying to love. It was then he began to drink. He got drunk every day.

This one gets drunk with him. They like each other. They are nice, in some queer way, together. It wouldn't satisfy you or me.

We had had fun before they came in and everyone tried to start it all over. With them came a queer couple. There was a rather sensual, sharp chin New England woman who had married a preacher & had had 6 children by him & then had left him. She had got a new man, tall and dark and forceful.

The talk swung to the impulses of 20 years ago, myself, Dreiser, Jack Reed, Floyd Dell, Paul, Margaret Anderson etc.[6]

What was to have been the great movement.

The dark, forceful man said we had accomplished nothing. He kept attacking me all evening but liked me as I did him. He was having fun as I had earlier.

The talk played and swung about. I wanted you there. I thought, "If she were here I would match this man, for the fun of it, blow for blow and at the same time would be light and happy. I would be in her, a part of her." It's hard to say what I mean.

I felt we had been strange together but very very nice. We played off a bit away from each other. We will have to do that lots of times.

I want to talk to you all day, dear. I mustn't. I must work now. Go away, dear.

The cane is so nice standing over there. I bullied it out of you but did want it, at your hands.

About Phil[adelphia]—dear, be free and feel free.[7]

If you can come, come not as a woman to her sweetheart but as a friend. No, not that. If you can, come as one who likes to be near me—close.

We won't think of love making. Let what will happen, happen. Being with you is always, to me, a sweet bath in the person to be with whom is sweeter to me than anything else that has ever happened to me in this world.

I will go to the Sylvania. Call me there when you get off the train.

1. W. Colston Leigh was head of the Leigh Lecture Bureau, which arranged SA's lectures.

2. An autobiography, which had just been published.

3. He had married Margaret Canby, his second wife, in 1930.

4. Wilson met Edna St. Vincent Millay in 1920 when he was managing editor of *Vanity Fair* in New York.

5. He married actress Mary Blair in 1923; they were divorced in 1928.

6. John ("Jack") Reed wrote poetry, short stories, and essays before achieving fame with his account of the communist revolution in Russia, *Ten Days That Shook the World* (1919). Floyd Dell was editor of the *Friday Literary Review* of the Chicago *Evening Post* before moving to New York in 1913. Margaret Anderson began the *Little Review* in 1914; her autobiography, *My Thirty Years' War,* appeared in 1930.

7. They had arranged to meet there that weekend at the Hotel Sylvania.

[Philadelphia, 17 May 1931]

Notes for Eleanor

A clean, sweet feeling all through my body. I feel light and happy. I went out immediately after my lady's voice came over the phone.

I walked down a side street—artists (you know what kind) in little old houses. A sign (Stumble Inn—good food—interesting atmosphere).

Thinking of Paul's description of such places—("Slightly antiquated maiden lady in smock. Blue vase with single flower. Slightly stale whole-wheat bread.")

Came back—broad-hipped maid doing the room. She was down on all fours dusting the furniture. It will be a day when I love all life, go out to it.

We began to talk—she laughing. "Anyway, at this job," I said, "you ought to have kept that girlish figure."

"Did your husband ride you too hard?" I asked her. "No," she said. "He didn't ride me hard enough. He left me with two kids and then he went and died on me."

I was curious. I showed her the miners' coins lying on the dresser[1] and we talked of labor. Then, as she went about in the room dusting, cleaning the bathroom etc., she spoke more of her husband. He was a mechanic and got his chest crushed.

"Did you ever want any other man after he died?" I asked her.

"No," she said. I gave her a good tip. She was nice. "You've got a wife, haven't you?" she said. "Yes, she just left here."

"I'll bet she's stuck on you," she said.

I hope she is.

Thinking about it some more, I don't, as you know, dear, really want to try to argue you into coming and being my wife. You will or you won't, as you feel, in the end.

You have been clear-headed with me. I do force my stroke. There is something so eager for all sweetness, all life, all sounds, sights, tastes, smells.

That sensual eagerness about everything. You hold me. Something inside you quiets me. I am one thing when I have been trying to go it alone and another when I have been with you.

I feel a kind of quieter, surer thing in you that becomes a part of me too.

It seems to me I grow nearer and nearer being ready for love. There is a kind of blind instinctive faith in what I can be with you as partner and lover.

You are on the train now.[2] It's hot. You should be sleeping quietly now.

You are strong and beautiful.

You are a marvelous lover.

1. SA had acquired them while touring coal-mining areas around Charleston, West Virginia, with Tom Tippett on 29 April; he stopped there on his way back to Marion from Chicago.

2. EC was on her way to Reading, Pennsylvania, where she was to attend a series of meetings on 18–21 May.

[Elizabeth, 18 May 1931]

Monday morning

Darling—I am still a bit on edge. For two or three nights I haven't really slept. When I am as I am now, I guess a bit oversensitized, everything gets in so.

I slept fitfully last night. Perhaps sometime I'll tell you the strange dream I had about your mother.

Being with Paul was like this . . . how shall I explain?

We did have something in America once. We spoke of it yesterday as a bird's egg renaissance. One little blue egg laid in a robin's nest perhaps.

Margaret Anderson, Dreiser, Paul, Waldo Frank, Sandburg[1]—I could name 20 men. Someday you and I will write a book about it. Perhaps I will tell it to you in long letters.

It got jammed up—lost. Did the egg go rotten?

Paul was not the most prominent among them. He came to me through Van Wyck Brooks[2] . . . whom we both admired extravagantly. They were the two most subtle minds of it all—a Jew and a Yank. Brooks went to pieces—that queer thing that happens to Yanks sometimes. He just faded out. He's half insane now—dementia praecox I guess.[3]

Paul had the faculty of giving love—as from man to man—a man thing—a mind thing. There is a kind of persistent Jewish sturdiness & health in him.

We'll talk of all that time later. I'll tell you about it sometime. The whole movement went blind or got swamped by prosperity—the war—the hard-boiled men—the smarties. It went anyway.

I have been afraid of Paul a little. For some reason—as you, dear woman, know better than anyone—I myself went off.

You gave me back life. I had stayed away from Paul nearly 3 years. It seemed to me I couldn't go near him—another dead man—not building—not hoping—not living (myself I mean).

The evening at his house wasn't so good. Yesterday was a test.

We were both older. You wonder, dear, that sometimes, when I come to you, I act queerly. You laugh at me. You think I'm surprised that I love you.

It isn't that. I'm really a little afraid.

I think the point yesterday was wrapped up in the question—did I really have, for Paul, something living to give—that he should still love me?

I sensed at once that he was alive. I knew I had been dead.

Was I a reborn man?

I think it came out all right. I felt him alive and happy and healthy when he went home. He kept saying it was the best day out of doors he'd ever had.

We even dared to map things out a little—what he would dare to try to do yet—what I would dare to try to do.

It means something almost terrible in its importance—that sort of thing—between two such men who have had that man's feeling for each other—saw it almost die.

I think he shares with me the feeling—you in it.

I mean by you the woman—

The thing a man seeks to help him live and work. He has, at bottom, my kind of blind faith in you women.

I was tired afterwards. I wouldn't be today if I could have come home to you last night to lie beside you—tell you of it.

Paul spoke of something I mustn't do—"forcing," he called it. It's hard not to. I'm always afraid, dear, that when I come to you after an absence, I'll be so eager—like a hungry kid, that what I want to give will explode—run away before you are all open and ready to receive.

The fear hurts too. It is like the fear that I will have nothing to give to you or Paul or anyone.

It is the death that was in me.

All this to make you know how little I am.

When I can be with you more, day by day, I'll have more to give because health comes from you always to me.

Men can only be, after all, minds to each other but we can be mind and body.

That is the birth of the queer thing called "art," dear. It has to be born there. I'll never be an artist alone anymore, perhaps never was. I can be one only in you, out of you, a part of you—you in me.

I can't say it but you know. If I am frightened—a bit shy and queer inside Tuesday night, be a little the mother, the sister, the sky and the field to me until I am again your man.

1. Waldo Frank was an editor of *Seven Arts,* which published some of SA's *Winesburg* stories in 1916–17, and a close friend of SA's during that period. Carl Sandburg, a member of the Chicago literary set, published his first volume of poetry, *Chicago Poems,* in 1916.

2. Rosenfeld and Brooks at the time were editors of *Seven Arts.*

3. Brooks had been in deep depression since 1926 but recovered in 1931.

[Indianapolis, 21 May 1931]

Notes for Eleanor

It is interesting about Ralph Barton who shot himself in N.Y. Did you read about it? He is said to have shot himself about a woman named Kresge—a 5 & 10 fortune girl. That's pretty much bunk.[1]

I know why he shot himself. It is because he went cheap as an artist and could no longer live with himself.

How do I know? I had a talk with him one night. I was with John Emerson & Anita Loos.[2] We went to Barton's apartment one evening. That was five or six years ago.

He & Anita & John were making a sort of Rabelaisian movie to amuse themselves. It was all about the impotence of certain other successful actors, painters, writers, etc.

It wasn't funny really, although they were trying hard to think it was.

I was pretty much disgusted although I didn't say so. All of these people, dear, are really sensitive people or they wouldn't be in the arts at all. At that time I was in an odd position. You know about John Emerson & me. We were boys & young men together. We were friends like you and Lois [MacDonald].

You said something the other day—about how—if everything went wrong with L—her eyes or something—you would have to stick to her. Of course I loved you for it.

John Emerson had got rich out of the arts. As I say, he & I had been boys and young men together. We were both interested in the arts. We made each other vows—you know—to stick together etc.

If either man prospered we were to divide etc.

John had become a millionaire. He felt guilty about the old vows, thought he ought to do something about me etc.

I foolishly let him try.

I had gone to N.Y. at his request. He had begun with music and had gone from that to the stage & then to the movies. He had got ahold of & married that clever little Anita. He was at bottom a shrewd business man. He worked her like a mule.

Still he felt he ought to do something for me. He did loan me a little money, a few hundred I never paid back.

It's odd. You & I never would get in any jam about money. It would never mean enough to us. But then we'll never have any money.

So there we were—the 4 of us—Barton, John, Anita and me in that room. Something happened. They were all getting rich on movies & hated movies. So they were shitting on the movies by making this excessively ugly one, pretending to themselves they were amusing themselves.

I guess they sensed that it made me sick for they all stopped suddenly. John, Anita & I went away.

I was living, for the time, over on 22nd Street, in a room I think.

Barton drove there late that night in a taxi.

It was a queer performance. Sinclair Lewis and a dozen others have done something of the sort to me. (In hotel at Indianapolis waiting for train to Lafayette)[3]

Barton came rather drunk and wanted to talk to me. We got in the cab & rode.

He talked only of how rotten he was, how he had debased himself. He wanted to debase himself some more before me. He had picked me out. He had got my address from John.

So that's why he shot himself. He felt so dirty.

There is something tremendous about this success thing. It isn't a question of money only. I don't know just what it is.

At that time I was being cultivated. Crowninshield,[4] all of the procurers, were after me. I was undeveloped property. They wanted to build on me.

I may have wanted to build against it. At that time Elizabeth was a book clerk in Lord & Taylor, really a department store clerk, dear. You know all of that grand lady thing she afterwards got. I don't intend to be hard on her.

Her very obscurity did attract me. I was playing about with actresses etc., successful people of all sorts.

And then she got it. I wrote *A Story Teller's Story* & *Dark Laughter.*

Money came in.

It raised hell with her too. She wanted, I guess, to be something grand.

When I first knew her, she was tired and discouraged and rather nice, you know.

She got more and more the other way—wanted to be refined—build up the aristocracy idea. Don't blame me if I hate that sort of thing, dear.

It's another form of the same sort of thing as the success, money thing.

When Paul and I were out riding last Sunday, we saw a bitch in heat.

A lot of male dogs trotting after her, that peculiar look on their faces, determination, self consciousness, shame, ugly male pride. Henry James spoke of the "bitch"—success.[5] He knew something.

There is a tone to life, more subtile, more difficult to get. I've never got it. I don't care. I'd rather try and try for it until I die.

It's something balanced, not sure of itself, lost and lost and then found again. I've got a certain pride, dear. That's where all of these wise psychologists go wrong. I have fought not to accept second-rateness. Elizabeth wouldn't stand by. She said she wouldn't. "You can go to hell," she said. "I'm going to have what I want." She didn't get it.

It meant breaking me. What? I don't know.

Some willingness in me to throw everything overboard, try again.

All of this brought home again because of that Barton's ugly death. It's the whole American story—in a queer way.

Gee—my love.

1. Barton, author and illustrator, committed suicide on 20 May. He was said to have been depressed over his third ex-wife, Carlotta Monterey, who had married Eugene O'Neill. Barton's fourth wife had divorced him the previous month, and he was reported to have wanted to marry Ruth Kresge.

2. Emerson, after his boyhood in Clyde, Ohio, became an actor, playwright, and movie producer. His wife, Anita Loos, was a playwright, screenwriter, and author of *Gentlemen Prefer Blondes* (1925).

3. SA was on his way to Lafayette, Indiana, to speak at Purdue University.

4. Frank Crowninshield, editor of *Vanity Fair.*

5. William James, Henry's brother, in a letter to H. G. Wells, refers to "the exclusive worship of the bitch-goddess SUCCESS" as "our national disease" (*The Letters of William James,* ed. Henry James, vol. 2 [Boston: Atlantic Monthly, 1920], p. 260).

[Elizabeth, 24 May 1931]

Sunday morning
Dearest Woman

After Mr. Jim Farrell—ex-laborer—set Mr. Charlie Schwab down rather hard in his seat, the *Times,* editorially, starts building Schwab up again.[1] I suspect Schwab's point of view is a lot nearer what the industrialists like to think of themselves.

I went to bed early—trying in fancy to follow you into the rich man's house. In the evening I wrote letters to John & Charles [Bockler] & to Maurice [Long], you & your mother and Bob. I slept and dreamed of you again. In the darkness I tried to draw you close.

I awoke at midnight and, as I was restless, read Huxley on *Evolution and Ethics.*[2]

I was very very lonesome.

There were so many things other than direct love making about having you so close that night. There was the sense of you in the room.

There is a kind of whole to you I love—having nothing to do with the parts of you I also love—your eyes, lips, breasts, Clarisse etc. It is you aside from me as lover, wife and my woman. Everyone I know who meets you speaks of it. It is the warm out-going energy of you.

It is such a tired time and you are not tired.

There is in you the same indomitable thing your mother has.

You laugh at yourself—call yourself lazy & sleepy. You do not tend to details as you should etc. It's nice, your blaming yourself so, but my dear.

The giving out of something warmly and constantly, as you do. It is the sort of thing that can't be measured. There is no foot rule made for that.

Your mother—having the same thing in her—has driven it all into the channels of mind. Well, not all. I am onto her.

There must have been fear of daring to be warm—that old puritan thing. And the rather slow and limited Germanic peasant thing in your father.

Why pardon me, dear, for analyzing it all so. That isn't my purpose. I just don't want you to blame yourself that you can't be like Lucy,[3] always at hand for meetings, always getting your reports made out etc.

You need to rest and draw in again too.

I've said before that you were the artist's woman. You are the artist as woman.

Your beauty shines. You are so much, my darling, proof of something that I also have, in my own blundering way, fought so for.

You went away from me yesterday along the street and I stood to watch you go—a flame along the street. It wasn't just your red coat.

There was, however, something good in the fact that the coat was red. Warm colors speak for you. If I were to paint you I would wash all the world about you in warm colors.

With your little dark body, the quick vital step, the athletic strength of your little legs.

You having had all that warmth to leave with me—taking more away.

How can you report what happened at the meeting at Reading—the working girls' meeting?

You can't say—"I came in among them. Something happened."

You can't say it—sweetest of all women—but I can know it.

I came slowly—stupidly—to knowing that, as your lover, I want most to have the warmth of you to go on undiminished—not to hurt you—not in any way to diminish what you are and can be to others.

I love you whole—all aside from me . . . sweetest one . . . purest of all people I have known . . . warmest . . . cleanest.

I love you very very much today.

1. James A. Farrell was president of the U.S. Steel Corporation, and Charles M. Schwab was chairman of Bethlehem Steel Corporation. Both were speakers on 22 May at the American Iron and Steel Institute. Schwab, the president of the institute, upheld the practices of management, while Farrell objected to self-congratulation and criticized wage reductions. SA refers to an editorial in the *New York Times* on 24 May (3:1).

2. English biologist Thomas H. Huxley published this work in 1893.

3. Lucy Carner, EC's immediate superior on the YWCA national board.

[Elizabeth, 29 May 1931]

Darling woman . . . There is always in the morning a little uncertain flurry. "Will it go well today?" It isn't only the writing. It is everything. Will life sing or will it drag heavily? Everything is in tone. It is a silly ambition, the one I have, and it is having it that makes me such a child sometimes. I do so want things nice, real. There is so little of life. I can stand up to real tragedy well enough I think. I believe I could stand starving, real illness, death all O.K. I can't stand the little pecking at life, spoiling it minute by minute, as I go along. I feel the same thing in you. I have seen you absorbed, worried, even a little angry sometimes. Do you remember driving over from Baltimore to Philadelphia when you got angry at me? That was O.K. It was a misunderstanding.

I believe we can live together sweetly in a real way. I feel more and more sure. The whole experience, loving you, is as new to me as though I were a young boy.

I walk about the rooms here, in the morning, listening. Often I catch something. You have seen a musician feeling for a tone or a painter for a tone in color. There is always something like that wanted. A man might make a bit of real music.

Prose is a complex thing. It should always, dear, have music in it but the music should not be obvious. I think it would always be better if, in as far as a man is a poet, he hide the fact. The important thing is the poetry not the poet. That is the real glory of prose . . . that down inside these slowly marching lines a man may, occasionally when no one is watching, plant a bit of poetry. It should be like Johnny Appleseed, walking through the wilderness, planting here and there an apple tree to bloom and bear fruit maybe after he is dead.

[Black Mountain, North Carolina,[1]
11 June 1931]

Thursday—Two young men have come to sit at my table. They are the sort that are afterwards made into professors. There is a kind of mildness in them, too much mildness. Already at twenty-two they are like apples that have been in the cellar two years.

I think of things I want to say to you after I get into bed. I hold imaginary conversations with you.

How greedy I was last night, after the sweetness in you like a little pig. I smile at myself remembering.

I watch the people eat. Most of the guests here are thin women, the kind you see going to church on Sundays. They store away quantities of food though. It is surprising. Perhaps all day they haven't anything to do but digest. What a quantity of refuse must come from them. You must not miss taking the picture of the privies at Marion.[2] I could pass them about here. Some might be sold.

Suppose you do not like some of the things the communists do. You look up Sam Adams and some of the other men who got up the American revolution. They were slick ones. I always remember what you said to me that the old socialist said to you—to stick to principles. More and more, as I think of it, I think it will have to be done in the communists' way.

I should be kinder, thinking of such people as surround me here. The kind of young girls we picked up in the car yesterday will likely be turned into this meaningless sort. It's a shame. Men make such meaningless whores out of women. They aren't real whores, wanting to go fuck sweetness into the world. That could be a dream like a poet's dream. Obviously most people just submit to life. That is what is terrible. I was a lucky boy after all. My father [Irwin Anderson] and mother never were this sort. My father lied and bragged. Anyway he was always full of life. It rolled through him. I myself use up so much energy in little passing thoughts and impulses. When I have worked for a time I am like a violin string drawn tightly. Yesterday after working I sat on a bench and suddenly began to cry. It was just something in my thoughts. At times a little thought can be like a whip hitting on raw flesh. When what I write is most quiet, most balanced, then I am often most shattered.

Going about as I did as a boy with rough, profane men, liars, braggarts, etc. was perhaps better than being brought up among good church-going people. If I had been the son of a Jack Sheffey[3] I might have shot him before I was fourteen.

Being with you puts me in a lovely mood. Last night, after leaving you and getting into a bed, I suddenly began thinking of something I once saw. It was a man whose wife had died. He was on a boat on the Mobile River, a little dried up old white man. He was going to a little town up river and had a fat little dog with him.

He was lying on a bench in the sun and talking to the dog about his wife. He didn't see me. The thought came that he had no one close enough to him to talk to about the death of his wife and what it meant to him but the fat little old dog. It is, dear, one of the thousands of stories I have never written. I am with you, I come into you, I sit with you, I hold your hand, I am greedily at your sweet breasts as I was last night and there seems a little current of sweet life coming out of you into me. It is a sweet spring to a thirsty man. It is tapping some inner sweetness in you [that] you have managed to keep sweet. I am like dry parched earth. As the sweetness comes into me, things begin to grow. There is an ever new spring in me. The lover of you in me is the poet in me.

1. SA rented a room at Black Mountain and worked on *Beyond Desire* while EC was at camp at Blue Ridge.

2. A reference to the primitive living conditions of striking workers at Marion, North Carolina.

3. A well-respected farmer and lawyer in Marion, Virginia.

[Black Mountain, 12 June 1931]

Friday

The woman who is in the next room rolls about in her sleep and groans. She must have an indigestion.

There is a big negro servant here named Jim who has more dignity than all the guests put together. I notice, in the paper, that when someone over there speaks on race relations they are careful to explain they do not mean negroes and whites sleeping together. Wouldn't it be nice if some negro would get up and say, "Shut up. I don't want to sleep with you."

You could take this room I am in as an example of everything lower middle class and ugly. It is in the beds, in the furniture, in the paint on the wall, in the curtains at the windows.

The woman of the house works all the time, never stopping. She is in the kitchen, in the dining room, the yard. Yesterday she explained to me. "I must give everything in the yard a good start. Presently I will have a house full of guests. I can't do it then."

I dreamed a whole short story as I sometimes do but when I awoke it got away. I do not dream the stories when I do this, I dream I am writing them. They are outside me. I am sitting writing them. I can even see the words.

I awoke and dreamed of George Mitchell.[1] He had gone in with some sharp men to run a lottery, had got permission from the state to run it if half the profits went to labor. So they fixed it up. They arranged that one man should put up one dollar and win eight thousand. That, they said, will start everyone putting money in. So they let the man win the eight thousand. He took it and walked away. Then they started the lottery and everyone just laughed. When Mitchell starts his paper it will be like the time I had a convention to establish a commercial democracy. One man will come with a dirty faced child and a bag of bananas.[2]

I keep thinking of the next camp, rather dreading it for you.[3] I thought of this. Would it work? Can't you call for volunteers among the factory girls? "Are you any good at entertaining? What can you do?" It might result in the development of some hidden talent.

If I were teaching people to mould with clay, here is how I would do it. I would put before each one a mass of clay. It is just a lump.

"In the lump is concealed something. It may be the face of a man or woman, a child, whatnot. It is in there. You do not mould the face. You cut away the superfluous clay so that it may come out." It is only later you should let them look from some face they want to mould to the clay. They must, by the power of the imagination, thrust it into the mass and then help it to emerge. It was in this way I made a sculptress of Tennessee Mitchell.[4] Within a week she was doing strangely alive things.

Self-consciousness must be got rid of. We are all more artists than we know. It is a curiously fine feeling to see something at last grow under your hands. Refinements may come later. I could be a fine teacher of such things.

1. Earlier in the year SA had exchanged letters with Mitchell, an economics professor at Columbia University, about a proposal by Mitchell to establish a weekly newspaper for the cotton mill areas of the South.

2. SA gives a more detailed account of the incident in *Sherwood Anderson's Memoirs: A Critical Edition*, p. 294. "Commercial Democracy" was a scheme to promote the sale of stock in SA's paint company in Elyria, Ohio, the failure of which contributed to his disposing of the business in 1913.

3. EC's next assignment was at Camp Merrie-Woode, beginning on 17 June.

4. This oft-repeated claim had been a source of some annoyance to Tennessee Mitchell.

[Black Mountain, 14 June 1931]

Sunday

It's nice, darling, to be able to come up to the room and find the bed all made after coffee and toast. The fact that I have been able to write a little, really, in here and have loved you in here has made the room nicer. The negro woman who makes the room has giant hips, very black skin and a voice like a little complaining child.

Suppose you were like that. Me riding the great waves of such an ocean of woman. A continent of woman.

I got out my newly laundered blue pajamas last night and put them on to celebrate such a glorious day and evening. I was full of slender young tree tops waving against a blue sky, your face up there, the waves, the fluttering tendrils of your blue-black hair, your eyes amid leaves.

Then a silent dark place by the river.

You in a telephone booth in a drug store.

Waves of loveliness, coming and going when perhaps even you did not know.

Your white skin, your smooth lovely hips against the sky there by the stream. Glory in myself too. I live. I see and feel such loveliness. Who am I to question whether I am a success or failure in life? Am I to be a bourgeois, counting pennies of time, experience, my woman's breath coming and going? I wanted something. I knew I would come home and want to lie on my back and wave my legs in the [air] and be nice and silly and laugh for a half hour before sleeping, and I did want you here, also waving your legs and laughing. O.K. God.

You will read this on the morning of your birthday.[1] God's blessing on you. I will be loving you.

1. Her birthday was 15 June.

[Black Mountain, 14 June 1931]

Sunday

I'll put this in the letter I mail to Sapphire.[1] It has been a glorious morning. I had a hunch it would be. I guess that was why I didn't let you have the car last night. You said, "I'll come in the morning." I thought, "She may get a tire blown out or something going home." It wasn't that. Some little voice said inside, not up in my consciousness, "The little river may want to flow in the morning." Something like that. I love you.

You have just phoned.

I thought while I shaved . . . "The other women were always hurt and jealous of the little river. She will never be. I said to you last night that I had come to perfect frankness with you. I haven't quite yet. I will.

The fragrance of you has made my thoughts and fancies fragrant again. The sentences become fragrant again.

The sentences are like the tree tops that were playing about your head when you made love to me.

To explain something . . . you say, dear, "You do not have to produce for me to love you." I know why you say it . . . so that I shall not hurry, spoil things. I do have to produce. To produce is to live, it is life, real life, flowing through. It isn't acclaim I want any more. I want as you do, darling, to do something nice to the life that has been good to me.

1. The mailing address of Camp Merrie-Woode.

[Black Mountain, 15 June 1931]

Later Monday[1]

I flowed again, softly and nicely, into the farm country, in Kansas, as the branch of the Kaw River flows into the Kaw. I hope my flowing was as Red, and as yellow with Kansas earth.[2] I won't try to do too much today. I just wanted to know it was going on. It's late morning and I'll quit now and go along. I love you . . . and Red.

Thinking, stopping to think in the midst of work, that we also . . . if we believe in our relationship . . . ought not worry about the future . . . whether we hold that Y job etc. The best defense is a belief that our lives together will amount to something. If we have to be poor what the hell.

One of the things I want to say in this novel is something that I have been trying to say a little in the lectures . . . super college kids etc. . . . folks like you and me too . . . were destined to be quite booted out. Suppose we had to go somewhere and live with workers, on the worker's scale . . . like in the little cabin at the turn of the road to which we walked yesterday. What of it?

They'd say . . . "Romance."

Why god damn it, love, that is what we have got to get back . . . that is what you and I are after . . . the romance of life.

We are going to get it too. Happy birthday.

1. This was his second letter of the day. Since it is in an unaddressed envelope, SA probably gave it to her directly.

2. In the opening pages of *Beyond Desire,* protagonist Red Oliver visits the Kansas farm of his friend Neil Bradley.

[Marion, August 1931]

I dread the days coming when I will not be able to see you, hold you, be near you. As I have you near I get new courage. When you are not near sometimes my courage goes down and down.

I am getting a new kind of love, though, deeper and better than any I have ever had.

Yesterday was good, good. The work went well. I loved seeing you on the horse and with people. Your father seemed happier. I am always made unhappy inside when I think he is upset and hurt because of it. I don't know what to do about it.

It isn't right that we should stop because of his feeling—if our love goes on getting stronger and better, as it seems to be doing.

I shall be dreadfully impatient and upset sometimes this winter. I will honestly try not to be. This morning I can't quite get hold of the mill girls, Doris, Grace, Nell and Fanny.[1] It seems almost as though I were in the mill myself, too close to them.

It seems to me though always to be too cynical about life. I wish I could live a thousand years, and you could, and we could go a thousand places and see everything that happens.

1. Characters in "Mill Girls," which was published in *Scribner's Magazine* 91 (January 1932): 8–12, 59–64, and later in *Beyond Desire*, pp. 69–102.

[Marion, 6 August 1931]

Thursday . . . Thinking all the time that after Sunday I can begin thinking of seeing you. The papers are out for this week. I wrote a short article for a magazine in Pittsburgh called *The Scholastic*.[1] It rained again today. I went, after the paper was out, to see your father and Miss May.[2]

Your father was sitting with a school teacher. She was a woman of perhaps thirty-five. It was a story. I sat down a little to one side. What I heard made me understand your father.

She is a good teacher. She married a man who went to pieces and got into the penitentiary. Before that she had been one of your father's teachers.[3]

She had three children. He gave her a job again. She is a good teacher. People have begun talking about her.

There is a man coming to see her. People say: "He isn't an all right man." They say: "She married one bum man now she is going to marry another." They don't want her. It's like people saying that about me. She was discouraged and wanting to cry.

Your father was wanting to stick to her. He said: "I'll give you another school as good." Just the same her pride was hurt. It was one of those curious situations in life, two good people trying to understand together the difficulties of life. Your Dad's job isn't an easy one. He is a good man.

Is he too cautious? I don't know. If he told them all to go to hell, as I would want to do, he couldn't hold his job.

O, my darling.

1. "How I Got My Literary Start," *Scholastic* 19 (17 October 1931): 6, one of a series of eleven articles by various authors.

2. May Scherer, dean of Marion College and sister of Laura Lu Copenhaver; she lived at Rosemont.

3. B. E. Copenhaver was superintendent of schools in Smyth County.

[Marion, 15 August 1931]

Darling . . . There wasn't any letter yesterday but a mighty nice one came this A.M. I guess it really came late last night. Anyway it set me up.

Burt D[ickinson] and I went in the late afternoon over into Washington County hoping the water would be clear in the South Fork[1] over there but it wasn't. Anyway we waded and fished and I found a lovely spot to take you to.

I wish to God I could have gone with you to the strike. That is what I now need for the book, some more actual contact. If I could only go such places with you, see it through your eyes as well as my own. Perhaps we can next year. It will be great to talk to you about it. I am trying to say to myself that, if it takes two years to do the book, it will be better than to go off half cocked with it. You'll agree on that.

[Louis] Jaffe is coming on the morning train.

Last night when I got home there was a long distance call waiting for me. It was from Maurice [Long]. Bob and Mimi were there[2] and he had fallen for Mimi. He was determined to keep them over Saturday so of course I said O.K. I spoke to Mimi. They will be at home on Sunday evening. Your mother is going to have Jaffe to dinner.

I ran up there and sat talking with her for an hour. She seemed quite her old self. You will find in this letter a copy of a note I wrote her and didn't send. I began telling her part of its contents and she then told me how much conversation meant to her. How skillful she is at it. I realized suddenly how much she has always wanted to lead just such a life as you lead, meeting people and having live adventures. Part of her love for you . . . this old dear without taking anything from you, as you know . . . is that she lives a great deal in fancy in your life. She is so grateful when I talk of your life, telling her some of your adventures. You should do it and not be bluffed by your father's fear that you will be doing something not regular. He also secretly has admiration for the part of your life he seems to condemn. His love for your mother is partly due to his feeling in her the same spirit. Toward me it is a little different. I am not his, not of his blood. He is a bit jealous of the fact that your mother and I have such fun talking and glad for her too. How mixed life is.

You see, the kids were really not so hot to get here. I might have come on. We—I'll—come on Wednesday evening and we will go and see about Jack's stuff[3] etc., whatever is up.

I think I will take Jaffe to the farm. It will be a nice ride and I want to take the lawn mower over there and mow the front lawn and put up the croquet set for the Jaybird's kids.[4] They expect him Tuesday and I will take him over and get him established. He will still be here when you come home. It will be good to have Jaffe here. We will go to Frank Copenhaver's[5] Sunday night.

About the songs.[6] Can you just tell her that when you were at home this summer I spoke to you about such songs, wanting to use a few of them in a novel I am trying to write about the death of a young communist. It seems to me that would be O.K. and not involve you too much with me, eh, eh, eh.

Yes. Yes. Yes. I love you. I adore you. I love you more and more all the time.

1. The south fork of the Holston River, a few miles south of Marion.

2. In Washington, D.C.

3. John ("Jack") Cronk, EC's cousin, who had inherited furniture that she bought from him, to SA's annoyance.

4. J. J. Scherer, Jr., and his family were visiting from Richmond.

5. Frank Copenhaver, a cousin of EC's father, was a Marion grocer. He and his wife, Ruth, were good friends of SA's.

6. SA had requested the texts of some strikers' songs collected by a speaker at a meeting EC had attended in Gastonia, North Carolina.

[Marion, 26 September 1931]

Saturday

It rained all night and is still raining. I have caught a slight cold. It is nothing. When I work rather intensely when you are here, it passes off quickly. It is because being with you in some odd way refreshes me so much.

When you are not here it goes more slowly. I shall lay off today, having, I am sure, got perhaps another forty or fifty pages of the book down.

Did you take *Merry Go Round*[1] with you? If not let me know and I will send it.

Please remember that you are in honor bound to spend that dollar I sent some time ago for the soap.

I have been reading a terrible book called *Sons of Cain,* by an Englishman,[2] the most intensely horrible story of a man's actual experience in war.

I have an odd experience about you, dear. You are so closely connected with my thoughts and I write so much to you that I am always thinking I have written you thoughts that I perhaps have not.

Yesterday, after working and feeling the cold coming on, I went out at 1:30 and went to a dahlia show at the hotel. There was a football game at the Rich Valley high school and I went over there, a long, interesting drive. I saw your father there. It was a rather interesting game in a lovely spot. I drove back over Walker Mountain, having gone over by way of Lyon's Gap. I saw a place where one Sunday evening we stopped beside the road, when I had first begun to love you. You will remember. We got off the road and had a flat. It was Sunday. We came over Walker Mountain. Do you remember it?

I have a new name for John. I call him Cousin John. I don't know why it fits so but it does. It in a queer way defines our relations. Father and son doesn't quite do.

I went in the evening to your mother. She was in one of her gentler moods, very lovely and almost girlish. She had thought out a scheme. All money was to be repudiated and new money made and distributed, a fresh start made. I challenged her, in fun, to start the distribution of new funds to make the machine go again and she got all mixed up. Your father had gone to sleep in his chair and when your mother woke him up he got up and stumbled off to bed, slamming the door as he does sometimes.

I was suddenly terribly sorry for him. He seemed to represent so truly the American man at his best. For some reason the American man has resolutely closed his mind. He simply will not admit the necessity of culture. I remembered that several European men I have met have said to me, "Why, you are not an American man. You are open. You are the European man." They must have meant that.

I remember once sitting on the porch when your mother was so ill. Do you remember when she was having that sinking spell and Bob played blithely on the phonograph? I sat out there with your father and Randolph. Some Tchaikovsky was being played. "What stuff," your father said. "What stuff," Randolph said. There was in Randolph the same kind of determined refusal to open his mind, the beginnings of the same thing. What does it? It is a strange mystery to me, a kind of queer prolongation of childhood . . . so determined, such an odd perversion. As though one should deliberately go to work to make himself a withered arm by refusing to use it.

I can't quite make out what your father feels about my coming there . . . I mean when you are not at home. There is a way, I'm sure, in which he resents the relationship I have with your mother, the fun we have, etc. At the same time he loves her and wants her amused. I'm sure of that. It would be lovely, and so characteristically American, if he both admired me for letting my mind and fancy go and play over life and at the same time rather disliked me for it.

An odd thing. A long telegram from the advertising men of NY asking me to come to New York and speak at a public luncheon. Why, I wonder.

I brought home *The Adams Family*[3] to read. I shall stay out doors a lot today and shake off my cold. After a day or two I am sure there will be mushrooms. It will be something to go into the woods for. The change here has definitely come. Fall is in the air. It began the day after you left.

Last night, when I left your house, your mother walked out on the porch with me. It was one of those perfect moonlit fall nights that come here, one of the kind that make you catch your breath. It made me hunger for you so that it hurt clear down inside, like sometimes when your hand touches me, lover.

1. By Albert Maltz and George Sklar, who also wrote *Peace on Earth*, first produced in 1933 and published in 1934 with a foreword by SA.

2. Wilfred Saint-Mande. This 1931 account of World War I experiences was published in England with the title *War, Wine and Women*.

3. A biography by James Truslow Adams (1930).

[Marion, 29 September 1931]

Tuesday

Darling . . . an unsuccessful day. I could not write. Perhaps, after all, I have not recovered from my cold. It seems to have passed into a second stage of stopped-up noses, hacking coughs, lassitude, falling of the womb of the spirit, glanders, sleeping sickness and string halt. I went to Frank's and we made more wine. I now have a half interest in 30 gallons there and twenty at another place. Frank and I also propose to make a lot of cider wine at which I am an expert. Let's say twenty gallons of that . . . 70 gallons a half of which would be 35. Now will you marry me? If you get tired of me you may stay drunk on my wine.

I have this definite impression of you these days . . . always when you are in NY . . . as fluttering from place to place. You are on the wing. Life and beauty are in your hands. You fly far overhead. I stand here dumb and I must admit stupid. I wish you could fly down where I am and make me alive and well again.

Darling, I am not dissatisfied with the way *PW* has been received. I thought the *Times* was O.K.[1] Again I am surprised. After all, on the whole I am always treated with a certain respect, perhaps more than I deserve. I believe in my soul that the central point of my thesis . . . that industrialism, as at present handled, leads first of all to impotence . . . beginning with spiritual impotence and leading to physical impotence. Of course I laid myself open. It can't be helped. I believe we are in an impotent age. I believe you have never committed yourself as to whether or not you think I am right.

It pleases me that, if I haven't first-rate brains but have sincerity, the fact of my sincerity is recognized and respected. I am always having a false hope that some day I shall sing some great song that will sweep all before it, like a storm at sea. I am childishly disappointed always for a moment, after every production, that I have not done it. At bottom I have never quarreled with American criticism. It has always placed me higher than I deserve.

A soft and very quiet evening. If we only had a room, any quiet place into which we could occasionally go for an hour. If I could have such an hour with you now.

I think I shall always have for you, dear, a kind of worship. It isn't, I'm pretty sure, sentimentality. There is a kind of inner sweetness in you that sweetens me. I need you every day. It is a beautiful evening, full of the touch of fall. I need you very much this evening.

1. On 27 September the *New York Times Book Review* published a mixed review of *Perhaps Women*: Rose C. Feld, "Mr. Anderson's Vision of a Machine Age Matriarchy," p. 2.

[Marion, October 1931]

Notes for Eleanor—

Two things saving me from prolonged silliness yesterday—the hard good sense of your mother and your own sweetness.

Your mother has got something that is invaluable. It is what I mean when I speak of the possibilities of woman. There is affection in her—what men have always meant by "woman's fineness."

But she has let her mind develop. She sees through and around things—judges swiftly and accurately.

I slept, dreaming of a ship—myself a sailor. We were plowing through a storm. I had to help pass a rope through some posts on deck. I worked

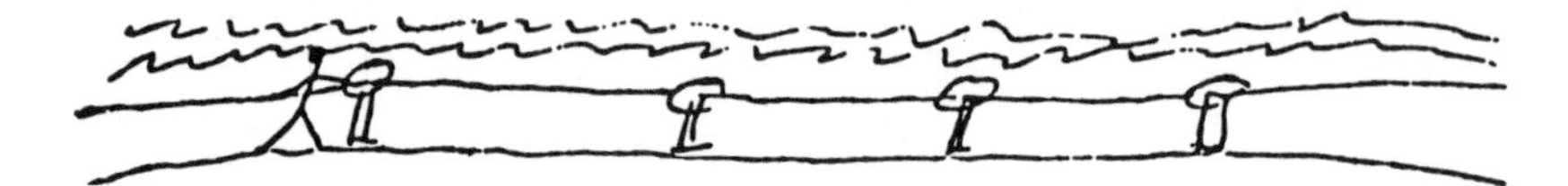

and worked at it, enjoying it. Now and then a wave knocked me down.

Last night, lying on the couch, a time of faces again.[1] If I wanted to make out a case for spiritualism I'd have it.

Who are these mysterious people who appear at such times? I see them as clearly as I see this hand held here before my eyes.

The man from California says they are indications of a new kind of communication.

An old man cracking walnuts by a fire in a cabin. He is alone. He has a long beard and watery eyes. He does not look at me. The fire is getting low. He disappears—a click—as of a camera.

A man—evidently a worn-out old pugilist—sitting on a stool. There are canvas walls about him. He is disfigured from old blows, a smashed nose, a misshapen mouth.

A young girl walking along a beach.

I won't go on. Often 20 or thirty of such figures pass thus, all clearly seen.

There is a kind of mysticism. I blame myself. It may be that, now and then, I have told some story of some obscure person. Others see it or hear of it.

They may not see it.

There may just be everywhere obscure persons—living lives they in some way want dignified. As a painter might say—"Here are a thousand scenes wanting painting."

The painter feels guilty always. "I have not done what might be done with that barren hill. The hill cries out to me."

The painter stands helpless before his tubes of color as I am so often helpless before these sheets.

Now these hard things—the factories—the machines—to be in some way dignified—so they can be accepted as dignified things in life.

I am always hoping I have done it.

I have. I haven't. I get silly, feeling my defeat again.

1. See letter of 29 October 1930.

[Marion, 2 October 1931]

Darling . . . Friday . . . A wasted week I am afraid. I have written some pages but am half afraid to look at them. In the meantime the skies have been clear and the weather fine. It is a shame to lose such days. I am still in the fallen womb stage of my damn cold.

"Beatitude there is none. And your only Mardian happiness is but exemption from great woes—no more. Great love is sad; and Heaven is Love. Sadness makes the great silence throughout the realms of space; sadness is universal and eternal." Herman Melville[1]

I am really needing you pretty much, dear. It seems to me that an hour of you would shake this off.

I have put in most of the time reading *The Romantic Revolution*.[2] What a drifting array of figures. I went to your mother in the afternoon and talked to her of Calhoun and Lenin.[3] It has amused me to compare the two men, both so sincere, both so puritanic. On the evening before your mother had gone both to prayer meeting and the movies and it was too much. She declares she will give up movies. The prayer meeting must have been pretty dull too.

She showed me the famous letter from Katharine about the dollar that had not been handed into the auxiliary and your father came home as I was reading it. I think he was annoyed that she had let me see it. It is a kind of perfect exhibition of what small town life can do, a rather terrible picture.

It seems to me that the big fellows are gathering themselves together. There will be universal cutting of wages. The time of good will, as between capital and labor, of which so much was made during the boom times, will pass. The challenge will be more direct. "We have to rule. Let's drop all of this nonsense. It's time now to cut and slash." That will be the new tone.

In the meantime a movement toward new consolidations. It will be a shaking out of the middle class that has ruled for so long. I can see all this coming.

I imagine that in the end such people as you and I will have to line ourselves up definitely or step aside. I wish I knew in what way a man could serve best. I am sending you the thing from the book I call "Mill Girls." Am I serving best in doing things of this sort or in such moves as the Danville speech?

I don't think my own life matters so much. There is so often the lack of the mental activity I love so much and when my mind and spirit are not active, when I just sit here letting the days pass, I get a queer ironic feeling.

If death should come in the door there, out of the bright sunshine, saying, "Well, my boy, come on," I really think I'd laugh . . . not when you are here I wouldn't but when you are gone, when I think of how few blessings I can probably ever bring to you, when I am here and you there . . . this feeling of isolation and of wasted days on me, dear lover . . .

It might be that I could love you more truly a ghost walking about and looking on. Ghosts pass swiftly from place to place. I might sit freely beside you, walk beside you in bright fall sunlight.

This, darling, as you know, will all pass away when I can see you again. A man goes from heights to such depths. We pay for moments of joy, of real love.

It is sad to be sad and to feel so useless in the bright sunlight.

1. Quoted from *Mardi,* near the end of chapter 84.

2. The second volume of Vernon L. Parrington's *Main Currents in American Thought* (1927).

3. John C. Calhoun is discussed in Parrington's chapter 2. In a letter the previous day SA explained that "the notion of Calhoun was exactly that of the communists—that a special class be built up—of generous-hearted men devoted to government—Calhoun having his eye on the plantation, slave-owning class and Lenin on the best of the workers."

[Marion, 3 October 1931]

Saturday
Notes for Eleanor

The strikers' songs—seen in cold print—seem particularly not inspiring, don't they.[1] They surely do need their poet, some Bobby Burns of labor.

I can't see anything to it, Eleanor dear. A backward step now, on the part of the women, would be such a betrayal.

We have all been led to believe there is a chance women may stay on the line.

Labor itself is so defeated just now. It is at such a low ebb. To deprive people like you of taking part in the struggle, as at Danville or Paterson,[2] would be deadly.

I myself feel so ineffective. That is one reason I grow so depressed. But, I'm afraid, I'm a bit like Emerson when he faced the abolition issue. He went to walk at night—wanting to be a man like Garrison but realized he couldn't. In the end he had to come back to his desk, in the hope he could there be most effective. I am struck, in reading the book on the Romantic Movement, with the likeness of the situation now to that men faced before the Civil War. Men saw it then. Horace Greeley, invited to go to an abolitionist convention in Cincinnati, refused saying—"When there is such terrible wage slavery here in New York, why should I go to Cincinnati to protest against bond slavery?"[3]

It seems terribly important to me that people like you not be hushed up. When you are fighting that battle I do not blame you when you haven't time to write me.

As regards my cold. I got it foolishly fishing and wading in the cold stream when I was exhausted from work. I stayed too long. Night came on and I got too cold. I was too much fascinated by the changing light on the water.

I went to the house yesterday but your mother was not at home. She had gone to the preacher's house. I talked for a time with your father and then came away.

I tried to work yesterday after the rather dismal letter to you. I am not sure how I came out. If I ever get this book to where I am satisfied at all with it, [it] will have been torn out of me.

Perhaps, dear, I need a stimulant I don't get here. When you are gone I am too much affected by the low, rather self-satisfied, middle-class tone of life here. I try valiantly to get up conversations with men.

They respect me—too much. The town has recently seen my picture in *Time*.[4] In *Liberty* some writer referred to me as one of the intelligent men of America, etc. Half the town must read *Liberty*.

When I try to talk to men it is as though they said—"Let him talk. He is too deep for me, etc." There is a softness to their minds, no hardness.

As regards *PW* to return to it again. We ought to think of it, I fancy, as a shot in the dark. It may come into its own in time.

This industrial thing will not [go] down. It will have to be met. I watch the dailies. All of the plans suggested by the so-called leaders, the American big men, are futile. None of them go deep enough. The best of our leaders now are as ineffectual as Webster finally became.

I think the only hope for me, while I am marooned here, when I cannot, for some obscure reason, give myself in work as I would like to do, is to try to forget myself all I can. I need actual love, felt in the person of another, of you. I can't have it now. I do try, dear, to divert my mind, to get off self and my own struggles and disappointments in this elusive stuff I try to work in.

I went yesterday to a sorghum making. It is amazing how like peasants many of these people are. There was the cane being crushed and the strong, sweet smell of the syrup boiling. I stayed an hour there.

I have still, almost constantly, the feeling of you in a maelstrom out at sea while I walk up and down on a beach, on a deserted island, watching your struggle.

Wanting to come and swim in the sea with you.

Perhaps I'll be allowed next year.

1. EC had sent the songs SA had requested on 15 August (see letter and note 6).
2. Paterson, New Jersey, scene of labor problems in the silk industry.
3. SA is paraphrasing part of a letter by Greeley quoted in Parrington, vol. 2, p. 248.
4. SA's picture was in *Time* 18 (21 September 1931): 55, accompanying a review of *Perhaps Women*.

[Marion, 4 October 1931]

Sunday

Dearest WW

Such a quiet warm day. My mind leaps away from this Sunday to others I have spent with you. On two or three Sundays at least we have been leaving here at about this time together. Places flash up before me. For some reason, all morning I have been thinking of the Sunday when we drove down into what proved to be Randolph County, N.C., and I sang you the song about Naomi Wise.[1] Afterwards we went to a little open place beside the road. Do you remember the brown leaves and the little flowers just coming up through the leaves? There was such sweet love-making there. It was one of our sweetest days.

I constantly have experiences such as you suggest. Something about some woman, a gesture, a way of carrying the head, suggests you. My heart jumps.

I suppose it is true that it doesn't change you. That is why I have such doubts for you sometimes—saddled with me I mean. But companionship, having someone near you love, going out of yourself to the one, does change one. The evidence of that is in your mother. There isn't a doubt that something goes out of her when you are all gone.

I went to her last night after a futile day, a futile week. Found her lying on a couch, the phonograph going, your father gone to the movies. She began to talk of it, how much she had missed real companionship all her life, what she spoke of as her late awakening to a new kind of conception of life etc.

It was really a protest against a middle-class world that becomes so self-satisfied, on the whole so dull. I couldn't help thinking of her young womanhood. What gorgeous possibilities in it.

The restrictions thrown about her, her marriage, the influence of her father, his possession of her mind, associations here, her marriage, restrictions about money. She thinks yours has been the better start in life. She lives a lot in you.

She loves being read to so I read in *The Romantic Revolution,* [John] Taylor, the early agrarian of Virginia, who got things so straight so long ago and saw so clearly what was going to happen to an exploited and exploiting America, and then Daniel Webster.

I read aloud until ten and then came away. Your father had come in and had gone off to bed. He said he went to sleep twice at the movies. I thought: "He must have felt a good deal this thing of life wasting away and slipping away under your hand." The man who feels that perhaps goes off to the movies as a kind of relief as I read books when I cannot work. I consume books, wade through them. What is it all worth? Is it at least laying some foundation for work in the future? I hope that.

My present difficulty seems to be largely a question of nerves a bit out of tune. I have so often, darling, the feeling that if you could just walk across this room or come to me and put your sweet arms about my shoulders . . . I might cry a little . . . something inside would break up. It has happened before. You have always been the one who could do it to me.

The communist girl leaves something out. There is a terrible need to love. There is no God. They have taken God away. There is need of the definite one you love, who is beautiful to you, to go toward, to go into, to be with.

You will know when my nerves are in tune again and I work. It will get into the tone of my letters to you. I am ashamed of their present tone, lover dear.

Your letters are such a relief to me. They are more intimate, sweeter, more full of you than they have ever been before.

I hate the thought of your having to work as you do. I wish I could do the studying for you.[2] It would be something for me when I cannot be with you.

There is a book here, Veblen . . . *The Place of Science in Modern Civilization.*[3] Are you needing it? This morning I am not very manly. I am a child, loving you as a child might love and want for its mother.

[Across margin] If you are in a new room, hadn't you better give me the new room number.

1. An American folk ballad about an actual murder in Randolph County in 1808.

2. EC had begun graduate studies in political economy at Columbia University, where she received her M.A. degree in 1933.

3. Thorstein Veblen's *The Place of Science in Modern Civilisation and Other Essays* (1919).

[Marion, 4 October 1931]

Darling . . . In the afternoon, after trying to work, I went out alone. I did not go to your mother yesterday, the first day I have missed. I thought of you, probably studying most of the day. John was in the shop all day, stretching new canvasses. Bob stayed at the linotype all morning and the afternoon took his Mary on a picnic. They went out to your father's place, by the spring, where we have spoken of some day having a house. In the evening John was at the linotype so the machine clattered away all day.

I went out almost to Shanklin's and turned into the little road that goes up into the hills, just out of town, I think on the Hull land. The road is only open a short way from the highway.[1] It is where the old stone chimney sticks up. You will know. I went just over the first hill from the highway and getting into the field spread out a blanket. I had a book with me.

I think the reason Sundays are so terrible to me is that I have a queer feeling there should be some kind of religious feeling about life in people. Our present Sundays are like bad poetry. There is such a dull heaviness about the pretense of worship. It in some queer way gets into the air. Even the people, intent on money making, on week days are better. I lost sense of its being Sunday or any other particular day out there. I stayed from two until dark. I had a book with me. I didn't read much. There were two horses feeding on a distant hill, not a house in sight. A man came across a field and spoke to me. He said he had just come to this part of the country and didn't know many people. We talked for a time. He goes through the country buying logs and shipping them. He said he and his wife had agreed not to speak any more of the hard times but that it was hard to keep still.

He had been in the South, in Mississippi, and spoke of the Poor Whites. He doesn't think they are any good. "It has gone on too long with them," he thinks. "It would be better if they were destroyed." He went away.

A man walked across a distant field with a woman. She seemed a mere girl while he might have been thirty. They went into a little hollow and stayed there a long time. When they came out he walked along in seeming indifference while she clung to him. They might have been father and daughter although he didn't seem old enough for that.

Two men came along a path, each with a tiny baby in his arms. They walked along with their women following them. The women looked stupid. They were all young.

I lost the sense of Sunday out there. The hours passed in a queer consciousness, just of the fields and the hills and the people coming and going across paths, that seemed, like the horses on the distant hills, all a part of some still, strange world.

The book I read kept talking about men and women. The writer thought that no woman could possibly care for a man when he left her and went off into the world of ideas, into the still, strange world such as the one I had stumbled into. Again in me there was the old desire to be a painter. I think it is because the world of inanimate matter, seeing a little into the heart of nature, the strange beauty of it, the terror of it . . . all of this seems so much less complex, after all, than the world of men.

I did not come back to town until night. I had not taken anything to eat since breakfast but wasn't hungry. I felt better than I have for ten days. Something out there seemed to have touched me, like your touch. As though a soft hand reached up out of the dry grass. I went and got a sandwich and walked awhile. I went by your house but it was dark. Perhaps your father and mother had gone to church. I went over to Frank Copenhaver's and got almost to the door and then turned away. I came home.

John came upstairs from the print shop and we drank beer. That little blue girl I have of Alfred Maurer's[2] seemed suddenly to spring at me out of the wall. John's portrait of himself was all alive. We talked painting. All day I had been in love with you as I am now. It is just a settled feeling that I won't lose you, can't lose you. I mean I can't lose my feeling of love for you. I have never loved before, not in this sense.

I went to bed. Immediately I dreamed of you. You were lying beside a wall, seemingly on a public street, on a sidewalk, but there was no one in the street. I stood over you and looked down. Your legs were drawn up as you draw them up when you sleep but you were not asleep. You smiled up at me, an odd, understanding smile. Your hair was all mussed but it was lovely. Your eyes seemed to understand my mood and your lips to say, "Don't touch me just now. Love me like that." I woke up.

Afterwards in the night I dreamed of you again.

It was deep in. It was hard in. Your eyes had that other lovely look. I had to get out of bed afterwards and walk around. It was hard to bear that you were not actually there. I had to get a book and read. It was hard to get to sleep again.

1. SA was west of town, off U.S. Route 11.

2. Alfred H. Maurer, American artist; in 1924 SA had written an essay for a New York exhibition of Maurer's paintings.

[Marion, 10 October 1931]

I keep snatching another word with you before working, before sinking into sleep at night. If I were with you I should not talk so much.

I take you as dearest friend, closest comrade, beloved. I expect you to be patient with me—knowing what a child I am.

I appeal to mother, friend, lover in you.

If you were here I would touch you instead.

To me you are all women. You are the essence of it all to me.

I don't at all expect to do anything of all I dream. I dream of an ordered world, of beauty understood, of music.

All of the discord and ugliness of life is in me too.

It is only as poet that I am worth anything. It is as poet I must utterly fail.

I forget what I have written to you. I express my moods at the moment. I have faith in your love. I feel free with you. It is a sacred thing, a common thing. It is every day, every hour. I was dead when I began to love you. In my love of you, Eleanor, I live.

[Marion, 11 October 1931]

Sunday morning
Darling—

Up early. The streets are deserted. I keep thinking of other Sunday mornings when I have been able to meet you.

You are evidently right about "Mill Girls." Your mother thought it did what I had wanted it to do—make the picture, so that you sensed and felt the girls.

Scribner's sent it back.

It is amazing how little that sort of thing affects me.

It is amusing though—people thinking I am a successful man . . . young men coming to me.

Everything accomplished is accomplished with such slow pain, dearest, waiting impatiently for the mood—the color not coming right—the innumerable discouragements—the thing you want so hard to get.

I think of Van Gogh, Gauguin, Cézanne—innumerable men who have tried for it.

In the end is the world taught anything? Is it all nonsense?

I can't think so. Again another day, a new try, loneliness.

These other lives—in dreams—the faces of people calling to me—"Try, try." They wanting to be painted, not with sentimentality—as they are—now grey, now red, now yellow—

As the hills and fields call out to me too—my wanting also to be a painter—

Some little bit of something made sacred, Eleanor—dear friend—dear lover—a life, the fragment of a life.

I remember once going to the British Museum—the Elgin Marbles—fragments dug up somewhere—

A few fragments suggesting motion, feelings, hope in humans dead hundreds of years ago.

They standing there—the artist unknown. They are named for a Lord Elgin who dug them up.

This passion to make life come out of itself and live. I can't account for it.

A man measures himself against time, weariness, unbelief, indifference. Often when all the love, all the courage in him is given, he is only cursed for it.

It's the way of things. I don't seem to care. I'm working again. Every moment, when I do not, cannot work, I am wanting you. You and work . . . the two things always desired.

I took what I have done on the new book—a part of *Beyond Desire*—to your mother and read it. I call it "Ethel."

It is another figure trying to come out, a baffled woman who tried to use the boy Red for her own ends—but was a bit too decent to do it in the end.

She seems sharp and alive to me so far. Your mother thought so.

It was an exquisite day here yesterday. I didn't see your father. Your mother is as she is sometimes, gentle and very lovely.

This morning is clear and lovely too. I wonder about you, where you are at this hour—8:30 Sunday morning. Are you just coming out of sleep? I can't make a picture of you in your house.

Another week to be faced without you. It's long, long.

[Marion, 12 October 1931]

Darling—I was so funny yesterday—the two letters. "Mill Girls" came back from *Scribner's* without comment, just the ms., as though they had just thrown it back at my head.

I was working on the new thing[1] and didn't want to be thrown off. So I was silly, compared myself to poor Gauguin, Van Gogh etc. I had really got myself out of the shock of it—as I had thought the thing touched the real life of these girls.

Then in the afternoon an enthusiastic letter came from them. The suggestions they made were all good. It is really written not to stand alone but as a part of a whole. They wanted it centered up a bit. They say, "It gives a picture that has never been given before with such reality."

I presume I did think—from something you said—that it did not hit you. That hurt a lot—because I thought I had caught something of the spirit and the lives of the mill women and I knew you cared about them.

I understand—in the distraction of your life—your always having to write hurriedly, in the midst of meetings etc.—that you can seldom say all you want to say.

I am pretty well pleased about *Perhaps Women.*[2] It will take its place. What I hoped it might do it has done.

The new thing is different—more sophisticated. It may run to 30000 words so don't expect it too soon. I am hoping the Russell thing is off[3] so I may work steadily on it. It is very different from the "Mill Girls."

Your two letters arriving this morning gave me life—"a little touch of Harry in the night."[4]

Too much last night in bed—thoughts of you again, longing. I had to get up and sit reading for an hour.

The Sunday went off. I worked until noon. Funk came and we went in his car to a hill back of the golf course and lay in the sun until four.

I went to Frank & Ruth [Copenhaver] and we all got in the car and went for mushrooms—got a few. We cooked them up and sat talking until ten.

After that the sleeplessness—wanting your presence. In the end I slept without a pill but did dream of you all night.

I talked to your mother on the phone. She said she was O.K. Will see her today. Dearest Wop.

1. "Ethel," book 3 of *Beyond Desire.*

2. Published on 15 September.

3. SA was to debate Bertrand Russell on the issue of the rearing of children—by the family or the state—in New York on 1 November. Despite some uncertainty about arrangements, the debate took place as scheduled, with SA taking the side of the family.

4. At the beginning of act 4 of Shakespeare's *King Henry the Fifth,* Henry visits his troops on the eve of the battle at Agincourt to give them "a little touch of Harry" (l. 47 of the chorus).

[Marion, 18 October 1931]

Sunday

Darling—

Don't worry about the Russell affair. I'll probably come out O.K. It will probably do me good, shake me out of myself.

My general line of attack I think will be this—

The coming of some new kind of socialistic or communistic state is perhaps inevitable. Russell probably—not being an American—doesn't realize our problem here.

Here we have all been brought up with very highly individualistic ideas. There is tremendous emphasis on money. A man has but to read a writer like Mark Twain. Even so short a time ago as Twain's day, having money meant refinement. It was the road to culture, etc.

We are getting somewhat disillusioned about that. Everyone has begun to realize now that that kind of individualism must go.

However the surrender of individualism doesn't mean anything if it doesn't mean an opportunity for the development of a higher, a finer kind of individualism.

As it is, the whole tendency of present-day industrial life is to pour all people into one mold. We do not want that.

As for the family . . . before we begin to institutionalize the child, we had better try to see what can be done with the family under new conditions.

The family should be given a chance after economic fear is taken away. Such men as Russell, instead of giving time and energy to trying to destroy the family, would be serving better in giving all their energy to making the new economic state.

There is the general outline, darling, as I have it in mind. Think about it, dear. If you have any suggestions, make them.[1]

I hope you can come down to Wash. next Sunday. It would be wonderful. Here is what I think I'll do. I'll go over to Maurice on Saturday evening.[2] I have already sent addresses. Maurice, 920 Rhode Island Ave. N.E. I'll stay there until about Wed. I thought I might go somewhere—for two days—to try to pound my ideas into shape—perhaps to Elizabeth [New Jersey]—the same hotel. It would be wonderful if you could come there.

Then I'll go into town about Saturday.

I just called your mother—and she said she felt bully. I am to go spend the evening there. John and I are to spend the afternoon out of doors.

I've been depressed and no good. I'm ashamed of it. I will get over it. So much of it is the constant wish I could be near you.

1. EC seems to have provided him with information on sociological studies supporting his side of the debate.

2. Maurice Long died suddenly on 18 October. Several subsequent letters express SA's shock.

[Marion, 20 October 1931]

Tuesday morning
Dearest sweetest one—

I think the acceptance of Maurice's death has come. I shall quit speaking of it now. It is as though he also had let go a little. There has been something—as though he were constantly here at my elbow saying . . . "I counted on you."

For what?

As in some way we do count on our dearest friend to know some secret unsullied part of us. It may be, darling, that, with us men, when we find that belief in a woman—a belief nothing can shake—we have [the] most a man can have. Maurice didn't have that from a woman, never had had it.

It made him not at his best with women but with men.

In some way, dearest, I do feel I had been faithful to our unspoken love in that—that to me he had always been, underneath all the muddle of his life, business, getting money, his not too nice affairs with women, underneath all this, an odd, talented, generous Irish boy.

A kind of flame deep down in him, burning, burning, like the little light at night in a Catholic church.

All of this as true and real as the other side of him. It was the side of him I always saw. He knew that. Perhaps his haunting me, after death, as he has the day and two nights, was his wanting assurance.

He must have got it. I do now accept the fact that I shall never again see the actuality of him.

As for Dreiser, dearest. When you said he would not come to a meeting—because he was afraid they would ask for money—your not saying it as your own but quoting it . . . there is in the radical group too always this ungenerous thing—jealousy and back-biting. I knew that wasn't true.

I don't know how he is about money. Perhaps his background, the hard years, have left him tight and niggardly. He has been almost terribly honest in his books.

Last night I read his *Dawn*. It is sordid in a way, low keyed. The terrible sentences.

As I read last night I couldn't help think how alike our own early experiences and yet how different.

Nothing sordid happening to him that did not also happen to me.

And yet

I remember coming from an older woman who had without a doubt seduced me. I had gone through it with her. It hadn't been nice—

Exciting in an animal way.

There was something outside of it all that night—stars—the sky—myself dumbly groping.

Dreiser doesn't always get at that—what we so want and need.

Next week somehow in some way I shall be at last seeing you. You are more and more to me.

[Marion, c. 10 December 1931]

Darling—I'll be back at Ethel today. Will go see your mother again this afternoon. Your little note came & made me happy. As I have told you, dear, I have this feeling that we are already bound to each other and will inevitably share with each other all kinds of moods.

It is wonderful how a flash of stark realism can sometimes clear the air. We were speaking of your father. I spoke of the difficulty of being on a give and take friendly basis with him. I spoke of his objections. You said—"Of course he would feel better and safer to have me as an economic asset."

Your saying it thus—in plain terms—was like a flash of light to me. I knew it of course. Did you know it?

When you are a bit sophisticated you can know such things and yet not look down on a man. To think that as a picture of the whole man would be silly of course.

It is a different sort of life, conservative, careful, living in a narrow circle. He has had to spend his life cultivating these small county politicians, Emmett Thomas, Frank Copenhaver, Doc Dave [Buchanan] and others.[1] He has been frightened a lot, fear of poverty, fear of these men too. Every election he has to put up his share . . . a small Tammany Hall.

There is a bit of tragedy back of it that, even with these men, I would have more power now than he has. Why? Because I would be a better poker player—a thing they understand. They know I wouldn't give a damn. They think I would say anything. They know that, no matter what your father might think privately—about some of their methods—he would keep still.

God, how you pay for all that.

I don't quite know whether it is fortunate or not but the truth is that, with all your own people, your relations have already changed. Before, with all of them, there wasn't any very definite notion of where you stood. Now they know. I haven't definitely intended this. Once in a while, in conversation, I have burst out—"What do you think Eleanor is? Where do you think she stands? What do you think she is up to?" I couldn't help it. The sort of half-formed picture of you as a weak little Christian gal, helping little factory girls to say the Lord's Prayer. It was too absurd.

Perhaps all that has been indiscreet.

And there is this other thing. I can't quite make out whether it is fine or foolish of you, dear—the notion, in the family, that it was important that Randolph have fine clothes, a fine position in life etc., same with Mazie and Katharine, but that you did not care for nice things, nice clothes, little lovely things etc. I don't mean they didn't love you. You are the most loved one in the family, except your mother, but there was a touch—as one might love a willing work horse.

Why my dear—if I ever have you as mine, I shall want more than anything to emphasize for you and about you the little nice things. You have so much woman's loveliness.

All the poet in me cries out that all of that side of you shall be fed too. My dear lovely one.

All of this little sermonette. It isn't intended as that. It is just an assertion that, as two people loving each other, we can have our own secret point of view too. My woman.

Now I shall go to work. I feel guilty about the bags. Be sure to wire. Remember I have 2 fine large ones. I guess I'd better just send one of them.

1. Emmett Thomas, Frank Copenhaver, and David Buchanan, a retired physician, were all prominent in the local Democratic party.

[Marion, 30 December 1931]

Note

I really think we should try this. I'll have my divorce—if nothing happens—in Feb. Early in March I go west. I'll be gone until well into April.

I should give you a chance to cut free of me—no letters—none of me at all.

I've been terribly insistent, writing you long letters every day, bringing my life and thoughts into your days.

You should have a time of standing off from me . . . thinking of the whole thing as impersonally as you can.

I'll come home ready to go to Europe. If you decide against me I'll go on . . . I'll stay for a year or two.

If I have luck with my book and have some money and he wants to come I'll invite John over. There will be no particular reason why I should come back to America for two or three years.

I've done about what I can for my kids.[1] They don't need me. Anything I do for John will be done, not for my son, but for an artist.

About New York. I mustn't now any more push myself on you. Maybe I've done too much of it. Do you remember Hugh—the night of his marriage—in *Poor White* . . . his creeping out over the roof to escape . . .

Not because he didn't love. You'll understand, dear. You don't miss things.

The whole point is that we can't have our cake & eat it I guess. You'll have to know soon whether or not you want—not to surrender to me—but to make up your mind whether you want to take your chances sharing with me what life I have to live yet.

1. SA and Bob had signed a contract on 12 December that turned over 14/15 of the assets of the newspapers ($15,000) to Bob, who was to pay John and Mimi $5,000 each by 1940, whereupon SA would sell his remaining share to Bob for $1.

[Marion, 30 December 1931]

Night

I am too much awake just now to sleep. There are things I want to say.

About marriage—it's a gamble of course. How much character I have I don't know. All those who predict disaster for you, if you marry me, may be right.

I have rather a queer feeling—that I have emphasized too much my need of you. I don't want you to marry me to save me from myself.

What I think is this . . . I am a somewhat different man than the man who first began to love and want you. I can work in a sustained way again—a lot of the self-pity has gone out of me.

You have done all this for me. I know that. If you decide not to marry me, you perhaps will have given me, during these three years of loving me a little, the guts to stand up and take the blow.

I have realized all the time I might not get you—I presume.

There is even a kind of program. I'll get out of here. The place is too full of memories of you.

I don't know what I'd do . . . try to work. I ought to have ten or fifteen years of work yet. I'm a man of talent. I know that. My talent should ripen.

I cannot conceive of ever loving any other woman. I do not believe I ever before knew what it meant to love a woman. But that is my story. I do not want you to marry me, dear Eleanor, unless you can be satisfied that, of all men, you would rather have me as your man. There is this to be said of those women who are so dead sure they would never marry me. There isn't a one of them that would ever have the chance.

Morning

An alive night again. I like them. I slept until two, got up, walked about the room, had a cigarette, thought some more then got back into bed. I really must be nicer in these lovely pajamas.

Thinking—I have had my hopes dashed before.

Still all related to you and the necessity, it seems, now soon, of putting it up to you.

I'm sorry.

I mean, dear, that some of the most delicate work I've done has not yet registered really, perhaps never will.

And that all of this new conception of a relationship with a woman I have been building up these three years . . . it changing all the time . . . it may not mean to you what it does to me.

You are hardly in the position of a woman stuck in a small town, in uninteresting work.

You won't even be in a bad position—the woman who turned S.A. down. They'll say—"He sure deserved it."

You ought to think of all the background of your own life. If it will be more interesting, alive, absorbing without me, you should not marry me.

That other thing you were a little afraid of—Channing & Mazie. I'm not Channing. You must remember that my absorption is different. It involves all my emotions . . . exhausts them at times. I don't want anyone to get my breakfast, mend my shirts etc. I've always attended to that and will. I'm much more likely to be awake and running to get your breakfast.

I want a play fellow, a work fellow . . . a lover.

I can tell you what will be hard. I sag terribly but, when I am rested, I begin again. I am terrible. I never get enough of anything, never love enough, work enough. I want everything, absolute beauty, perfection.

I've tempered that impulse a little in myself. I'm a little more reasonable, even with myself. I'm even a little more of a good workman. I only mean to say that most people . . . women too . . . want to stop. They want to get to a quiet place and rest there. I wear them out I guess.

If I could say all I feel. I can't.

I'm grateful, grateful. I do not want to go into a marriage that isn't fine for both of us any more than you do, dear.

I mean what I have said to you. If you decide against me, you will owe me nothing.

You found me defeated, I thought done for. Your whole family has had something to do with carrying me through. Your house has been a place to come, to feel people. Your mother has been wonderful.

All those drives with you . . . a new sense of earth . . . work again . . . lovely days remembered.

You have all helped to make me rich again.

You mustn't feel any obligation for any, what you may think of as, implied promises . . . my own need. You have paid your way with me every inch, owe me nothing.

I just want you to feel free of me in making up your mind. If you can't get free, all right. You're mine then.

[New York, 10 January 1932]

I think, dear, my sadness this morning was partly Fred's death.[1] He was a man with something of Maurice's flair for life (they would have loved each other)—the same vividness—love of life, people . . . a rare and beautiful story teller—his story telling, by word of mouth, always far richer than his writing.

He knew it.

He came and talked sadly to me about it several times.

"I haven't kept the faith."

He knew what it was. He wanted money, riches, travel, wine, clothes, houses. "We're all whores," he told me.

The last time I saw him was in New Orleans. He came and stayed a week with me.

I remember a Sunday morning on the docks at New Orleans the day before he left. Men, like men and women, get tender about each other. We talked of our two worlds.

His a world of travel, seas, ships, brown men, yellow men . . . far distant places.

Mine little towns, streets, cities, factories—

There was, I remember that morning, dear, a queer mutual feeling of mutual inadequacy.

It might have been the brown river flowing past in the sunlight that morning—making us both seem small.

Fred haunting me this morning, as Maurice did after he died. I'll have to go out and see people this evening. I'd better. Lover. I wish it were going to be—just touching my arm with your dear hand.

1. Frederick O'Brien, journalist, lecturer, and author of *White Shadows in the South Seas* (1920), who died on 9 January. SA included the *New York Times* obituary with the letter.

[New York, 17 January 1932]

Darling—I had left my glasses at Paul [Rosenfeld]'s. Got up on the elevated platform before I discovered it—had to walk back.

The young man who came in last was there & walked up with me to 23rd St. I did not like him much.

I was full of you. Came to my room here but could not sleep. Later in the night I did sleep and, after daylight, slept until 11.

Lying in bed last night—thinking of you. Besides you Mrs. [Edmund] Wilson was the only woman there I liked much. I would get out of patience with the very naive Walkers.[1]

Thinking about our marriage, lying in bed—wanting you here to talk. It seems like this to me, dear. How shall I say?

When I am with married people—so often—there is something they do to each other, about each other. Mrs. Walker did it several times . . .

little digs at her husband . . . as though to say . . . "There he is . . . he is so and so . . . well, he's my husband."

As though also to say—"I might have done better."

At any rate we are mature I guess—if we are ever going to be.

I think that—if we marry—you should always be . . . in company and out of company . . . dearer to me than any human being. I shouldn't care who knows it.

Once last evening Wilson got up and went across the room to his wife. He sat holding her hand a moment. I loved them both intensely at the moment.

Life is so difficult at best. Why, I even think there is where 1st classness really lies. If someone would make a new marriage ceremony—saying, "This one I take—to make it the purpose of my life to make as many as possible of her (or his) hours pleasant and fruitful."

I have never had patience with those who have big showy virtues etc. but growl and fuss and grumble their ways through life. Once I said to Cornelia—"Why—as long as you live with me—do you seem to work to make hours in the house disagreeable and unpleasant?" She and Elizabeth always did that. They said—"I am disagreeable to those I love." They both said that.

Intimacy meaning that—the privilege of being disagreeable.

I used to wonder. There would be a disagreeable scene. Then a guest came in. Smiles—pleasant talk.

"If you could so get control of yourself when that stranger came in, why not before?"

It is terribly important to me. I think I am as you are. I am not living to make a reputation for posterity or to get to Heaven—but for every precious hour of life. You give me such precious ones.

As last night . . . sitting there in that room.

In another world it is as precious as when you give your body to me.

I think there is the possibility of the lover in me. When beauty comes thus—winging—and lights on you, I want always to be aware. I want to feel, see, be alive. I want you always to be willing to be beautiful. That's why I love you so. You are willing. I want this kind of secret pact with you. We two—we are trying something.

When it grows difficult we will try to say so—coming to each other . . . "It's getting difficult for me."

Like a ship that has got stranded—two pairs of hands trying anyway to get it afloat again.

It is so much more important to me than big virtues. I tell you this because I got stranded on these rocks before.

I don't believe we will. I am willing to try so hard to be a good sailor with you—lover.

1. Adelaide and Charles Rumford Walker, who were active in labor organizations.

[February? 1932]

Dear One—I have again been, for two or three days, in a curiously depressed state. It was odd to come across, in Mill, a chapter in which he speaks of just such a time.[1]

It has been with me I believe as it was with him, with a difference of course. I wish I could define it for you, dear. It might help me to do it.

I think he, as a young man, must have depended a great deal on a kind of intellectual conception of some kind of good end toward which he thought he could help men to go. Do you remember when one day he began to question that? Everything suddenly fell away.

I think with me it has been the same but for a different reason. I reacted bitterly against all my early life.

Art opened out before me. There was sensual pleasure in that. I've been thinking, dear. I would like to be honest with myself. I think I must have had women as a kind of reinforcement to art.

The art also was to be "my art." I never did drop that notion. I wonder if I only wanted these women to be emotional channels for me.

Did I only want to use them? One by one they accused me of that.

Did I finally realize it was true? Has my long depression been due to that?

Did I come to feel that I could not love for another's good—wanting another to help me find [a] channel for my own emotions—not to help them find it for themselves?

I think it must be true. I have these terrible questioning times about you . . . not about my love for you . . . but about its purity in this real sense.

I think you ought to help me all you can, dear. You are sharp and critical too. If you feel falseness in me, tell me. If you feel the other, tell me.

It has got to the place now I think where I am healthy when I am with you but often, when I am not with you, doubts attack me. The doubts take all of the life out of me, all the spirit. It isn't, dear, a question of loving you. It is a simple question of being able to really love.

When I am near you all this goes away. I feel such health, such reality in life. That is why I am always wanting to sleep near you. It seems such a crime sometimes that we can't have daily, and nightly, hour by hour, closeness.

To get all this clear.

I think I am coming to feel—not as I used to that all depends on production, production—but that all depends on my feeling about you . . . that all I shall have of life will depend upon that.

1. Probably chapter 5, "A Crisis in My Mental History," of John Stuart Mill's *Autobiography* (1873).

[Marion, 6 February 1932]

Saturday

Dearest Woman—lover—It was a queer lonely night. Why are the nights so much the worse? Is it because, every night for so long, I have thought about you?

Again I try the little trick of having imaginary conversations with you.

I awoke at 2 wide awake. I read a story of Balzac's.

The little valentine, by Stein, I sent you the other day is from this month's *Golden Book*.[1]

I have about $1100.00 in [the] bank here and $200 owed me yet by Leigh[2]—$1300. I'll start west with nearly 1200 and should make at least $1500 clear.

When it comes to Russia I'm all for doing our own thing over there, in our own way.

We'll begin by not trying to do anything big. We'll go to the factories. The man at Washington suggested that we go off to the seashore with one of the groups of Russian workers sent on vacation, have the vacation with them.[3]

It's odd the queer effect, darling, of living just where I do here, looking out my two windows to the [J. C.] Campbell house, the [R. G.] Goolsby house, the [Blaine] Richardson and B. F. Buchanan houses.[4]

The houses sit there fat in the morning, telling me things. They come up out of the night. You are lucky, darling, having come out of that charming house you did come out of.

I think so often of your girlhood, regretfully—that I did not know you, wasn't your boyhood sweetheart.

Your mother and I talked. She thought perhaps there never could be real understanding between men and women—she herself understood women—her daughters—better than her husband and son, etc.

I wondered. You yourself do not seem so dominantly feminine, dear, although sometimes I want you to be. Sometimes I want you to be soft in my hands, yielding.

You seem to be sometimes.

Mostly comrade, though, darling.

I was awake at six, lying in bed, the window up, looking at the day breaking over the hills—a very soft, rich light.

Some days the whole world seems to float in unreality. This will be such a day. A week ago today we walked and were on the river and I was very happy walking with you in the ferry house at Weehawken [New Jersey].

The sweet hours you have given your lover.

A charming letter from a factory hand of 23–about *Perhaps Women*. He said it was all something he had wanted said, etc. I am so near the divorce that I refuse longer to destroy your letters.[5]

1. "A Valentine to Sherwood Anderson from Gertrude Stein," *Golden Book Magazine* 15 (February 1932): 100.

2. Leigh Lecture Bureau.

3. On 31 January SA had gone to the Soviet embassy in Washington, D.C., to discuss a possible trip to Russia.

4. Bob and Mary Anderson had taken over the printshop apartment after their marriage on 18 December 1931, and SA had moved into an upstairs room at the Onyx C. Sprinkle house, which was close to Rosemont and some of the other imposing houses in that section of the town.

5. His divorce from Elizabeth Prall was granted on 22 February. None of her letters prior to that date and only a few after it have survived.

[Marion, 2 March 1932]

Wednesday

Dear Woman—I slept hard, worked all morning and went to court in the afternoon. I will be leaving here a week from Friday for Detroit. That will be the 11th. Your ring is found. Your mother left last night. It is warm, like early April.

In court, a young boy with a rather nice face. He went up on a hill back of the hospital with a girl. She became pregnant.

In such cases, if you get the girl to do it by promising marriage and if she is until that moment a virgin—it is seduction—a felony—carrying a sentence of from 2 to 10 years. The boy seemed rather nice. Pat Collins[1] handled his case. He did not put the boy on the stand.

That was probably a mistake. There was testimony that she had been with other men. The witnesses weren't however very reputable. These cases become curiously dramatic. It was evident that the boy was determined he would not marry her. He was sore.

On the other hand, if she had been fond of him she now hated him. She sat there, big with a babe in her, swearing him away to the penitentiary. He was sent for two years.

There is a thing about the jury system, very interesting. Although so many of the cases tried come from among the poor, there are no poor men on the jury list. They are all solid men—upper middle class.

So, you see, there is a boy, only 18, made into a penitentiary bird. I went out of the place really wanting to cry.

I am thinking of you as perhaps in the desert now. The town here seems terrifically empty. I have made a cut on Mr. Sullivan at Ripshin. I really had to. He has so little to do. He has really been over paid.

Later—it rained in the night. This morning the sun came out then went and hid itself. I've been reading again Turgenev—the Sportsman Sketches. How I love them. They are like low fine music to me.

It's a queer life, being a writer. You think, "Am I any good? What use do I serve?" Sometimes you are so sure of yourself, so egotistical, and then, an hour later, you want to crawl.

You see anyone doing anything and you think—"There he is, being a merchant, or a judge, or a farmer. He amounts to something."

I stood before the court house, talking to two men, old Squire Farris and Sam Zimmerman—a Jewish merchant. They both agree life has gone all wrong.

The Squire said, "Once there was a man came here for the day from Wytheville. He had scarce got off the train when suddenly there rushed up to him a man & paid a $20 bill. It had a corner torn off.

"So he took it & spent it. It was spent ten times that day, $200 spent, debts paid. At night he was going home and a man paid him the same bill. It had a corner torn off."

"So you think, if we would all get money from the bank, begin to pass it around, good times would come again?"

"Yes."

We talked of Russia. Sam Zimmerman says, "It is good, a good country. I have a nephew there. He does well, splendidly. He likes the new government. He writes enthusiastic letters but it will not work."

"Why?"

"Because, you see, it is socialistic. It isn't the style. It is different. It is out of style. It won't work."

I love you. I'm lonesome.

1. L. Preston ("Pat") Collins was a Marion attorney, later lieutenant governor of Virginia.

[Marion, 3 March 1932]

Thursday

Darling—Your note came from N[ew] O[rleans] after crossing the Mississippi. I have sent off letters every day to S.F.[1] by air mail so you will have some when you get there. You should have given me a Pasadena address.

This Lindbergh baby affair here turned out to be one of the most vulgar, most cruel affairs imaginable. Here were these poor people with their baby.[2] They were in one of those cold little cabins in a tourist camp—about 3 miles east of town. All evening the road was filled with cars flying out there. The camp was surrounded by a mob of people.

At last they all went to bed leaving the poor people to sleep. Then at 3 A.M. Crockett Gwynn[3] went fantod. He sent officers up there, roused the people out and brought them down & threw them into jail.

Then this morning—such a procession—a thousand women rushing to the jail to look at the poor people. The poor working man has become suddenly a felon. Fat old middle class town women shaking heads. "He looks bad to me. If it isn't Lindbergh's baby, I bet he stole it." What a civilization, dear. Indeed it needs a shaking. It makes you sick at the thought of being a human being.[4]

I am still unable to get just the feeling and movement I need for Red.[5] I have stopped pressing. In the afternoon I went to Funk's house and helped him trim his grape vines. We worked for an hour or two and it begin to rain. Funk, myself and an old workman Funk calls his secretary went into the cellar where we sat drinking wine. I went to Frank [Copenhaver]'s to dine.

I was walking on the rr tracks in the rain when a powerfully built workman stopped me. "How's Dresser?" he asked. He meant Dreiser. "Well," he said, "I read your speech about him in N.Y."[6]

"What about it?" I said.

"Well," he said, "I knew you had the brains. I did not think you had the nerve."

It is an occasional little incident of this sort that makes you think, after all, that there may be hope that there is material for revolution here. A man gets, must of necessity get, so much of the middle class viewpoint. They can conceive of a civilization not founded on possessions as they conceive of their Heaven—or Christianity—something outside actuality—sometimes to be talked of—as not practical.

As though the present civilization was at all practical.

I think, dear, this present thing hurts all of us. There is something deadly in the air. For example, there is, in the paper this week, a call to the republican convention to assemble delegates to renominate Hoover. Funk is the republican chairman. He will make a speech.

I spoke to him, "Funk, you are not a republican. You do not believe in Hoover, the tariff, any of the things the party stands for."

"No."

"Yet you will get up there. You will get off that old falsehood." It made him a bit uncomfortable but he will nevertheless do it.

I think it is this appalling thing in men that is so paralyzing to our life now. There is a kind of terrible sickness of the spirit. I do believe, dear, that it is this thing in the air that is so paralyzing to all of us now.

You must be nearing the Pacific. The ride up from Los Angeles to San Francisco is lovely really. How I wish I were with you, lover.

1. EC was on her way to San Francisco, where she was to conduct a ten-week study of women's working conditions.

2. The people were suspected of being the kidnappers of the Lindbergh baby.

3. The mayor.

4. SA reported in another letter on the same day that the parents "took it all good naturedly—seemed even a little flattered."

5. Red Oliver in *Beyond Desire*.

6. SA spoke in support of Dreiser in New York on 6 December 1931 at a "Harlan Terror Mass Meeting" called by the National Committee for the Defense of Political Prisoners, which was headed by Dreiser.

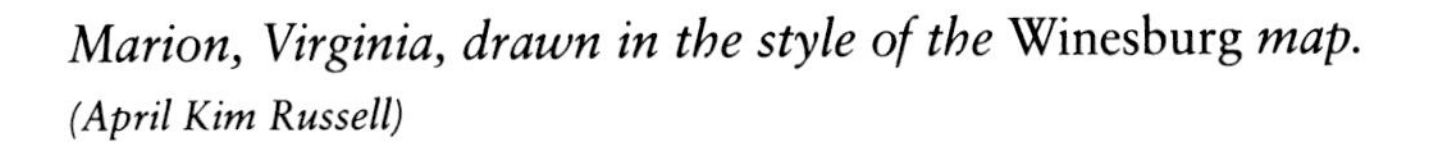

Marion, Virginia, drawn in the style of the Winesburg *map.*
(April Kim Russell)

Sherwood Anderson in front of the printshop about 1928.
His apartment was upstairs.
(Sherwood Anderson Anderson Literary Estate Trust)

Ripshin, Sherwood Anderson's home near Troutdale, Virginia.
(Sherwood Anderson Literary Estate Trust)

Rosemont, the B. E. Copenhaver residence in Marion, Virginia.
(Sherwood Anderson Literary Estate Trust)

B. E. Copenhaver, Eleanor Anderson's father.
(Sherwood Anderson Literary Estate Trust)

Laura Lu Copenhaver, Eleanor Anderson's mother.
(Sherwood Anderson Literary Estate Trust)

Eleanor Copenhaver in the mid-1920s.
(Sherwood Anderson Literary Estate Trust)

Sherwood Anderson in San Francisco, summer 1932.
(Sherwood Anderson Literary Estate Trust)

Eleanor Anderson.
(Sherwood Anderson Literary Estate Trust)

Eleanor Anderson at Ripshin.
(Sherwood Anderson Literary Estate Trust)

In the driveway at Rosemont in 1940. Left to right: B. E. Copenhaver, May Scherer, Sherwood Anderson (in car), Laura Lu Copenhaver, Katharine Van Meier, Eleanor Anderson, Randolph Copenhaver.
(By permission of the Newberry Library)

Eleanor and Sherwood Anderson at Rosemont in 1940.
(Sherwood Anderson Literary Estate Trust)

Sherwood Anderson in Marion, 1940.
(Sherwood Anderson Literary Estate Trust)

At Ripshin in 1940, from left around table: Eleanor Anderson, Sherwood Anderson, Katharine Van Meier, B. E. Copenhaver, Laura Lu Copenhaver, Katharine Wilson.
(By permission of the Newberry Library)

The dining room at Rosemont in 1940. From left around table: B. E. Copenhaver, Randolph Copenhaver, May Scherer, Mazie Wilson, Eleanor Wilson, Laura Lu Copenhaver, Katharine Van Meier, Sherwood Anderson, Eleanor Anderson, Henry Van Meier.
(By permission of the Newberry Library)

Sherwood Anderson at the front porch of Rosemont, 3 January 1941.
(Walter Sanders, Black Star)

Sherwood Anderson in the foyer at Rosemont, 3 January 1941. The portrait to the right is of Laura Lu Copenhaver, who had died on 18 December 1940.
(Walter Sanders, Black Star)

Eleanor and Sherwood Anderson as they boarded the Santa Lucia, *28 February 1941.*

(Sherwood Anderson Literary Estate Trust)

[On train in Ohio,[1] 12 March 1932]

Saturday morning

Darling—Your note of yesterday I carried with me on the train as far as Columbus, figuring it would get directly into the western air mail there. It turned colder during the night. I have just had my breakfast. I shivered in my berth. I awoke, demanded another blanket & felt more comfortable. There were only 2 other passengers in the day coach, Marion to Roanoke, and there are only 3 others this morning—Roanoke to Detroit. I think I can get a sleeper tonight, Detroit to Chicago, after I speak and can stay in Chicago Sunday & Monday. If I miss any letters from you I'll leave forwarding address.

I speak in Tucson, Ariz. on the 23rd and do not have to be in Salt Lake City until the 28th. I've an idea I can stay in Santa Fe two days—the 25th and 26th of March. Put it down—DeVargas Hotel, March 25th, 26th.

I imagine Nick [Carter] will be on hand to hear me in Chicago—the 17th. I have engaged 2 single rooms and am having Mimi down to the hotel to stay with me the 17, 18, 19th. At any rate, whether they like it or not, I am going to say a good deal to the advertising men about the social implications of what they are doing. Also in Detroit.

We are in a dead flat section of Ohio as I write, more like the country around Chicago than the country I knew as a boy. There you would find soft stepping little hills and gullies. There were many beech forests, the trees with soft grey trunks. Here, in this section, the central Ohio plain, there is another thing—the horizon—always a mystery, as it is about Chicago. This morning all the little ponds and rivers are frozen over and you can see the marks of skates where boys have been skating. It is in this country, not I'm sure 25 miles from where I sit on the train writing, that I was born—at Camden, Ohio—a tiny village I imagine, where my father once had a harness shop.

I have been reading again Turgenev—*A Sportsman's Sketches*. It is such lovely, quiet, assured prose, darling. I've been thinking . . . I wonder . . .

He was a land-owning aristocrat. He lived about half his life in Paris, half on the Russian steppes. There must have been a kind of sureness. I am quite sure he went off hunting primarily to be with common people. He was a tall, bearded, broad-shouldered man—I'm sure with a kindly eye. He slept in little peasant huts and in stables. I am sure all writers want that close touch with common people but perhaps then the terrible injustice of life did not seem so blatant and apparent as it does to us.

Perhaps he could be quieter inside, not always being hurt as we are. How else can you account for the smooth grandeur of his prose?

Don't forget to have me tell you the story of John and the car. It's nice. I love you.

1. SA was on his way to Detroit to begin his lecture tour.

Chicago, [13 March 1932]

Sunday morning

Darling—After writing you yesterday at Detroit a young newspaper man came running into my room & said they were holding the funeral of the workers shot at the Ford plant. It was a communist hunger demonstration march, got up by Foster,[1] although he was not in it. 3000 paraded through the streets. Dearborn, as you perhaps know, is a separate corporation. They marched out there and when they got to the Dearborn town limits the police were drawn up across the road. They began using gas but the wind blew it away so they began to shoot. The crowd threw stones. Four marchers were killed.

The liberal mayor, however, allowed a huge communist funeral parade which I saw. They carried striking banners—"Down with the Ford terror," etc.

There were many banners that spoke of the speed up—of its speeding all the life out of men etc.

My own speech was queer.[2] I've an idea—after they engaged me—then all this communist agitation sprang up. The manager of the lectures had hurried home from Florida. He got me in a room & tried to get me to give him an outline of my talk in advance. I wouldn't.

We went ahead. He introduced me as briefly as possible & then went & sat in front with the pres. of the club—a man named [Herbert B.] Trix.

Trix turned out to be a rather good sort.

They were both nervous, however, and sat glumly there. A lecture is an odd thing, dear. You become an actor. With the same groups of words you can be cynical, threatening, optimistic or pessimistic. I made it as serious as I could.

The long poem on the automobile at the end, however, got them. I think they were all relieved really that I didn't shoot or anything.

You see, my Dreiser speech in NY and other things had come since they engaged me.

After the meeting the pres. & his wife & two or three more intelligent men of the club took me in a room. We had drinks and talked frankly and in a very friendly way. He was much more a man than the rather craven lecture manager & said he was glad they had got me, that a change had to come & that some of the rich needed straight talk etc.

I felt glad, however, to get it over as I hate unfriendliness.

I am seeing Mimi this afternoon & she and Ferdinand [Schevill] will go to supper with me. It is very cold. I was a fool not to figure out that I would be here today—as I might have had a letter. I'll go to Evansville tomorrow.[3] Gee, I'm loving my little wop.

By the enclosed you will see there is also trouble here.[4]

1. William Z. Foster, a leader in the American Communist party and presidential candidate in 1924, 1928, and 1932.

2. SA spoke on 12 March at the Detroit Athletic Club.

3. SA was to speak in Evansville, Indiana.

4. A reference to a disturbance following a political protest on Michigan Avenue in Chicago, in which five people were hurt.

[Salt Lake City, 28 March 1932]

Darling—It is evening (Monday) and I am all dressed and waiting for the man to come and take me for my first lecture here.

Black sox O.K. Coat full of moth holes, but they don't show at night. One or two of them did gape open so that white showed through, but I darned them with black thread found in a hotel room.

There is one more lecture put in at Los Angeles which will make 6 there—next week.

I worked a lot today—saw the Mormon museum, the Mormon Temple & Brigham Young's Beehive[1]—where he had 19 wives under one roof. I call that being a damn hog, don't you?

Just the same, he had one with a big grand house of her own—called "Amelia's Palace"[2]—just across the street from the Beehive. She was, of course, his favorite and I presume he didn't dare keep her over there for fear one of the 19 would poison her. It must have been the gay life.

An English professor—from Ohio—from near my own birthplace (not a Mormon) came this P.M. and drove me up on a mountain 11000 feet—to where you could see the whole valley here, Great Salt Lake, etc. stretched out before you.

There is a big Catholic college here and one of the nuns, a Ph.D. by the way—University of California—and the best known woman Catholic poet is at the head of it.[3] (Sounds rather like best writer in the taxi industry, doesn't it?) However, we went up to call on her and she proved to be rather witty, alive and good looking. Eleanor, I hope for the sake of the salvation of her soul I'm mistaken—I rather thought she gave me the eye.

She told me how much she loved my works and I wanted to say—"Did you read *Many Marriages*?" but didn't. There goes the phone. He's here. Just at the page end too.

1. Young's official residence.

2. Named after Young's twenty-fifth wife, Amelia Folsom.

3. Sister M. Madeleva Wolff, head of the College of St. Mary of the Wasatch, which closed in 1959.

[San Francisco, 11 April 1932]

Darling—

I find I cannot really write much of the two days[1]—in my notes—just a few high spots to remind you some day. It may be I only write these notes knowing that the chances are ten to one you will live far beyond me. I am a hopeless egoist. I want to live on in you then.

The thing I feel deeply today is that we must, must, believe in our love. The two days were a kind of testimony from the gods of the poets—as though the gods had said—"If after these two days you cannot believe, then you are no poet and no woman."

For the two days with you I would have given my life. What memories they have left, chief of all you under the oak at the edge of the orchard sunning your lovely gracious body, so full always for me of hillsides, earth, flowers, soft, rich smells.

If we can doubt now that love is the great gift, we are hopeless. For what we had alone in the two days I would so gladly go through again all my blunders—and yes—(it's a terrible word but true) my suffering.

Never for one moment think I have ever before known such love as I give you, darling.

1. SA arrived in San Francisco on the ninth, and he and EC spent the next two days together driving through the San Joaquin valley.

[On train,[1] 14 April 1932]

Darling—

What I want to say about what just came up this morning I should say. As you know, darling, since I have known you, I have been trying to return to something a long time lost. You have helped me in that more than any other woman ever did.

I always did have the capacity for making money and have it now. I could begin making money tomorrow. I could make enough to take away all fear for your father and mother. I could get on a train this afternoon, go to Hollywood, show them things I saw when I was down there. I could convince them in an hour that they would be ahead paying me $1000 a week.

Of course, I won't. I have come to feel this—that if someone gave me $50,000 outright tomorrow I would at once give it all to the revolution.

For myself I actually want to be and stay on the edge. As long as millions of other men and women are living as they do—and will—I do actually think there is a kind of ill health in being safe or wanting to be safe.

You see, dear, it's like this. I don't want you, except as wife. Something has been growing in me lately—the determination—hardening in me—to devote the rest of my life to the revolution. I think it's time. I do not intend to go into the communist party for the simple reason that I think the communist party in America is too Russian. I think there has to grow up a new kind of American communist now, out of American life. I think I have the background for it.

I really am, dear, proletarian at heart. I have had such experiences. The Prall family here for example.[2] Where did they get their money, their respectable safety? They got it out of the patent medicine business.

Then they became a professional family—with pretensions about family blood—daring to be ashamed of me because I wasn't respectable. Elizabeth always stayed half on the fence. She never did come to me, backing me in an inner sense, in my inner life.

I think all these things—her failure to really go with what might have been her man, your father's present position, the present position of thousands of middle class American men, now frightened, worried, upset, is all a part of a dirty evil in the world that men have got to begin to fight.

I don't think Americans are any more cowardly than other people. I only think they are more confused. I think even Dreiser and men like that are only expressing confusion now.

What I am trying to say, dear, is that I don't want you to come with me unless you come all the way. I think there is a certain talent, a certain ability in me. I have passed, or am passing, through a great confusion. I am trying to see clearly. One of my weaknesses now is that I see so much, feel so much, so much has come upon me so fast that I am no more the simple man who wrote *Winesburg, Poor White* and *Many Marriages*. Everything in me is more diffused, confused. I have to try to learn to think out of a new confusion.

I think it is going to help to accept fully a belief . . . as a man would accept a religion. I want to accept belief in a revolution in America, an American revolution, in that way.

Just as your father accepts a future life—in Heaven—I want to accept a future life on earth—live the rest of my own life for it, think for it, work for it, with my talent, with my head, with my feeling.

Never forgetting it, never giving it up any more while I live.

The point is, dear, that I am not going to take you in any half way. I have done that with other women—my need of warm, physical, personal love being so great . . . it blinds me at times . . .

I don't want, with you, as with the others, to have the wreck come later. Better now . . . no matter what it costs.

There isn't any question. You can go on being a social worker . . . you can play it safer for yourself and your father and mother and Randolph. It will never be safe, I'm afraid, with me.

With me it's like this . . . by some odd chance I have escaped something. Being on the edge of it a thousand times—I never have really sold my talent into slavery. I remain a figure in America. Underneath all this talk about my failure with women etc. I am something to young talent in America. I am more to them than any living American man. I do carry a banner for them. They all know it. They are all conscious of it. I have a chance I think also to carry some of the talent in America toward the revolutionary impulse.

Perhaps all this seems egotism. It isn't. It's my artist's manhood. You, my dear, or any woman taking me only as a man, aren't going to get much. I've been through too many emotional battles, have been to the wars too long to have much left.

The whole bet, if there is a bet for you, is on the poet and if you are going to be my woman you have to take that elusive, always getting lost poet as the first thing in the world for you too.

It's that poet, the white running boy of "The Book of the Grotesque," who gets hurt when you say casually you have to throw him overboard because an old school teacher in Virginia needs you more. I can't help it. It's that way. You see what I mean. It wasn't just your casual remark. It was that it seemed to me that, having got this letter from your mother, your first impulse was to feel guilty because you loved me.

I don't want you to feel guilty. I want you to be proud, being my lover, being the lover of the poet in me.

1. SA was on his way to Portland, Oregon, where he was to speak on the fifteenth.

2. Elizabeth Prall Anderson's family lived in Berkeley, California.

[Portland, Oregon, 15 April 1932]

Darling—

I am writing you at once, on getting in at 8. I find that I do not get into S.F. on Sunday morning until about 10.[1]

I'm a bit ashamed of the letter of yesterday—too much SA again. Well, don't mind it, darling. That chestiness in me will always be popping out.

We came, almost all day, through a country not unlike the long valley we drove through—down by the immortal Patterson[2]—last Sat. & Sunday . . . gorgeous color, whole fields of the yellow poppies. There were two interesting brakemen on the train—one literary who discussed Eugene O'Neill and the other an incipient communist. Also a big Russian with a beard and a rather cruel mouth who kept writing in a notebook.

At three o'clock we began getting into hills, all bare and wrinkled. The brakeman told me they had once been wooded but that the fumes from copper smelters killed all vegetation. It was a copper country. Now they do not let them release the poisonous fumes and growth is beginning again. Besides most of the mines are abandoned.

We followed the Sacramento River until dark.

In the night once I woke up and we were in the mountain tops with 5 or 6 feet of snow beside the train.

I had rather let down after all the tenseness I had felt in SF and I suppose the emotional thing—seeing again my dear lover—after so long. I felt weak and queer & do this morning but am O.K. It will pass.

Up here it is early spring and all the fruit trees are in bloom. I love you.

Until Sunday—my lover.

1. I.e., he was to return to San Francisco on the seventeenth.

2. Their trip the previous week had centered on Patterson, a small town near Modesto.

[Columbus, Ohio, 22 May 1932]

Darling—I haven't been able to find Ferdinand.[1] There was only a boy at the University switchboard Sunday evening and he knew nothing. I got the names of 2 history professors but they were not at home. University Club N.G.

I have been taking a walk—sad that this party is at an end—it has been so lovely—paticularly San Francisco.

I have come to the above hotel[2] to bring my notes up to date—a memory haunted place. I came here as a young soldier boy—as a young business man. Restless nights wandering about here. More than one evening sitting perhaps in this same writing room.

I wonder what I hoped then, dear, what I dreamed.

There must have been nights of lust here. They came frequently, driving me to walk restless perhaps half the night—looking at women hopefully.

I don't believe I wanted ever to just lie with one of them as you know I never have with you.

I was so stupid today trying to say what I wanted and know I don't deserve—wanting it the more hungrily because I know I don't deserve it.

Perhaps, dear, I want in myself a dignity and maturity I don't deserve. I become so frightfully a kid—resent so when I am not loved. I guess I want to feel that you are my woman, my woman, laughing at me when I'm foolish, lifting me up a little when I go down, down.

That's all dear and you do it so wonderfully. As today, when I felt you warm toward me, love coming out of you toward me, all the dark evil thoughts went away and I was warmly happy.

You know when it happens to me, dear, must know, as all the world becomes at once livable again.

Perhaps there is a deeper story told by the present physical aspects of a town like this now than by volumes written. I walked quite a long way. It seemed to me, dear, that I felt a very loosening and slump in the bricks of factory walls. The advertisements seem to shout without belief in the words shouted. The town was very dirty—something rather sad and dead in people met.

The feeling always in you that everything is at pause, old gods dead, no new gods born yet.

I cannot, cannot, dear, feel that there is any advantage to you in me but for every moment you can love me or feel warm toward me I will be as grateful as any man could be to a woman he loves.

1. Ferdinand Schevill, who was a visiting professor of history at Ohio State University during the spring quarter.

2. The Chittenden Hotel.

[Marion, c. 25 May 1932]

I started to write an amusing satirical piece on the subject of marriage with me—to amuse you—but it wasn't funny.

Up to now the whole question to marry or not to marry—between us—has been put up to you.

It is rather unfair.

As I have been lying here, for these two or three days, ill, I have been trying to be a bit realistic. I have been balancing—or rather trying to measure—my own chances against the world.

How good are they?

Certainly they are not very good.

Would I be handicapped in my work by marriage with you? I ask this because I know you ask it.

No.

The record of my work since I have had you shows that I have worked better.

But it has brought me less.

That is largely due to circumstances. It is no time for men like myself. In a disturbed time of transition such as ours, the artist is out of place. Things shift and change too fast for him. A few generations ago a man like myself—with the bulk of work I have put behind me—the influence

I have had on writing etc.—would have been a national figure. I am not. In such a time of transition there is too much restless hunting for the new—the right note. The world cannot stop to measure the whole bulk of any man's work. More subtle things become unimportant.

If you were just a little, rather meaningless female thing—to help me on the physical side of my life, mend my sox, keep house for me, lie with me at night.

You are so much more than this.

With me out of the way you can be more. Really the present, with things disturbed as they are, is an opportunity for one like yourself. You are pretty shrewd and canny. You have what few people have—a mind. You already have what is needed, a good deal of ground work laid in economics—and in experience. Your field is going to grow more and more important now.

You ought really to shake yourself out of a kind of laziness you have. (I may have brought that on you. I have confused your life more than it ever was confused.) What we think of as your mental laziness will probably go away with me out of the picture. I ought to get out. I rather think that this present illness of mine has been brought on trying to face this fact.

You are not like any of the other women I have had. You have more importance in yourself—outside me. You do not need me.

Even physically you do not need me as I do you. It is probably because I am more quick to express myself physically, have always done it more. If I had got you as a younger woman, you would be more like me in this.

What I am afraid of now is that my clinging to you, insisting on my need of you, is just another expression of the individualist egocentric me . . . that ought to be put away now if it can be.

I do think that I can be a help to you if you want to go ahead now, get away from me, stay by your organization, build yourself up. Perhaps I can learn to love in a new way. I don't know. I can try.

I really think that just now—with a little fire of purpose built under you—you can make yourself more important to the world than I can . . . and I have to face the fact that marriage with me will handicap you in that as it won't me. We ought, I suppose, to do what is most important.

Why, I know, dear, there is another side to you—the just woman side, very precious and lovely—you ought to know how lovely it is to me.

I will feel that sometimes I have let that live a little.

As for my own road.

It is confused. At my best—as poet and story teller, I presume I have been able a little to release people. I even dare think that sometimes I have been able to do that for you more than anyone else ever did. There was an odd combination—the mature woman in mind with the immature girl in body. It's gone. You are much more a complete and real woman.

I suppose I can't do this anymore, physically, with any other woman. I won't be wanting other women after you.

The other side of it—to try to be content to go along—do what work I can—put up with my loneliness—go through my blue times and work times.

Do you suppose I might get some happiness out of the thought that I played square with you—stopped trying to seduce you into something that wasn't right for you?

I suppose it ought to be definite—a physical parting. I'll try to go through with the thing down there this summer—with people about. I'll try not to make any long-range plans. Everything may well go to the bow wows by fall.

[Marion, 6 June 1932]

I have been trying to put down a little in my notebook[1] these days my feeling about my relationship to you—a thing you wouldn't need to do but which is as necessary as breathing to me.

I'm thinking that, at last perhaps, dear, all my inner defeats and beatings have at last whipped something into me a little so that I can see you and love you not even wanting you to feel as I do about things or follow me in anything.

You seem very lovely & still inside these days.

I keep thinking about your marrying me. I mean it when I say I can't see any advantage to you in it.

I'm not a fool and I know that we will have delicious hours & days.

But I know the risk—

For example the risk of fading out of power of mind and spirit in me—the thing that must come of course—as fall comes after summer.

Or your having to think about my health and be careful for me. All that.

I have a queer feeling—that if the new thing that must be born into the world now—if the new generation were actually springing up . . . if it were of your generation—then you should find a lover in that.

I think sometimes that what I can do, if anything yet, is to furnish a kind of mental and spiritual seed bed. You'll know what I mean.

Sometimes I think that if I had the courage to be sure—if I do begin to slip and be just a hulk of a man going about—if I could be sure I could know when the hour of the end of my usefulness had struck—so that I could take the hulk that might be left—

An old man perhaps like the pictures of those old wrinkle-necked men in the pictures of *Winesburg*.

If I could take that off somewhere into a quiet wood or on a lake—

A shot perhaps—like an old horse that can no longer plow.

The difficulty is that I'm not sure I'll know when the time is.

It's dread of saddling you, dear you I love so, with that—keeps me so fearful sometimes of letting you take the chances with me.

1. The journal that he kept throughout 1932, called "a letter a day" for EC.

[Marion, 19 June 1932]

Sunday 12:15 P.M.

Darling—I was really disappointed not to receive a note from you today—yesterday one of about 12 words. It is really inconceivable to me that you can't get time (I suppose because I scribble so naturally on all occasions). Again I get the feeling that—if it is all a matter of time—you can't possibly be able to look at all the long letters I send you & that I do wrong to bother you with them—

But when you are gone I miss you so bitterly & letters are a sort of cord between us—to me anyway.

I have got all but the last chapter of Red down and I think rather beautifully. I sent off a great packet of stuff to you today. I feel a bit guilty about it but perhaps at King's Mountain you will not be too busy for your lonely man.[1]

It has rained all morning—gray and warm. I am however going to the farm with the Funks.

There is a little scene in a barn—Red lying in the loft above—a woman milking in the light of a lantern down below—he looking down through an opening in the barn loft . . . her hands on the teats of the cow, in the circle cast by the light.[2]

I think it's nice. I think you will be liking all this.

It is doing what I like most to do—a glamour over the so-called "commonplace."

You must know how I am always writing—when I write—with the sense of you at my shoulder—earth in you—rains and all growing things.

You also in the ink bottle & in the pen.

One reason I sent you Roger Sergel's letter[3] was because it expressed so what I felt when you came along—and in me—and of me—I want so to think—

My own loneliness and isolation too that you broke up.

It does return sometimes when I do not hear from you or when you tell me no—or so few—details of your days.

You can't think they are not of importance—to your lover.

1. EC was going from Camp Merrie-Woode to King's Mountain, North Carolina.

2. *Beyond Desire*, pp. 311–12.

3. Sergel had written on 15 June about the separation of people, observing: "I have today more *things* than I ever had, am solvent, out of debt, yet lonelier & more discontented than I have ever been." He adds, "You are one of the few men I know who seem to me to be *alive*. I couldn't name another."

[Washington, D.C., 10 August 1932]

Wednesday

Darling . . . I hate having you miss days like this. There was Cohen, Waldo Frank, Rorty and a negro editor from Baltimore.[1]

A letter had already been sent to Hoover & he had replied—through a secretary—that he could not see us but we went at once to the White House and made a demand. We were kept waiting for an hour. Newspaper men flocked about. Three or four of them knew me personally from old days in Chicago. They were all personally sympathetic.

At last we saw one of Mr. Hoover's secretaries[2] who told us again that we could not be seen. A newspaper man had slipped us a list of his appointments. (It was his birthday.) There was the head of a big steamship company who brought him a cake, some movie people, some children who recited a little poem—some insurance men etc.

The secretary led us into a big room. The odd thing is that he was pale and upset. There were several politicians sitting about. The secretary said he was not speaking for Mr. Hoover, or [but?] in his capacity as a citizen and a fellow writer. He said he had been a writer for 25 years. It was gaudy. His voice actually trembled. Waldo and I were protesting. We wanted Hoover etc. The man began to read from a typed statement.

A lot of communists and disorderly characters, etc. had taken advantage of the soldiers being here to become disorderly. They attacked the police. The citizens of Wash. appealed to the president. It is a president's duty to maintain order, etc.

"But aren't we as important as these people Mr. Hoover is seeing?"

"He will not see you."

We went out to give our story to the waiting crowd of newspaper men.

That was that. It was rather gaudy. We had apparently scared them.

I got my passport in 10 minutes. Three newspaper men went with me to the state department & made them put it through at once. I am running to the boat now.[3] I can't phone. I wired.

I love you.

S

1. Elliot E. Cohen was secretary of the National Committee for the Defense of Political Prisoners; James Rorty was a poet from Westport, Connecticut; the "negro editor" was William Jones of the *Baltimore Afro-American*. They had all gone with SA to the White House to protest President Hoover's treatment of the veterans' "bonus army." SA subsequently wrote an open letter to Hoover, "Listen Mr. President," *Nation* 135 (31 August 1932): 191–93.

2. Theodore G. Joslin.

3. SA was about to leave to attend the World's Congress Against War, which was to meet in Brussels on 27–29 August; the site was later changed to Amsterdam.

[At sea, 18 August 1932]

Thursday

Darling—I think I will only try to put down little notes. First—when you had to leave like that—suddenly—I knew but it hurt.[1]

The evening went off. We nearly missed the boat. We are 3rd class but it is about the same as the all one class boats I have sailed on in the past.

They have given me a large room with an open window out to sea. There is a big writing room, a swimming pool etc. The crowd is all working class—A.F. of L., a negro,[2] socialists, a woman representative of the Amer-Lithuanian Society,[3] a Dana from New England[4] etc.

The meeting has been switched suddenly from Brussels to Amsterdam. I understand there is a big general strike on in Brussels. I will go to London after the conference & come home by Southampton. I think my ticket is good on any Cunarder. I am loving you very much. I go about thinking of being to sea with you later. Have been offered 1st class passage but will stick with this crowd. I like them. In the excitement forgot to tell Miss Z[5] not to release anything about the divorce. I'm afraid she will. I must have seemed terribly helpless to you last night, darling.

Sat. Aug. 20. It turned cold and there was a blow but it has cleared again. Much cooler. I haven't yet entirely recovered from the last strenuous week. I have begun now to think of you as at home. I will mail this running letter on the boat to be sent ashore at Southampton.

We land at Cherbourg—and go through Paris to Amsterdam. Perhaps we will have a half day in Paris and if we do I shall spend it taking these two working women about the city—the little Jewess[6] & the Lithuanian woman—

The Lithuanian woman is the interesting one. She is quite beautiful. She began working in a cotton mill at 13 and at 17 married a cotton mill worker. She is just Doris of the book.[7] She had one child that was sickly and so took it to the hospital and left it at the waiting room. Then she went out & phoned the big surgeon of the place saying, "The child will die if I keep it. Cure it or kill it."

The doctors got interested and the child was made well.

I gave her the book to read and she came to me with eyes shining. "I would never have believed anyone could know how we feel," she said. It has been a fine test of the book.

1. EC had come to see him off.

2. Joseph Gardner, a worker and army veteran from Chicago.

3. Sonia Kaross, representing the Lithuanian Working Women's Alliance.

4. Harry Wadsworth Longfellow Dana, grandson of Henry Wadsworth Longfellow and Richard Henry Dana.

5. Probably Leane Zugsmith, a novelist with Liveright who wrote some press releases for SA at the time. The reference is to SA's divorce from Elizabeth Prall.

6. Belle G. Taub, assistant secretary of the American Committee for the World Congress Against War.

7. Doris Hoffman, a mill worker known for her strength in *Beyond Desire*.

[At sea, 21 August 1932]

Sunday

Darling—This is the 1st morning I have felt really rested. We are to have a peace meeting aboard ship today at 2 at which I am to speak.

One of our party is Harry Wadsworth Longfellow Dana, a New England blue blood but a real fellow. I like him. I think I can get passage out of Liverpool on the *Scythia* on Sept. 3 and still have a day or two in London. The meeting will be over at least by the 31st and Amsterdam is only 6 hours from London.

The weather continues fine. I miss you every hour of every day. I wonder if you feel as queerly separated from a part of yourself as I do.

Tuesday Aug. 23.

Darling—The sea is like a quiet pond. It has been so cold that we sleep with blankets. We now pass ships every hour and by night will see land. I will mail this at Cherbourg. We get off the boat there early in the morning Wed. and go up to Paris. Should be in Paris by noon and I hope can stop over for the afternoon. I would like to get a Fiat and take some of these workers about the city.

I begin to understand better your life. We have meetings every afternoon but they have been good for me. I listen. Dana really knows the international mixup fairly well—has been a great deal to Europe and lately much in Russia. There is a rather roughneck lawyer named Brodsky.[1] I saw him at that luncheon at the New School[2] sometime in Dec. or Jan. and took a strong dislike to him. Now I have come to like him. He is an old labor fighter and really gentle underneath his bluster. Dana is all culture but unafraid and fine.

The negro is our surprise man, with real intelligence coupled with the natural negro ability to speak. His speeches are loaded with negro life & negro poetry.

We have a red haired sailor of the fighting type but he is also sensitive.[3] Yesterday he managed to get into the forecastle of this ship and spent the afternoon with the English sailors. He is from what is usually called a good family in the South, from Alexandria, La.—a sugar raising family of planters—ran off to sea etc. He has acquired his own kind of education and it would be shocking to many southerners to see the real friendship between him and the black man Gardner. They bunk together.

I have been sad these last two days, dear—I think because I cannot escape the constant longing for you. I have come to want you with me in everything.

I will be writing again from Paris. I love you.
My love to everyone at home.

1. Joseph Brodsky, chief lawyer of the International Labor Defense.
2. The New School for Social Research in New York.
3. James McFarland.

[Paris, 25 August 1932]

Thursday—I am up early to write to you, darling. It is after 8 and we take a train at nine for Amsterdam. There are two sides to this thing—a certain amount of excitement & amusement out of this group of people and also this going about Europe with all officialdom suspicious. When we got here there was some question as to our getting into Holland at all and, as it is, I am sure the Russians will not get in. Although Romain Rolland[1] sent out the call for the meeting, the communists are given credit for doing it. It may be true—I don't know. I think there are not more than 3 real party people in our group.

They are all very nice to me but I do, whenever I am alone, become sad, thinking of the quiet drives about Marion—you there—the porch at night etc. I am given a separate room in the hotel[2]—this I rather insist on—even though I have to pay for it out of my own pocket. They have so little money to go on. I dare say the trip must cost me at least $100.00 out of my own pocket.

My arrangements are made. I sail on the *Scythia*—from Liverpool on the 3rd, arriving in New York on the 11th.[3] Perhaps I had better cable you. Today will be rather a hard day—with 12 hours to be put in on a 3rd class train—with some uncertainty about getting in. We may be stopped at Brussels. Over 600 are going in from France.

Darling, I love you very much and when I am separated from you feel that all the best of me is lost. O dear woman.

1. French author, musicologist, and leader of pacifist causes. He was chairman of the International Committee of the World Congress Against War.
2. Hotel Fournet.
3. As it turned out, he landed in Boston on 14 September.

[Amsterdam, 26 August 1932]

Friday

The fine weather holds. Roth[1] fell in the canal. I go everywhere with Joe [Brodsky], who is a bit crude and noisy but arranges everything.

We went to the public library, a large quiet place, to find Waldie Van Eck, my Dutch translator, but she had gone off to England. We went wandering along tree-lined streets and sat in sidewalk cafes in little clean squares drinking brandy & coffee. The people drift past by thousands on bicycles. Without Eleanor I feel constantly that I have lost my mate—the other 1/2 of me. Everywhere I go I want her.

Saturday—Again it was such a day for me as you must have seen many of. We went from meeting to meeting. The big press meeting was in the late afternoon—Barbusse[2] was in charge. There are conflicting reports about Rolland. He has cancer of the intestines. It is touch and go whether he can come. Gorki[3] is in Germany and will probably not be in. I went to the big press conference and when my name was mentioned I think you would have been pleased. The journalists of Europe are much more likely than our own to be scholars. They are nearly all doctors. There was a sudden murmur at the press table. They kept getting up one by one to shake my hand. I stayed at the meeting but a few minutes and when I left a German, a Lettish & a Hollander came running after me down the stairs. They said many nice things in broken English. "You are one who has helped me to understand America better. You have made me like your people, etc." It was very nice.

Barbusse is long & lean and too verbose. He talks beautiful French, everyone says, but too much of it. There are also three very verbose and, I'm afraid, stupid Indians. One who was president of the Indian Nat'l Congress is the most stupid.[4] He will talk of nothing but his hatred of England.

I am made one of a ruling group of 100 to run the convention. I dare say I shall have to speak. The convention opens today at 1 and if Rolland is too ill to get here his speech will be read. [George Bernard] Shaw and [H. G.] Wells have not come. The French and Germans will be here in a mass. They will far outnumber all the others.

There are also many doctors. One yesterday made a talk saying the next war would be one of poison gas. I like the tone of the meetings so far. I talked to some of the leaders. The plan is to let the workers do most of the talking. I am loving you.

1. Joseph G. Roth, a machinist from Ithaca, New York.
2. Henri Barbusse, French author and journalist.
3. Maxim Gorki, Russian author and playwright.
4. Vallabhbhai Patel.

[Amsterdam, 27 August 1932]

Saturday night

Darling—Your letter (the 1st) came at last. The congress opened today in a great hall here packed to the door. I should say it is about 1/2 & 1/2 communists & non-communists like myself. The meeting is dominated by the French and German, as it should be, they having each several hundred delegates. Our American delegation numbered at the last about 30. None of us have spoken yet—except the Scottsboro woman Mrs. Wright[1]—after all a very charmingly simple negro woman. Apparently all the fuss made about her all over Europe has not spoiled her. She has the real negro laugh. Of course, she is having a gaudy time with everywhere crowds about her, flowers, & money for the defense.

The intellectuals have as yet not come off well. Barbusse is a bit thin, a long, lean, very excitable & nervous Frenchman. I thought Romain Rolland's long letter flowery & tiresome. Tonight as I write an old Chinese revolutionist is speaking.

The hall is crowded. The great thing is the sense of youth and life. They sing gorgeously, making the very rafters shake. I have been approached by people of all nations—they are very sweet. They speak to me of *Winesburg*, of *Poor White*, of *A Story Teller's Story*. Already word of the new novel[2] seems to have crept over Europe. Already the Dutch and French ask for the privilege of translation. A man came from the University of Leyden. It is very sweet, very satisfying—as they all seem so very very intelligent—to know what I have been driving at in my books.

I have refused to be on committees that go about passing resolutions etc. It is better to wander about, get the sense of it all, talk to individuals. Nearly everyone, darling, has some English. I feel very very stupid. I cannot help them.

The whole Russian delegation is shut out.[3]

I am to speak tomorrow—for American writers, but will speak very very briefly. There have been too many intellectuals & writers speaking. Harry Dana speaks tonight. The negro Gardner speaks with me tomorrow. After each speech a translator redelivers the speech in the other languages—voices sounding from all over the hall. It is half a bedlam. I have crept away to write this to you—my lover. I love you.

I did not give you an English address because I have not known when I would be there or where. It is too late now. I sail on the Cunarder *Scythia* on Sep. 3, landing in N.Y. on the 11th. I hope, dear woman, you will have had your talk with Lucy.[4] I hope you may be in N.Y. and that you can go home with me. I hope you may be ready to go to R[ussia] with me by Oct. 10th. I love you.

1. Ada Wright, mother of two of the defendants in the Scottsboro, Alabama, rape case.

2. *Beyond Desire.*

3. The Russians were barred from entering Holland by the Dutch government.

4. EC was to discuss with Lucy Carner the possibility of marrying SA.

[Amsterdam, 28 August 1932]

Sunday—I am writing you at noon. Sunday—in the big hall—in a bedlam. This is the big day. I am to speak sometime during the day. It is a bedlam. Outside, in the streets, marching bodies of communists & socialist youths. It is insufferably hot. These Europeans have no wish for fresh air. The hall is wonderful. I get so many impressions that I am wrecked emotionally. After all, my dear, these workers have something. The intellectuals have shown up but poorly against them. They speak briefly and with great fire. Yesterday the intellectuals were predominant. Today the labor men speak. I have never been in a worse bedlam, and then suddenly out of it all emerges some little old French peasant or an Italian boy and suddenly it is all galvanized into order.

I weep, darling, that you are not here. I do not want to have experiences without you.

[Amsterdam, 29 August 1932]

Darling—Monday—I am again writing from the rostrum of the congress. Speakers are crowding up. The chairman is surrounded by hundreds struggling forward wanting to speak. I have not spoken. I am in an odd position. It seems to me more important that workers speak but the English and Americans here clamor for me to speak, hoping even a few words may get some play in newspapers. It is probably all folly. The newspapers will no doubt utterly play down the congress—which is nevertheless a vast success.

I have spoken—only 1 minute 2 minutes—to say that in America the fight now was all for the imaginations, the minds of men & women in America.

[On train, 31 August 1932]

Wednesday
Darling—I am on the train—Amsterdam to London, by Flushing & Harwich, and expect to be in London about 9 tonight. In Amsterdam it is the queen's birthday and crowds are flocking into the city—many peasants in their native costumes. It is rather too bad to leave.

A sweet letter came from you—the 2nd. I'm afraid I shall miss some. I left word for forwarding.

I have left the party. Only big fat Joe Brodsky is with me.

Yesterday—in the morning, I went with a native Hollander to the plant of the big social-democrat newspaper here, a huge plant and the most modern and beautiful I ever saw. I was carried away by its perfection, beauty and cleanliness and stayed all morning, going from room to room. It was breathtaking.

Barbusse and the others wanted me to go to Paris to serve on a permanent proletarian peace bureau. In the congress I must say I did, darling, keep myself in the background, not because I am so modest but because I prefer it so & get more. Harry Dana pushed himself forward, being very ambitious. He did not even introduce me to Barbusse & Barbusse had to come & seek me out.

Then later, when the congress was about over, the newspapers began to come in from France & Germany and newspaper men from Russia began to get wires to see me. The situation was amusing. Our own crowd were all resentful of Dana's attitude. Of course I am not going to take the place he so wanted but now I doubt if he will get it—(the train has started).

I have not written you enough about the city & its beauty—I went yesterday to the Rijks Museum to see a special Rembrandt show—very fine—and got some fine Rembrandt reproductions for

John. The ship models also were gorgeous. In the evening I went out with some Holland literary people, who had come to the hotel with me.

I feel grand starting toward you at last. Darling, I love you.

[At sea], 3 September [1932]

Saturday

Darling—Just a word—to try & have some sort of contact with you. I am wondering if you know yet that I am sailing today—will you be in NY when I arrive.

It is bitter cold. We left Liverpool in a sleet storm at 1 P.M. I am sharing my room with a stolid looking Englishman named Jones. At table I am to sit with two quite attractive women from Ohio. One of them knows Karl.[1] They were in my train compartment coming down from London. I am loving you and O so eager to see you, darling.

Sunday—Sep. 4—We have just left Queenstown. The sea is quieter. I have slept a lot. I stood for a long time last night watching the sea and the gulls flying after the ship.

Rest in me . . . thinking of you too . . . saying to myself . . . "I want her." Thinking I ought to make it clearer if I can.

It isn't marriage—don't give a damn for that—

Nor children—that to be your own thing—if you want it. It hasn't much to do with my maleness. I grow more male thinking.

Possibilities of disaster for us together. I know that too.

I look at the sea thinking my own thoughts aside from you—my own mysticism—

As though the sea had made me say to myself—"Are you, Sherwood, afraid of death?"

Death being like the sea, cruel, quiet, raging, changing, endless. If I can say "no," I can go on living. That's the contradiction.

Wanting you for my loneliness, my apartness—that is the strongest thing in me but that always hurts and hurts.

You are the only one that makes it quit hurting. That's all I know.

1. Karl Anderson, SA's brother, an artist.

[At sea], 9 September 1932

Friday Sep. 9—Dearest One. We are in a heavy fog & have been all night—feeling our way through the Newfoundland Banks—the fog horn going all night. It was a day—yesterday—and an evening and a night full of you. Sense of you about everywhere—as though all day I could pass, by some miracle, through a door or a wall and find you. It kept up all day and night and I still feel it.

Sat. Sep. 10—'32. A gorgeous day. There are plenty of quite pretty women aboard & one—a cabin passenger, a slender blonde—has a yen for me. People tend to get intimate in this close, huddled life so I walked with her and we had some frank laughing talk. She was a man-hunter wanting excitement. She didn't tempt me. I passed it off in playfulness.

The positions of the man and woman in such a case are reversed. The woman is presumed to be reluctant, the man bold. I see no reason why a man also should not keep himself to himself.

Sunday Sep. 11. We were to have been in Boston today but we are still far out, 200 to 300 miles, and in the grip of a great storm. I am afraid I will not be at home to see you, darling, on my birthday. I do not know whether you are in NY or in Marion.

The storm is the most magnificent I have ever seen with waves like the hills at home, often the ship seeming about to dive down into the sea. I stayed out all day hanging to the rail, fascinated. Last night I was as tired as though I had been in a fight. Often the waves washed clear over the 3rd class deck forward—the water rail high. I am terribly hungry for the sight of you—my lover—but it may be 3 or 4 days yet.

Monday Sep. 12. We should have landed in Boston yesterday and in NY today but, because of the great storm, will not be in Boston until tomorrow—my birthday.

I had I presume what you would call a temptation. It was the woman Mildred—who on Saturday night got ginned up and got a man to come with her from the cabin (1st class) and wanted me to go with her. I sent her packing but yesterday in the afternoon, as I felt guilty having been rude, I went to call. I went to her cabin and knocked and, after asking who it was, [she] said come in. I went in & she was in bed so I sat down. She was lying there in bed, a rather shapely blonde, and told me in so many words I could have her. I admit I was aroused—the animal in me. "Get up & dress," I said and she did. She has had a flock of men at her heels, being hot for it like dogs after a bitch in heat. I made her dress and we went out. She had determined upon me because I didn't want her and was hurt, thinking it a lack of charm in herself etc. I tried to explain to her that I had my own male self-respect too etc. but doubt if she understood. I mull all this over as a writer does. It's unimportant. I love you. Had I taken her, I would have felt very unclean today. I sat talking with her and realized she was just a rather twisted child and so left her but am glad to have had the experience because now at least I know that I am not the casual man I was before I met and loved you.

I wish I knew where you are.

[Marion, 24 September 1932]

Saturday
Darling—

There is one thing sure in me this morning—Saturday. The book isn't going to go.[1]

To have it go at all there would have to be in people a wide acceptance of some new world. There isn't that, no acceptance yet of the thing as inevitable, no willingness yet to accept responsibility for it, try to go with it.

I have tried, as you know, to catch if even faintly some new music of a new world—

In which the factory is accepted as a part of all life.

It might be—perhaps some day will be—a place to which we will all go—accepting thus, all of us, the responsibility of feeding and clothing these masses of people.

The point will be missed—that all of this is a plea in song for acceptance—acceptance.

They won't take it because they won't want to.

I've watched—Mimi, John, Bob, your mother—all of us. They are perhaps right. The whole picture may be too somber yet.

We are all children in the face of a terrible thing. Lankes writes this morning. He is sure mankind is done for. "We can't make it. We can't make it," he cries.

I will be blamed for having dared to try to throw the doors of the factories open even a little.

They don't want to go in there.

"What, go in with that outcast crew?"

The book will be dismissed quickly, forgotten as soon as possible.

The adjustment, when it comes, will be slow and cruel and ugly I'm afraid.

You will see what Hansen says.[2] I'll show you. A quick dismissal.

Always a woman.

A cheap fling really. I'm a man in the modern world. The puzzle of it all is on me. I have turned to woman after woman saying—"Be my comrade." I have turned to men saying it. Have I been too bold, too daring? The fragment of a man. This morning I feel like saying—Eleanor—my love—flee from me.

I am afraid I will bring you only defeats.

I am afraid no precious hour I can give you can pay you for sharing with me in my defeats.

I love you though.

1. *Beyond Desire* was published on 19 September.

2. Harry Hansen reviewed *Beyond Desire* in the *New York Herald-Telegram*, 19 September, p. 23.

[Marion, 25 September 1932]

Dear Eleanor—I guess I had better cut out. I have waited two days, tensely, for the result of your interview with Lucy—thinking of course you would have a real interview and tell her everything and then decide.[1]

After the two days I got only a brief letter from you saying only that you were more uncertain than ever, wanted another interview with her and hadn't had a real talk with her at all. It is doing me up too much, dear. I can't go on with it.

Perhaps it is impossible for you to be more direct and final. You have many things pulling at you. The whole tone of everything is against me and perhaps they are right.

I don't know what I'll do. The idea of facing this loneliness the rest of my days is unbearable but there never has been the frank straight acceptance of me—with all my faults on my head—that would give me the happy freedom I need with you and perhaps there can't be.

I think you are more attached to your family than you know. In your heart you know that they would all be more comfortable if I had never shown my head. I do not believe you would leave either your father or mother as you have left me here—not at all realizing what you are doing.

I think now you ought to say, frankly and directly, whether you will marry me or not and when. Everyone in the world has been consulted now. More talk would not make anything clearer between us. Your mother, father, Randolph, Mazie, Katharine, Lois [MacDonald] and Lucy [Carner] have all been consulted. I have never consulted anyone and don't intend to. I do not believe it is a matter that can be settled in conference. It is you and me that have to do the living together.

My dear, I have always gone on the plan of living first and consulting the economics of things later—when I was compelled to. It has got me into some bad tight holes but I have lived until now after this plan and I shall go on.

Certainly—my dear woman—I respect your desire not to be economically dependent on me but there are two sides to that too. A man—even the man who must live the uncertain, precarious life of the artists—likes to feel that his woman will take a chance with him. I do not believe you have quite the right—no one has—to decide for me whether or not it may hurt me too much to have to go to work for my woman.

And in this matter too, dear, I have, as you know, tried to clear the boards. I have made a definite settlement on my children—giving them all the economic security they have a right to expect. I think I have done enough for them. I suppose and I think have a right to suppose that I can support my woman.

As for going on without marriage—in our society—I simply won't do that to you. As I have thought for a long time now that, before this, I would have definite word from you, I have not pretended to anyone that I didn't want you.

I have known all along that it would come to this moment between us so I have always left you an out, dear. Bad as I may be, I do not believe that any woman need be ashamed of the simple fact that I am in love with her and always, from the beginning, I have let it be known that I was the one committed to you and that you were not committed to me.

Now, if your doubts are too strong for you to go ahead, I promise you that I shall always let anyone interested know that you are the one who refused me. I can't deny my love and wanting for you.

What I propose now, dear, is this. Read this letter and take an hour or a day or a week to decide. Please, dear, don't do any more consulting with anyone. Then, if you will have me as your man, for the rest of our days (or my days), for better or worse, come what may, say so and when—by wire please, dear.

If not I'll cut out. Everything I need to do here can be done in a few days. I'll make it as easy as I can for you by staying out of sight. I know it will be a basic shock for you too, a long hard time to go through, and I'll stay in Europe until you have time to adjust yourself, through work or another love.

I've been tense and bitterly lonely ever since you left and will be until I hear from you.

The uncertainty has gone on too long, dear.

I think I have a right now to ask—yes or no?

When?

If it is to be, don't put it off, dear.

We'll do what we have to do together afterwards.

I'll not write any more. You say the word now, Eleanor.

If it turns out that you want to marry me now and want also to hold the job—and can hold it—I'll gladly give up the Russian trip—altogether if necessary—

Or put it off.

I'd be glad to go out to Kansas City to be with you while you work there.[2]

I'm not going to join the communists or depend on them.

1. See letter of 27 August and note 4.

2. EC was scheduled to go to Kansas City, Missouri, in November to conduct a study of labor conditions there; because of her illness, the trip was postponed until January 1933.

[Marion, 26 September 1932]

Monday

It is still morning—now late morning. I have already written to you twice. I have worked a little, in a fragmentary way. Bob came in to tell me that the NY *Times* review of the book was unfavorable.[1] I cannot get you out of my mind.

I walked twice down Main Street thinking. It is a cold bleak day. I thought—if this thing happens to me—as now seems likely—perhaps I shall go on working anyway.

This union of two people . . . if we had been able to do it long ago . . . before I so muddied my life in other people's minds. It didn't happen.

If I could get the feeling . . . this is what happens to people in life.

That man there . . . it happened to him.

That woman . . . it happened to her.

If I could get a new tenderness—and sustain it . . . pride and arrogance gone.

Always to know that you didn't want to do it . . . didn't do it. I did it . . . long ago, before you knew me.

As though I had secretly killed someone long ago and now it came out—

A man in jail, or a rich man, or a man to be hung.

To merge it into a kind of general tenderness.

If I didn't want so—physically—the touch of your hands, your lips and your breasts. I so want you to know that you have given me more than I ever had before or ever hoped to have. I do want you not to be hurt.

Miss Belle[2] brought me a dish with some ripe tomatoes & salt—to eat in my room.

I have spoken to no one of my own particular dark garden I have been living in since you went away except to Miss May. When I had written you the rather arrogant letter saying, "Decide, decide," I went to drive & there was Miss May in the street so I picked her up. I told her a little of my feeling—my uncertainty, fear etc. Then this morning she called me and I went there. We sat and talked plainly for a half hour. I think she made me understand her love for you and that, frankly, she wasn't much concerned about what happened to me. Oddly enough I liked that. It didn't hurt, rather pleased me.

I think, dear, that a man might eventually get to that place—a final and absolute giving up of the notion that he is to have personal love or that there is any reason to expect it.

It would be easier going today if the sun would shine. I presume you went to Washington. No letter came from you in the late morning mail. I was with Frank & Ruth yesterday and had a little feeling all day that they liked me a little and even had something like tenderness for me.

Perhaps a man can get these little fragments of feeling from people and live by them.

There is strength in a phrase—in maliciousness. I keep saying to myself . . . it helps me oddly in what I am trying to build up . . . some kind of inner foundation for a life without you . . . "Fourth wife of Henry the Eighth."

Night—steady rain.

I managed to work a little and then went out. Your father was in Washington & I knew I wouldn't meet him there so I went to the mountain farm—where the blind woman is, where we have picnicked often by the spring. I walked clear back beyond the broken-down house where we found the mushrooms. It was a little like being near you. The hills were lovely. I stopped in the little broken house and stood there.

It began to rain hard. I had left the car in that place where we turn around in the lane. The rain seemed good—I got soaking. The whole little inner valley in there seemed full of you.

I have got boxes and am having Grace[3] pack books. I had enough so that I could take what I wanted and still leave plenty for Bob's house and John's house. Whatever happens I'll have to put them away.

I've had a queer feeling all day of the soil here, the Killingers[4] & Copenhavers—all kinds of people in the families—the soil in them and in you . . .

Even though you have been so much in the cities. As you know, I always have visions when I make love to you—of the out of doors, of hills and fields—as though the very blood of your earth people came into me through you.

I haven't given up hoping that it will be but have convinced myself that, for you, it shouldn't be.

I saw stones sticking out of the ground and remembered when I wrote about the farm girl pregnant and how the stones in a field became to her the heads of buried children.[5]

Tuesday morning—

I slept—this time without dope—an exhausted sleep. I read until midnight in the Harlan miners book[6]—to keep from thinking. It was raining steadily. I dreamed of people fighting with the captain on a ship in a storm.

I keep saying over and over to myself—"She shouldn't she shouldn't." It isn't hard to convince myself you shouldn't. I go with all of them on that.

What is hard is to convince myself I can get ahold of life again now without you. That's my side of it. I tell myself that you can really take hold of your work again and do it better than ever. You have told me yourself—a lot of times—how you took hold of it better and did it better before I came along to distract you from it. Distractions, things to do, help. They say everything wears out in time. I suppose it does.

I figure this—that at bottom I guess you don't want to. I haven't any right to decide anything like that but I take little indications—as they seem to me.

It's a part of something. I've taken too many risks in the past. I guess I've had a side all the time but I've given the other side too many guns. Just now I don't feel that any work I've done—although I guess I did it—that it is any part of me—any more than this town or any person I know. I can't take any credit for it and make any claims to anything. I feel for the time just bare-handed, cut off—N.G.

[across left margin] I think back to when we began it. It's easier when it's a year off or two years. You don't have to decide. You can kiss, feel the other in you, feel the sun or the night. Let it go. Marriage is quite different.

1. John Chamberlain reviewed *Beyond Desire* in the *New York Times Book Review,* 25 September, p. 6.

2. Belle Sprinkle, SA's landlady.

3. The maid.

4. Relatives of EC's. Laura Lu Copenhaver's mother was a Killinger.

5. "The heads of little stones stuck out of the ground like the heads of buried children" ("Motherhood," *The Triumph of the Egg,* pp. 169–70.

6. *Harlan Miners Speak: Report on Terrorism in the Kentucky Coal Fields* (1932), a collection of essays prepared by the National Committee for the Defense of Political Prisoners, which included contributions by Theodore Dreiser, John Dos Passos, and SA ("I Want to Be Counted").

[Marion, 28 September 1932]

Darling—

By this time you will have got other letters, sent after the strangely unfair one.[1] Within two or three hours I must have known of its unfairness.

I think the trouble with me now is that I cannot escape the constant feeling of guilt in asking a person like you to take a chance with me. It presses in on me from all sides. I think it must be the fighting of this sense of guilt in me that makes me assertive. When I am with you or near you I seem to be all right. Something in you balances me. Then I am left alone. I am jealous of those who can be near you. I grow unfair. I am terribly ashamed afterwards.

I think there has been a misunderstanding about money. My letter wasn't entirely honest. I thought it was you who did not want to take a chance on my being able to support us and, while I didn't like it, I thought of all the times I have been poor—as when you first knew me, and of dragging you into that.

You see, dear, I have all kinds of thoughts. My mind goes like a race horse. People before now have said I was a trifle mad. All the time of course, dear, I have wanted you not to have to think of a job or anything but then, when I wanted to speak out and say that, another thought would always come—"Are you going to try to trick her out of safety into unsafety?"

The truth is, dear, that, a great deal of the time for the last two years, I have been as I was all that summer when your mother was ill—the man with his hat in his hand.

These last few days I have tried hard, darling, to strip myself down to bare bones. I guess I can't see much, when all is said, worth your bothering about. Every accusation you make in your letter today is true.

Except this—that if you had been where I could have seen you for an hour, or if it had been possible for you to have reassured me a little. I know you want to. I know that you wouldn't bother with me if your affections weren't in it but it is very hard for you to say the little warm things on which I might build and live.

May I say this too, dear . . . I did, dear, put a great deal of love and feeling into the novel. It has hurt me more than I have let anyone know that it hasn't apparently awakened the response in others I secretly hoped for. It has been rather a black time about that.

I am just frightened, dear, about your going off to Kansas City for two or three months if I can't be near you. Do you think . . . if you are not through with me for good . . . that it would be possible for me to go there and be in the city as I was at San Francisco?

Or would that interfere with the work too much?

When would you go there? How long do you think you would stay?

Just now everything, dear, is centered on this one question. Can we make it or can't we?

If we can't it's my fault and I'll take it.

I'm a little like a child trying to learn to walk these days—trying to take it for granted that the chances you would have to take with a person so moody, flighty, often so unfair, are a bit too much, and trying with all my might to get ground under my feet.

I'd like to promise, dear, that I won't be unfair again but I can't. I'm terribly impatient. It has seemed so long, waiting, waiting.

You know I have often spoken to you about letters unsent. They have usually been unfair as that one was. I became clear headed again before I sent them or I saw you.

That's how it seems to be with me.

I'll give up the Russian trip—do not want it without you. If you decide—after thinking everything over—that you can go on—that there is a chance for enough happiness—I'll try not to be like that any more.

I ought to quit writing. I will. I think you ought to know that I am jealous of your family—that's the reason I say such unfair things—simply because any one of them can be in a house with you, go freely about with you, be a part of your life as I can't and as I want to so much.

The whole thing is just a twisted thing in me, dear, due to the fact that I want you so much. If you decide, dear, that it is worth your while to go on with it, won't you try hard—

To tell me more little things about your daily life—give me a few more little pictures to cling to—

I'm dreadfully lonesome.

Tell me oftener if you have any little warm feelings for me as you go around.[2]

It is still rainy here. Your mother looks well. I think they all know, without much being said, that everything is in the balance just now. I am embarrassed about going there.

I have things half packed—ready to go—I don't know where. I hoped it might be to you—somewhere.

I do feel, darling, like a man waiting at a railroad station.

Later—

Dear—I can't remember what I have written since the assertive, demanding letter. It has been a sick time . . . a terrible feeling of guilt and uncertainty in me. I've been doping myself to sleep. I have felt such an outcast.

Perhaps it would be better if I didn't write and bother you until you have thought your own way through the muddle—if you can.

1. I.e., the letter of 25 September 1932.

2. The following paragraphs are crossed out: "I have never taken it for granted you were going to marry me at all. Time and again you have asked me not to.

"Perhaps, after all, if you could say 'I will' or 'I won't.' "

[Marion, 29 September 1932]

Darling—I have certainly gone about today realizing what a fool I've been—and a brutal one too. I can't quite understand it in myself. After I did it I got too low. I thought I had lost you.

I went out into the country. The sun came out after the rain. I began to think maybe you would forgive it. I got great quantities of field mushrooms, enough for your father & mother, Pat Collins & wife, Frank and Ruth [Copenhaver], Bob & Mary, Burt & Clara [Dickinson].

I kept thinking of myself. I thought I would say these things.

That, to get at what I am, you do have to go far back. I think it was like this, Eleanor.

When I was a young boy—& just went up to the city—I was a young laborer, with two young children & sister to help support. There wasn't any way to get out of that except in business.

I got in. I was 20 years an advertising man.

Advertising was worse then than it is now. I guess you have seen pictures of me as I was then. I guess I was a sensitive boy. Maybe I was even a young poet.

I had to deal with slick men—say like Ben Geer.[1] I began to hate them and my work but kept thinking I was wrong. All the men I knew & thought big men were slick ones.

Then I got married. The woman[2] was all right but she did think that any expression of love through the body was nasty. She couldn't help it & I was ignorant but she did spoil that side of life for me—so that finally I couldn't bear to touch her. A good many people have said that in my writing I have had a sex obsession. Perhaps I got it then, a determination to assert the purity of sex, the wonder of it.

I used to have fits of unreasonable anger in the advertising office. If I had not been pretty talented they wouldn't have stood for me.

When I went away from the woman & the children finally—she kept wanting sex at the same time she was asserting its ugliness and nastiness . . . I couldn't stay—it cut me deeper than anyone will ever know.

Why am I telling you all these old things? I felt all the world against me when I left my family but had to leave to protect something precious to me in myself. That advertising world was foreign & hateful to me.

It got a queer assertive streak into me—unreasonableness too.

I wish, dear, as much as any man could that you could have had me when I was younger. We would have made a life. But now I have to bring you this older scarred man. What happened wouldn't have happened if you had been near. I'm not sorry you saw that side. If it is too much for you to take on, I won't blame you.

I think if we could have been living together you could have laughed it away.

Seeing your mother has helped a lot. She told me things you do not often tell me—how you were hurt that the critics didn't get the real point of the book, how you had identified yourself with me. I suppose you have been reluctant about telling me things that most show your love thinking you might not, in the end, take me.

I just do think that, if we had been together, you could have taken away this whole black time—turning on you, taking the critics too seriously temporarily etc.—it would have passed in a half hour. It did pass in a few hours but because you weren't here I sank down too low perhaps into the desperate feeling you could never forgive.

These times have really happened much less, dear, since I have known you.

Your mother said something that lifted me more than anything. It was about the books. I had to get them out of Bob's as he is moving. I was going to put them in the attic at your house.

Then I thought—"I've killed my chances with Eleanor." I thought I shouldn't embarrass anyone. I thought I'd leave. I was distracted.

Your mother said something about the books—"You can store them up there," so I told her. She said you had told her about my dreadful letter.

"She may not marry me now. I'd better not put them up there," I said.

"Well," she said, "whatever happens between you and Eleanor, we were friends before you loved her and we will be friends as long as either of us live."

It was the most curative sweet thing that has ever been said to me. I love you, dear, but I also love her.

I am sending copies of the book to Katharine, Mazie & Randolph and I gave one to your father & mother & one to Miss May.

[across margin] Don't you think, dear, that I do sometimes anyway have sweet nice sides—something to build on? Don't you think so, dear one?

1. A mill owner in Greenville, South Carolina.
2. Cornelia Lane Anderson.

[Marion, 29 September 1932]

Darling—Your dear letter came—two in one envelope—both gorgeous—except that they made my arms ache for you as they have ached all along.

Don't you dare be sick.[1] Please, dear. If you are it will be because I have been such a beast.

I have been happier all day than I have been for years. You had never, dear, told me like this.[2] I feel your arms open and warm for me. The dreadful sick loneliness is all gone.

Don't be mad at poor Miss May. I don't care what anyone says if they love you.

Yes, dear, I got the gorgeous Stallings review.[3] He got it. What happened was that, when I thought perhaps, by my dreadful impatience, I had lost you, the book and everything else I had ever done seemed to go away from me. Nothing existed. It all seemed to have nothing to do with me.

So many things to say to you and I want to hold you and kiss you.

I think my letter of today (this is night Thursday—too late for mail)—I think my letter will make everything clear.

I don't want to go to Russia without you, dear. I can't. I'd like terribly to go to KC and be there while you are working there. I'd rather go as your husband. If I can't, can't I go anyway? I'll try so hard not to hang too close. I'll work. If I can just see you now and then. Can you tell her how I feel? Would it do for me to write her?

I want you to do what you think right with them. Now that I know—as your letters make me know—that you are my woman, everything is different, darling.

You work out what you can.

I don't want you to be sick. Please don't.

It's horrid I can't be holding you and telling you all this.

Best of all, I think now, would be for us to go off south—for some months real rest for you—before we go to Russia. We won't make or destroy Russia.

You must have a rest. You must you must.

I have been as happy as a kid all day. I worked. I went and got John. We went to the country and again got great quantities of the most delicious mushrooms.

We went back to his house. We made cans of mushroom pickles. We made mushrooms au gratin—with cheese & bread-crumbs. We had Dave [Greear], Mary & Bob for dinner. Then your two letters came.

The birthday present came. It's just right. It's perfect.

Dear, make any arrangement you can—except for me going to Russia without you.

Let me be near you if there is any way. Darling.

What a shame I can't mail this tonight. If I dared I'd call you. Darling. Darling.

1. EC was having problems with a wisdom tooth.

2. She had written him that she would definitely marry him. Because of the responsibilities of her job, however, the wedding did not take place until 6 July 1933.

3. Laurence Stallings's favorable review of *Beyond Desire* had appeared as "The Book of the Day" in the *New York Sun* on 20 September, p. 28. It was subheaded: "Sherwood's Himself Again and Shows the Young Men How to Write."

[Marion, 6 October 1932]

Darling—Your letters grow shorter & more rare but I know it's wisdom tooth and rush and perplexity.

When he couldn't write, [D. H.] Lawrence scrubbed floors and made orange marmalade etc. and I wouldn't mind things like that. So there's a hunch—if we get stranded.

I thought, over night, about the Lawrence thing[1] and know I've got to work on it some more. I think I'll let your mother see it.

A queer half intimate letter came from a woman who was once—for a year—my secretary out in Chicago and now suddenly you get the impression, from the letter, of a person mature—as she certainly was not—and almost cultured.

Just the same, dear, don't you give up writing me just because you're rushed and, if you feel love, you go ahead and say it. It isn't going to hurt you and won't spoil me and it's as hard for you to say a little as it is perhaps for me to keep from saying too much. So I presume I ought to train myself to say less—and you to say more.

I spilled a whole bottle of ink all over my desk & made a hell of a mess.

Thinking—this letter writing—the only form of communication we have these days—unless something flows through space—as I sometimes half believe—it's like love too. Where my training needs to come is in holding back and yours in coming forward. You'll know what I mean.

Lawrence is fine it seems to me in his rock-ribbed belief in love between a man and woman that could go on in spite of hell. I guess they fought like hell, he and Frieda,[2] and hurt each other but they hung on and you can't help believe got a lot.

You know, dear—I say this to you but wouldn't to anyone else—I feel and have always felt that L and myself belonged, by some queer chance, to the same gods. I wonder what it would have been like had we known each other. I was tempted to go to him once, when I was in England when he was, and am sorry now I didn't.

In his letters again I feel so much I myself feel—

Reading this morning—"If when he enters her house, he does not become simply her man of flesh, entered into her house as if it were her greater body, to be warmed, and restored, and nourished, from the store the day has given her—"[3]

You see, dear, I feel that way now—and have since I have loved you truly so that, every morning when I awaken, I turn half hopefully, as though you might be lying there.

The hunger being to just lie very still and close beside you for an hour before getting up for the day.

It's bitter emptiness always that I can't do that. I have to fight for something—courage maybe—that has always—the few times I have had the chance—flown from you to me.

If only I put something into you in return which I feel I must or it wouldn't be so perfect and good for me.

I wonder if you'll read all this, dear. You tell me if I write more than you want to read—or, as suggested—save them to read when you aren't so rushed.

Of course I don't mean that, I guess.

1. SA was working on an essay about Lawrence, "A Man's Song of Life," which appeared in *Virginia Quarterly Review* 9 (January 1933): 108–14.

2. His wife, Frieda von Richthofen Lawrence.

3. The passage is from a letter by Lawrence in *The Letters of D. H. Lawrence*, ed. Aldous Huxley (New York: Viking, 1932). Lawrence goes on to say that if a man does not come home to his woman in the manner described, "she shall expel him from her house, as a drone" (p. 104).

[Marion, 21 October 1932]

Friday

O darling one. Your letter has just come.[1] I have been afraid. O my dear one.

I wasn't nice yesterday. I wasn't bad. I went & thought—why doesn't she wire when she'll come? You see, illness never came into my mind. I thought it was a meeting.

If I were only there.

I went & told your mother—let her read your letter. She cried a little. She said—"I wouldn't be afraid if it weren't Eleanor." She is afraid, as I am, that you haven't told us the worst.

I sit waiting for your wire. O dear one.

My only sister went to a hospital for a slight operation. She died.[2] I'll not let you see this until you are well.

Is it Clarisse? Have I done anything?

O precious sweet dear woman. I can't live without you. Don't let it be bad. Don't let it be bad. Dear one. Dear one.

You are so in me—all through me.

I was at your mother's yesterday. We were talking. She said—"Mr. C doesn't like any of his sons-in-law. He has no use for them in his heart.

"He likes you as a man but does not like it that I like to talk to you.

"He will never want anyone closer to Eleanor than he is."

I said—"He cannot have both you and Eleanor. He can have a father's share of Eleanor but she will be of my very flesh. There need be no talk of closeness. She will be a part of me."

Afterward I was almost sorry I had said it. I think though she understood.

She said this morning—Friday—your letter only came an hour ago—that she would not tell your father until she had a letter from you.

This so he wouldn't be hurt that the news came to her through me. I went away quickly so he would not see me there.

I've been praying—a kind of blind prayer. I've been trying so hard to get at God in my own way. I need. I need.

I keep thinking—"It may be now—this minute—she is under a knife." My flesh quivers.

Will it be somewhere I can come & be near you? O, dearest lover. Your flesh. Your sweet flesh.

1. EC canceled plans to come home because she was scheduled to have an operation for the removal of an ovarian tumor at the Harkness Pavilion in New York on 22 October. SA took a train to New York on the afternoon of the twenty-first and arrived there the next morning. He visited her shortly after the operation and each day during the following week.

2. SA's older sister, Stella Anderson Hill, died in 1917.

[New York, 30 October 1932]

Eleanor dear—

I have been reading two or three novels, evidently followers of Hemingway. There is a certain attitude toward life now.

For example—

I was talking yesterday to Tommy.[1] We were in his bedroom. When I got there, for breakfast, he was in his bathrobe, a short, strong, half-fat man.

He went to shave and I stood in his bedroom talking with him—of Hardy. (I have suddenly a passion now to reread Hardy . . . I think because Lawrence admired him). Suddenly Tommy began speaking of an incident of a few nights before. "Sherwood—what do you think. I had a virgin in there 2 nights ago.

"The first one for years," he said. He came to the bathroom door and pointed to the bed, smiling.

You see, Tommy is really a NY man about town. He has been connected with several big publishing houses, is cultured, well read, likes people, has good manners.

I got the impression that the woman (of 28) had given him an opening perhaps thinking that through him she would get to know so-called famous people etc.

He described the experience. "It wasn't any good. She was frightened and inexperienced. I felt like a surgeon."

Just that, dear. Even in this man who has experience of a sort, really intending very nicely toward people, the whole thing taken merely as well done or not well done.

The shock to that woman—her first trip down that road, perhaps her own sense of inadequacy in it—all missed. It was as though Tommy had said, "I took a trip to Washington. I was disappointed in the city. I didn't have a good time" etc.

It is this dreadful casual thing that has got into life. I think we love Lawrence because he never had it. Think of the depth of the insult to that woman, Tommy standing there and telling of it—not knowing what he was doing.

I feel this everywhere now, dear.

When I said I was not going to follow Waldo Frank, Cowley, Dos Passos[2] and others into active communist work I meant that I was not going to address meetings, etc.

I've got a sense in me that, although people may not know it, I can do most by story telling.

I believe I have got respect for life . . . it all strengthened and made all alive in me again by you.

I can't become a life hater.

Formerly, long ago, when I wrote *Winesburg* and *Poor White* —I had in me real tenderness for all life that now is all coming back. I think it can be now more mature.

You will never know half of what you have done for me.

1. Thomas R. Smith, editor in chief at Liveright.

2. Malcolm Cowley, critic and literary editor of the *New Republic,* and novelist John Dos Passos.

[On train, 1 November 1932]

Tuesday morning

Just running out of Pittsburgh.[1] It is a cold raw morning. We had 30 minutes and I breakfasted in the station.

Not many people on the train . . . a large man covered with diamonds who looks like a sporting politician.

I wonder if it is the same with you, darling—the whole thing—from the talk with you on the phone from Marion—seems like a dream—the sudden queer terror, the first 3 or 4 days—my walking in the streets with Mazie, confidence fighting all the time with fear, the distorted dreams at night and then, suddenly again, sureness.

Anyway you can't dismiss such experiences just because loose-talking fools use words loosely blathering about the spiritual. They do bring it home to a lover—where he stands.

Nothing I have said to you has quite got at what I feel about life and you and work just now but it doesn't matter. If it has integrity it will come out in work and in an attitude you'll feel. I never knew you to miss things.

I believe I'm going to take the point of view now—have suddenly come back to it stronger than ever—not that the communists are not right, or that I want individualism, but that I ought to go, with all my strength, my own road. Even if we had a revolution I'd think that about everything in personal relations we have in the world now would carry over.

If you tell the story of lives lived in any civilization I guess you tell your whole story of the civilization.

I just mean I'm going back wholeheartedly to story telling now.

Lordy it was nice last night. You were so gorgeously beautiful. I've never had anything happen so sweet to me as just the feel of your arms about my head and shoulders for the little minute, dear.

Don't bother to save Mimi's letter. Anyway I'll never let you marry a grandfather.[2] Figure that out.

1. Feeling that his continued presence at EC's bedside was resented by her family, SA left New York to visit Roger Sergel and his wife, Ruth, in Chicago.

2. Mimi had written that she was expecting her first child, Karlyn, who was born on 28 February 1933; thus EC did marry a grandfather the following July.

[On train, 1 November 1932]

Monday morning[1]

Darling—I am writing on a tablet bought in Amsterdam and using an envelope carried off in my portfolio from Chicago a long time ago.

These dreary industrial towns—Ohio—Salem, Alliance, Canton, Mansfield etc.—it is all so silent now. The industrial thing is only splendid in action. There is such despair in a mill standing idle, groups of idle men walking along the streets of the towns, that queer feeling of futility, of men not feeling themselves a part of anything.

Dear, I almost saw this thing born in Ohio. When I was a small boy it was getting under way. They had got oil at Lima. Gas came spurting out of the ground at Findlay. A case of stomach distention. Mother Earth with gas on her stomach.

It was going to be such a gorgeous thing. Just why no one asked. Forward. Progress. Up and at 'em.

The factories coming. I remember when I was a newsboy, young men on the streets of our town—"By God, you can get four dollars a day."

"At Lima they got a whole street of fancy houses."

"On Saturday night you go out. Get yourself a fancy Jane."

I guess most young American workmen's dreams were about like that.

I went to Findlay once but only stayed a few days. I had a job in a glass factory, pushing trucks loaded with glass dishes into a packing room. I had got into such an ugly little street, an ugly room I shared with another man. He got drunk almost every night. I just got up and left. Shortly afterwards I went out to Chicago.

You have such a feeling now that it never did have any purpose. It was just an ugly scramble. You find out what you can about the place of the scientists, architects etc., how they think they can do it.

I haven't seen a plant in any of these towns that looks as though it was doing a thing.

1. An error; it was Tuesday morning.

[On train, 1 November 1932]

Monday afternoon[1]

Darling—The day is still grey but occasionally the sun comes through. We are going through a part of Ohio a little like our country—the hills lower but having that same rounded, firmly sensual quality.

Like your hips and your breasts and shoulders and neck.

I've been thinking and feeling all day that all the years since I was a boy in this state have been like a queer, adventurous, a bit distorted pilgrimage.

As though, dear, I had not lived for any actual happening, achievement, relationship I've had, but for an actual connection that might come some day.

I'm getting almost afraid of the word "love." I've used it too many times falsely.

Anyway, whatever it is I've all this time been hunting for I've found.

The farmers are in the fields husking out corn from the shocks. It lies, little heaps, like gold against the grey-brown earth.

1. Again, it was actually Tuesday.

[Chicago, 2 November 1932]

Wednesday

Darling—I am sitting in Jackson Park. The day has turned cold & raw. It is four o'clock. I have been for a long walk. All of this part of Chicago is filled for me with old associations. This morning, at breakfast, we were talking of revolution and I made the remark—rather banal—that I wanted it to come while I was alive. I hated to miss anything etc. "You'll live a long long time," Ruth [Sergel] said.

"O, I don't know."

"It's odd about you," she said. "It's ten or twelve years since I first saw you. There is something eternally young in you. It hasn't much to do with the Lady. I don't know what it is."

I wonder if it is true.

A queer sense as I walked. I have walked with women many times in this park, half in love with some of them. Today I had the odd feeling that they were all you—some part of you in each of them—half things snatched at—waiting for you.

I think I must really have come out here wanting terribly just now to be near someone I felt had genuine affection for me. I was a little afraid to go on home just yet. I may go early in the week.

Later—back in my room—one of the boys' room, given up for me during my visit. I'll bet he doesn't like it.

Do you remember the man on the train, coming from the west, who wrote the letters, one after another, to be mailed at every stop—his sitting and reading them over & over? Anyway I don't do that.

[Chicago, 5 November 1932]

Saturday

Darling—It was marvellous to get your letter when I only expected a card. It came when I had been for a walk with Ferdinand [Schevill]. He was as you always find him, alive and at work. The terribly depressing modern thing—questioning all life, the feeling of being thwarted—in so many men now—hasn't touched him. He has, more than any man I know, a thing I always feel in you, dear, a kind of loyalty—willingness to be loved—power to love. You feel, once you are his friend, that nothing on earth could change his feeling for you.

It was good also to see Clara [Schevill] for a moment. She had been to a concert and we only had a few minutes after our walk before I had to come back here, where I was engaged to dine. It had begun to rain and we came in wet and Clara, who is always very reserved . . . she is tall and has remained beautiful, with a kind of stately beauty . . . she threw her arms about my neck and kissed me.

I started to say that it was good to find again and be again with these two people who have managed to love through everything—after this house—where this strange struggle is going on—even though it will come out O.K.

I have decided I will go home Wednesday, next week, get back into my room[1] and straightened out. You will be going to the apartment at least by next weekend—even on the 3 weeks schedule—and at home, I pray, by the following weekend—so that perhaps ten days wait there . . . I'll not say any more about the waiting.

One thing Ferdinand impressed on me. He was insistent. I had told him about your being through an operation. We didn't, dear, go into any details. Clara has been through a lot that way. I think they found something malignant but finally she has got well. He said, over and over, "Make her rest. Don't let her hurry." I told him of my dream, of taking you off somewhere down south by the sea, and he kept saying—"You must do that—you must."

I don't want you, dear, to have it on your mind about me and marriage.

Certain things have worked out. You have become dearer to me all the time. In some way, your going through all this has made me know how I am all colored by you and live in you.

You also, dear, make me feel again a workman. If there were any way by which I could go on living near you—with you—without your having to bother about marriage—the odd thing it seems to do to some people.

Like you, sweetheart darling, I have sometimes fears of that—the tricky things in me I mean.

I'd rather go through the hell of loneliness than be a hurt to you. I mean that.

You see now, dearest, *Beyond Desire*—a really fine piece of work—has fallen—well, rather like throwing a stone into a still pool in a wood—nobody there.

It will sell, say 10 or even 15000. Enough.

The point is that there isn't much response in life now. Everyone is too puzzled, hurt, distracted.

At the same time it makes it difficult for the workman to go on working.

He needs—

At least the one. Just your putting up your little arms and holding my head a few minutes—dear sweet one.

Anyway you know how I feel.

1. At the Sprinkle house.

[Marion, 10 November 1932]

Thursday night

Darling—I suppose I am all wrong to be so nervous about things. You will be very very sensible, won't you, dear?

I sent a copy of *Beyond Desire* to Brownie [Jones].

I went for a long walk—in the moonlight—a cold clear night. First I went out to Bob's place, just before dark. The place lies beautifully between the hills and there was a gorgeous sunset. Bob and little Dave [Greear] were riding two horses up and down in the fields and they made nice figures against the brown of the hills. There was an N&W train going along and the smoke stayed—not lifting, greyish white against the brown hills—a long time.

Afterward in the moonlight a long walk over the hill by the cemetery and out that Scratch Gravel road we often rode on. It was cold and clear and the shadows black. I kept thinking how lucky we are that you could have a good hospital and a good surgeon.

I always know, dear, that, for one reason or another, I may not get you and I try to think how I can put in the days and years if I don't. It's so damn lonely.

My room is nice again. Won't it be fun if I ever can make a place for you. I'd have such delight in just the details, putting up pictures, getting effects.

Do you suppose you can darn some sox for me while you are convalescing? I'd so love to have you, dear.

Dear, can't you have some unemployed woman come, just to be in the other room, get things for you? I'm afraid, thinking of you over tempted to do things. Please please, lover, be careful.

(Morning)

It drives me crazy that I can't do it, have no right. I dare say Lois [MacDonald] is doing it. That isn't me. It doesn't help my loneliness. How does it seem to have people jealous of the right to do things for you?

In Chicago I felt—regarding the times—it really is no time for such people as me. The man in *Nation* made out that all my life had been a retreat.[1] First a retreat back into boyhood, then to woman, then to art, etc. But the outer surface of life now, dear. Is one to accept the impotence of a Hoover or a Roosevelt, or the tiresome smartness of the day—

Or to produce a literature that expresses only disgust of life? One book I read recently went on about the refuse of the body going down the toilet.

I keep feeling that so much of life now wants you to be dead. So many critics go on performing funeral services over a man. It's disgusting really.

At any rate, dear, I have moments here. Last night, standing on a hill, I was simply glad to be alive among the hills and to see Bob & Dave on their horses—the life in the horses.

I can't go to the house much. Older people have been dying here—Gil & Dr. Dickinson[2] & others. Your father has just now one of his obsessions.

And it annoys him profoundly that your mother—so alive as you are—has fun talking with me. I feel it constantly so I must not go there much.

There remains, during this waiting time, for you, who give me so much of life, just to try—standing off a little, seeing people—the hills, cattle in fields etc. Today I am going out into the fields with Funk to see his dogs run. He is getting them ready for the hunting. I feel pretty helpless.

You must get well. You must be very careful.

1. Clifton Fadiman in "Sherwood Anderson: The Search for Salvation," *Nation* 135 (9 November 1932): 454–56.

2. Gil Stephenson, typesetter for the printshop, and S. W. Dickinson, retired Marion physician.

[Marion, Thanksgiving,
24 November 1932]

Night
Dearest darling—

I haven't any words to tell you, dear, what happens when you come back to me.[1]

It's such a silly word but there is, at last, lightness of the soul.

My body too, dear—the sweet sense of you near—

Your hand touches me—O darling one . . .

Something dancing inside me, dear—

I'm not what you see. O dear, I wish for you I could be Apollo. There is a white, swift, soft-running thing—man, boy, lover—

Softly—on the carpet of the night—run—run—run—

To her—to the dear sweet lipped, sweet breasted one.

You are sweeter than ever. Can you love me? Is it possible? Your eyes shine with love. O the sweetness in you—

Dear darling woman.

1. EC arrived in Marion earlier that day.

[Marion, 4 December 1932]

Sunday morning—

Darling Woman—How I wish there were some way to say all I have to say so that it would not disturb you at all. I am afraid you have the matter of our marriage on your mind. Don't, dear. Not now.

I am very very happy—having you near. At night I sleep happily, like a child. I know you love me.

I know how puzzling it all is to you. You will get well rapidly now but there will remain the problems. Never did I so wish that I had money. I haven't. My earnings are precarious—I know.

Then there is your father and mother . . . the uncertainty about your own future.

I think, dearest one, that when it seemed that what stood in the way of our life together was the question of the reality of our love—my own ability to be faithful to it etc.

I couldn't help knowing that more or less ugly things were being said against me.

All this made me terribly impatient.

I am impatient by nature and then, darling, I know myself well enough to know that without warm affection close to me I grow twisted in my mind, imagine all sorts of things, become quite impossible.

But we do not have to think of all that just now. You are here. I feel the warmth of you. I look out of my window and the earth seems good.

All I want to say, dear, is that I do realize how difficult all this is for you but please, dear, try to put it aside for the time.

Let's have these days. I'm working. You are here. Life is glowing and real to me. You make it so. Let's try to float on life just a little now.

No man ever had a sweeter, warmer lover.

[Marion, 10 December 1932]

Saturday

Darling—I have a great pile of new white sheets, having used up 500 of these sheets and a bottle of ink since you came home. It is nice and cosy here in the room. I wish you were in here, lying over there on the bed.

If we ever have a place, you will let me come sometimes and work near you, won't you?

Sometimes I like to walk up and down the room—muttering words. My father always hungered for the stage—to be an actor—and I'm sure, although, alas, your mother says I am a bad actor—I'm sure there is some of the same hunger in me.

That's what makes this writing for the stage such great fun.[1]

Usually when a man comes fresh to the stage he begins by wanting to revolutionize the stage. It is a little like the group of young writers in Paris who think, to write good prose or poetry, the language itself should be revolutionized, so they write—

Ezeech he bobbins in elfish lovelace,
Laskar segundi—etc. etc. etc.

You see, I am talking to you as I would like to be walking up and down and talking to you in your room.

I remember that when I began to write I realized that I had, because of lack of formal education, a very limited vocabulary. I do think there was a kind of wisdom in me. I took what vocabulary I had and did not try to force its extension. I think I did achieve color in simple words and sentences—

Then later here with the papers I tried again to work with the materials right at hand.

So I would approach the stage. I would like to go sometimes into the empty theater, go to rehearsals. All my life I have been gathering a wealth of materials outside the theater. Now to learn to cast some of this material inside the world of the theater just as it is.

I remember being on the lot, in the movie studio at Los Angeles, the place where they put discarded movie scenes—a fantastic place—and suddenly I wanted to have them let me make a movie—not buying one single new piece of property—a fantasy made of 1/2 street cars—a river propped up against a tree—a college campus—a South Sea island village.

Well, I must go to work. I've bragged enough. This is but a substitute for running in to you and talking to you for ten minutes in the morning.

1. SA had begun working on a dramatic version of *Winesburg* in an ultimately unsuccessful collaboration with Arthur Barton, a New York playwright.

[Marion, 15 December 1932]

I haven't seen anyone yet I want us to be like.

I couldn't sleep for a long time. I wanted you near me very much but that wasn't all the reason. I wanted to lie and think quietly and hear the storm rattle the windows and groan and sing. The bed was cold. It took a long time to warm it but I didn't care much.

Thoughts at night—

That my feeling for you has grown, seeing more of you. The passion is as strong, perhaps stronger, but now there is something else—

Nameless—belonging in a room with you, in a bed with you.

Belonging to breath[1] in the same place—walk and sleep in the same place.

I had passion before but not this thing—whatever it is—with another.

I know as well as you can, dear, that not any 5 & 10 cent store words, preacher, document signed, marriage, can make or break it one bit. I'd avoid it if there were any way.

I look at you differently than I ever looked at any other woman. I don't see you with their eyes.

We are so curiously alike. You have a certain thing to the face of the world you have carried so long that I sometimes wonder—do you often yourself believe in it?

You can be very cruel. You can be hard. Quietly you can sit and hurt someone and laugh. You could send someone to death.

You are an aristocrat, really, with the best kind of aristocracy.

I often sit and see you measuring, feeling about, with something inside yourself—as I do.

Only you hide it more—keep it more secretly put away.

It was cold in the bathroom this morning but I didn't care. I was thinking of something.

It was a realization that, in myself also, I have a kind of power. Some few people have noticed it.

It is that I can be very old and suddenly young—as young as a new world in which no man has ever walked. I shall not stiffen or harden much ever. I shall be old—then young—then old—then young.

Then, when I die, I shall die suddenly and you won't mind so much because you'll know I was ready.

Why am I saying these silly things?

Because I love the intimacy of singing to you—intimately, as I never was with another—

It's a substitute for talking softly in the night—in bed.

Who cares whether the things said are true or not?

It's so silly—silly and useless—living alone when you have found the other to live with.

1. SA may have meant to write "Longing to breathe . . ."

[Marion, 17 December 1932]

I have a queer feeling of approaching one of the strange crises of my life. It has happened before.

As when I walked along a railroad track one afternoon long ago leaving my wife and children—leaving a factory where I could have become a rich man.[1]

Later—one rainy night in Chicago—leaving a house there to get into a Ford car. I drove blindly that time for two weeks praying & thinking.[2]

That was Tennessee and myself. She wanted something that was her right—her own career—not willing, or perhaps not able, to merge something with me—the fling of the dice.

Eleanor dear—

I haven't slept all night. It doesn't matter. John is right about me in a bed. I don't lie quietly. A few times I have with you. I will never lie quietly alone but there is a queer strength within me. I can go on unquiet a long time. Then a black time comes—despair.

Then I begin to hope and work a little.

Then it repeats itself again.

I have to quit blaming anyone. I have thought it out again. I am—happen to be—a man in a civilization to which I don't and can't belong.

It is a civilization based on money. All through my youth and young manhood I tried and tried to fit in. I couldn't.

Perhaps a man cannot be a man who cannot fit into his civilization. I stayed in that advertising business so long, so long.

Then I tried being a manufacturer. It was the same thing.

I got queer obsessions. There were times when I wanted to fling money away. I used to sit in advertising conferences thinking—

I thought—if I only had a handful of hard silver dollars to fling at the heads of all the other men here in this room. I even went once and got twenty-five dollars worth of silver dollars for the purpose.

Then I realized I was going a little crazy.

Silly—silly.

I got out—started again.

Starting—starting—always starting.

Last night I lay in bed trying to hold on to something—

Facts.

Yourself—to face it—what you can and what you can't—your civilization. I thought a long time about your father. I have come to admire him as much as any man I've known.

Why?

He is hurt by his civilization but not too deeply hurt. He has his God so he can sit tight, have his woman, his son, his daughters, his land and house.

The doubt didn't get him, didn't destroy him, so he can sit tight.

He doesn't belong to my day, my time.

Your father—

My father—

The doubt got my father and destroyed him. He lost his dignity.

I will always remember him, Eleanor dear, as a man forever apologetic to his woman.

Then he went outside his house to other men and was a clown—so that his own children were ashamed.

He was, I guess, one of the men at the beginning of the time when men were to have no God.

I thought in the night about Lawrence too. I suppose I could begin that—myself alone in a room—thrusting up an arm—breathing deep—trying to make a God exist in some inner darkness.

But I can't.

Unlike him my faith is in a closeness I can't achieve. My dream is of a merging—a thing made of many men and women—something to which they all contribute.

I see the possibilities of it always in every man or woman I meet, a spark of it—but it is broken and fragmentary.

It won't combine.

I have thought—my faith has been—it is—my only hope.

I have thought—these little fragments I have picked out of lives—in stories and poems—

As though I were gathering and trying to shape a little a few stones for the builder when he comes.

What has all this to do with us?

Only that, like a child, I want the impossible.

You watch your mother, Eleanor dear. Your father is like a rock of fact to her.

Can a doubting, floating man be that rock to a woman?

I'm afraid not.

On every side of your mother there is your father—a fact.

It isn't just love we want.

I am trying to pour myself into my own groove—

Men of the doubting time—the time between—

Men without women.

Women without men.

I keep asserting and asserting—only a confusion to you.

I reach into the past too much—into your father's world. It is an unreal world to me.

Economics—face facts.

The chances are that now—until it is broken and something new emerges—if it can emerge—I can't be sure even of that—until then perhaps you—woman—have to float alone and I—crippled man—also alone.

All this hesitation you now feel—inability in you to throw the dice—for which I also blamed poor Tennessee—besides you the only woman who ever counted with me.

It's so silly to blame—or perhaps to hope.

I sit here—in my room—alone.

I am in my bed—alone.

I want men.

I want my woman.

I have as yet not made myself worthy of either. My only hope is to make myself a singing voice out of this time of loneliness and doubt and defeat.

Because we—my men—I could love—love is possible in me—because we—my men and myself—have now no roots in earth or air.

No gods. No women.

I think it is as hard for you as for me.

Facts—

Economic interpretation of history—

John Dewey.

Lois [MacDonald]—

Channing [Wilson]—

Y.W.C.A.
Me.
Abe.[3]
They are all as much lost souls as I am.
Perhaps you are. As regards us that is my only hope. That you are and know you are—with me.
Then for a dream.
I am afraid I can only be rag-tag—on the edge.
Perhaps I can make a few building stones—
If the builders ever come.
As regards my children, I guess I've about done all I can for them. I have set their little asses down on what seats I have been able to find for them. I have done for them what I can't do for myself or you. I have given them what I had. Just now they aren't anything very special to me. I can't, couldn't, am unable to live in Bob or John as your father can live in Randolph, in his uniform,[4] bringing one of their pictures in—then going off to sleep—
In faith in a world already created.
France will have to pay because of dishonor.
I'm ashamed every time I come in—my voice even—breaking down a little that faith—
When I—and my men—haven't even begun to make our own faith.
I spend too much time being ashamed.
Facts—
I've got a car.
$ 550 here.
$ 600 there.
$ 385 another place.
$1000 promised.
$2535

I guess I can't go to K.C. I can't believe much in Y.W.C.A.
I can't believe much in—
John Dewey.
Abe.
Lois.

1. Referring to his nervous breakdown and departure from the paint factory in Elyria, Ohio, on 28 November 1912.

2. In early July 1922, SA's marriage to Tennessee Mitchell was breaking up, and he left Chicago for New York.

3. EC's taxi-driving friend. See letter of 27 March 1931 and note 3.

4. Randolph Copenhaver was an army air force physician.

[Marion, 22 December 1932]

Thursday night—after leaving you—before sleeping.

Thinking that it exists as much as a stone, or a street, or a tree—

Our own world—I mean—in which we both breathe.

We can make it exist and keep on existing by believing in it.

We can destroy it.

It will always be destroyed.

The point is can we rebuild it, and rebuild it, and rebuild it.

Flesh and blood, and thought and little outbursts of laughter down inside and moods and stray thoughts—

And the beauty that is in you—

And sometimes in me—

To build with until our world comes to life again and keeps coming to life again until we die.

That is what I think marriage with you can mean to me.

[Kansas City, 19 January 1933]

Darling—

This you see is the city—as I see it from my window.[1] I went and got a coffee pot, cup and some coffee. I tried it. You put the plug in and have coffee—hot—in five minutes.

I didn't go to the river after all, putting it off for another day. I went and looked in neighborhood stores etc.—took a walk in the street. I came back to read.

I like lying on the bed—if only I could have you to talk to—to express thoughts as they come. I'll get to work soon.

I like to court you like this—being near you. It's so much better and I know I'm better and saner. In some way you've made me that and make me more so with your confidence in me.

Little things mean so much. At lunch once I could just see the soft sweet line of your breasts. It isn't like seeing any other woman's breasts. There's a different feeling—sweeter and more real. I can't say all it means or how sex means what it never did mean before—only you see, dear, it's a part of me to keep trying to say.

Partly my way of singing to you.

I know you won't feel harassed by me here, near you. It's pretty sweet to be allowed to watch you a little, that you don't get too tired.

And I've a growing confidence that, in some way, if what you are doing becomes too hard, you can cut it and we'll manage. I'd love to have you able to feel me a little back of you like that. Can you let yourself feel it, dear?

I have inquired. You are some six blocks away. When I went to the elevator to go to lunch, a drunken woman—in soiled pajamas—staggered out of a room and addressed a remark to the negro elevator man.

He is fat & smug & has taken me under his wing.

It is, I imagine, a place to which have fled down & out automobile salesmen etc.—while they weather the depression—they in the meantime getting what joy they can.

Darling—the whole trip was one of infinite inner peace and sweetness to your man. Last night was very lovely. I am so proud and happy to be your man.

1. SA and EC had come to Kansas City on 18 January; he was staying at the Puritan Hotel.

[Kansas City, 10 February 1933]

Darling

You went off, up the hill, after breakfast, without looking back. I sent off the letter to your mother and wrote Paul [Rosenfeld]. Again last night I dreamed out an act of a play.

I am going to try to find the river and walk by it this afternoon. During the day I'll read over what I have done on the novel[1] and see if it takes hold of me.

The Lawrence letters[2] move me a good deal. He is nearer to me than any other writing man of my day. I think our mysticism lies in the same direction.

I wonder if there isn't a kind of puritanism in this feeling—that we mustn't get too much dependent on each other etc.

I think I have some right to say that I am a somewhat different man than the man you first knew and who said many things you now remember. I admit it was confusing—my speaking to you constantly out of the confusion of that time.

But I have somewhat cleared myself. Perhaps, dear, I shall need from you, presently, the act of faith. I've an idea that's what our marriage will have to come to be—on your part.

It can't be very long now. We both know that.

In the last few years—as you must know, dear—I have really tried to thrust out—to try to find something—someone—really to take the burden off you.

I seem now to need very much direct love, faith in me by another person. Something—just before you knew me—shook my own faith in myself terribly. I was a little like a building, its walls cracking, ready to fall down.

So I asked, did ask, men to help me. I went out to Chicago—when you were ill in New York and when I was scared—and when your brother and sister (perhaps thoughtlessly) made me feel I was in the way, being near you in New York—and I directly asked Roger to give me love. I don't think he understood—may even have thought—or Ruth may have suggested the idea—she was in a state of dreadful fear of losing him—he may have half thought I had turned homo.

Anyway I'm sure I only confused him.

Darling, when I say things I do say about the kind of work you are doing now . . . I don't want to take the fun or the sting out of your work.

It's like this—you see, in walking about here—I've only been looking at the outsides of buildings—seeing people rather in the mass—noting faces—the queer American droop of them—

It would be absorbing to take any one building and make a survey of what—of real importance—is going on in them.

You get a queer feeling about buildings too—as though they wanted to be something—to have something real going on in them—like people now. They, like people, seem to cry out—fill me . . . fill me.

Why, I think the trouble is that none or few of us have faith in the revolution—to really want it yet.

So we've got to get that—to begin perhaps to say to ourselves every morning—"Does this I am feeling, doing, thinking relate to it? It's got to come."

So that might bring us to the question of our own real values—where they are etc.

That could bring us to you and me—marriage and everything. We can't go on always just questioning—

So I have to admit here that this brings up, for you, a delicate question.

You take the things I have done since I loved you—*Perhaps Women* and *Beyond Desire*. You have said several times that you believe that such work is more truly revolutionary—in its implications—than any kind of direct propaganda can be. Your mother says things like that too.

But do we not say such things, most of us, as we say we believe in revolution?

Not deep down inside ourselves I mean. Rather as men go about nowadays saying they believe in God.

Yes—as your father says it. With all his faith it isn't a real faith, is it? It hasn't lightened his life.

You see, dear, I am talking about a faith that lifts a little. I feel myself heavy too much. I looked at both of us this morning—as we sat in the restaurant—and I couldn't help feeling that we both sat too heavily in our chairs.

I mean there was nothing under the wings of us, lifting us at the moment.

I admit it's a fight to get it—a terrible fight. I left you and went and got the flowers because the blossoms seemed like butterflies wanting to sail away. I felt so discouraged. I went to get my shoes shined by young negro boys and felt like apologizing to them. I bring so little into any room any place I go.

It's time now that there does seem a terrible load to lift against.

How shall I say what I mean? The other night—in our two bodies—I did suddenly feel the light—lightness—the singing, living thing.

I suppose what I want is for us to marry in this faith—that it is worthwhile—if we must go down to go down in faith—

You see, it's so hard to say. Most of the time I'm so heavy.

But there has to be something—outside our two selves—we strive for together. It's the only real sense and purpose of marriage—as I see it now.

Am I only beating my own wings senselessly in this little room here? It's a kind of fight against skepticism. It always has been and will be that.

Do you think it is all silliness—or do you believe?

You have to answer presently. I can't keep asking—beggar man—if you don't presently answer—positively.

1. "Thanksgiving," never completed.
2. See letter of 6 October 1932 and note 3.

[Kansas City, 12 February 1933]

Darling

I am quite sure I am getting the disease licked.[1] I presume a part of it is this dreadful feeling of depression. Just at present nothing I have ever written seems any good at all, nor does it seem at all likely I ever will write anything that is any good.

I am trying to be as sensible as I can and put all this down to the disease but I do keep thinking that really I am only a nuisance to you here and that perhaps I should light out. You can't, I presume, do the job you have to do here without having it as your central interest and all of this having to phone me, see me etc. must be a pest to you. All good sense tells me I'd better go.

You see, dear, I do not want quite to get into that relationship to you. It amuses me a little—although it hurts too. Your attitude for example last night. I smiled afterward thinking how rather characteristic we were of the American middle class man and wife—the husband coming home—rather tired of the day of hustling—to pick up the newspaper—rather rigid and apart—and the wife sitting and looking at him.[2]

She with such a sharp sense of not having done much—being middle class you see—someone to do her cooking, make her clothes, do her house work etc., as I have.

Me, you see, inevitably in the position of the middle class wife.

It may be only for a period. If presently I can begin to take you places, go to meetings with you etc.

That may be difficult, however—too difficult.

Mind, I don't blame you for all this. You warned me.

My difficulty is the strength of my feeling for you—need of you as woman—my woman—to lie with you, hold you.

I almost called you on the phone last night . . . at 2 A.M. I had just had you, in a dream, and your presence seemed so real.

You see, I guess I am an outcast. They all say—you say—poet—and so it must be.

But a man is only poet at times and it isn't a day or an age for the poet. No one really wants him.

And when he isn't poet he is likely to be such a stick.

I don't know really what I can do—New Orleans I presume—as well as another place.

I'm even pretty gloomy, dear—thinking that perhaps between us it may always be so—you in the active whirl of things—me outside—rather helpless—most of the time meaningless.

Poet eh—in an age when poet isn't needed or wanted. What is wanted, needed now is active fighting revolutionist and—obviously—I'm not that.

At least I could get where I would not be a constant daily bother to you—the worker.

1. SA had the flu.

2. An *X* follows, referring to this continuation on the back of the sheet: "At the moment I was even jealous of the handsome outdoor advertising man with the ability I thought to really interest you— thinking he might really be the important one . . . man of his times etc."

[Kansas City, c. 4 March 1933]

Darling—It is curious. I do think that perhaps the letter from Roger threw me off.[1] It isn't at all, I think, that I resent the implications of the letter—implications not new to me—I have often had the same from you but, for the moment at least, I am in a state of uncertainty—the implications being—somewhat at least—that all the motivations of my own life are somewhat romantic—even silly.

This in relation to the novel I am trying to write. I think it must be rather this way with such men as myself—that we move from level to level. "Now I am in a certain frame of mind—in a certain relationship with life." It may be true or false. How am I to know?

What we do—such men as myself—is to try to project something forth—from that level. A figure is imagined, having a point of view.

Often, my dear, I have asked myself whether or not there is such a person as S.A. It may be not.

I think I do try constantly to create one and it may well be, dear, that all my struggle in life, uncertainty etc., is but an effort to come to some sense of reality in self.

A dreadful confession to make to a woman but anyway it is honest—at least honest to me and my feelings today at this moment.

I am often curious to know if you go through the same struggle but you are not like me. You do not constantly speak of yourself. It is very seldom that you show me inner workings of your self.

Is it because you do feel something solid and real—a self—Eleanor? I can imagine it at least. "Here I am—Eleanor. Today—at this moment—I am beautiful but an hour from now I may not be."

It doesn't matter. You exist. You are. At least I fancy it must be so from the very fact that you do not speak often of yourself. I may be all wrong.

I wonder if you know, dearest, what it means not to exist at all. I have had long times of that. The feeling keeps coming back and back.

What I think of Roger's letter is that it does, in a certain sense, destroy me—at least for the time—and so this morning, instead of writing on my novel—living for the time in this Frank Blandin—I sit here quite shattered—unable for the moment to live in him or in anyone.[2]

"But why not live in self?" you say.

"But is there any self?"

I am very curious. Do such times at all come to you?

I think this thing in myself might explain a good deal. I have gone about seeking love. You know about that.

Why?

What is it we want in this thing we call love?

You see, my dear, this morning there is no creation in me. I want to tear down, destroy.

Not you—my dear. You are rather a rock to me.

There is this eternal question of my own existence. It does not bother you. Very well. It does me.

Often. Often.

Often when I am with you, walking with you, dancing with you, dining with you, I have this sudden feeling of unreality—never in you—always in myself.[3]

And so I am always seeking—what?

There are two things—the darkness of utter nothingness—oblivion—or self-realization perhaps—life—to go awake and aware. It must be what your mother means. She has perhaps achieved it.

"I am living. There is something inviolate in me. I exist. I am."

But it may be that your mother also—being so keen about me—putting her finger on me—has not done so.

Now as regards woman, a woman. You say over and over that I must not depend on her.

But I am speaking of my own need, or what I think my need. I won't go now into what has done this to me . . .

Do you remember when you first knew me, how I asserted and asserted? Did you realize it was the voice of a child, crying in darkness?

Not complete darkness. That would have quieted all the assertion in me. Death—why should a man fear that?

Instead of that a grey meaningless half death, half life.

You see, I think now that Roger also has not understood as completely as it seems at first.

After all, what is this hard common sense? It is merely acceptance, isn't it?

Can't you conceive, dear, that there are people who cannot stand alone? If you and Roger can do that—perhaps you can—I admire but do not understand.

I say frankly I can't. If I were to try to stand alone I would simply be a tree with its roots out of the ground.

You say, you think, I too much glorify woman but is it not legitimate for me to say frankly what is true that, if I am to go toward life—not death and nothingness, I must go toward that thing that is source of life to me?

I think sometimes that it would be better for me to pass all this up—all pretense that I can stand alone. For you who can the glory and richness of that. It is not for me.

Something left out of me when I was born perhaps . . . too much of something else put into me—need, constant hunger? I do not myself quite know what it is.

You know what I have been saying to you lately. You know how it came up. You yourself had said that you could be either of two things to me. You spoke of what you called an honest life together—to be disagreeable when you felt disagreeable—never under any circumstances making any pretense of need of me except when it was natural—I got it that way—or, as over against that, another way—to play with me a game. "I can be always sweet to you, always loving, if you wish it so," and to that I said quite honestly—"Yes, I want that."

What you may not have understood quite was the real and altogether sincere humbleness back of that, for had I thought, been at all sure, I had in myself the grace of mind or body, strength, sureness in life, to compel your affections—

Who wouldn't have taken the first alternative?

Why, I do not mean to say I am wholly weak. At long periods in my life I have endured life unloved. I believe I do, as much as people like you and Roger—if you are alike in this—and from your accord with his letter I take it you are . . . I believe I do as much get from nature—trees, skies, rivers—incidental people met—little oddities in them . . .

What I take to be this romanticism is then—isn't it—assertion beyond reality—resulting I dare say always in lack of balance.

I never did claim much balance.

But there is something else. I wonder. Could it be that after all I am the true communist? That those of you who are inwardly stronger, more integrated, perhaps are the real individualists?

You see how Roger has misunderstood. You take for example what I have had in mind for Ripshin. It is a beautiful place and of course I wanted to share it. It was silly for him to talk of honeymoons. Men past 50 do not go on honeymoons. There was even—silly romantic notion—the idea of men and women with children about—why should they need to be our children—at least for a few months a year.

I saw your own smile when I talked of it. "It won't work." You were willing enough.

Tell me the truth—was it not indulgently—as one would indulge a child?

"You will awake from this dream too."

O, my dear, how many many times I have awakened.

I am awake this morning—jerked out of my world of assertion of what is probably impossible.

But nevertheless I do challenge. Something in me keeps saying—

Communism rather than individuality.

It may be only because I cannot perhaps achieve anything alone—not even self.

1. Roger Sergel had written SA urging him to be bolder in stating his values.
2. Frank Blandin is the main character in "Thanksgiving."

3. SA here inserts "*X* over" and adds on the back of the sheet: "You know sometimes when we are together and I speak to you—you being gone off somewhere with your thoughts and you are annoyed—you compare me with the woman Tallulah [Bankhead]—but it is not often egotism—thinking what I am saying important—but rather desire to live in you—refresh myself in awareness of self in you."

[Kansas City, March? 1933]

Darling—

I always have a strange feeling when it happens as it happened last night. I am to blame. I am more impatient than you. That may be the maleness that goes forward and demands. I am writing this in the very early morning—not wanting to sleep.

Last night I had and I still have a sense of your great sweetness in trying to give me what you think I want.

I guess it is wrong though for you ever to give me what you think I want when you do not want it.

If we are after anything I should think it would be marriage and I do not mean by that just a ceremony. There is a marriage. It is a possibility. It cannot happen between two males or two females.

It cannot happen in the half world either. In its essence it is the poetry of existence.

I expect, dear, you blame me sometimes for so much speaking of it but, as between us, I am the proclaimer.

We talked last night of romanticism, you saying you wanted it—to be worshiped by some man—thought always beautiful etc. Of course, as in all such talk, you were half in fun, half earnest. When you turn such a conversation afterwards, saying it is your wit, you only half tell the truth.

Then what is it?

I know a little. We had stopped in that little street end. There was the slim girl who came to the door to look out, the car that passed, the light in an upper window.

What I am now trying to say may sound a little silly to you.

I presume I am poet, dear. Life for me consists in moments. It is the thing called overtone that sometimes gets into my work.

Where does it come from?

I will tell you a secret. None of it ever came from me alone.

I mean that had we two, man and woman, in that same spot last night, been truly lovers (I admit the impossibility), but had it been possible and happened—there would have been for me a fertilization as real as though my seed had gone into you to fertilize you.

What happens then?

Does it sound silly? Sometimes you say you are a materialist. What I mean is that I might have got so sharp and penetrating a sense of the house in which the light came in the upper window—the man in the passing car—the slim girl who came to the door—the light flooding out—that it would all have been like a beautiful painting hung up. It is already half that.

There is this sharpening, intensification. Poetry doesn't consist just of words put down in rhythmic sequence. It is life drawn up, sharpened and made to sing.

With me it happens, dear, that I have to get this through and in a woman—myself lost, something born that is not the woman nor myself—but something made of we two—marriage.

Do you want to stand free of this? Do you remember how I have told you that Elizabeth finally couldn't bear it? She kept saying—"You want to make dust of me." She began talking of being a slave. That was when the inner self in me rejected her as it has others.

In a sense that is what you are saying when you say, "I want romantic love from a man."

What?

When you are romantically loved by a man, you are, for him, the center of the universe. All beauty is contained in you etc. It is, rather an atrocious thing to want, isn't it? I guess though it is ultimate ego boost.

Or each of us could set ourselves up in another way. After all, dear, you must give me a kind of credit. With my position I could have surrounded myself with worshipers . . . disciples etc. I haven't. I have always rejected them. The permanent friends I have made and kept have been stronger men like Charles [Bockler] & Roger [Sergel] and Ferdinand [Schevill], and you too could—you are strong enough—have the charm to get women under you—half equals, not quite. You can live that way.

Do you know, dear, I have thought sometimes—or I mean I did think before I loved you—that—after my former failure—if I loved a woman again I would love one who had blundered a lot in relations as I have. I find that thought developing in this novel as I write.

I mean one who had tried out romantic love as I have . . . and perhaps—in that time you like to refer to—when I said that about your going out to take lovers—there was something of that sort in it.

I really didn't know you very well then. I know you better now.

For you are not virginal and never have been. There is something in you too earthy and unromantic for virginity. It is not for nothing I have always found in you—in all closeness to you—a new sense in myself of the sweet reality of ground, skies, trees, cornfields—everything I've seen with you. If you were the pure, lovely, virginal thing who inspires romantic love in men, you would have taken me away rather from all this—all concentrated rather on you.

You will get the implications of all this. I really don't want you or any other woman in a romantic sense anymore—to let her exist out there in her lovely isolated splendor. To hell with it.

Regarding the Lois [MacDonald]—what really and completely soured me on her was not the things she said about me. She was probably right in most of them but in conversation with your mother, again and again, she did spit upon my work.

As though I had made a beautiful painting and had hung it on a wall and another disliking me had dared to go throw mud on that.

It comes partly, I dare say, from the 1/2 scientific mind, which is like 1/2 poetry or 1/2 maleness or 1/2 femaleness—that is to say it is 1/2.

You see I do feel . . . you may not like this . . . that, in the time I have known and loved you, I have done "Loom Dance," "Lift Up Thine Eyes," *Beyond Desire*, "Machine Song," "Brother Death"[1]—all basically beautiful things that belong to you as truly as to me—as none of them could have existed without you in them.

I mean that I can't find the road to poetry alone nor exist alone and I can when I become something that isn't you or me but is us—and that is marriage to me.

1. "Brother Death" appeared in *Death in the Woods*, pp. 271–98, which was published on 8 April 1933.

[Marion, 6 April 1933]

Thursday Eve

Darling—A day of April showers. I have been in twice to see your mother. Dear one, you will understand that my hint—that your father should be told definitely—as soon as you feel definite—was not to butt into your relations with him (you may understand each other too perfectly for it to be necessary) but was only an idea that his feelings should not be unnecessarily hurt from being left outside. I remember to have heard him complain of that.

I went with Mary [Chryst Anderson] to get wild flowers in the woods & got wet. Took some to your mother & came home to change my clothes . . .

I know I am getting well because I have been full of physical hunger for my sweetheart all day.

Your letters are charming.

Friday. A man lets himself get into such queer foolishness. It was raining. I had nothing to read. I drove up to your house. It was all dark there, except for a light in your mother's room. Your father had gone to the movies or to church. The town is closed like Sunday nights. There are a swarm of fat, stupid-looking evangelists here. Even the Lutherans have got into it.

I went to John's but he had gone off walking in the rain. I picked up a book there—*The Strange Death of President Harding.*[1]

It is utterly ugly—a record of ugly men—Harding a poor sheep of a victim in their hands. Maurice [Long] knew a good deal of all this ugly business. Once he also was dealing in whiskey permits. He had dealings with Daugherty.[2] I never knew exactly that money side of his life. He didn't want to talk about it. Once or twice he began and then stopped.

I shouldn't have begun reading the book at night. Why is it that, once launched in such a mess, you go on? I did—until midnight—such a queer slimy feeling and afterwards distorted dreams. How much of the baseness of human beings should be realized.

More and more you get the fixed idea that money is accountable for most of the ugliness of life.

There was that poor sheep of a Harding with the ugly, half insane, ambitious wife. Then he fell in love with the girl—Nan Britton. Evidently she was loyal to him. He kept fooling with other women and lying. I dare say he didn't want to.

There would be a man like that—strong physically, with no mental processes going on in him to burn up a part of his energy. You must pardon me for thinking of him in connection with myself. At least I have escaped something.

I guess it is true that I could have made money, handled men etc. What an escape that I did not go into it, or become ambitious—for that kind of power.

And really, dear, how foolish of Cornelia & Elizabeth that they—for some odd reason—did not want me to absorb myself in an art—

Anyway—there I was, last night—1st of all restless for you, all afternoon and evening—then, like a fool, letting my mind get involved with that mess.

So I was walking up and down the room when I should have been sleeping—at midnight & after.

There was one thing I could hold to myself. Before—in all my experience—I have never felt, regarding another person (a woman) that she belonged to me. It was a satisfaction to feel—in my very bones—that I would never be a liar to you, nor be disloyal. I could believe that.

How essentially sweet you seemed to me and real. I remembered how many times you have steered me off from my bad times—of self—by being really sweet about it—letting it pass quickly.

My hip is about well[3] but I haven't worked yet. I do miss you so terribly. It has got so that I feel that—for some queer reason—things will never be the same since I have loved you—in that, now, always, any work done has to be, in some odd new way, never my own, but ours.

I do love you so.

I have just called Viola[4] who says your mother is much better and has been up & walking about but has not come downstairs. V promised to try to keep her in bed today. I'll go up later.

1. From the diaries of Gaston B. Means, as told to May Dixon Thacker (New York: Guild Publishing Corporation, 1930).

2. Harry M. Daugherty, who managed Harding's presidential campaign in 1920 and became U.S. attorney general. He was later charged with involvement in the Teapot Dome scandal but was never convicted.

3. He had twisted a muscle.

4. The Copenhavers' maid.

[Marion, 10 May 1933]

Darling—

I got your letter after your visit to Lucy[1] and do rather know how you feel and how confused you are. It adds to my own confusion. I can't well ask you to throw all aside for me and come to me. Once I could have done that but the day when I can do it has passed.

You must know how I am now. The physical need of you keeps coming but, as I guess you know, that isn't the most vital thing between us.

In New York, when I was near you, I had confidence. Life wasn't fearful and confusing to me and here again it rather is. I have plunged into this thing here, knowing well enough the danger and the chances being taken—I know nothing else to do now. The house is there—so lovely—in a way the work of my own hands. I can't sell it. It seems so criminal not to be using it—for myself and others.

On the other hand I have been going there, working and arranging, seeing about beds, dishes, towels, sheets, curtains, chairs—a kind of blind going on—

I feel isolated and strange. I go touch a chair or lie on a bed and it doesn't exist, isn't quite real to me.

I don't want to bring this into your already great confusion but I have to tell you.

Away from you, dear, I simply feel helpless and half frozen. Is this love? It is, dear, more and more a new kind of thing to me—as though, having at last found you—in some half mystic thing another part of me—I find existence too confusing without it.

I make plans blindly now. I have to, dear. I can't feel that the situation there is likely to change. I think that two weeks from now—or three weeks—it will be the same. They probably can't promise anything but I feel that, with me put aside, you would be one of the logically last ones to go. They also will probably do things just out of confusion—in the brutal way things seem to have to be done now.

You do understand my position—my love for you (silly word), my keen realization of the shortness of any road before me—the great danger of my leading you into something that might be a mistake for you.

Do you believe—as I do now, dear—that marriage does exist? I mean that a union does sometimes happen between a man and woman—a union so vital that one torn from the other is a cripple? I didn't used to believe in all that but I know it now.

I won't say more. I know you are tender toward me and will give me comfort and make things real to me again when you can.

Your mother seems well again. There is no cause to worry except the constant one. I feel very tender about her too.

I've a sort of feeling sometimes that—in getting his last appointment—your father did something—made some compromise with a certain rigid thing in himself that startled your mother. Perhaps something she clung to slipped away. This is a guess—some few words dropped—a wistful something in her. I have a really strong love for her.

There is nothing that has ever been in me like the feeling I have for you, dear, but I feel very helpless about doing anything to really bring you to me.

1. EC had again consulted with Lucy Carner (see letter of 27 August 1932 and note 4).

[Ripshin, 20? June 1933]

Morning

Dear One—I am going to arrange the working here in a new way. I shall give a scene to B and let him work on it alone in his tent.[1] There are two tents—the Bartons living in one and he is having the other for a work tent. This will put him on his mettle to see what he can do. I want to smoke him out—see if he can contribute anything real. Louis[2] has a good stage sense and I think would like to write plays with me. I do not think he has much sense of people but I have plenty of that. We were discussing me the other night. Joan says I get intimate with people too fast.

Answer. "I know that. It has been an advantage and a disadvantage. People are my materials."

Louis—"You are too tender about that."

Answer—"It may be I am tender and it may be just a fool."

Joan (laughing)—"I think it is partly that."

Afterwards (walking with Louis)—"Of course men like Barton—and Kraft[3]—will try to attach themselves. They are trying it all the time with me. Sometimes they succeed. You need a wife. You need Eleanor. You need someone, beside yourself, who has the interest of the work at heart."

I think Louis and I will get somewhere with "The Mississippi."

Soon now—lover.

1. Arthur Barton, along with his wife and child, had come to Ripshin the previous week to work with SA on the dramatization of *Winesburg* but had not produced to SA's satisfaction.

2. Louis Gruenberg, a composer who had written the music for an opera version of *Emperor Jones,* had been living since 18 May, with his wife, Joan, their child, and her mother, in the "green house" across the road from the main

house at Ripshin. SA had hoped to collaborate with him on an opera based on the Mississippi River.

3. H. S. Kraft, a New York writer, who earlier in the year had interested both SA and Gruenberg in a joint dramatic project. See *Letters of Sherwood Anderson*, pp. 279, 282–85.

[Ripshin, 26 June 1933]

Monday morning
Darling—

Yesterday morning I had Roger, his son Chris,[1] and Barton into a room and went through the 1st two acts of the revised play. I believe it is quite tight and O.K. now and that, as soon as we come back here, I can start dictating. Roger is enthusiastic. He was good enough to say that there were a half-dozen devices I had invented that prove to him absolutely that I am a dramatist. As he handles and reads plays constantly[2] and has cool clear judgment, I counted a good deal on his judgment. Barton again was of no help. Poor cuss, he is so defeated that what he may have of superficial stage cleverness is paralyzed.

Like your mother, R is indignant that B should sit down on me here but that is near an end. He will be so much better off away now. It is rather cruel but these new acts he had not seen or heard until I read them yesterday—this because his dabbling in the materials only confuses my mind now. I shall leave here on Wednesday—but will not come into camp until Thursday and not then if you tell me not to. I'll go to the hotel in Hendersonville (Skyland) and look there for word from you.[3] I am leaving on Wednesday partly to give the Bartons a chance to get away while I am gone and before leaving will tell them to go—doing it as gently as possible.[4] It is the best thing now.

It rained in a mile-round circle all about us yesterday but we had only a light shower here. After dinner I took Roger in the car and we drove over beyond Mouth of Wilson and spent two or three hours lying on our backs on the banks of the New River (there are so many places I want to take you here) and had good talk. He and Louis like and respect each other.

In the evening Bob, John, Dave [Greear] and Mary came and we had a big croquet match.

Alas everything is very bad and sad for poor Barton. All of the ordinary conversation between the rest of us leaves him out. It is extraordinary how little background he has.

And then everyone suddenly began on Roger—urging him to stay longer and making plans to get him back. I kept trying to change the subject, as did Roger, but it did no good. It went on and on.

R was up and off at daylight. I got up to take a last plunge in the creek with Chris and to breakfast with them. I gave him a letter to you to mail at Bristol.

Darling—only a few more days now and we will be together. I have been tense again with the waiting. I'm so glad it is near an end.

1. Roger Sergel and his son Christopher had arrived on 21 June.

2. Sergel was head of the Dramatic Publishing Company in Chicago.

3. SA drove to Hendersonville, North Carolina, on Tuesday, 4 July. He picked up EC at Camp Merrie-Woode on 6 July; they drove to Marion and were married at Rosemont that evening.

4. The text of the letter he left for Barton is in *Sherwood Anderson: Selected Letters,* pp. 169–70.

[Ripshin, 26 July 1933]

Wednesday morning

My Darling Wife—I will be at Lynchburg at 6 on Sunday evening.[1] If you are not too tired we will drive on to Marion that night. I guess there is nothing to do about the situation (as regards my books). It was your mother's notion that you go to Scribner's—with an idea of publishing all my short stories—but it was not mine. She has an idea—flattering to me—that I might become a kind of college text-book for short story writers, but I do not certainly want to go to Scribner's as a petitioner, begging them to take me up etc. I guess they, as well as other publishers, know what the situation is.[2]

It looks dark. Things have been badly handled in the past. In the past I have over trusted publishers, just as I over trusted Barton last year. They got my name to bad contracts and such things do come home to roost.

The man who wired was, as you know, a literary agent. He has probably found out how tangled my situation is and has dropped it. Let it all go until we are in NY this fall and I will take it up and try to work something out.

As regards Roger's letter about the play. He wrote not having seen the 3rd act. I have now sent him the complete play to see. I have done all I can with it now and will wait until I hear from him and you see it complete.

Darling, I'd rather you didn't bother about my birthday.[3] Birthdays are not such cheerful occasions for the life lover who begins inevitably to think—on all such occasions—of the time when springs must come, trees bloom and the grass grow green and he not here to see.

Also, darling, I do think of the time when you will be going about, your voice heard, and I not there. I can't help it.

It's better when I'm with you. Then I only think—"Now I am with her. She's mine."

I think, dear wife, that there is an essential difference in the attitude toward life and particularly toward our marriage between your mother and myself. We spoke of it a little the other day. It is hard to define. She believes, essentially, that no one person should fix dependence upon another. She says that it was her notion that you go on living and working under your own name and that she suggested the idea to you.[4] I must have heard it discussed without the inner import of it quite coming into my consciousness.

I do not believe even you, dear, can know how essentially lonely I am. I cannot take your mother's road but must identify myself. Something—some mystic part of myself—must continually flow into another and I must get such a flow also from them. Without you, whom I love more than I ever loved anyone else, I am actually like a plant with its roots out of the ground—

And in using that figure I don't intend either to represent myself as a flower or you as earth but merely to get at truth.

I think in a broad sense your mother has got, in the adoration of her husband and children, something she essentially wants but I think also that some subtle, real thing has been let go.

Perhaps I should let it go. I would be of infinitely less bother to you—perhaps more self-reliant—but I guess I'll hang on.

I do know that with you there is health and that, away from you, I become a different person—not so nice, slightly irritable—inclined to build up notions of wrongs done me etc. I don't know whether or not we will have a child but I do know you are constantly a source of life to me as I am always hoping I may be, a little, to you.

I won't say any more. Thanks for all the clippings. Thur., Fri., Sat., Sunday. 4 days & 4 nights yet. If you must go Sep. 15th then I'll manage to break up the life here when you go and follow you. There will be nothing in the Gruenbergs to hold me.

Sunday sure—

Your anxious waiting lover & husband.

P.S. I did not tell you but I really went to Floyd, with Doc Brown, to bring some whiskey. There is some fine whiskey made there by an old man who sells only to a small group in Richmond, another in Roanoke & one in Marion. Frank Emmett, Doc Dave and Doc Brown are the Marion group and they take turns bringing it in. They have always let me have any I wanted so I thought it only fair I take my turn in bringing it.

1. ECA was returning there by train from a YWCA meeting.

2. The Liveright publishing firm had gone bankrupt and was sold on 20 July. SA did later go with Scribner's, which published *Puzzled America* (1935), *Kit Brandon* (1936), and *Plays: Winesburg and Others* (1937).

3. On 13 September.

4. ECA considered keeping her maiden name at work but decided to change it, as SA wished, to Anderson.

[Ripshin, 5? September 1933]

Darling . . . I am certainly sorry about the mood I was in yesterday and the day before, your going being quite inevitable, but at any rate the mood was not personal and the hatred that was in me was directed toward no one person. I was all the time afraid of what I might say to someone . . . as though all life had got in some way quite hateful. The man said I had criminal tendencies in me and I guess I could do murder sometimes.

We went out to Bob's and Bob was not at his best . . . myself talking away out at the end of something, as though some sort of business were going on at the front of a house, on the front porch of the house, having nothing to do with you inside the house.

When I got home I couldn't sleep so read for a long time and then suddenly I knew that you were loving me and everything got better. There was an actual physical experience, not unlike an experience I used to have long ago in the period of my life I am now trying to write about in my book. Then at night I used to feel my mother's hand come and touch me sometimes at night and last night your fingers began playing over my face, caressing me into quiet so that I did sleep after midnight.

About work. Perhaps it makes no difference. I suppose a man can work in times of misery and loneliness and in times of happiness but I fancy that what happens is that his mood gets into the work so that it has a swing and jump to it or it has a bitter tang.

In the night I thought again about the question you asked me yesterday . . . as to whether or not you should write to New York, saying finally that you would not travel this fall. Dear, you must see that I can't answer such questions. There is always the fact staring me in the face . . . "If I tell her to do so and so there should be, in the telling, the implication of being able to take care of her under any circumstances," and I presume, dear, that, long ago, I gave up that right. To have it would necessitate in me the adoption of a bourgeois point of view I've lost. To get security in money matters you have, apparently, to think in terms of money and I can't do that anymore at all. You must know this, dearest. I know you do. Think of the opportunities I have had, a bit of flattering and fawning and the money would come I guess. Really you see the feeling I have got for the G[ruenberg]s, so that I shall be tremendously relieved when they leave,[1] is that now I see and feel them only as slaves to filthy little sums of money, ten cent pieces etc. and the spectacle sickens me but I guess it is in this way that you get security so that you can tell your woman, "Rest in me. I'll take care of you."

I tried to write you yesterday a little of how I have come to feel about you, a fine kind of aristocracy in you that accepts me in my vile and my nice times, and that is the greatest comfort and help to me I've ever known.

Try to rest a little, dear, and for God sake, if there is any cement man or other sort of man there who will give you any fun or amusement, take it as I would. I am a bit sore at your mother just now . . . not a personal feeling . . . I love her . . . but because she happens to be the instrument of your being taken away when I want you so much. As you know I love you both more I think than I ever loved any other two women.

1. They left a few days later upon urging by SA.

[New York, 2 October 1933]

Monday

Darling—I am pretty tired. It was hectic but rather grand at Dreiser's.[1] I kept wishing you were there. He is really a great person and it was a joy to see Wharton again.[2]

We did not get into town until noon and I went to lunch with Moley.[3] I like him. He came from a town near mine in Ohio. I proposed to him that I do the traveling thing in the South & he fell for it head over heels. This for after Christmas. The proposal will be expenses & $300 a week—

We worked it out on the basis of a kind of super reporter—

Then he sprung on me the idea of going down to Washington and doing an article on Wallace[4] and I wired to find out if I could get at Wallace this weekend and wired you. As soon as I hear from Wallace's office I will wire you again.

The later things are to be in the form of a full and running letter each week—an open letter to Roosevelt.

Moley wanted me to go talk to Roosevelt but I told him I could probably do them better not seeing Roosevelt.

Then to see the producer who wants to do *Winesburg* & found him a swell guy.[5] You are going to like him—he is all eagerness about the play and wants to produce it before Christmas. I liked everything about him. He is alive, a man of culture and so overwhelmingly sold on the play. I'll call Nathan[6] and ask him about the producer in the morning.

Nathan & Lillian Gish,[7] also [Floyd] Dell & wife came to Dreiser's Sunday afternoon.

Dear, I think I am getting my city legs under me. I'll be better when I see you again. I wanted you every moment while I was away.

I got from Nathan the story of the Guild & *Winesburg*. They were enthusiastic until they got [the] O'Neill play[8] & then felt that the two plays were too much down the same street—both small town plays etc. They didn't want to do two in the same year & of course could [not] turn down O'Neill.

I can get along swell with Moley.

The new man has some good and intelligent ideas about the play.

I'm going to crawl in bed early tonight.

I love every hair on the head I was so shabby about rubbing.

1. On Sunday, 1 October, Dreiser gave a party at his country home at Mt. Kisco, New York.

2. Wharton Esherick, wood sculptor of Paoli, Pennsylvania, was a friend of SA's.

3. Raymond Moley, born in Berea, Ohio, had recently resigned his position as assistant secretary of state in the Roosevelt administration and had become editor of a new periodical, *Today*, for which SA wrote a series of articles during the next two years.

4. Henry Wallace, secretary of agriculture, who had visited at Ripshin the previous summer. SA did visit him in Washington the following weekend and wrote an article about him, "No Swank," *Today* 1 (11 November 1933): 4–5, 23.

5. Benjamin F. Kamsler, who produced *Foreign Affairs* in 1932. This and subsequent efforts by SA to present the *Winesburg* play on Broadway were unsuccessful, in part because of complications arising from a contract he had signed earlier with Arthur Barton.

6. George Jean Nathan, drama critic and an editor of *American Spectator.*

7. Stage and movie actress.

8. *Ah, Wilderness!* which opened on 2 October, produced by the Theatre Guild.

[New York, 27 September 1934]

Thursday evening

Darling—I do not remember what files were brought to Marion. There were some letters between me & Roger when he was in trouble with Ruth. Your mother thought I said something in them. If they are there bring them along.

Braver-Mann's plan (very good I think) is to address some actors who have had rotten enough parts in movies and to tell them about the part of Hugh in "Poor White."[1] He will address—experimentally—Walter Huston, John Barrymore, Paul Muni & possibly Wallace Beery.

Really poor B is rather fine. He wrote a letter to these people that is very stupid. I rewrote it for him & he was childishly grateful.

He has made a synopsis of the play—for quick reading—that is very intelligent & clear. After all he is a sincere and even humble worker and there isn't apparently any of the Barton trickiness about him.

He is very eager to outline a play from *Poor White* but I am stalling him on this until I have talked to you.

At last apparently, darling, my cold is almost well. I am very eager to see you—too eager to sleep well until you again sleep beside me.

Friday morning

After writing the above I went to Dreiser. He had with him a lawyer and a literary agent. He began at once talking of his regret that he hadn't got down this summer—taking it for granted that we were eager for him (for which I was glad).

He has just got clear of Liveright's[2] and told me it had cost him a good deal. The fact is that they had advanced him a good deal of money which, I imagine, he had to give back.

No doubt they had cheated him on records of sales. They probably cheated everyone.

The literary agent went away and D, the lawyer and I went to Charles,[3] where we dined. D is going to Simon—called Schuster.

It turned cold. My poor cold had got almost well but now my head is stopped up again.

We had really delightful conversation at Charles but afterwards the lawyer went away & the literary agent joined us. Dreiser is wonderful in many ways. He doesn't at all mind the business side of writing. He has been down in Wall Street trying to get a hundred thousand dollars to make pictures from his own novels.

We went to a saloon and drank beer. Suddenly for some reason the two men began speaking of whores and whore houses. D knew the famous Everleigh sisters of Chicago.[4] They ran a famous place out there. Men came from all over the west and paid huge prices. One of them wrote to Dreiser. They had got rich and had retired. She wanted him to write her story. He and [H. L.] Mencken used to go to her house—she had retired to NY—and drink her champagne.

D told a little story of an experience as a reporter in Chicago. He was looking for some man and went to a laborer's house near the stock yards. The blinds of the house were closed and when he knocked on the door no one answered so he opened the door.

There was a dark room and 15 or 20 men were asleep on the floor. On a table in the room a man and woman were making love. He stood and looked at them but they didn't stop. The man grinned. He said they were all workers of the night shift in the stock yards.

The literary agent, an Austrian, began talking. He was a newspaper man here on a German daily when the war broke out. He got $10,000 from the German government to give to some American newspaper man who would go to England as a spy. He got his man.

"He had the $10,000 in cash.

"So we went to a house. We paid $300 for the night. We had champagne. We had women."

The American who went to England got caught but escaped death by telling on other spies. The literary agent was himself arrested and interned—at Chickamauga Park. He talked a long time about his experiences there.

D—"They did right to lock you up. If you were not a spy you were a potential one."

Literary agent—"Yes. I was pro German. I would have done anything. They did right to lock me up. I am in luck to be free now."

The lit. a. went away & D walked to my hotel with me. He got into one of the moods that makes us all love him. As we walked along he touched me on the shoulder and said—"A—your writing is different than that of any other man. You see and feel life differently from any of us. It is in every page of everything you write. It is distinction."

I myself had a sudden feeling. I was glad that, in the face of so many reasons at various times to be annoyed and even disgusted with D, I had always been loyal to him. I felt suddenly that many things he had been through would have dirtied me beyond ever getting clean again but that in some way he had kept clean.

Wharton [Esherick] is in town and is coming to lunch with me.

I won't be writing any more. Thank God you will be here.

1. B. G. Braver-Mann was planning a film version of *Poor White* that never materialized.

2. Dreiser's year-long case against Liveright had been decided by arbitration.

3. A Manhattan restaurant.

4. Minna and Ada Everleigh came to Chicago in 1899 and ran the lavishly furnished Everleigh Club before it closed in 1911.

[New Orleans, 11 March 1935]

Monday

Darling . . .

I paid income tax $82.46, so I think we got out pretty well. Jimmy's[1] financial man fixed it up for me. I am sending your black belt under other cover today.

You wrote a letter home and one to me and mixed the envelopes. Don't worry. You said nothing that would startle or shock anyone. I got mine from your mother and sent hers on.

I was tired today and did not work long. Got the 250 for the Texas story[2] and by the way are you all right for money? Don't hesitate to use the Amalgamated money.[3] I'm not spending much these days.

I am pretty sure that, about Saturday, I'll go on down to Grande Isle[4] and stay there for a week or more. I want to get back outdoors and also away from the people here. It isn't that I don't like them. Well, you know.

Tuesday

Went alone to a prize fight last evening. Some very beautiful work by a slender young Filipino boy. It was a joy to see. I see that the Libby Reynolds matter is front page again.[5] Libby surely shows up well and decently against the Cannon crowd. In front of the Roosevelt, a young man selling, for thirty-five cents, a pamphlet . . . "Why Huey Long Should Be President." I stopped to speak to the young man. "What are you trying to do, get money to finance Huey's campaign?" "Hell no. To hell with Huey. I'm trying to finance myself." It seems to me that Huey is digging his own grave. He is beginning to try to explain his Share the Wealth plan.

I haven't seen the young communist you spoke of. Dear, my experience is against it. Just because a young man is a communist doesn't stop his being a bore. And they are usually so terribly self-righteous about it all.

I think, dear, that if Roger is not coming at once[6] . . . and I think he isn't, I'll go on down to Grande Isle. I should know by Thursday and if my plans change I'll wire you. I speak of it now because I do want your letters.

It has turned cold again, a norther. The room here is full of moths but the woman says that it isn't the moths that do it. It's the grubs that come later. Before I leave I'll have everything sent to the cleaners as we do not want to take the beasts home. The leather jacket came and I'll wear it today.

My chapter went off yesterday and I'll have to rewrite that one. I got the Sheean book[7] but have not got into it yet. Did you read it?

At the prize fight I was recognized. "Well, I swear. How are you? I haven't seen you for a long time." "And who do you think I am?" "Why, you are Mr. Bradley, the chicken merchant, aren't you?" "No, alas, I'm not."

"Well, you're a dead ringer for him."

About once a week a kind of terrible hunger for you comes over me. It's almost unbearable. Last week one day I walked all afternoon, trying to shake it off or wear myself out so that I would sleep. It's one reason I want to get out of doors. I feel it coming on again alas. I love you, dear.

1. James Feibleman, philosophy professor at Tulane University and friend of SA's.

2. "Valley Apart," *Today* 3 (20 April 1935): 6–7, 22–23, SA's impressions of travels in the Rio Grande valley in Texas.

3. SA had a checking account with the Amalgamated Bank of New York in addition to one at the Bank of Marion.

4. On the gulf coast south of New Orleans.

5. Libby Holman Reynolds, a Broadway actress, had played Belle Carpenter in the Hedgerow Theatre performance of *Winesburg* in 1934. She was the second wife of tobacco heir Smith Reynolds, who was a victim of either suicide or murder. SA's reference is to her involvement in a lawsuit by Reynolds's first wife, Anne Cannon Reynolds Smith, who was making an unsuccessful effort to acquire his entire estate for her daughter.

6. Roger Sergel was planning to meet SA in New Orleans; he and his wife came later.

7. Probably Vincent Sheean, *Personal History* (1935).

[New Orleans, 22 March 1935]

Friday
Darling

Morning of the 28th. That I think will be Thursday. It is hot here. I slept late. I brought Lucile[1] some trout and went there to dine. Jack McClure[2] had called up. I hadn't seen him yet and it was his night off. Went with him and some other people to a night beer garden. A man in the party is heavily in politics here, a young lawyer, very bright, and the evening was spent hearing tales of [Huey] Long. The man, by these tales, can be nothing less than a paranoiac, insanely ambitious, unscrupulous, tricky to the nth degree and full of audacity. In such times as ours he might go anywheres.

I am to dine with Tom [Tippett], his Mary and the boy. The place called The Basement Bookshop, the place to which I took Gertie[3] that evening, announced a reception for me, Roark Bradford[4] and others for tonight but forgot to invite me or say anything to me about it. Now they are on the phone but I have my phone plugged.

Truth is I would go if you were here to go with me. I don't mind such things when you are by.

In some way Grande Isle refreshed me and I think I can work again. Being here, working here and you gone . . . the association, inevitable, with the little group here . . . a kind of staleness in it . . . I think had got me, and the open air, the craziness of that queer hotel, even the drunken landlady, gave life a new freshness.

Jack McClure said . . . he is [a] queer little man, a royalist . . . "I want to meet your wife. Everywhere I hear it, how fine she is, everyone speaks of it." I hear a good deal of such remarks and don't know what to say. "Yes," I say, "she is nice." I love you, dear.

1. Lucile Antony. She and her husband Marc were old friends of SA's.

2. John McClure, a poet, a founder of the *Double Dealer,* and a member of the editorial staff of the New Orleans *Times-Picayune.*

3. On a lecture tour of the United States, Gertrude Stein had come to New Orleans in February and had visited with SA.

4. Author of *Ol' Man Adam and His Chillun* (1928), *John Henry* (1931), and *Kingdom Coming* (1933).

[Valley Cottage, New York,[1]
18 October 1935]

Darling

Here is a little check you might cash.

There is and has been something on my mind for some time. It is about the matter of pregnancy. Of course I know, darling, how much you want to have a child. Why should I dissemble? It doesn't really matter so much to me. Just the same I want you to have what you want. I don't know whether or not it's my fault or yours that you have not become pregnant. When the doctors reassured you, and me, at the hospital when you had the operation[2] . . . that you know I never did believe in, I had my doubts. They'd be pretty likely to say what they did say. At the same time it may be my fault.

I suppose, just because I have so wanted you to have what you want, I've been a little extra sensitive. It has rather seemed to me lately that when any other male comes around I see in you, in your eyes, a hunger, even tenderness, I no longer seem to arouse in you. I just don't feel it being awakened. I don't blame you and of course you do constantly make me pregnant, as I really love you. I get all the best of that.

Yesterday it was just something . . . not at all that you are or would be in love with Paul [Rosenfeld] or any other man I know but I came out there and you were feeding him grapes out of your hand and there was that thing in your eyes . . . the male I presume, what you want now from the male. And then you went off to the other arbor, to where the white grapes are, and I said, rather wistfully, "Bring me some." You did bring some and went to Paul and gave them to him and I felt suddenly shut out . . . in a rather silly way I admit. It is just because I so want you to have what you want and am discouraged that I don't give it to you so I wanted to stay by myself and think. And I did think and wanted to tell you to follow your impulses and that it might be worth trying some other man to see if you could get what you want.

I could go through it. I don't think anything will ever touch my love for you and I do think we have got something we won't lose.

And so there it is said and don't take it as sentimental and don't you be sentimental about it.

The truth is that I didn't want either Elizabeth or Tennessee to have children and never gave them the chance because I never loved them as I do you.

I really think, dear, you might do me a kind of honor to take this liberty from me. I am really a sophisticated man and, at the bottom of me, in spite of fuss about such little things as poison ivy,[3] etc., rather childish, it doesn't really mean much.

And I want really the tenderness you used to express to me more than you do since you have begun to be a little hopeless about this thing.

Your lover

You wouldn't need ever to tell me who it was and if you wanted to could pretend it was me.

I'll mail you today the script of the Lindsay, to be typed. Book, out of which part of the article is taken, under other cover.[4]

Find out the first name of the painter Hopper—the man who loves to do those absurd mansard roof houses . . . I'm uncertain. Call up the Museum of Modern Art. They'll tell you. Also check on spelling of Burchfield's name.[5]

1. The country home of Mary Emmett, near Nyack, New York. After Burton Emmett's death on 6 May 1935, SA and ECA frequently stayed with her.

2. I.e., on 22 October 1932.

3. SA was recovering from a severe case of poison ivy.

4. "Lindsay and Masters," SA's review of *Vachel Lindsay* by Edgar Lee Masters appeared in *New Republic* 85 (25 December 1935): 194–95. It quotes six paragraphs from the book.

5. In his review SA suggests that an artist such as Edward Hopper or Charles Burchfield should do a painting of the Lindsay house in Springfield, Illinois.

[Valley Cottage, 13 November 1935]

Dearest Eleanor

I must try to put down a little more definitely about my talk with M[ary] my feeling about the whole thing etc. etc.

In the first place of course you know that it was sheer luck that I had the *Today* thing last year. That is of course off. In any event the magazine won't last.[1]

And, E, I do not get younger. I do feel that my powers as a writer still grow. In some way I have managed to keep young in that regard but I cannot any longer do the work I'd like to do as a creative man and at the same time do the scratching around I've always had to do. Before you knew me I went on for year after year doing as much work as you are doing now at your job and doing other work nights and at odd moments. Some of my best stories were done in a crowded office, interrupted every few minutes as you are. You'll hardly believe this. It's true anyway but I cannot do it any longer.

You also may not believe that the hardest thing about this present thing to me is that the only way I can justify taking money from anyone is by a good deal of egotism . . . that is to say by bringing forward the notion that I am of enough importance as an American artist to be so taken care of. Believe it or not that isn't easy either. You often hear me speak in a big way but it is really no more than an outside swagger.

And it isn't easy for you. When the idea was first suggested[2] . . . it came up one day when I was driving M from Ripshin to Marion . . . I had been talking quite innocently as I would to any friend about the problem before me and mentioned the ambition to some day go to work on the Civil War . . . when it first came up I went and talked to Mother. She said that, if it were her in your place, she did not think she could do it. She said it would involve the idea of another woman doing for her man what she would like to do and that she didn't think she could do it.

She, however, had something the same impression of M that I had . . . that it wasn't a matter of sentimentality . . . that wouldn't come in. I had thought that I could be friends with M as I could with any man, Funk for example, or Roger. I think we both saw M pretty clearly, the funny little greedy spots that will show, little queer ways of saving money, things like her grabbing of the things at the flower show.

All of these balanced against a bigness that is there. I am sorry you have not heard some of these talks we have had when that side came out.

Her saying that for example about money earned in advertising and now used by one hurt by advertising.[3]

I think she is really anxious not to be on our hands too much so as to bore us. She said, "I will frequently run away on trips," etc.

At the same time frankly saying she is frightened at the idea of trying to live without us.

She is very anxious that as few people as possible know about the arrangement, knowing as well as we do that it would affect such people as have been about her . . . they feeling that we were working her . . . not to have that brought in . . . her friends think, because of the way we live, Ripshin etc., that we are well-to-do. It's better to have them think so etc.

She said frankly, "There is no use our trying to have a nice relationship without Eleanor in on it." She wondered, as I have wondered, how much your position and the feeling of being useful in a world outside my world . . . how much that would mean to you. She thought maybe you might get interested in the history and be content in that way.

She even spoke of her fussiness about me, wanting to do little things, saying it was a carryover from thirty years with Burt and also a way of keeping busy and feeling herself of some importance in the relationship.

I think we do have to balance against her retelling of old tales, little funny economies etc., this bigness in her, which I am sure is real.

It isn't easy or simple. I admit it. For me, as a worker, it is terribly more important than to you. There is a fighting chance I may do my best work in the ten years ahead. I may, in order to use what talent I may have to the uttermost, be compelled to live differently, even go off South for parts of winters and things of that sort.

You have a feeling of being outside all this, I know. You'd like to be able to do yourself what M because of her money can do. You can't. You'll have to be pretty big to make it a go.

I did . . . you will forgive me . . . tell her, in our talk about the winter, when I had made over the papers to Bob and was broke, how you practically supported me, etc., put me back on my feet, and did try also to make her feel how terribly important you were to me, that my marriage with you be a success etc. etc. It is.

And to this she said frankly . . . "Well, if I am to live with you two from time to time, share some in your lives, you know I could not do it without her." She pointed out that it would be practically impossible for me to be here now but for you and then spoke, I thought with real feeling, of her admiration for you. There was the suggestion that if she was to make a contribution . . . and she did say it was not to me personally but to something she felt I stood for . . . she could only do it if she felt you were willing.

I think that is about the net of our talks, its shades etc. I wanted to write it all out for you the best I could. At any rate from the standpoint of opportunity to work it's pretty lucky I feel.

1. In February 1937 *Today* ceased publication and merged with *Newsweek*.

2. On Sunday, 8 September, Mary had proposed giving SA $3,000 a year to work on a book about the Civil War as a memorial to her husband. SA hoped to work on the project with ECA at the Library of Congress, but she was opposed to taking the money.

3. Burton Emmett was a New York advertising executive. SA gave up his advertising work in 1922.

[Valley Cottage, 18 November 1935]

Darling

What a day. The sleet of Saturday night turned to rain. I got up at six to work. Built a fire downstairs, not to disturb the Wolfs.[1] Worked until ten and left to get Tommy [Smith] before they were down. Should have had sense enough to call Tommy. Had a blowout going down and ruined a tire. Had picked [up] a nail, I presume down somewhere in Jersey City. Simply had to run on it to a garage as I pictured Tommy waiting in the cold and rain.

He wasn't there . . . too much weather . . . didn't blame him. I finally called him and he had called Mary, begging off. It still rained and the wind was so strong that it seemed about to blow the car off the road.

The Wolfs seem very nice . . . he a rather irritable gentle little man, unhappy in his work. I fancy that Mary would like to do something for them but he's a hard one to do anything for, I fancy. She has been tubercular. She formerly wrote publicity for a bank. I get it that [they] are one of the kind of couples that go together for years and years before they marry.

There is a doctor . . . I had heard of him . . . who made a study of human faces. The idea was to try to create a science of faces. He got quite a reputation, was employed by American Express and others to try to select people and also place them in different positions according to natural talents etc. I understand he was very successful. So Alice Wolf has studied with him.

She got at me. Well, my dear, she told me some things you would perhaps like to hear. Things I shall not tell you. I must get her at you. She didn't particularly mention my criminal tendencies but did say some things about ruthlessness etc. Oh dear, oh dear.

I wonder if you will like what I wrote yesterday morning. It was pure patter. Will have to decide later whether or not it goes in. I remember that George Moore[2] said that the acid proof of a writer was his ability or inability to write patter. Well, anyway I can sure do that.

The Wolfs left early Sunday afternoon and in the evening M and I to our cards. She forged ahead but before the evening passed I had again knocked her off. Alice W says that Mary has no skill with people. It's amusing. She wants to take the grey kitten to town but the wop man here, Angelo, has turned her down cold. AW also says Mary could be a sculptress, that she has a feeling for that sort of thing etc. I guess I'll start her. It would be something for her. I made one sculptress and why not another?[3]

Will get the money off to Mother for Mazie and Mr. C and to Mazie for Mother . . . this today. It is to be moving day and M and Harry will take the two cars and a load today. I'll take the Austin and go to Nyack for a haircut. The wind is dying and the snow melting but winter is here.

Things about your husband . . . He cannot completely love or depend upon one other person. He has a very highly developed social sense and needs people terribly but can rapidly substitute one for another. The feeling he has is the very thing he is always denying . . . that is to say it is for people in general rather than the individual. He has the word sense extraordinarily developed, is extremely apt in managing others, gets what he wants . . . is altogether devoted with grim determination to some ideal or principle, AW presumes it to be his art etc. There is more. Be a good wife and don't be too tired. Have what fun you can. In spite of AW he loves YOU I believe with absolute devotion.

She admits what may be true in general may have exceptions. She does not know how apt you are sometimes in making yourself loved.

I hope I have not gone too fast. In writing Mazie I suggested that John & I would probably be going down about 10 days before Xmas and that we could stop and pick her up. My notion was that you & M could then perhaps pick up and bring Channing. It would save them r.r. fares.

I hinted to Mazie that we were, in general, laying off Christmas. This to stop them spending anything on us.

1. Eddie and Alice Wolf of Melfa, Virginia, friends of Mary Emmett's.

2. Irish novelist whose works included *Esther Waters* (1894) and *Evelyn Innes* (1898).

3. See letter of 12 June 1931 and note 4.

[Marion, 31 December 1935]

Darling—I know your loneliness and confusion. It is in me too. It may be I attempt too much. You say sometimes . . . you know when . . . that you are like a violin string drawn to the very breaking point.

I am so driven by ambition. I want to break this thing. When I am angry or irritated with Aunt May or your father, it is more than half because of insistence upon isolation. Nothing in the world is true if it is not true that there is in every human being terrible need. The difference between me and some of the others is that every work I have ever done is an attempt to break it. When I fail, as I always do, irritation comes. I get angry, unreasonable, I know often unbearable. Forgive it when you can. Believe, dear, in the essential attempt I am making if you can. It may enable you to forgive much. Do not hold onto your hurt. Try to throw it away, dear.

It may be that together we may in the end get to laughter, knowing that the ultimate perfect thing we want cannot be attained. One of the causes of Mother's distinction is the final attainment of this inner laughter. But for it she would long ago have been dead. By holding to it she will live longer than you think. I am not sure but that association with her has really taught me, at least up in my head, what I [am] trying to say here.

[1935?]

The woman's article on aloofness etc. you sent interested me and I wondered if you thought, in sending it, that my own hesitations about going in for things like government in art, or for example "Descendants of the Revolution" etc., were indications of my aloofness.

Seems to me that all such movements are the movements toward aloofness. Who so aloof and sure of himself as the average radical—the [Malcolm] Cowleys, Waldo Franks, Mike Golds?[1]

I think we only want that our reactions to life shall not be made for us by a party or by any group.

I have been rereading *Winesburg.*

Pretty far from aloof, darling.

1. Michael Gold was the editor of the *New Masses*, a playwright, and the author of *Jews Without Money* (1930).

[Marion, 14 January 1936]

Tuesday morning
Darling . . .

It's another fine morning but I didn't sleep and I'm mad at myself. It all happened yesterday afternoon. It was such a grand day and I'd asked your mother to take a little ride with me. The car was caked with mud because of the trip to Ripshin Sunday so I'd had it washed. I came up from town to take your mother and she was mad at herself. She'd asked your father to go with us and he'd said yes . . . we could take him to the farm to feed his cattle.[1]

Your mother didn't want to do that. "We'll just have to stand around," she said. I said . . . "But my car's freshly washed."

"We'll take my car," he said.

So we went and we had both already admired the steers from Texas and it was deep cold mud and we stood and stood, like two fools, both catching cold and I mad at myself that I have got to be the kind that takes cold too easily. You know how you do. You want to go and don't. His man out there, that nice fellow who used to work in the garden last summer, had quit, had got starved out, and we went into the little house where he had lived and I thought of us getting excited about mill villages and here was this, about like John and Dave's place,[2] thin boards and old dirt etc., and Pop saying over and over that it was a fine house for such people and Mother whispering to me how the man had really starved and we both catching cold standing in the deep cold mud.

We fled finally to the car and sat . . . god knows how long, mother talking as she does of how foolish it is, out of some notion of kindness, to do what you don't want to do, and then he came.

It was rather beautiful because a conversation started on the way in that did tickle me. It concerned her always calling him Mr. C. He said he liked it. He said there should be some one way in which a woman acknowledges her inferiority to a man and he thought the kind of respect shown was just right.

I'll shake off the cold and if it doesn't clear right up I'll go to a nose man in Richmond.

I've been reading Hemingway's *Green Hills of Africa*.[3] He's a queer bird all right. I think they really did destroy him. He's so determinedly egotistical. He's got an idea . . . that you chuck the imaginative world . . . look always hard and straight at what he calls the real world . . . so he romanticizes that all out of focus and doesn't know he's doing it. My own notion is he's a mess.

But who isn't?

The best thing, coming home at night and up into the room and you not here, is the photographs of you. They are like you asleep, when you are so lovely and a fellow stands and looks at the sweet line of your neck and at your face changing from minute to minute and loves you so.

But for Christ sake, darling, take a note out of my experience of yesterday. There's no use your writing me any more, asking me to check up on what you are to do for this one or that one, because I won't do it. You've got sometime to realize that you are you and that your natural loveliness has its own value and that you are not a servant destined to spend your life running errands.

So I love you very much.

1. The Copenhavers owned a large farm just outside Marion.

2. John Anderson and David Greear were renting a house on land owned by the Copenhavers.

3. Published on 25 October 1935.

[New York,[1] 3 June 1936]

Darling—

I am trying to devote the day to thinking. It concerns this money matter. I think, when you 1st knew me, I was in a terribly defeated state. There were two or three bad years. I think myself, dear, that I am a man like Lawrence who could never live really without a woman at his back.

There is the constant terrible demand for love and I do not mean just being loved. I mean having near me someone I can love blindly, constantly, as I have come more and more to love you.

I was defeated in that by 3 women. They were in no way to blame. It wasn't to be. When you first knew me I was in the midst of one of these defeats and so spoke perhaps a good deal of money, fear of poverty etc. I don't believe it was my true self. Surely you know you have cured me of that.

It is all I think in the little poem "Tandy"—in *Winesburg*, written long ago. The man's woman, "strong to be loved," did not come in his time. You did, darling, come in my time.

It will be a little cruel but better for M[ary] in the long run. Do not blame me that I have been too hopeful as regards her. It is my way. I can't change. I throw the door wide open. If the person invited doesn't come in it goes shut.

It is my economy of existence, my way.

By rejecting M's money and help now I shall help her more than by any other thing I could do. It will disturb her, perhaps set her thinking.

I think the door went shut Sunday and over a little thing, the lovers in the grass.[2]

And after all, dear, even you, sensitive as you are to wrongs, don't quite see or understand all that meant to me. When we went out to dine that evening, I walked, both ways, to the restaurant. I did because for just a moment I wanted to be in the road with those people, the big-legged Jewesses, laughing stupid youngsters. It was me in the grass with a Jewess in my arms, me ordered off the land, me hurt. The blow struck was directly at me. I am much further what you call left than even you dream of, darling.

And then, it may be because of that, suddenly I can no longer work or live here in this house with these possessions. They crowd in on me, both here and at Valley Cottage, and suddenly I know that they killed Burt Emmett, that they have made it impossible for this child woman M to ever really even glimpse the clean wind-swept world that the poet can never live in but must always, if he is to remain a poet, go toward.

They press in, these silly possessions now, cry out, hurt me. I can't live among them anymore. I doubt, when I go out of this house in a few days now, if I'll ever come back to sleep here again. Poor M is bound, tied to these possessions, as Burt was. The illness I've been having came out of them and into me. Don't think, dear, this is just some kind of silly mysticism. I no more blame M for the disease she occasionally gives off than I blame you for getting amoeba in that hotel in Chicago.[3]

The possessions become simply the filth of life.

1. SA was staying with Mary Emmett at 54 Washington Mews.

2. SA and Mary had quarreled over her chasing away some young people who were trespassing near the house.

3. ECA had contracted amoebic dysentery at the Auditorium Hotel in Chicago in 1933.

On train, [22 September 1936]

Tuesday
Darling,

I am leaving Marion and Mary.[1] She brought me to the station. It all passed off very well but the train was some 10 minutes late. I thought to say something nice and thanked her again for all her care of me etc. Then it came, the curious, half-insane look in the eyes, hard voice, the thing that in some strange way sends a queer trembling weakness through the body, as though you had been hit a blow or had taken poison.

"I know you have been annoyed about this diet.[2] I didn't want to do it. Eleanor asked me to."

From that launched off into a tirade. You have heard it. You know, I felt myself growing again weak and upset, as I have seen you upset and trembling after such a session. I begged her not to. "Please, Mary, don't. I am very grateful. Now I'm sick. Let's not."

I really wasn't sick until that moment and now, the train going, I breathe deeply again. I know now that what has held me back from recovery has been the constant dread, at any moment one of these evil explosions.

Well, it is over, ended, and I am happy and at the moment very hard against her but I will not write anything, as I have not said anything rude. I'll write nothing without thinking it over carefully and when, before I leave, I let her know that any intimacy is at an end, I'll put it on the ground of temperament, on my part, having to have my own place etc.

The danger at home was May, who had begun to dream of getting money out of Mary for the college,[3] but I think Mother and I have her checked.

Poor, poor Burt. Bill is right. She did kill him. After illness came, he must always have been on a strain.

I'll see no one at Knoxville but Moutoux[4] and, as soon as Mary is gone, will go back home & begin to clean up. God, but I do love you.

1. Mary Emmett was visiting at Ripshin, and SA, who had suffered from the flu since the first of the month, had suddenly taken a train to Knoxville, Tennessee, to escape her.

2. Mary had insisted that SA follow the Hay diet, which was popular at the time.

3. Marion College.

4. John Moutoux, a newspaper writer, had visited at Ripshin on 16–17 August and wrote "Week-Ending with Sherwood Anderson," *Knoxville News-Sentinel Magazine,* 30 August 1936, p. 1.

[Media, Pennsylvania,
22 October 1936]

Darling—

This was one time when I was in luck to start early.[1] Just did make the 6 o'clock 7 Ave.—a jam—my driver a hot baby—full of fight—

Bumped another cab & both drivers in the street—"Sons of bitches" being hurled back & forth.

At entrance to the station a negro boy, several boxes on a hand truck, tried to dodge in front of us. We hit the hand truck—smashed a box.

Negro on the running board. "Come out of there, you white son of a bitch."

Out jumps my man.

"What, you black bastard."

He has negro by the throat, shaking him.

Negro reaches for hip pocket.

"After a knife, eh." Throws him to the street, jumps back in car.

Negro hops up. Is on running board.

"God damn you, gotta get your number."

"Let's see you get it." My man punches him, knocks him off—we sail on, arrive at station 5:54.

Hot dog. Big town life.

Sweetheart, I ought to be telling you 50 times a day how much I love you.

Rest.

Get well.

If you don't I'll quit loving you.

1. SA, staying with ECA at the Royalton Hotel in New York, had taken a taxi to the train station and the train to Media to spend a few days at the Hedgerow Theatre.

[Marion, 18 December 1936]

Darling. I am sending this to the house . . . along with a note written yesterday and not mailed. I had a pretty good day, in fact seem to be working again. I went to Funk's to eat birds[1] . . . delicious. I made a cocktail . . . an orange blossom . . . and took it over.[2] The birds were fine. Mother says she is going to write you . . . that I am having a big time in your absence etc. etc. I am going to stay home now for several evenings. I suppose a fellow occasionally does get rather fed up on so many females. He says to himself . . . "Well now, I'll have to go find some men." My new short story, not yet finished, is about that.[3]

For some reason you do not count as female in this sense. You are simply the one loved.

I believe, dear, that this new way of living . . . eating very little . . . a good deal of orange juice . . . practically no drinking, makes the mind clearer. And then I find it is time for me to be outdoors more, walk more. Yesterday, after work, I walked to Lincoln Hill[4] and then made a great loop around the town. I have promised to take Mazie with me on such a walk today but it is better to go alone. You go along thinking things out.

Regarding January . . . if you work in February . . . I presume Texas will be too far. We'd better perhaps go to Florida . . . anywhere we can find a beach to walk and loaf on. We can be together outdoors . . . that's the main thing. Well, I'll keep myself fluid. I'll wait and see how it turns out.

Mother seems very well. Aunt May is flying about. All is as usual. Your father sighs, insults God by the way he says grace at table, starts the radio at five in the morning etc. etc. and has a good time. I really do like the man immensely. Yesterday the biggest of the rocks in the driveway got down under his car so that he had to jack the car up, sweat and groan for a half hour. Did he remove the rock? Not he. He had it put right back where it had been. A man of character, I say.

I'd give an arm to hear your peculiar hurried footsteps on the stairs. It won't be long. Only one Sunday to be got through.

1. Quail and pheasants.
2. SA had been ill and was drinking large quantities of orange juice.
3. "Man to Man," apparently never completed.
4. To the north of the downtown.

[New York, 4 April 1937]

Sunday
Darling—

It's ten and I've been out to breakfast—the 1st time I've been able to slip past Ethel.[1] Think I had a pretty good day of work yesterday.

Got your wire last night and so thought I'd better send this to Louisville.[2]

Had K[atharine] to lunch at the Brevoort and who should be sitting at a nearby table, with a man, but Mildred.[3] I lied and said I'd called her.

Went with Mary for a drive over the Triborough Bridge and on up through the layout for the World's Fair.[4] It is going to be magnificent & the bridge is magnificent now. We must really drive over it.

M[ary] continues very very nice.[5] We plan a trip up to the farm today.

Did I tell you that Mary and I went to that opening of the Raleigh cocktail bar at the Warwick Hotel but it was so jammed we could get no seat & could hardly move. There were a great many names on the wall so we didn't find ours.

I dined last night with Ted and that bright little kid sec[6]—Ted, as always, very fine. I think he has less money as he is in a hotel not nearly so swank and the little gal looked thin & said she had a touch of tuberculosis. She is going away somewhere to the country to be cured.

No word at all of Helen[7] and, under the circumstances, I didn't ask. Ted seemed mighty glad to see me. He's on a diet but we dined in a little Italian place and had a delightful evening.

Think I'll go on over to Jap's[8] on Tuesday night & spend Wednesday & Thursday there, taking the train Thursday night.

The weather has been fine here.

Don't expect K[atharine] before the 10th or 11th.

Give my best to Randolph.

Am dining with Max and Tom Wolfe tonight.[9]

Feeling O.K. and getting a good deal of work done.

1. Ethel Miller, a friend of Mary Emmett's who also lived at Washington Mews.

2. ECA had left Marion by train on 30 March for meetings in Chicago, Louisville, and Des Moines. SA went to New York on the same day.

3. Mildred Esgar, a friend and YWCA associate of ECA.

4. The New York World's Fair of 1939–40 at Flushing Meadows. The Triborough Bridge, connecting the Bronx, Queens, and Manhattan, was completed in 1936.

5. In his diary entry for 31 March, SA wrote that she had "made great strides in getting command of herself" (*The Sherwood Anderson Diaries, 1936–1941*, p. 94).

6. Theodore Dreiser and his secretary, Harriet Bissell.

7. Helen Richardson, Dreiser's companion for many years, who in 1944 became his second wife.
8. Jasper ("Jap") Deeter was the founder and director of the Hedgerow Theatre.
9. Maxwell Perkins, Scribner's editor, and novelist Thomas Wolfe. This was the first meeting of SA and Wolfe; on the next day SA wrote to ECA: "He's huge. You'd like him. He has a fine generous feeling for others . . . extremely sensitive and rather combative, but in a good way. I think he's great."

[Philadelphia,[1] 12 November 1937]

Darling.

I am writing this so it may greet you when you reach Chicago. I just want to tell you again how much I love you and how happy I am being your husband & lover.

It has been a grand time these last few weeks. Don't think I don't know that you work too hard. I wish it weren't so. I wish it were possible for me to make your future safer.

Really, dear, I don't quite know how I lived before I got you. I guess I didn't.

I adore you.

S.

1. SA attended the Hedgerow Theatre on 11 November; on the twelfth ECA joined him in Philadelphia, and he gave a speech there that evening. They went on to Baltimore the next day and caught trains—ECA to Chicago and SA to Charleston, South Carolina.

[Marion, 26 May 1938]

Thursday

Darling.

In regard to the matter of that job[1] . . . I presume it would mean living in NY most of the year. It does not appeal to me.

It would mean practically giving up our home.

It would mean that you would constantly be doing beyond your strength. The idea that they will get someone else to do most of the work, etc., is piffle. They will forget it of course.

I think it is important that one of you children live nearer Mother at least some of the year. She gets no younger. May looks like hell. Your father is pretty helpless.

I am going to say as little as possible about my own feeling in regard to N.Y. For years I have been trying to hang on to something. It has been a struggle. It is hard to define. The whole trend of thought and feeling now—as expressed in the arts and particularly in writing—is a kind of unbelief. If it is true, dear, that there is, as you sometimes say when I am closest to you, when I am making love to you, that I am a poet, it is also true that I am a mystic. I can't figure on what will happen next year. I was, as a boy, in the country. Most of my life has been spent in the country or in small towns. More than I can say without sounding silly, I get something from the sky, the trees, the silence of country nights by which I live. I presume for me the city will always be connected in my mind with those years in business. I do not much like the present day intellectual and radical crowd with whom, in the city, we seem destined to be. They choke and kill something in me.

Although I have always, even though not much figuring on the future, managed to live, I can't naturally superimpose my point of view on you.

This is as near as I can say what I feel. I can't, naturally, ask you to take risks that any artist who remains alive must I guess take.

I know that I love you.

1. ECA had been offered the position of head of the industrial division of the YWCA. In July she accepted it and served in that capacity until 1946.

[New York, 26 October 1938]

Wednesday
Darling

I want, if I can, dear, to tell you how much I love you. I am really in a bad state. If it were not for you I think I would gladly give up living.

The outlook is so hopeless, dear. What am I to do, where turn? It doesn't seem to me, dear, that I can go on living on two women.[1]

Perhaps if I were producing, it wouldn't matter, but it is obvious that it is not in me to produce the glamorous stuff now wanted.

And I cannot blame people for wanting it. There is so much in life now that is terribly depressing.

What I want to say is something about the way you must find me now—so often sunk into myself, uncommunicative, silent. This absorption in books—the terrible constant effort to escape from myself and my own present ineffectiveness that leaves me so little to give you.

I am like a child clinging to you and want rather to be a man, standing on my own feet with something to give. My darling.

1. ECA and Mary Emmett.

[Fremont, Ohio, 7 January 1939]

Saturday morning

The weather still continues wonderful. I find that Olivet is near Marshall, Mich. and I will very easily make Marshall tonight, where I shall stay, going up to Olivet probably on Sunday afternoon.[1]

I didn't stay in Clyde after all as there is now no hotel there. I drove over here and returned to spend the evening with Herman Hurd—a very short, broad man, my best boyhood friend. The Hurds have kept a grocery in the same building in Clyde for 110 years. He has two sons, one a young architect, the other a painter.

It was very sad seeing poor Miss White,[2] who knows she is only waiting for death and is suffering constantly but doing the job nobly. She has a very fine head.

I miss you every mile I drive.

The country has been very beautiful and I have had a nice feeling about the people.

Clyde hasn't changed much. I drove about in familiar streets over which my fancy has played so much.

Darling, I am very very much your husband, and your lover.

1. SA was on his way to Olivet, Michigan, to serve as Resident Lecturer in Creative Literature at Olivet College for the rest of the month. He had visited in Clyde, Ohio, the previous evening.

2. Trillena White, a retired high school teacher who had been a close friend of SA's when he was a student at Wittenberg Academy in Springfield, Ohio, in 1899–1900. He visited her in the hospital in Springfield on 5 January; she died on 8 May 1941.

[Olivet, Michigan, 16 January 1939]

Monday

Darling—

There is a slow peaceful fall of snow on an already white world. The boy came early this A.M. with your Sunday special delivery . . . but I was up & dressed. I think that, after our heavy feast on Saturday evening, we were all heavy yesterday.

No, I didn't go to church. The library, where I work, was locked but I found a man to let me in, so I worked. It was well they let me in as I found a busted pipe and thus prevented a flood.

Went to a tea at five.

In the evening sat with the biology man and Gosling,[1] of the English Dept., until 11. Then we drove to Bellevue—5 miles—and had soup and sandwiches. To bed at 12.

I'm rereading *Moby Dick.*

I speak twice this week—to a small group and then to a large one. I have the lectures prepared.

I swear there is something nice here—the whole feeling. It may be the best out for us yet—that rather than the newspaper[2]—a connection with some college. I rather like the kids. They seem to like me.

In the end we might be able to do that and still hang on to Ripshin.

An industrial town—so completely one as Front Royal will be—would not be the same story as Marion and I'm not so sure about dependence on labor leaders.

I dreamed of you all night—making very violent and frequent love to you, darling.

1. Glenn Gosling, an English professor. The "biology man" was Charles E. Parkinson, biology professor.

2. On his way to Michigan, SA had stopped at Parkersburg, West Virginia, to discuss with Kenneth Douty, a labor union organizer, the possibility of starting a pro-union newspaper in Front Royal, Virginia.

[Olivet, 18 January 1939]

A prediction—something I get from the kids here—that my own life is not quite the failure I've been thinking it. There is something—there must be something buried away in my books that goes pretty deep into a great many people. There will be, someday, perhaps not in my time, a new demand spring up for the books. I feel that they do answer something these kids more and more want.

Thursday. Darling—

I wrote the above yesterday but wonder this morning if it's true.

So you have been having snow too. This morning the sky is clear and the sun shining. Deep snow everywhere but here they go right on, used to it, paying no attention. It is very quiet here and against the white the tree trunks very black. This morning all the little twigs are covered with frost & glisten in the sun.

I spoke last night to a big crowd of students. They seemed to like it a lot and afterwards a painter who is working here[1] brought a bottle over to the house and he with some of the men of the faculty sat with me until midnight.

The days, however, seem to go very very slowly. I seem to have been away from you for months.

1. George Rickey, then a young painter on the Olivet faculty and later a prominent sculptor.

[Olivet, 26 January 1939]

Thursday
Darling

More snow. It is really becoming quite deep. I went at noon to Battle Creek to address the combined business men's club (gave them anti-fascist talk—10 minutes—pretty good) from where I wired you about the summer writers' school. A letter had just come from Ted Davison and he wants an answer by wire.[1] They also say they want me here.

I gave the last of my formal talks here and it went with a bang. I found I had to write 2 new talks and revamp the one on Realism. There have been three formal talks and the crowd has grown constantly larger. I think, even though we get a bit less, I'd rather come here but will make no decision until I hear from you.

Something very interesting has [happened], as you perhaps have guessed from my letters. As when you first knew me, I find that I have been drawing more and more within myself. It is, darling, partly because of the Mary arrangement that is not, at bottom, sound. As it has turned out, it is you now who are constantly meeting and associating with people while I am in some way shut out.

Here I have seemed to open out. These youngsters like me. Again I see material that is living about me. It has been very stimulating.

And I am wondering if it isn't the out for us, say a seven-month arrangement with some such college, giving us enough on which to live, being together. I see here how easy, apparently, it might be to make some such an arrangement. It could give us a life together. It is certainly worth thinking about.

I love you.

You had better name a hotel, in Philadelphia, where I can meet you on Friday Feb. 3.[2] Send me word at Antioch College, Yellow Springs, Ohio. I will keep you in touch. This morning the snow is a foot deep here and still falling but I'm sure the roads will be kept clear.

We go to Lansing, to the newspaper men, tonight.[3]

1. Edward ("Ted") Davison, poet and English professor at the University of Colorado, was planning the 1939 writers' conference at Boulder and invited SA to take part.

2. After a speaking engagement at Antioch College, SA drove to Philadelphia and met ECA at the Sylvania Hotel on 3 Feb.

3. SA spoke that night in Lansing at the annual pancake supper of the Michigan Press Association, an organization of publishers and editors of weekly and small daily newspapers in Michigan.

[Washington, D.C., 7 March 1939]

Tuesday night

Darling,

Don't think I do not know that I am being a complete rotter to run away as I have done just as this time,[1] you not well, Mother coming, K[atharine] and H[enry] coming and the whole set-up. I guess I had to, dear. It has been very hard for me this year. I have seen you working harder and harder, showering presents and money on me and, in the midst of this, it has been for me, as you must know, a time of absolute ineffectualness. The only time for a year now that I have felt a little useful in life was the few weeks up there at Olivet.

It's pretty hard to face, the whole set-up, Mary's great kindness (and she is infinitely kind), you working too hard all the time, myself living on a scale beyond what I deserve—all living conditions too good, wearing too good clothes, everything.

It has nothing to do with my love of you. That's solid. It's the most real thing left in my life.

I wanted to be by myself, think if I can—try to face what I am and why. I don't know whether I'll succeed or not. I fear talk is n.g. now.

That's the reason I didn't go to Hedgerow or Mazie and won't go to Jay [Scherer]'s. I'll aim at Mobile first. Go to the little hotel there—the LaClede—facing the little park.[2] I'll wire you every night. Write me air mail there when you get this.

There has been, I'm afraid, too much kindness. I can't quite bear any more just now.

I guess I'll come out of it some way. It's a cross-roads.

I only want it to be clear that it is personal and has nothing to do with us as lovers.

I'll write a note to Mims[3]—tell her I'm drifting about the South etc.

[across left margin] I hated asking you to attend to the income tax but was too horribly ashamed that I had earned nothing.

1. Following a long siege of flu, which, he said, "left me weak and despondent," (*The Sherwood Anderson Diaries, 1936–1941*, p. 223), SA left New York driving south and stopped at the Hotel Raleigh in Washington.

2. SA may have been thinking of the Cawthon Hotel rather than the LaClede, which did not face a park. On 10–12 March he stayed at the Cawthon, which fronted on Bienville Square.

3. Marion ("Mims") Phillips, actress at the Hedgerow Theatre, a friend of SA's.

[New Orleans, 15 March 1939]

Wednesday

Darling—

This is the 1st grey, rather cold morning I've seen since I left New York.

The people from Olivet haven't shown up yet.[1] I worked well yesterday. Lillian Feibleman[2] invited me to dinner as did also Julius [Friend] but I went neither place. Stayed in the evening in the room here and went to bed early.

I have books borrowed from Marc [Antony]. Read a life of Goya, about whom I had known little. It's the old story of all artists. He lived when Napoleon was invading Spain and you might well think, reading, that it was the story of present-day Spain, Franco etc. The same killing of people, plotting with the church, starvation, etc.

In the late afternoon Marc took me to an amazing man—a Doctor Marion Souschon—a rich successful surgeon here who took up painting some five years ago. He is a Louisiana Frenchman and an extraordinary man—big like Joe,[3] cultured and, I think, a natural. His paintings are very exciting. He is going to give me one.

I think I miss you most in the late afternoon and evening—here in the room. I am on the 10th floor—a corner room, looking over a great stretch of the river and the whole French Quarter. It is certainly a very beautiful city.

Going back to M, I think I could stand the whole situation better if she really had any taste, any real sense of the arts, so that I could feel that what I got from her was something earned by my work and not due to a kind of personal attachment. I find that Goya had exactly the same problem, although he had no sympathetic, understanding wife as I have. When he was past 70 he had to get on a mule and, leaving all he had accumulated behind, strike off to try to begin life anew again.

I expect the Olivet crowd—2 men & two women—will be in today.

I love you very much.

1. A group of Olivet College faculty arrived later that day.

2. Wife of Jeff Feibleman, a distant relative of James Feibleman.

3. Joseph Girsdansky, a physician in New York, a good friend of the Andersons.

[Olivet, Michigan,[1] 21 July 1939]

Darling . . .

I think I must be very well. The first morning after I came here it was cold and rainy. I was restless and couldn't sleep and got up early. I got into the car and went for a drive. I didn't take my hat or overcoat and caught a cold. I took three aspirins that day and got a bottle of Vick's and by the next morning the cold was all gone.

Sounds like a patent medicine testimonial, doesn't it?

Carl Sandburg was to come for an evening but didn't show up so I have volunteered to fill in. I am simply going to give them the speech I made here this winter and that they later printed in the little booklet.[2]

Don't we feel rich though with the fifteen hundred?[3]

Neither Robert or Glenn can come now.[4] I wrote you about Padraic and Mary Colum.[5] I won't invite them unless you say so.

Then there is John Bishop.[6] I dare say he will be going back east. If the Colums can't ride with us, we might invite him.

Bishop spoke last night. It was a fine job. The man knows a lot.

I haven't figured out the Katherine Anne Porter.[7] I think she is probably a cold woman, pretty wise and foxy. I doubt she takes much to me. I presume it is my story telling faculty but there isn't much doubt they fall harder for me than the others and Olivet does rather star me. It's a little hard for such a one as the Porter to take. John and Padraic don't mind. They are bigger.

Several people have spoken wishing you were here. John Bishop was particularly enthusiastic in speaking of you.

I love you, darling.

1. SA was participating in the Olivet Writers' Conference, 16–29 July.

2. *A Writer's Conception of Realism,* a pamphlet published at Olivet College in 1939.

3. SA's royalty for "Discovery of a Father," *Reader's Digest* 35 (November 1939): 21–25.

4. I.e., to Ripshin for a visit. Robert Ramsay was registrar and dean of men at Olivet. Glenn Gosling did visit Ripshin for three weeks in August.

5. Padraic Colum, Irish editor, dramatist, and poet, and his wife, Mary, author of *From These Roots: The Ideas That Have Made Modern Literature* (1937), were participants in the conference. SA was considering inviting them to ride back with him for a visit to Ripshin.

6. John Peale Bishop, poet and novelist. As it turned out, SA met ECA's train at Sandusky, Ohio, and the two of them drove back to Ripshin.

7. Two days earlier he had written to ECA that Porter was "pretty literary—cold I think—I like warm people—about fifty, suggestion of anemia, a fading flower but still small and pretty in a faded way."

[Harrodsburg, Kentucky,
25 September 1939]

Monday morning
Darling

Did I tell you that I haven't taken a drink since you left?[1] I decided I'd give it a rest for a time, perhaps until I see you again. What about you?

I had a big sleep after the drive over here—went to bed at eight and slept without waking until seven. I had worn the heavy blue suit and it was hot coming over.

I think I'll be able to work here. Will drive over to the tracks at noon.

I finished *War and Peace*. Don't think you missed much as the later chapters are the weakest. As Mother had nothing new to read, I started her on it.

I'm trying the best I can to live up to my own preaching, not to let my own mind and imagination get too high on all the so-called big things going on—to see as much as I can of the small close about me. I really think that, if that could be done, the small might spread out and explain the big.

Effort to get a table in the room here to work on—

Me—A card table would be fine.

Negro boy—I don't think a card table would do.

Me—Yes it does fine.

Boy—Its legs are too weak.

Me—No it's fine.

Boy—I think you wouldn't like it.

Me—Yes I would. You get it.

Boy—Well, you see, mister, we ain't got any card table.

God only knows when you will get this letter or when I'll hear from you.

I am loving you strong.

I'll write Mary.

1. ECA had left Marion on 19 September; on 24 September SA drove to the Hotel Harrod at Harrodsburg, where he stayed while attending the trotting races at Lexington, about thirty miles to the northeast. He wrote an article on the experience, "Here They Come," *Esquire* 13 (March 1940): 80–81.

[Harrodsburg, 27 September 1939]

Wednesday morning

Darling.

I hope for a letter from you today.

I was certainly quite a boy at the trots yesterday.

I made 3 bets. Merry Mite—in the 3 year old pace—paid $7 for $2. $5 ahead.

Then I bet $2 on Princess Laurel in the 16 pace and lost. $3 ahead.

Then bet 2 on Gentleman Jim—2 year old trot—and it paid $28.80. $31.80 ahead.

I quit betting at that.

There was a huge crowd.

The starter bawled out my name from the judge's stand and, full of fear that it might be a wire and that something had happened to you or Mother, I went over there.

The race Gentleman Jim had won was a famous old race[1]—the 63rd renewal—and besides the purse a silver cup was given.

So out I went on the tracks before the grandstand with the owner, his daughter and the driver Curly Smart—and helped present the cup.

Then we all went up in the judge's stand and each talked over the mike. I said 4 words.

In the morning a two year old pacing filly Ann Vonian had set a new world's pacing record for 2 year olds—2.02 1/2—and I was taken over to the stables and stood at the colt's head while they took another picture.[2]

They released me then but in the evening I got into big society—dining with a man named Dick Case—secretary to Harriman the railroad man's son, who is a big trotting horse man, and Dunbar Bostwick, the young millionaire polo player, who has gone in for the trotters.[3] He seemed a nice healthy chap. We all then went together to a big sale of yearlings at Walnut Hall farm.

And you wouldn't believe what gorgeous places these farms are or what beautiful colts they raise.

They sold only yearlings. I got back to my hotel here at 11 P.M.

Sore that you weren't here to see me being so horsey.

It was fun though. The crowd is so different from that you find at the running tracks—so many country town men, doctors and lawyers etc. who are in racing as a fad because they have the same kind of admiration for these beautifully trained creatures I have. There is betting of course but it is the same sort of betting I do.

The weather remains wonderful.

The races end on Friday afternoon so I will go home Saturday.

I wish you were here.

I love you.

1. The Lexington Stake, begun in 1875.

2. The picture of SA posing with the horse and its owner, Ethel Wengler, appeared on the front page of the *Lexington Herald* on 27 September.

3. Case was publicity director of the U.S. Trotting Association and editor of a magazine on trotting, *Hoof Beats*. William Averell Harriman, the son of Edward H. Harriman, was then chairman of the board of Union Pacific Railroad and an official in the U.S. Department of Commerce. Bostwick, owner of one of the winning horses, was treasurer of the U.S. Trotting Association.

[Olivet, 19 July 1940]

Friday

Darling.

So one of the weeks is almost at an end.[1] I'll be at the early morning train on Saturday all right—we'll come over on Friday afternoon.

As for the life here—it is—on the whole—pretty much a grind. The 1st 4 or 5 nights there was a good deal of sitting about and drinking until 2 or 3 a.m. but I chucked it, going to bed at eleven.

There is a little clique of the more precious ones—the Porter, John B a good deal, Warren etc.[2] who get away with it by analyzing everything.

On the whole I tell stories. I think probably they all have more fun with me but whether or not they learn anything I doubt.

I find I can't work at my own work here and probably the whole thing doesn't pay—a waste of time.

Anyway I'm very hungry for you and our own life—my darling.

1. SA had returned to Olivet for a two-week writers' conference, 14–27 July.

2. Katherine Anne Porter, John Peale Bishop, and Robert Penn Warren, who also attended the conference.

[Marion, 20 October 1940]

Sunday

Darling.

I went off last night to a football game at Emory & Henry[1]—very nice out of doors under the lights. I wore my new heavy overcoat. I sent the raincoat in your bag by express but am leaving the light coat here. I'll buy a light overcoat in New York.

Had your father and mother to dinner . . . met them at the restaurant and, as I sat in the window waiting for them (they had wanted to walk down) and saw them cross the street, I realized that they really did look an old couple.

Your father has certainly aged fast this last year but how much of it is real and how much a bid for attention and affection I can't make out.

When he is, as he is at this moment, in Mother's room, looking so like a small boy, Mother getting or rather explaining his Sunday School lesson to him, his naive questions, simple belief in the words of his Bible, he is wonderful, but the part he is playing now, holding back from this necessary operation, keeping Mother keyed up trying to push him on, the lack of courage and ordinary manhood about a thing that must be done, it's pretty bad to see going on. It's going to take a team of oxen to get him into that operating room unless he changes.[2]

Darling, tonight will be the last night here and I'm glad. I hate leaving Mother but will be so happy to be again with you.

You mustn't do as you have done, report a horrible headache and then not tell me when you are out of it.

Another very beautiful day. I am loving you.

1. Emory and Henry College in Emory, Virginia, about fifteen miles southwest of Marion.

2. After strong urging from his wife, Copenhaver had the operation, for cataract removal, on 8 November.

[Marion, 2 January 1941]

Friday[1]

Darling—

I am getting this note off to you so you will have it when you get to Chicago. Darling, I know how hard everything has been to you and wish I could have helped more but thought the best thing, in the end, would be to stay out as much as possible and not bother any of you much with my advice.[2]

I do not believe I ever loved you so much as I do now, and often wonder if you feel our marriage, after these years together, as complete and satisfying a thing as I do.

It seems to me that my love of you and appreciation of all you are grows on me all the time.

Write as often as you can.

Your lover

1. This letter was apparently written on Thursday, 2 January, the day before she left; see the beginning of the next letter.

2. Laura Lu Copenhaver had died on 18 December and the family had been occupied with matters of her estate.

[Marion, 3 January 1941]

Friday

Darling,

I wrote you yesterday, so you would have a message of my love when you got to Chicago. I haven't been worth much here. Last night I was pretty ugly, growling away at you about your generosity. I think that was what kept me from sleeping later.

Back of it all, of course, is a kind of fear. Your father is at the back of it. I have so definitely the fear, the dread, that he isn't going to buck up.

And then I am afraid that one by one, for this or that reason, will fall away and that it will end by your father and Aunt May clinging to you. Of course I know that is what he wants.

I rather think that, more than you know, you, more than any of the others, have your mother's patience. It has been rather gigantic, darling. I can't conceive of his ever quite standing up to what fate has dealt out to him. She has, I'm sure, always carried the load and I don't want it to fall on you and am afraid of the generosity in you that may bring it about.

As for myself, darling, I don't know how long I could stand up to it—the curious whining voice, the eternal howl of the radio, the inept talk of poor Aunt May. I'd get ugly, as I was last night I'm afraid, scolding at your generosity with all of the possible result of it in my mind.

Well, I suppose we must just live from day to day and not fear too much.

I have the background of your sacrifice of yourself before I knew you. Mother often spoke of it, saying that for a time she was unaware.

I do want so much some happiness, some ease [for] you.

As for the insurance, when it is spoken of there is a kind of sickness in me. I keep asking—"Why should her money go into that?"

Of course I know that it is 10 to 1 I'll go first and I'll certainly want to.

All my love, darling Eleanor.

[New York, 5 January 1941]

Sunday

Darling—

The room is on the 8th—805—so we have Mauda back.[1] They come at 9 on Sunday now so already at 9:30 I have had breakfast and the room is made.

John E[merson] called, and, after seeing Stryker[2] (I am to see him again on Wednesday to talk more of the child's book), I went to dine with him [Emerson] at the Algonquin. He seems quite his old self. He had a woman with him—I'd say a certainly undistinguished one. He wanted to try to get me a seat at the theatre, where he was going with the woman (he not expecting me until tomorrow), but I was polite and came home.

Anyway I was ready for bed.

Ferdinand [Schevill] has moved to some hotel away uptown. There is a note from him saying it was too noisy for him here.

Saw our Greek[3] at breakfast. It turns out he writes poetry and, as I breakfasted, he stood over me reciting his poems and giving me a dissertation on thought, life and the general condition of life in a rather unsatisfactory world. He is charming and boyish but I'm afraid, alas, might grow tiresome. We are rather terrible people, you and I, both, I fancy, rather up to the same trick, wanting to be nice to people and so unconsciously inviting them and then too quickly tiring of them.

I only hope to God we don't ever tire of each other and I don't believe we ever will.

Chinita del alma mía. Me amas tú?[4]

1. A favorite maid at the Royalton Hotel, where the Andersons often stayed. She was probably French, since SA later had her translate a note from Jean Renoir, French playwright and son of the artist, who was also staying at the hotel.

2. Roy Stryker, an official in the Division of Information of the Farm Security Administration, who had provided the photographs for *Home Town*. SA had in mind a book that would show a "child in simple, direct prose, and in pictures, the drama back of the production of almost everything that makes the child's life comfortable" (*Sherwood Anderson: Selected Letters*, p. 248).

3. A waiter at the Algonquin Hotel.

4. SA's later translation for ECA: "Mistress of my heart. Do you love me?"

[New York, 12 January 1941]

Sunday

Darling—

Far from having a riotous time, when I am away from you, it is hell to know what to do with myself.

So I work. O.K. About 2 or at the most 3 hours. I dictate in the afternoon or the Spanish lady[1] comes. She has come twice. Well, she is nice but, alas, I fear I have caught up with her. She has no more of the typed lessons. I've consumed all she has.

She gives me, elaborately, certain Spanish verbs to work on. So. There they are all in Terry.[2] All right. I have her for something to do.

So you are bored with having to see the Sergels—my unfortunate impetuosity.[3] You should understand it. Dear Mother had it too.

But darling—do you think that Ferdinand or John E are entertaining?

Why do people get old? Your pa is old. John E is old. Alas, Ferd is old.

I am not old. If I were old, how could I love you as I do, dreaming of you at night, making love to you in dreams?

You, darling, not being here.

It's unfortunate. It's terrible. Why are you the only other human being, among so many, that it is always fun to be with?

Are we both too goddam sophisticated or too dumb?

You are really the only one.

Oh, I know that, as lover, I am sometimes inadequate but, damn it, woman, how is it? When I am inadequate it doesn't too much matter to you.

Because you love.

Really, darling, you're a wonder. You are a real lover. How in Christ's name did I ever happen to find you?

You utterly sweet thing.

You are in a jam now, dear, but don't get too involved. Keep your head as clear as you can.

Lordy, I do love you so much.

1. Margarita Madrigal, who was giving SA Spanish lessons.

2. Thomas P. Terry, *Terry's Short Cut to Spanish* (1938).

3. SA had arranged for ECA to visit the Sergels during a busy period in Chicago.

[Marion, 29 January 1941]

Wednesday morning
Darling.

It was so sad leaving you last night.[1] I cried a little later too. I have felt so low and n.g.—so blue, so worthless. You say you love me. How can you?

But I'll not talk of that. I'll come out of it presently.

Mazie says she doesn't plan to [go] home. The child E2[2] is better—much, but I presume this may have something to do with M's wishes. May is up and about, Elsie[3] at home. They say your father—I haven't seen yet—is much better. He has taken charge, it seems, of the younger child.[4]

It seems so strange here without Mother. It will always be so. You will always be expecting her to come through doors.

I wish, darling, you could believe that, in spite of these times when I do not live, how deeply and really I love you and you only.

1. SA had gone south to recuperate from a case of the flu. In another letter he wrote that he left because "I was so discouraged and ashamed that I could not be a better lover."

2. ECA's niece and namesake, Eleanor Wilson.

3. Elsie Groseclose, ECA's secretary.

4. Katharine Wilson.

[Sumter, South Carolina,
30 January 1941]

Thursday
Darling

We really should spend every winter in this country or in country like this. All day I have been packed full of memories of our days down here, the negroes plowing, the red clay side roads, the burning off of old fields, memories of our U-Drive-It days down here, golden days to look back on.

I guess I misunderstood a little. You spoke so often of my going away if the trip was put off.[1] I came to think you didn't mind.

And then, at the station, I knew you did.

It was an easy drive, sunshine all day and quite warm . . . no snow on Fancy Gap. I came by Mt. Airy, then straight south to Salisbury and Charlotte, and from there here.[2] It should be an easy drive into Jacksonville. I am loving you very very much. I feel so much better.

1. SA had originally hoped to leave by the middle of January.

2. He was staying at the Claremont Hotel in Sumter.

[Tampa, Florida, 8 February 1941]

Saturday
Darling—

I think that if you are going home next weekend—the 15th—I'll meet you there, leaving here the later part of next week, this because, after the experience of last night, I have about made up my mind that I am not going to get what I came here for. Your Miss Tabor got me into touch with a Mrs. Cortina, a Spanish teacher here, and I dined last night with the lady & her husband[1] in one of the restaurants at Ybor City.[2] The truth, however, is that Ybor City has become something rather special. It's a kind of Coney Island for tourists & soldiers here. In the restaurants there are Spanish (Cuban) waiters but the patrons are middlewestern tourists and army people. This is becoming a big new flying field.[3]

As for these people, I haven't been able to get it into their heads that I wouldn't mind rooming in, for example, a workingman's family, only wanting to hear Spanish spoken, to try my own etc. I think they have got it into their heads that I'm too much a big shot for that and, as regards the few older Spanish families, they either haven't heard of me or are shy, thinking they aren't intellectual enough. If I were to stay here for some months of course it could be worked out but, as it stands, and if you are going home, I'd so much rather be with you.

I think I'll not tell Roberto[4] of my failure here and of course I have got something as I have worked away at the thing every day. I am to meet the editor of the Spanish newspaper tomorrow and dine with some Spanish people.

So, darling, when you get this, tell me, if you can, definitely whether you do plan to go home the 15th and I'll make my own plans accordingly.

I wonder if you would mind calling up Roberto Rendueles, either at his office, "Editors Press Service," or at home RE 4–2495, and ask him if he would mind checking with Mr. St. John[5] to be sure that everything is O.K. about the trip, state room etc. I am a little fearful yet that something may go wrong and, if there is any chance at all of its blowing up, we should know it now. I don't think he'll mind. I'm writing him today.[6]

I love you.

1. Mary Cortina, who taught Spanish at the University of Tampa, and her husband, Joseph.

2. A large Hispanic section of Tampa.

3. MacDill Air Force Base.

4. Roberto Rendueles, director of the Editors Press Service in New York; he had helped to plan the Andersons' trip to Chile.

5. A vice-president of Grace Line, who was arranging complimentary passage for the Andersons.

6. SA met ECA in Marion on 14 February. They arrived in New York on 23 February and boarded the Grace Line ship the *Santa Lucia* on 28 February. SA became ill at sea and on 4 March was taken to a hospital at Colón, Canal Zone, where he died on 8 March.

Bibliography

Works by Sherwood Anderson

Windy McPherson's Son. New York: John Lane Company, 1916.
Marching Men. New York: John Lane Company, 1917.
Mid-American Chants. New York: John Lane Company, 1918.
Winesburg, Ohio. New York: B. W. Huebsch, 1919.
Poor White. New York: B. W. Huebsch, 1920.
The Triumph of the Egg. New York: B. W. Huebsch, 1921.
Many Marriages. New York: B. W. Huebsch, 1923.
Horses and Men. New York: B. W. Huebsch, 1923.
A Story Teller's Story. New York: B. W. Huebsch, 1924.
Dark Laughter. New York: Boni and Liveright, 1925.
The Modern Writer. San Francisco: Gelber, Lilienthal, 1925.
Sherwood Anderson's Notebook. New York: Boni and Liveright, 1926.
Tar: A Midwest Childhood. New York: Boni and Liveright, 1926.
A New Testament. New York: Boni and Liveright, 1927.
Hello Towns! New York: Horace Liveright, 1929.
Nearer the Grass Roots and Elizabethton. San Francisco: Westgate Press, 1929.
Alice and The Lost Novel. London: Elkin Mathews and Marrot, 1929.
American County Fair. New York: Random House, 1930.
Perhaps Women. New York: Horace Liveright, 1931.
Beyond Desire. New York: Liveright, 1932.
Death in the Woods. New York: Liveright, 1933.
No Swank. Philadelphia: Centaur Press, 1934.
Puzzled America. New York: Charles Scribner's Sons, 1935.
Kit Brandon. New York: Charles Scribner's Sons, 1936.
Plays: Winesburg and Others. New York: Charles Scribner's Sons, 1937.
A Writer's Conception of Realism. Olivet, Michigan: Olivet College, 1939.
Five Poems. San Mateo, California: Quercus Press, 1939.
Home Town. Edited by Edwin Rosskam. New York: Alliance Book Corporation, 1940.
Sherwood Anderson's Memoirs. New York: Harcourt, Brace and Company, 1942.

Collections, Letters, and Critical Editions

The Buck Fever Papers. Edited by Welford Dunaway Taylor. Charlottesville: University Press of Virginia, 1971.

France and Sherwood Anderson: Paris Notebook, 1921. Edited by Michael Fanning. Baton Rouge: Louisiana State University Press, 1976.

Letters of Sherwood Anderson. Edited by Howard Mumford Jones and Walter B. Rideout. Boston: Little, Brown and Company, 1953.

Letters to Bab: Sherwood Anderson to Marietta D. Finley, 1916–33. Edited by William A. Sutton. Urbana: University of Illinois Press, 1985.

The Portable Sherwood Anderson. Edited by Horace Gregory. New York: Viking Press, 1949; revised edition, 1972.

Return to Winesburg: Selections from Four Years of Writing for a Country Newspaper. Edited by Ray Lewis White. Chapel Hill: University of North Carolina Press, 1967.

Sherwood Anderson: Centennial Studies. Edited by Hilbert H. Campbell and Charles E. Modlin. Troy, New York: Whitston Publishing Company, 1976.

Sherwood Anderson: Early Writings. Edited by Ray Lewis White. Kent, Ohio: Kent State University Press, 1989.

Sherwood Anderson: Selected Letters. Edited by Charles E. Modlin. Knoxville: University of Tennessee Press, 1984.

Sherwood Anderson: Short Stories. Edited by Maxwell Geismar. New York: Hill and Wang, 1962.

The Sherwood Anderson Diaries, 1936–1941. Edited by Hilbert H. Campbell. Athens: University of Georgia Press, 1987.

The Sherwood Anderson Reader. Edited by Paul Rosenfeld. Boston: Houghton Mifflin Company, 1947.

Sherwood Anderson's Memoirs: A Critical Edition. Edited by Ray Lewis White. Chapel Hill: University of North Carolina Press, 1969.

The Teller's Tales. Edited by Frank Gado. Schenectady, New York: Union College Press, 1983.

The "Writer's Book" by Sherwood Anderson: A Critical Edition. Edited by Martha Mulroy Curry. Metuchen, New Jersey: Scarecrow Press, 1975.

Index